TRINITARIAN DOGMATICS

TRINITARIAN DOGMATICS

Exploring the Grammar
of the Christian Doctrine of God

D. Glenn Butner Jr.

Baker Academic
a division of Baker Publishing Group
Grand Rapids, Michigan

Published by Baker Academic
a division of Baker Publishing Group
PO Box 6287, Grand Rapids, MI 49516-6287
www.bakeracademic.com

Printed in the United States of America

Library of Congress Cataloging-in-Publication Data
Names: Butner, D. Glenn, 1989– author.
Title: Trinitarian dogmatics : exploring the grammar of the Christian doctrine of God / D. Glenn Butner Jr.
Description: Grand Rapids, Michigan : Baker Academic, a division of Baker Publishing Group, [2022] | Includes bibliographical references and index.
Identifiers: LCCN 2021053970 | ISBN 9781540962232 (paperback) | ISBN 9781540965554 (casebound) | ISBN 9781493436507 (pdf) | ISBN 9781493436491 (ebook)
Subjects: LCSH: Trinity.
Classification: LCC BT111.3 .B88 2022 | DDC 231/.044—dc23/eng/20211130
LC record available at https://lccn.loc.gov/2021053970

Unless otherwise noted, Scripture quotations have been taken from the Christian Standard Bible®, copyright © 2017 by Holman Bible Publishers. Used by permission. Christian Standard Bible® and CSB® are federally registered trademarks of Holman Bible Publishers.

Scripture quotations labeled ESV are from The Holy Bible, English Standard Version® (ESV®), copyright © 2001 by Crossway, a publishing ministry of Good News Publishers. Used by permission. All rights reserved. ESV Text Edition: 2016

Baker Publishing Group publications use paper produced from sustainable forestry practices and post-consumer waste whenever possible.

22   23   24   25   26   27   28   7   6   5   4   3   2   1

*To Elias, who has already begun
asking questions about the Trinity.*

Here is my answer. May it one day move you
to knowledge and worship.

Contents

Contents

Acknowledgments

I am indebted to many individuals who have helped make this book possible. My understanding of the Trinity has been shaped by sound teaching and by critical feedback on my writing in graduate courses and examinations, especially that offered by Robert Doran, D. Stephen Long, Marcus Plested, J. Warren Smith, and Wanda Zemler-Cizewski. I would not be the theologian that I am today without such fine theological instruction.

A number of scholars provided input or resources at various stages of this manuscript's production, each improving the quality of the text. Fred Sanders proposed adding annotated bibliographies and glossary. Pete Kosek, Roy Millhouse, Aristotle Papanikolaou, and Gene Schlesinger offered brief feedback on key points. Madison Pierce and Adonis Vidu graciously provided me the opportunity to view their publications in advance of their release dates so that I could incorporate their ideas into this text. James Dolezal, Brandon Smith, and Mitchell Stevens provided feedback on a full chapter, Jordin Greer read several chapters to help me assess whether this book was accessible to graduate students, and Richard Barcellos kindly volunteered to review the first draft of the entire work. The resulting proposed edits sharpened my thinking and my prose. My friend and colleague Tim Gabrielson answered hundreds of questions regarding issues in the field of biblical studies. Each of these fine scholars has left an imprint on the final form of this work, and I am truly grateful for their kindness and keen insights.

A good portion of this work was written during the COVID-19 pandemic, when much of the interlibrary loan system had ground to a halt. The astute reader may notice several peculiar absences of key works by major figures, which resulted because the books were impossible to acquire during periods of lockdown.[1] Such gaps are so infrequent thanks to the tireless work of the library staff at Sterling College, especially that of Mikki Millhouse and Laurel Watney. I truly could not have written this book without them.

I have enjoyed the support of the fine team at Baker Academic, especially David Nelson, James Korsmo, and Sarah Gombis, and I am thankful for their effort to bring this work to press. Baker has an excellent team and publishing process, and they improve the quality of the work while preserving the author's voice perfectly. The copyediting of David Doherty greatly improved the style and syntax throughout this book.

Above all, I am thankful for my wife Lydia's support in pursuing my career as an author, professor, and scholar, and for her grace during the more than a few late nights spent writing instead of socializing with her.

I am blessed to have such fine friends, colleagues, editors, and family. I deeply appreciate their influence on this book.

1. I remain confident in the final product and believe that I have presented a sound doctrine of the Trinity, even though in some cases my route to certain key insights was atypical because it bypassed certain major figures.

Introduction

How does one begin a book on the doctrine of the Trinity? To write of the Trinity is to write of God, eternally Father, Son, and Holy Spirit, eternally one, unique, and indivisible. It is the triune God who creates, who redeems, who will come to renew creation, from whom and to whom are all things (Col. 1:16; Heb. 2:10). To write of the Trinity is therefore to write of that ultimate reality that lies behind all things as their source and whose tripersonal coming is awaited as the fulfillment of creation (1 Cor. 13:12; 15:28). To comprehend the Trinity, one must know the infinite, a kind of knowledge proper only to God. Thus, knowing the Trinity is, as Karl Barth famously insists, contingent on God graciously taking humans as the object of his self-giving, an act that enables them to participate in God's knowledge of God.[1] Using the older language of Francis Turretin, our knowledge of God is finite and is "the image and ectype of the infinite and archetypal" knowledge that God has of himself.[2] It is a bold endeavor that would make no headway apart from the grace of the God we seek.

Yet, it is necessary to write an account of the doctrine of the Trinity, to attempt the impossible, and to draw as close to God's knowledge of God as he will graciously permit. The formulation of such doctrine is a means of fulfilling the evangelistic work of the church, since we may use the doctrine to describe the God whose mercy and grace we proclaim and the trinitarian structure of God's self-giving for our salvation. It is also a means of ensuring proper worship. There are timely reasons to pursue the doctrine of the Trinity, for in modern times some argue that the Trinity is not biblical[3] or claim that

1. Barth, *Church Dogmatics* II/1, 63–178.
2. Turretin, *Institutes of Elenctic Theology* 1.2.6.
3. E.g., Leander Keck sees aspects of the Gospel of John, Hebrews, and Paul's Letters as closer to the views of Arius than of Nicaea, where trinitarian theology began to coalesce (*Why Christ Matters*, 149–55). There have also been a number of exegetical challenges to specific

1

traditional formulations of the doctrine were corrupted by Greek philosophy or are philosophically incoherent.[4] Even among those who defend the Trinity, there has been a tendency, as we shall see in later chapters, to shift the meaning of key trinitarian terms like "**consubstantial**," a key descriptor of the sameness between Father, Son, and Spirit, or "person," the fundamental term for describing what the Father, Son, and Spirit are in their uniqueness. Such shifts arguably stem from a general lack of understanding of key historical sources in the development of trinitarian thought. Much of this book, then, will be concerned with the exegetical foundations of the doctrine of the Trinity and with an accurate historical analysis of concepts that have become fundamental to any dogmatic account of the Trinity.

Despite the emphasis on historical theology and biblical exegesis—perhaps also partly because of this emphasis—this work is not a properly historical or exegetical work. This is a work of trinitarian *dogmatics*. It falls to me to explain how I am using the term "dogmatics" in the title. According to Emil Brunner, dogmatics emerges from a "threefold root," the polemical struggle of theologians against heresies, the effort to develop a genre suited to instruction of catechumens and students, and the systematic exploration of the Bible.[5] A dogmatic theology exceeds mere biblical exposition in that it requires attention to the historical development of various interpretations of Scripture, some eventually deemed orthodox, others deemed heretical, and still others seen as open to varying degrees of disagreement. Yet, there remain contemporary theological positions that this dogmatic account will engage with in polemical fashion—often briefly, given the extensive scope of this work—so dogmatic theology is not reducible to historical theology. This theology, like all dogmatic theology, is intended to serve instructional purposes. It is targeted to the seminary and to other graduate-level classrooms, though I hope and anticipate that it will also serve professional theologians. In other words, this volume seeks to convey the fundamental dogmas or doctrines that those who study theology in preparation for ministry ought to understand. Many speculative, constructive, or applied aspects of theology must

---

aspects of the doctrine of the Trinity, including eternal generation, the inseparability of divine operations, and divine simplicity.

4. This argument was most famously developed by Adolf von Harnack, though we will see similar challenges from more recent theologians to various trinitarian loci like divine simplicity and inseparable operations and to classical definitions of the divine persons. Harnack is prone to see a sharp distinction in Christian history between an earlier, more Judaic stage and a later Hellenistic stage marked by an emphasis on philosophy, particularly Platonism. While he admits that this shift made cultural sense at that time, he disallows such concepts in a modern context, considering them implausible (Harnack, *What Is Christianity?*, 200–209).

5. Brunner, *Dogmatics*, 1:93–96.

be neglected in dogmatics, as instruction in the fundamentals must precede the theologian's attempt to do something with those beliefs.[6] The polemical and instructional dimensions of this dogmatic account of the Trinity should never draw us away from the biblical dimensions of a dogmatic theology, and yet dogmatic theology considers historical-grammatical interpretations of Scripture along with theological interpretations, word studies and analyses of narratives, canonical readings, and reception histories of texts. Dogmatic theology ought to be biblical through and through, yet it often engages the Bible in a manner distinct from the commentary or biblical theology, which, in order to meet the instructional and technical needs of the biblical-studies discipline, favor the analysis of discrete books or themes. In writing a work of trinitarian dogmatics, I am intending to write a systematic account of the Trinity that is normed by Scripture and shaped by centuries of polemical debates going up to the present, my purpose being to create instruction that benefits the church. How is such a task possible?

Knowing the Triune God

With audacity do we claim to know and speak of the triune God! God "lives in unapproachable light," so no one can see him (1 Tim. 6:16). The God who appears to Isaiah is so holy that the seraphim surrounding him have to cover their eyes. Isaiah cries out that he is ruined for having seen the perfect God while being an unclean and sinful man (6:1–5), but God provides a way of atonement so that Isaiah can speak on his behalf: a glowing coal from the altar brought to Isaiah by one of the seraphim to purify his mouth (6:6–7). This atonement that enables one to know God is a type of Christ, who alone has revealed the Father (Matt. 11:27; Luke 10:22; John 1:18) and whose death provides access to the holy of holies where God dwells (Heb. 10:19). The Holy Spirit more perfectly fulfills the role played by the coal-carrying seraph in Isaiah's vision, bringing the benefits of the atonement to the believer in order to cleanse us from iniquity so that we may know God (1 Cor. 6:11). Drawing on dialectical theology more than typological readings, many modern theologians, particularly those influenced by Karl Barth, have rightly argued that our knowledge of God is rooted in God's self-revelation in Christ.

6. Here I must admit that I do not think the doctrine of the Trinity is a doctrine that is meant to be used for other ends, since it is a conceptual framework meant to help us understand, as best as we are able, the God whom we worship as Father, Son, and Spirit. God is not an object to be used, but is to be enjoyed, as Augustine teaches. The point still stands for other doctrines, which can be and are used for constructive purposes. (See Augustine, *On Christian Teaching* 1.4.)

For example, Paul Molnar insists that the Trinity is known in faith but that God makes such knowledge and faith possible through the work of the Son and Spirit.[7] "If our knowledge of God is not grounded in the very being and action of God himself—and consequently in his Word and Spirit—then it is in fact nothing more than our own religious or irreligious speculation grounded in our self-experience."[8] The Trinity simply cannot be reduced to a threefold human experience of God, for such an understanding would leave us with more knowledge of human psychology than of God's being.[9] Any attempt to define the inner life of the triune God "from the human side" constrains God within the limits of human reason, limits that he exceeds.[10]

Karl Barth, who is often credited with reviving interest in the doctrine of the Trinity in the twentieth century, was well aware of the limits of human efforts to understand God. This is clearly evident in his early treatment of the subject in his commentary on Romans, where, drawing on Acts 17:23, he speaks of God as the unknown God, "the divine incognito," the absolute other whom we cannot reach with human reason. Any God discovered through speculative reason alone is the idolatrous no-God, a false human concept and projection.[11] Barth's point, and Molnar's like it, is well taken. Apart from the divine self-revelation found in the incarnation of Christ, God remains unknown, and apart from the work of the Holy Spirit, the self-revelation of Christ cannot be recognized. Barth takes this profound insight and uses it to develop a theology of the Trinity that emerges from God's act of self-revelation. For Barth, the Trinity is evident in the structure of the gospel proclamation that "God reveals Himself as the Lord," just as it is evident in the nature of this divine self-revelation, which involves a Revealer, the Revelation itself, and the Revealedness of that revelation.[12] God's self-revelation requires One who reveals himself (the Father), the revelation of the One (the Son), and the revealedness (the Spirit) that makes God's act of self-revelation "the effective meeting between God and man."[13] Yet, there is only one self-revelation. Surely, Barth's is one of the more insightful ways of presenting the doctrine of the Trinity.

Though I agree with the broad point that Barth and Molnar are making—namely, that we cannot know God apart from his drawing us into his own

7. Molnar, "Classical Trinity," 77.

8. Molnar, *Divine Freedom and the Doctrine of the Immanent Trinity*, 15.

9. Molnar, *Divine Freedom and the Doctrine of the Immanent Trinity*, 136–38.

10. Molnar, "Classical Trinity," 74. In context, Molnar is discussing the ineffability of the divine processions.

11. Barth, *Epistle to the Romans*, 35–48.

12. Barth, *Church Dogmatics* I/1, 351.

13. Barth, *Church Dogmatics* I/1, 381.

knowledge through his self-revelation—I will not follow Barth in constructing the doctrine of the Trinity from the threefold form of God's self-revelation in the Christ event, in part because I do not believe that Barth's method is the only means of being faithful to his conviction. Barth is clearly seeking to develop a biblical theology, to the point that he is often accused of biblicism, yet his emphasis on the threefold nature of revelation as a basis for the doctrine of the Trinity can seem a bit arbitrary.[14] As Maurice Wiles once quipped, "The whole argument sounds suspiciously like a later rationalization to support a doctrine really based on [propositional revelation] and now in search of a new foundation."[15] Wiles was quite critical of the idea of propositional revelation and therefore found Barth's entire project uncompelling. It is better, I think, to embrace the challenge head on, considering why it is that the very words of the Bible itself may lead to the Trinity, as they did historically, eventually prompting Barth to take his own approach in explaining the Trinity. Those seeking a full theological method here will likely be disappointed; this is, after all, an introduction. Though I may not convince all readers, I hope at least to provide some sense of how I will proceed in this work.

I share the conviction of Barth and Molnar that we can know God only through the gracious gift of his revealing himself, but I am convinced that God has made himself known from the dawn of history. Though the Christian faith is grounded in the belief that Christ is the ultimate revelation of the Father, I contend that Christ's life, ministry, and teachings are intelligible only within the framework of the history of Israel as recorded within the Old Testament. Christ himself drew on the sacred texts of Israel, and the earliest records we have of the incarnate life of the Son interpret him within this framework, sometimes by clear citation formulas—"Now all this took place to fulfill what was spoken by the Lord through the prophet" (Matt. 1:22)—and sometimes through less direct allusions, as when Matthew depicts Jesus as a new Moses. This fact prompts me to hold two principles. First, what I have elsewhere called the inspiration principle requires that we see these biblical texts as exceeding merely human records.[16] If these texts are necessary to understand God's self-revelation in the Son, and if true human knowledge of God must participate in the **archetypal** knowledge that God has of himself,[17] then Christians must take it as an article of faith that these

---

14. Watson, "The Bible," 59. Watson believes that these charges of conservative biblicism miss the main contours of Barth's project.

15. Wiles, "Some Reflections," 105.

16. Butner, "Probing the Exegetical Foundations of Consubstantiality."

17. This knowledge is archetypal in that it is the perfect original in which human theology participates **ectypally** by God's grace.

texts participate in God's knowledge by inspiration.[18] Second, the fact that Jesus must be interpreted within the context of these older texts prompts a canonical principle. Again, if these books are necessary in understanding Jesus, then they must be included in theological analysis and thus rendered as canon, while other texts that are not equally important in interpreting Christ within his historical context are excluded from having equal authority. Only the canon is fully normative in theology.

A dogmatic account of the Trinity thus begins with the affirmation of the Bible as Scripture—a specific canon of texts viewed as uniquely communicating God's knowledge of God in a manner appropriate to human knowledge. Human knowledge, like the biblical canon, is varied in form, so we can expect a wide range of possible approaches to deriving the Trinity from the Bible. Sometimes, despite Wiles's reservations, the Bible makes clear propositional claims about God. A dogmatic account of the Trinity must seek to systematize various propositions in the Bible so that we can hold them each as inspired. This act of systemizing can take the form of extensive exegetical analysis of a single verse or passage, or it can consist of surveying broad biblical patterns of speech. Yet propositions are not the only aspect of the Bible pertinent to our study. Human knowledge also consists of words, narratives, practices, and experiences, among other things. Therefore, at various points in this book I will use word studies, examine narrative components of the Bible as well as the overarching narrative of the entire canon, and consider the diverse modes of biblical interpretation deployed by Christians at various points in history. There is no single approach that could incorporate all aspects of the doctrine of the Trinity. The varied and sometimes eclectic ways of using the Bible that are necessary in order to understand the doctrine of the Trinity will become evident as this book unfolds. Yet, each approach is rooted in the same conviction: Scripture is inspired and supremely authoritative, though it is not alone in the theological task.

Tradition, too, plays a role in this quest for knowledge of the Trinity, at least if tradition is properly understood. Speaking anecdotally, I have often seen tradition treated at a lay level as dry, old, and outdated ideas from past generations, something that has limited influence on modern church life and for good reason. Such a perspective does not recognize the ways tradition has been guided by God, albeit not to the same degree as Scripture. A full account of biblical inspiration lies beyond the scope of a work on trinitarian

18. I appreciate the wording of John Webster, who argues that human authorship of Scripture must be seen as a kind of sanctification. "In briefest form, sanctification is the act of God the Holy Spirit in hallowing creaturely processes, employing them in the service of the talking form of revelation within the history of the creation" (*Holy Scripture*, 26).

dogmatics, but brief consideration of one model of inspiration can illustrate my point. A. A. Hodge, a noted American theologian, described biblical inspiration as a four-step process. Through *providence*, God brought the biblical authors to the right historical moment. Subsequent *spiritual illumination* provided by the Holy Spirit ensured genuine religious insight, opening the Christian to receive *revelation*, which was then accurately recorded through *inspiration*.[19] In seeking to ground our knowledge of the Trinity in God's self-revelation, we might be tempted to discard tradition on the grounds that it is rooted in human knowledge, not in God's knowledge of God.[20] Hodge's four-stage process of inspiration shows why this would be a mistake. In the Old Princeton theology that Hodge represents, illumination was thought to belong to all Christians who have received the Holy Spirit (see, e.g., John 16:13–15).[21] Hodge notes, "Spiritual illumination opens the organ of spiritual vision and clarifies it."[22] All Christians, then, having received the Spirit, have some clear sense of God as mediated in Scripture and therefore can guide one another in the interpretation of Scripture. Similarly, they can influence the way that we use philosophy to make sense of questions raised by Scripture yet not explicitly resolved therein. Tradition is not infallible in the way that Scripture is, so critiquing it is always a possibility. Still, Protestants have been wise in their use of tradition as a test of the truthfulness of a given interpretation.

Reason, too, has a role to play in dogmatics, and necessarily so.[23] When we engage in biblical hermeneutics, we are using reason, and it is often difficult, for example, to clearly identify the boundaries between hermeneutics and philosophy. Philosophy also contributes much vocabulary that helps provide clarity when speaking of conclusions drawn from Scripture. Here we must see philosophy as Anselm of Canterbury did, as a resource for faith seeking understanding.[24] The idea is not to impose a foreign framework on the biblical text. Rather, philosophy can help make explicit what was only implicit in the Bible. Yet, we must heed Barth's worries about human reason. God created the world of space, time, and matter, and he therefore exceeds that world and all our experiences of it. This truth should significantly chasten our confidence in our intellectual abilities. Without attempting here to explore the

19. A. A. Hodge, *Popular Lectures on Theological Themes*, 85–87.
20. Certainly, Barth did not take this approach to tradition.
21. See also C. Hodge, *Systematic Theology*, 1:155.
22. A. A. Hodge, *Popular Lectures on Theological Themes*, 86.
23. Even those Reformers like Martin Luther who are often depicted as rejecting the scholastic use of reason in favor of a more biblical theology in fact resort to much traditional scholastic method and the scholastic genre of disputation in their treatment of the Trinity. See the discussion in Helmer, *The Trinity and Martin Luther*, 53–59.
24. Anselm, *Proslogion* §1.

full ramifications of divine otherness or to resolve the philosophical difficulties that arise from it (such matters are more proper to other dogmatic loci), I must make note of one major dogmatic commitment that properly serves this chastening work. As endorsed at the **Fourth Lateran Council** (1215), the doctrine of **analogy** insists that God is different from the world that he has created but recognizes that creation bears some relation to its Creator. This similarity amid greater difference allows us to use human words and concepts of God yet requires that we always explain how their meaning differs when they are used of God rather than created realities. As Katherine Sonderegger remarks, Lateran IV's insistence on a "movement from likeness to unlikeness" is "the scholastic expression of Divine Holiness, the Lordly Act of setting Himself apart."[25] When grounded in Scripture, our use of reason does, by God's grace, lead to knowledge, but it remains a knowledge of the God whose holiness prompted even the seraphim of Isaiah's vision to cover their eyes. Even though our language is restricted by the principle of analogy, in our human knowledge of the holy God we see the Trinity, which early Christians glimpsed even in the recurring threefold affirmation of that holiness—"Holy, holy, holy is the LORD of hosts; the whole earth is full of his glory!" (Isa. 6:3 ESV; see also Rev. 4:8).

What, then, of human experience in a theology of the Trinity? Certainly, we cannot construct a theology of the Trinity on the foundation of human experience, for the product would be merely a description of human subjectivity. We would have no reason for believing that this description corresponded to the God who lives in unapproachable light. Yet, in a rather ironic twist, we must pay particular attention to human experience in order to avoid too subjective a theology. T. F. Torrance summarizes the matter eloquently: "The temptation of orthodoxy, and all scholasticism, . . . is to fall a prey to their own subjectivities through converting the truths of the Word of God into rationalized objects."[26] The cultural-embeddedness of human language means that our propositional descriptions of God can distort the objective revelation of God, hiding the objective truth behind a system prone to manifest our own assumptions. While this leads Barth to be somewhat skeptical of propositional orthodoxy as manifest in scholasticism, I see no reason why an account of God as Revealer, Revelation, and Revealedness is any less beholden to cultural influence.[27] Any treatment of theology is necessarily bound to certain human

---

25. Sonderegger, *Systematic Theology*, 2:xxv.
26. T. F. Torrance, *Karl Barth*, 101.
27. This is especially clear to non-Western trinitarian theologians who more easily see Western culture on display in Barth: Kombo, *Doctrine of God*, 106–14, 119; Miyahira, *Towards a Theology of the Concord of God*, chap. 3.

cultures and experience, and any good theologian, like Barth, will seek to center the objectivity of God's self-revelation. It seems to me that the best way to do this is to read widely from theologians whose cultural location, philosophical assumptions, and personal experiences are quite different from one's own.

I write as a modern white American male theologian, and these (and other) dimensions of my experience of the world, which is always embodied and bounded by history and culture, could distort my understanding of God, resulting in a theology more beholden to culture or personal experience than to the revelation so graciously provided in Christ and in the Holy Spirit. There-fore, throughout this work I will strategically refer to theological perspectives of people occupying different cultural locations, my aim being to identify cases where cultural difference may result in divergent theological assumptions or claims. I hope that such divergence will immediately prompt the reader to con-sider their own assumptions. Of course, this method is not intended to suggest that theological knowledge lacks objectivity. Nor do I intend to divide human-ity into a series of people groups whose common physical, social, or cultural location inevitably leads to homogenous thinking in a deterministic fashion. Here Ada María Isasi-Díaz makes a helpful distinction between "shared experi-ences" and "common experiences." The idea of common experiences held by all "seems to mask differences, to present that there is but one experience" for a given ethnic or cultural group.[28] In reality, there is no universal, singular voice of Hispanic women, of African Christians, or of the poor. Yet, the voices of particular authors from a certain cultural, gender, or ethnic group may help us understand something of the illumination given to members of these categories as they have sought to understand Scripture and tradition within their own contexts, because their experiences may be more likely to be shared by others within the same group. The more particular voices we hear, the more the per-spectives of the global church, or subsets of that church, can be understood.[29] I also do not intend to reduce theological perspectives of authors in a different cultural or social location from me to curiosities that I can instrumentalize for my own purposes. Many such scholars will be cited and referenced on the merits of their own work, not merely as a cultural foil.[30] Yet, I am convinced that attending to the possible distortions of theology that may emerge from my own experiences requires me periodically to compare my theology with that of Christians who differ from me in various ways.

28. Isasi-Díaz, *Mujerista Theology*, 67.
29. Isasi-Díaz, *En la Lucha*, 63.
30. At other times I must simply admit that my questions are different than those of other authors, a fact that will certainly be reflected in my answers.

Having explored, in an admittedly cursory manner, humans' ability to know the triune God and the evidence pertinent to this knowledge, I turn now to the way in which I will develop an account of the doctrine of the Trinity.

The Structure of This Book

Many texts introducing the doctrine of the Trinity, whether at the most introductory levels or in highest academic form, proceed diachronically, exploring the way in which the doctrine of the Trinity has been developed over time.[31] Such texts typically begin with an introduction to the biblical foundations of the Trinity; explore patristic debates that resulted in the ecumenical creed developed at **Nicaea** (325) and **Constantinople** (381); supplement this basic outline with a description of smaller debates in medieval Europe, the Byzantine Empire, and the Reformation; and conclude with an analysis of the ways in which modern trinitarian thought has modified these earlier categories. The historical development of the doctrine of the Trinity is certainly an important story and one worth telling, yet structuring an introductory text in this manner has certain shortcomings. Covering relevant biblical content in earlier chapters can leave later doctrinal debates unmoored from relevant exegetical discussions, giving the impression that ideas such as **eternal generation**, consubstantiality, or **inseparable operations** are the byproduct of later philosophy more than the close analysis of Scripture. For Christians who share my commitment to the principle of *sola scriptura*, this simply will not do. Moreover, I would distinguish between the way of discovery, which explores the manner in which biblical foundations of the Trinity unfold into increasingly sophisticated dogmatic formulations, and the way of teaching, which moves from more basic and logically prior concepts to more complex ones.[32] The way of teaching may require that we deviate from a diachronic historical progression in order to consider concepts from various periods simultaneously. Because I intend this work, among other purposes, to serve as a tool for classrooms, I have structured it according to a progression that I believe most clearly introduces the key concepts of the doctrine of the Trinity. Each chapter will explore one dogmatic locus of the doctrine of the Trinity. The first locus will be consubstantiality, which is, in my understanding, logically the most fundamental idea to the doctrine of the Trinity, yet one that raises more questions than it answers. The required clarification will come as the

31. See, e.g., Holmes, *Quest for the Trinity*; O'Collins, *Tripersonal God*.
32. This distinction is medieval in origin but has been developed more recently in Lonergan, *Triune God*, 63, 67.

book moves on to increasingly complex subjects, such as the divine **proces-sions** and divine **simplicity**. By the time I reach the question in chapter 8 of how Christians have **communion** with each member of the Trinity in a distinct way, I will assume knowledge of all content presented earlier.

Choosing to begin this work with the doctrine of consubstantiality immediately exposes me to an objection quite typical of modern theology—namely, that by beginning with the oneness of God I have already set the stage for the elimination of divine plurality. In various forms, modern theologians have argued that this allegedly typical Western approach of beginning with divine unity results in a number of problems. For example, Colin Gunton argues that the Western emphasis on the divine being reduces persons to relations within a logically prior, underlying being that is no longer identified with the interpersonal communion of Father, Son, and Holy Spirit.[33] I am unconvinced by these objections for many reasons, one of them being that the notion of distinct Eastern and Western versions of the Trinity, with the attendant accusation that the West lost the genuine distinction between and communion among the **divine persons**, is rooted in simplified historical readings. At best, this notion accurately describes reality during a brief period in the ninth century, after which the distinctions between East and West grew more complicated.[34] Moreover, the Bible itself introduces God's oneness first, in the Old Testament, before complicating matters with the Christology and pneumatology of the New Testament, which led Christians to develop the doctrine of the Trinity. Starting with God's oneness cannot automatically be ruled out as problematic, and I am convinced that the doctrine of the Trinity emerged from the early Christians' startling realization that Jesus was somehow united with the Father, a realization that eventually led to the idea of divine consubstantiality. Therefore, I have chosen to begin with a chapter on one way in which Father, Son, and Spirit are one.

At the same time, I recognize that any theologian attempting to explain the doctrine of the Trinity faces the risk of overemphasizing either the unity of the persons or their distinction, favoring oneness or threeness to the detriment of the other. I am quite aware of this risk, so under advisement from Gregory of Nazianzus, I have adopted a strategy to mitigate this danger. Gregory writes, "No sooner do I conceive of the One than I am illumined by the splendor of the Three; no sooner do I distinguish them than I am carried back to the One."[35] Therefore, chapters will alternate between emphasis on

33. Gunton, *Promise of Trinitarian Theology*, 10, 41.
34. I argue my case in Butner, "For and against de Régnon," 399–412. I will treat this subject more extensively in chaps. 2 and 4.
35. Gregory of Nazianzus, *Oration on Holy Baptism* §41.

divine unity and divine threeness. Chapter 1, which explores consubstantiality as the logically fundamental concept of unity, is followed by a chapter on the divine processions, the logically fundamental basis for differentiating the persons. Besides structuring the book in such a manner that plurality is placed to offset unity and unity plurality, within each chapter I will attempt to show the relationship between God's oneness and threeness. Wherever an aspect of divine unity is explored, a dogmatic account of this unity must be normed by a faithful commitment to divine plurality. Only then can the Trinity be maintained against the notion of a singular divine monad. In a similar fashion, where divine plurality is discussed, divine unity must regulate this account to avoid polytheism.

With these strategies in mind, I can now turn to the work of constructing a dogmatic account of the doctrine of the Trinity. I have added a glossary to the back of the work, as the vocabulary becomes quite technical at times. Terms are in bold the first time they occur in the text. Readers may also find they want a deeper analysis of certain subjects, so at the end of each chapter an annotated bibliography proposes further reading on various disciplines and the subject of the chapter. My hope is that the readers will find what follows to be a robust, biblical, and precise dogmatic account of the one God who is eternally Father, Son, and Holy Spirit. I remain convinced that this hope may be fulfilled only through the Father's gracious gift, through the Son, of the illuminating Holy Spirit, so I pray that that gift may be found in author and reader alike.

FOR FURTHER READING

The Trinity and the Bible

Bates, Matthew W. *The Birth of the Trinity: Jesus, God, and Spirit in New Testament and Early Christian Interpretations of the Old Testament*. Oxford: Oxford University Press, 2015.

> *The Birth of the Trinity* introduced prosopological exegesis to English-language scholarship and to educated lay audiences, resulting in a more robust analysis of the Trinity in the Bible.

Hill, Wesley. *Paul and the Trinity: Persons, Relations, and the Pauline Letters*. Grand Rapids: Eerdmans, 2015.

> Hill's text argues that debates over high and low Christology, which explore the extent to which the Son is considered equal to the Father, miss more important texts about relations between Father, Son, and Holy Spirit. Hill ably explores such relations as a basis for the Trinity in Paul.

Pierce, Madison. *Divine Discourse in the Epistle to the Hebrews: The Recontextualization of Spoken Quotations of Scripture*. Cambridge: Cambridge University Press, 2020.

>Pierce's technical analysis provides great insights into the trinitarian prosopological exegesis found in Hebrews. As an added bonus, she includes a close reading of Hebrews 1, a key text in debates about eternal generation.

Wainwright, Arthur W. *The Trinity in the New Testament*. London: SPCK, 1969.

>Though dated, Wainwright's survey remains one of the best introductions to historical-critical debates about the Trinity in the New Testament. Wainwright argues that the New Testament creates a "trinitarian problem" that demands a systematic theological answer.

Selected Major Treatments of the Trinity in History

Ayres, Lewis. *Nicaea and Its Legacy: An Approach to Fourth-Century Trinitarian Theology*. Oxford: Oxford University Press, 2004.

>Ayres's work on Nicaea revolutionized the way that scholars interpreted many aspects of trinitarian theology before and after the Council of Nicaea. I rely heavily on his schema of pro-Nicene, anti-Nicene, and non-Nicene theology throughout this work.

Muller, Richard A. *Post-Reformation Reformed Dogmatics: The Rise and Development of Reformed Orthodoxy, ca. 1520 to ca. 1725*. Vol. 4, *The Triunity of God*. Grand Rapids: Baker Academic, 2003.

>Muller's treatment of Reformed scholastic thought is invaluable as a historical resource that introduces many untranslated theologians' ideas.

Selected Western Contemporary Treatments of the Trinity

Barth, Karl. *Church Dogmatics*. Vol. I/1, *The Doctrine of the Word of God*. Edited by G. W. Bromiley and T. F. Torrance. Translated by G. W. Bromiley. Edinburgh: T&T Clark, 1936.

>No work dominated the twentieth-century landscape of trinitarian theology in the way that the first volume of *Church Dogmatics* did, with its unique presentation of the Trinity as rooted in the doctrine of revelation.

Emery, Gilles. *The Trinity: An Introduction to Catholic Doctrine on the Triune God*. Translated by Matthew Levering. Washington, DC: Catholic University of America Press, 2011.

>Emery's introduction is particularly strong in its extended theological treatment of the ecumenical creeds, which exceeds what is found in many texts of this nature.

Sonderegger, Katherine. *Systematic Theology*. Vol. 2, *The Doctrine of the Holy Trinity: Processions and Persons*. Minneapolis: Fortress, 2020.

Sonderegger's volume, which was published so recently that I could not engage with it as much I would have liked, challenges many points of theological consensus on the Trinity and is sure to spark much discussion.

Selected Majority World Treatments of the Trinity

Bingemer, Maria Clara Lucchetti. *A Face for God*. Translated by Jovelino Ramos and Joan Ramos. Miami: Convivium, 2014.

Bingemer's text is a nuanced presentation of many common modern ideas about the Trinity, including political and feminist readings of the doctrine. It also uniquely incorporates poetry in substantive ways.

Boff, Leonardo. *Trinity and Society*. Translated by Paul Burns. Maryknoll, NY: Orbis Books, 1996.

This treatment of the Trinity from the perspective of liberation theology is perhaps the most well-known Majority World treatment of the doctrine. Boff's methodology and conclusion are innovative and contested.

Kombo, James Henry Owino. *The Doctrine of God in African Christian Thought: The Holy Trinity, Theological Hermeneutics and the African Intellectual Culture*. Leiden: Brill, 2007.

Kombo illustrates that ideas of God as supreme essence, supreme subject, and divine community in unity are all shaped by culture. He then explores how a presentation of the Trinity shaped by African cultures might look.

CHAPTER 1

Consubstantiality

One of the most famous visual representations of the Trinity is the icon of Abraham's three visitors sitting at the oak of Mamre (Gen. 18:1–15) produced by the Russian Orthodox monk and iconographer Andrei Rublev sometime between 1392 and 1427.[1] The icon depicts three figures seated at a table. At the level of the Genesis narrative, this is a depiction of the guests resting, having accepted Abraham's offer of bread and some water for washing their feet (vv. 3–5). However, at a theological level Rublev discloses these three to be persons of the Trinity. The figure seated on the left, clothed in royal purple in front of a house, is the Father, that eternal King whose mansion has many rooms for the faithful (John 14:2). The Son sits in the center, his red and blue robes a traditional symbol of the incarnation: red represents the human **nature** of the incarnation, and blue the celestial and divine nature. This middle figure sits in front of the tree, which is symbolic of both the tree of life and the wood of the cross. The figure to the right, then, is the Spirit. Though the meaning and color of this figure's robes are debated,[2] the mountain behind the figure is likely an important symbol of spiritual ascent, which is made possible through the Spirit.[3] The figures themselves lack visually distinctive characteristics and are distinguished by their posture and garments alone, a diversity that simultaneously illustrates a unity.[4] The entire icon is situated within a circle, suggesting that the three

---

1. Strezova, *Hesychasm and Art*, 189.
2. Podles, "*The Trinity* by Andrei Rublev," 54.
3. Strezova, *Hesychasm and Art*, 196.
4. Strezova, *Hesychasm and Art*, 201.

are united, and their wings, their halos, and the curves of their hands form concentric circles that converge on the chalice placed on the table in front of them.[5] The eucharistic association is clear, suggesting perhaps that we can encounter the divine three through Christ's presence in the sacraments. The table itself is open to the viewer, inviting them to join the holy three by worshiping the Trinity in adoration.

This famous icon raises an important question: Why did Rublev, and many commentators and iconographers before him, interpret Abraham's three guests as being the three divine persons of the Holy Trinity? The careful reader of Genesis 18 should note several interesting features of the text. First, the appearance of the Lord to Abraham (18:1) is identified with the appearance of three figures (18:2).[6] Second, as Victor Hamilton notes, the passage "shift[s] back and forth from singular to plural."[7] At times the dialogue proceeds as if Abraham addresses a singular God (18:10, 13, 17–21), while at others it proceeds as if he speaks with three strangers (18:5, 9). Hamilton argues that this ambiguity is part of a larger "fluidity between God and angels" found throughout Genesis and other Old Testament texts (see Gen. 21:17–18; Judg. 6:7–24; 13:1–25).[8] Some modern scholars see the shifts between one and three as evidence of later editorial combinations of two different stories, one where Abraham was visited by a singular stranger, another where he hosted three individuals. According to this theory, only a later editor identifies this story as an instance of divine appearance.[9] Other modern commentators see in this passage a meeting between Abraham and God plus two angels, with Abraham only gradually learning the identity of the strangers.[10] Gerhard von Rad, a patriarch of historical-critical Old Testament scholarship, is skeptical of the latter solution. He argues that it would be peculiar for two servants to accept an invitation to dine with their master (Gen. 18:8). Noting that the three ask a "common question about Sarah" (18:9), von Rad concludes, "One is rather

5. Strezova, *Hesychasm and Art*, 189. Strezova suggests that these circles also allude to perichoresis, the subject of chap. 5.

6. The history of Jewish interpretation of this passage is interesting, ranging from Targum Onkelos's explanations for why three angels must be sent at once to Philo's belief that this is a threefold appearance of a singular God. See the discussion in Wainwright, *The Trinity in the New Testament*, 27–29.

7. Hamilton, *Book of Genesis*, 6. "Thus: v. 2, three men; v. 3, all singular; v. 4, second person plural; v. 5, again the second person plural; v. 9, plural; vv. 10–15, singular; v. 16 plural; vv. 17–21, singular; v. 22 begins with the plural but ends with the singular; vv. 22b–33, singular" (6).

8. Hamilton, *Book of Genesis*, 6–7.

9. See Westermann, *Genesis*, 135.

10. See Speiser, *Genesis*, 131; Wenham, *Genesis 16–50*, 53–54. Such interpretations typically point to the description in Gen. 19:1 of two angels leaving Abraham, which indicates that the third figure must be God.

inclined to think that Yahweh appeared in all three."[11] Von Rad, dependent as he is on the literal-historical meaning of a text, denies any connection between this triad and the Trinity, but if one assumes that the Bible's human authors were inspired by the Holy Spirit, as early Christians did, then it is only a small stretch to see at a spiritual level an allusion to the Trinity. This sort of move leads to the idea behind Rublev's icon.

I begin my dogmatic account of the doctrine of the Trinity with Rublev for three reasons. First, Rublev sets the stage for appreciating how difficult it is to depict simultaneously the oneness and threeness of God. What Rublev attempts in the form of three visually similar figures harmonized by concentric circles, systematic theology attempts through technical terms such as the subject of this chapter—"consubstantiality." Let the reader be warned that the transition from paint to technical vocabulary does not result in an easier task. If, for us, the triune God moves from complete mystery to partially understood, these words will have served us well. The second reason I choose to begin with Rublev is that his reliance on Genesis 18 illustrates a theological reading of a text. Such readings often exceed what we can expect the original human authors or audiences to have understood, yet these readings are nevertheless true and valid meanings insofar as they are based on the intent of the divine Author behind the composition of the Bible. A robust doctrine of inspiration requires that we accept the possibility of inspired meaning beyond, though not contrary to, the literal-historical meaning.

Third and finally, Rublev draws on angelic mediators and on worship to depict the Trinity, and both mediators and worship play an important role in understanding the consubstantiality of the Father, Son, and Holy Spirit. At a literal level, Genesis 18 relies on a certain ambiguity between divine mediators and God. The same ambiguity is present in the New Testament's depiction of Jesus and the Holy Spirit, and it led early Christians to worship in a trinitarian manner. Early Christians eventually had to seek terminology that made sense of this ambiguity. Rublev's icon moves beyond the literal meaning of Genesis 18 to represent the Trinity in art, but Christians at the Council of Nicaea (323) and the First Council of Constantinople (381) depicted God's unity through appeal to philosophy by drawing on the term *homoousios*, the meaning of which is represented in this book by the equivalent English term "consubstantiality." This chapter will explore how New Testament depictions of Jesus and the Holy Spirit fit within Second Temple Judaism's identification

11. Von Rad, *Genesis*, 204. Von Rad denies that we should interpret Gen. 18 in light of 19:1, since in his view, these two stories likely originate from different sources. He does admit that this narrative "is so strange and singular in the Old Testament that it must belong to the peculiarity of this tradition and this tradition only" (205).

of heavenly mediators with God. With regard to worship, the New Testament moves beyond other texts of that time by centering worship on the Son and Spirit, raising a question concerning how the Father, Son, and Spirit can be identified with one another and can be worshiped together. I will explain how the church historically answered these questions with the doctrine of consubstantiality by showing how Basil of Caesarea, Thomas Aquinas, and Christians engaging with Islam explain the doctrine. In the course of this discussion, I will also demonstrate how certain modern analytic treatments of consubstantiality lead in a problematic direction.

The Biblical Roots of Consubstantiality

Much in the same way that Rublev draws on Genesis 18 to depict the Trinity, many New Testament authors appear to draw on **mediatorial figures**[12] present in Second Temple literature in their depiction of Jesus Christ. While we must be careful to avoid overstating the case,[13] it does seem likely that the way New Testament authors deploy such mediatorial figures can provide us with some exegetical basis for the doctrine of the Trinity. What do I mean by mediatorial figures? James Davila explains that mediatorial figures can include "personified divine attributes" such as wisdom (to be considered below), "exalted matriarchs and patriarchs" like Enoch or Adam who are given an elevated status in proximity to God, and "principal angels," who are said to be closest to God among the heavenly host, like the mysterious **Metatron** found in some Second Temple literature. Mediators can also include more mundane figures like charismatic prophets or "ideal figures" such as the Davidic king. Such mediators can have a past, present, or future role, but all are thought to represent God to his people in some respect.[14]

The personified divine attribute of Wisdom helpfully illustrates a larger trend in Second Temple literature. As Gerald O'Collins summarizes, "Personified Wisdom or Sophia becomes increasingly related to the divine work of creation, providence, and salvation and grows in dignity and power."[15] We first meet wisdom in Job 28, where she is said to be established at the time of creation (28:27). In the later text of Proverbs 8–9, Wisdom, now personified,

---

12. Sometimes, language of "divine agents" is preferred. See, e.g., McGrath, *Only True God*, 14.

13. See the hesitation in Bates, *Birth of the Trinity*, 19–26. Bates does not deny the validity of this approach but rightly notes that the mediatorial approach on its own "requires urgent supplementation" (26).

14. Davila, "Of Methodology, Monotheism and Metatron," 5–7.

15. O'Collins, *Tripersonal God*, 24.

speaks to the audience and claims to have been generated before the earth was formed and to be a "master workman" beside God (8:30 ESV), sharing in the work of creation and offering favor from the Lord (8:35). Certain intertestamental literature like Sirach 24 (ca. 180 BC) continues to elevate personified Wisdom and associate her with divine attributes such as omnipresence. By the time we get to the later book the Wisdom of Solomon, Wisdom is still said to be omnipotent, omniscient, and omnipresent (Wis. 8:1, 4–5). She is now associated not only with creation (9:9) but also with the saving deeds of God, including delivering Adam from his sins (10:1), providentially guiding Joseph in Egypt (10:13–14), and powerfully freeing the Israelites in the exodus (10:15–19). In short, Wisdom is not only the one through whom God has brought deliverance but "a pure emanation of the glory of the Almighty" (7:25b).[16] "This is very bold language indeed for someone who is writing within the biblical tradition," remarks David Winston, and rightly so, for the line between creature and Creator has certainly been blurred here.[17]

These blurred lines between heavenly mediators and God have led to growing debates among scholars concerning the sense in which first-century Judaism was monotheistic. Today, the term "monotheism" is often associated with the claim that only one God exists, but it may be the case that first-century monotheism was characterized more by the worship of only one God (more technically termed "monolatry"). Even here we must be cautious. While it is certain that most Jews would have refused to sacrifice to Caesar, even to the point of martyrdom, other aspects of worship were less rigid. For example, some Jews may have prohibited bowing down to any figure who was not God (Esther 3:5),[18] but in other instances Jewish texts record humans bowing before heavenly mediators (1 Enoch 62:9). Though there is a common depiction of angels refusing veneration, as discussed below, it is also possible to find occasional instances of people blessing angels as a form of veneration performed in return for the angels' care for a community (11Q14 [Berakhot]; Joseph and Aseneth 14:1–12; 15:11–12).[19] Thus, while there is consensus that sacrifice was reserved for God alone, there is greater debate concerning whether such prostration and blessings count as worship.[20]

16. See the treatment in O'Collins, *Tripersonal God*, 24–30.

17. Winston, *Wisdom of Solomon*, 184.

18. McGrath, *Only True God*, 7. McGrath notes that the LXX of Esther 13:12–14 seems to deny that any prostration is permissible.

19. Stuckenbruck, *Angel Veneration and Christology*, 161–63. However, Hurtado notes that "there is . . . no evidence of an 'angel cultus,' that is, worship offered to angels as part of the devotional pattern of any known Jewish group at the time" (*Lord Jesus Christ*, 34).

20. See Hurtado, *Lord Jesus Christ*, 37–42. Hurtado contends that reverence would be paid to many authority figures in first-century Judaism but that such reverence may not equate with

Fortunately, our question is not historical but dogmatic. This means that we need not reach a clear conclusion on questions regarding how frequently worship of mediatorial figures was present in first-century Judaism, assuming it was present at all. Nor need we address the question of whether early Christian practices would have fallen outside of what was acceptable in other varieties of Judaism, leading to the parting of ways between these two religions. Instead, I must consider dogmatic questions: How are we to interpret canonical depictions of Jesus in light of the historical context of the human author? When we consider the worship of Jesus within the inspired biblical canon, what conclusions about Jesus can we draw? I turn now to these questions.

Heavenly Mediators and Christology

The New Testament depicts Christ as fulfilling all five mediatorial types. Jesus obviously fulfills the role of the ideal figure in that he is the awaited Davidic king, a truth that the New Testament establishes not only through genealogical claims (Matt. 1:2–16; Luke 3:23–38; Rom. 1:3) but also through the direct application of the title "Son of David" to Christ, particularly in the Gospel of Matthew (1:1; 9:27; 12:23; 15:22; 20:30–31; 21:9, 15; 22:42, 45). On several occasions Jesus is called a prophet (e.g., Luke 7:16; John 4:19), and he also clearly fulfills the role of a charismatic prophet.[21] Our focus, however, will be on the three other mediatorial roles: personified divine attribute, exalted human figure, and principal angel. At times, these roles blur in New Testament Christology, but I will attempt to highlight examples where one mediatorial role or another is clearly in view.[22] While we often cannot assume any textual

---

"'worship' in the 'hard' sense of reverencing a figure as a deity" (38). Fletcher-Louis disagrees, pointing to several counterexamples, the most persuasive of which may be Adam in what he calls the "Worship Adam Story" in Life of Adam and Eve 12–16. This account preserves a tradition of ascribing such glory to Adam that he is worshiped by angels as God's image. Context suggests worship is in mind, and traditions of Adam bearing God's glory seem to have been preserved in some liturgical contexts, including Qumran (see 4Q504 8) (Fletcher-Louis, *Jesus Monotheism*, 1:250–92). Though this does seem to be an example of worship, it is not fully cultic in the sense used by Hurtado, as Fletcher-Louis does not point to prayers, doxologies, benedictions, or rites like baptism centered on Adam.

21. Cullman, *Christology of the New Testament*, 13–50. Cullman shows that this is "one aspect" of Christ's identity, but it certainly does not exhaust early Christology, especially with respect to preexistence and Christ's eschatological role (49).

22. Thus, Alan Segal comments, "The Christological titles (and even Son of God) can be partially understood as a combination of traditions of exegesis about various angelic figures with messianic prophecies." Segal attributes this to a combination of messianic prophecy, notions of Jesus as an exalted human, and influence from apocalyptic angel appearances (*Two Powers in Heaven*, 208–9).

dependence on the apocalyptic traditions that emphasize mediatorial figures (the use of certain quoted Old Testament texts being an exception), we can at least acknowledge that such mediatorial concepts were possible in a first-century Jewish context.[23]

New Testament Christology clearly draws on personified divine attributes and exalted human figures. For example, Jesus is identified as wisdom in 1 Corinthians 1:30. Though some have been prone to downplay this as mere metaphor, Andrew Chester marshals evidence that Paul is probably drawing on wisdom tradition that the Corinthians would have accepted. Paul not only depicts Christ, like Wisdom, as the mediator of creation (1 Cor. 8:6; cf. Prov. 8:22–31; Sir. 24; Wis. 9:2), but he also identifies Jesus with the rock in Exodus 17 (1 Cor. 10:4), much as Philo identifies this rock with Wisdom and the Word.[24] John's treatment of Jesus as the Word of God also likely draws on such personification.[25] Paul's depiction of Jesus as the new or last Adam (Rom. 5:12–21; 1 Cor. 15:45–49) mirrors many apocalyptic Jewish accounts of an exalted Adam who stands as God's mediator.[26] In each instance, Jesus is closely associated with God, either as an attribute of God or as the one who most fully makes God present on earth.

Depictions of Jesus as an angel are less common in the New Testament. Perhaps the most interesting case is found in Jude 5–7, where a figure is identified with four acts: the exodus, the destruction of the Israelites in the desert, the holding captive of fallen angels, and the destruction of Sodom and Gomorrah. Though verse 5 in most translations identifies this figure as "the Lord," several important ancient manuscripts have the reading "Jesus" or even "God."[27] English translations and commentators tend to prefer the first reading, but even here interpretation is complicated by the fact that verse 4 has just identified Jesus Christ as the Lord, so all three readings could have Jesus in mind. Jarl Fossum argues that by the first century each of these four acts

23. N. T. Wright cautions, "We cannot assume that all or even most early Christians knew, or even knew of, the writings that we can casually pull off a shelf today and treat as 'typical' of first- or second-century Christianity. . . . With praxis and symbol we are on surer ground" (*New Testament and the People of God*, 359). We will turn to the question of praxis in the next section.

24. Chester, "Jewish Messianic Expectations and Mediatorial Figures," 72.

25. See Keener, *Gospel of John*, 1:341–63. Keener offers an exhaustive analysis of various possible influences on John's use of *logos* ("word") in the Gospel of John's prologue. Though some Hellenistic influence is possible and expected, Keener highlights parallels in the Wisdom of Solomon and 3 Enoch, as well as the Wisdom tradition already discussed, since Wisdom and the Word are overlapping concepts.

26. I have detailed my view on Second Adam Christology in Butner, *Son Who Learned Obedience*, 166–70, 173–78.

27. Another variant even has "God Christ" rescuing people.

was associated with an angelic mediator.[28] Wisdom saved Lot (Wis. 10:6–8), an angel of the Lord brought the plague in the desert (1 Chron. 21:12, 15), an angel (Num. 20:16) or Wisdom (Sir. 24:4) led the Israelites out of Egypt, and an "angel of the presence" bound fallen angels until judgment (1 Enoch 10:4–6). While we cannot be certain that Jesus is in mind in these passages, I find Fossum compelling when he claims that in Jude 5–7, "the Son is modelled on an intermediary figure whose basic constituent is the Angel of the Lord."[29] Though this example of angelic intermediaries is contested, it is still clear that Second Temple intermediary figures helpfully illuminate New Testament Christology.

The Worship of Jesus Christ and the Holy Spirit

Though there is some analogy between New Testament Christology and Second Temple mediatorial figures, there may also be differences. These differences center on worship and are heavily debated among New Testament scholars. It is certainly clear that the New Testament incorporates Jesus into what we might call **cultic worship,** defined by Larry Hurtado as "devotion offered in a specifically worship (liturgical) setting and expressive of the thanksgiving, praise, communion, and petition that directly represent, manifest and reinforce the relationship of the worshippers with the divine."[30] What is less clear is how distinctive such worship of Jesus Christ is in a first-century context and the extent to which the Holy Spirit is incorporated into such worship.

The liturgical structure of early Christian worship follows a clear trinitarian pattern. In a particularly important passage, Paul incorporates Christ into the **Shema,** that key confession of faith among Jews. Deuteronomy 6:4 speaks of the Lord God being one, and Paul insists that there is "one God . . . and . . . one Lord" (1 Cor. 8:6).[31] Such a confession was likely used in the setting of liturgical and corporate worship, and the use of the name "Lord Jesus," itself a confession, was probably a common liturgical practice (see Rom. 10:9a; 1 Cor. 12:3; Phil. 2:11).[32] The Holy Spirit was thought to inspire songs sung to God in the name of the Son (e.g., Col. 3:16–17), and Martin

---

28. Fossum, *Image of the Invisible God,* 50–61.

29. Fossum, *Image of the Invisible God,* 67.

30. Hurtado, "Binitarian Shape of Early Christian Worship," 190.

31. This passage is the subject of much debate. See McGrath, *Only True God,* 38–43; Fletcher-Louis, *Jesus Monotheism,* 1:32–59; Dunn, *Christology in the Making,* 179–83; Hill, *Paul and the Trinity,* 112–20.

32. Kramer, *Christ, Lord, Son of God,* 65–71. Kramer notes that Rom. 10:9 and Phil 2:11 link the acclamation with the word *homologein* or *exomologeisthai,* both of which can mean "to praise/applaud."

Hengel interprets the data to suggest that there was a growing practice of singing songs not only *about* Christ but directly *to* him (e.g., Eph. 5:18–20).[33] This practice may derive from early Christian methods of interpretation that sang the Psalms as if personally addressed to Jesus, though this is uncertain.[34] The Holy Spirit did not only inspire songs; he is directly invoked in benedictions in the New Testament Epistles (2 Cor. 13:13; cf. Rom. 15:13). Christ is invoked in such a manner more frequently,[35] and this pattern leads us to suspect that such invocation may have occurred in corporate-worship settings. Baptism occurred in the name of the Father, Son, and Holy Spirit (Matt. 28:19), in the name of the Lord Jesus Christ (Acts 10:48; 1 Cor. 6:11), or into the name of the Lord Jesus (Acts 8:16; 19:5; cf. Rom. 6:3). The latter two formulas imply Jesus had heavenly authority,[36] while the former provides an explicitly triadic Christian initiation rite. There are also New Testament examples of Jesus being addressed in prayer (Acts 7:59–60; 1 Cor. 16:22) and being the object of doxology (Rom. 9:5; 2 Tim. 4:18; 2 Pet. 3:18; Rev. 1:5) and benedictions (e.g., 1 Thess. 3:11–12).[37] Collectively, these practices demonstrate a remarkable inclusion of three figures in liturgical practice, praise, and reverence: the Father, the Son, and the Holy Spirit, particularly the Son.

How distinct is this worship of Jesus (and, less clearly, of the Holy Spirit) in its first-century context? That question is heavily debated. For example, there are a number of instances in the New Testament where individuals fall prostrate before Christ (e.g., Matt. 2:11; 14:33; John 9:38; Rev. 5:14), but the Greek term used in these cases can describe veneration given to nondivine figures,[38] including those who are members of devout churches (Rev. 3:9).[39] The New Testament prohibits the worship of angels (Col. 2:18), and there are examples of angels rejecting veneration (Rev. 19:10; 22:9), a motif found in other apocalyptic texts (2 Enoch 1:4–8; 3 Enoch 1:7; 16:1–5; Ascension of Isaiah 7:18–23; 8:1–10, 15; Tob. 12:16–22). Even the common angelic saying

33. Hengel, *Between Jesus and Paul*, 80–81.
34. Daly-Denton, "Singing Hymns to Christ as to a God," 282–85.
35. See 2 Cor. 13:14; Gal. 6:18; Eph. 3:17–19; 2 Thess. 2:16–17; Philem. 25.
36. "When Jesus was called 'Lord' in the baptismal formula, it meant that he was confessed as a heavenly authority, not as the God to whom the Thessalonians had turned, but yet as a Lord with divine power who was active among human beings. . . . A baptism 'into the name of the Lord Jesus' presupposed belief in a glorified Jesus who had power which he now exerted on earth" (Hartman, *"Into the Name of the Lord Jesus,"* 47–48).
37. On 2 Tim. 4:18, see Wainwright, *The Trinity in the New Testament*, 94.
38. Hurtado, "Binitarian Shape of Early Christian Worship," 188–89.
39. McGrath, *Only True God*, 19. McGrath makes a strong case that prostration before other figures was prohibited only in the case of pagan rulers who opposed God and in the case of angelic figures, perhaps because the prohibitions mean to convey an equal, not superior, status to humans.

"Do not be afraid" (Matt. 1:20–21; Mark 16:5–7; Luke 1:11–20; 2:8–12) may intend to prohibit fearful veneration.[40] However, there are examples in non-canonical texts of figures arguably being worshiped, though the evidence for cultic veneration as defined by Hurtado is quite limited in comparison with New Testament texts.[41]

Taken from a dogmatic standpoint, the New Testament treatment of Jesus as a divine mediator worthy of worship is a sufficient basis for establishing some form of identity between the Father, the Son, and (less clearly) the Holy Spirit. We can admit the historical point that some first-century Jews might not have moved from worshiping Jesus to believing in his full divinity. However, it is a different matter when we constrain ourselves to the biblical canon and ask, based on these holy texts, what we ought to conclude about Jesus. In other words, if we accept only the Old and New Testament texts as revelation, denying the inspiration of other first-century texts, what can we conclude about Christ?

Here four arguments are, in my mind, decisive. First, the New Testament consistently depicts Jesus as the only mediator between God and humans (1 Tim. 2:5). This is evident in the argument in Hebrews 1:4–2:10 that Christ is above all angels. When the Gospel of John argues that no one has seen the Father except the Word, who comes from God (1:18; 6:46), it likely intends to deny the ascension traditions that speak of other exalted human figures sharing in God's glory.[42] When Paul exalts the last Adam over the first (1 Cor. 15:45–49), he undermines the possibility of worshiping the first Adam, whether or not he was familiar with texts implying this was a first-century practice. Second, apart from the aforementioned worship of the Son and the close association of the Holy Spirit with him and the Father in liturgical practice, praise, and reverence, there are no New Testament examples of cultic worship offered to a figure other than God.[43] Third, this identification between Jesus and God that leads to equal worship is sometimes treated as the basis for Christianity's feud with Judaism. For example, when the crowds want to stone Jesus for blasphemy after he claims "I and the Father are one," (John 10:30–31), the reason is probably that, as Richard Bauckham says, Jesus's claim "echoes the terminology of the Shema" (Deut. 6:4).[44] Fourth and

40. Stuckenbruck, *Angel Veneration and Christology*, 87–92.
41. E.g., some Jewish funerary inscriptions invoke names beyond God's (McGrath, *Only True God*, 30). Angels are sometimes evoked to give a blessing (see 11Q14 [Berakhot]; Joseph and Aseneth 14:1–12; 15:11–12) (Stuckenbruck, *Angel Veneration and Christology*, 161–63).
42. Segal, *Two Powers in Heaven*, 214.
43. James McGrath sees cultic prostration before the king in 1 Chron. 29:20–23, but this falls far short of the sort of liturgical worship noted above. McGrath, *Only True God*, 50.
44. Bauckham, "The Trinity and the Gospel of John," 103.

finally, New Testament Christology is atypical in elevating a contemporary historical figure, rather than an abstract attribute, an ancient patriarch, or an incorporeal angel, to the point of sharing God's glory.[45] This leaves no ambiguity: the Son who took flesh was distinct from the Father who did not, yet he was identified with his Father in worship.

Read canonically, the New Testament gives us reason to affirm that God is solely revealed in Christ, who, with the Holy Spirit, shares God's exclusive right of receiving worship. Whereas some Second Temple texts blur the line between a wide range of heavenly mediators and God, the canonical account is that there are no others who can be identified with God in this way. Though some Second Temple texts show reverence, on rare occasions nearing cultic worship, to heavenly mediators, the entirety of the New Testament liturgical practice is marked by trinitarian forms suggesting that proper worship involves Father, Son, and Spirit. Because Christ, the mediator of God, is identified with him in worship, we have laid an exegetical foundation for the doctrine of consubstantiality. Whereas angels are mediators who reveal a God that is other, meaning that they cannot rightly accept worship, the New Testament account drives us toward what modern systematicians have called God's self-revelation and self-communication. In some sense, this is the entire dogmatic purpose of consubstantiality: demonstrating that when Jesus reveals the Father, he is also revealing his own nature. T. F. Torrance summarizes this basic function of consubstantiality nicely: "Apart from . . . oneness in Being there is no Mediator between God and man, and the identity of Jesus Christ has nothing to do with any *self*-revealing and *self*-giving on the part of the eternal God for the salvation of mankind."[46] The groundwork has been laid, but the case is not fully made. To complete the work of explaining consubstantiality, I turn now to tradition.

Nicaea and the Doctrine of Consubstantiality

The doctrine of the Trinity gradually developed in the centuries following the writing of the New Testament, but the doctrine of consubstantiality did not truly emerge until the fourth century, when an argument between Arius of Alexandria and his local bishop, Alexander, escalated into a dispute fought across the Roman Empire. Drawing on certain lines of patristic

45. E.g., Raymond Brown highlights the significant overlap between the Johannine Jesus and Wisdom, concluding that John introduces "a much sharper historical perspective" than what is found in other personifications (*Introduction to the Gospel of John*, 263).
46. T. F. Torrance, *Christian Doctrine of God*, 94.

precedent, Arius argued that the Son was the preeminent *creature*, a mediator between God and humanity, recipient of all the gifts of God by grace, not by nature.[47] A group of theologians that modern scholars call **pro-Nicene** developed anti-Arian arguments that will help illuminate the doctrine of consubstantiality. Pro-Nicene arguments drew on biblical texts that would soon become the New Testament canon to argue that the mediatorial depictions of Christ discussed above required Christians to view Jesus as the same **essence** as his Father. In fact, the New Testament canon was finally solidified for many Christian groups during this era, as inspired text and orthodox creed helped confirm the validity of one another. Though the pro-Nicenes were likely aware of Second Temple texts only to a quite limited degree, their arguments help us connect New Testament Christology with the doctrine of consubstantiality.

Pro-Nicene theologians argued that Christ could fulfill his mediatorial role only if he was the same essence as the Father. Arius tended to depict the Son as an exalted human figure, the first creature God made and one who had earned his status as Son through obedience.[48] In contradiction to his assertions, Pro-Nicenes could point to the canonical emphasis on all things being created through Christ (John 1:3; Col. 1:16) to argue that Christ could not be a creature. For example, Hilary of Poitiers argued that if all things came to be through Christ, then he must have been a Creator, not a creature, for creatures would not have the same nature and status as their Creator.[49] Athanasius of Alexandria would make a closely related argument: If the Son was created, we would either have to say that he created himself, which is illogical, or that someone else created him, which would mean that he did not create all things. Therefore, if the Son made all things that were created, he could not have been created.[50] Such arguments certainly fit with the New Testament emphasis on Jesus as the unique mediator. Furthermore, pro-Nicenes insisted that since Jesus was depicted as a personified divine attribute like Wisdom (1 Cor. 1:24, 30) or the Word (John 1:1), he had to be eternally divine in essence. After all, Christians could not have supposed that God did not eternally have his wisdom, for this would have made God unwise prior to the existence of the Son.[51] Also, if the Son were the very Wisdom of God, Christians would also have to deny that he earned and was given

47. For a concise summary of Arius's theology, see R. Williams, *Arius*, 98.
48. Gregg and Groh, *Early Arianism*, 21, 24.
49. Hilary of Poitiers, *On the Trinity* 12.5.
50. Athanasius, *To the Bishops of Egypt* §15.
51. Augustine, *On the Holy Trinity* 6.1.1. Augustine connects this argument with a discussion of appropriations, a subject I discuss in further detail in chap. 7.

wisdom, for how could one be given, in the course of one's life, what one is by very nature?[52] A possible counterargument could have been that Jesus was personified attributes in only a metaphorical sense, but the pro-Nicene position was guarded by the fact that New Testament texts uniquely combine the personified attributes with the exalted-mediator trope. If a divine attribute was also a real historical figure exalted at the resurrection, personification of this attribute was less clearly mere metaphor. In each of these arguments, the pro-Nicenes built on mediatorial images and the New Testament emphasis on the exclusive mediatorial role of Christ to argue for his consubstantiality with the Father.

At times, worship played a considerable role in the fourth-century debates around the Trinity, particularly regarding the Holy Spirit. Anticipating modern exegetical debates surrounding worship, Gregory of Nyssa acknowledged that because prostration could properly be performed before human beings, Christians certainly should not deny a higher reverence offered to the clearly superior Spirit. When performed toward leaders and rulers, this act of veneration was meant to elicit the giving of gifts, so how much more ought Christians to worship the Giver, the Holy Spirit?[53] Ambrose of Milan made a number of clear connections between worship and the Spirit's divinity. Baptism in the Spirit, Ambrose argued, was indicative of the fact that Christians were sealed in the Spirit (Eph. 1:13–14) and thereby given the grace of adoption and participation in the divine nature (2 Pet. 1:4). Ambrose further argued that the Spirit could not give such blessings unless he, too, was divine.[54] Baptism in the Spirit also signified a "sharing of honor or of working" with God,[55] such that Christians should not only worship *in* the Spirit but also worship the Spirit.[56] Ambrose's argument relied on some grammatical analysis of liturgical forms, but Basil of Caesarea's *On the Holy Spirit* was far more thorough in its liturgical analysis, arguing that there was no scriptural basis for allowing worship *in* the Spirit but prohibiting it *to* the Spirit.[57] He argued that the Spirit was consubstantial with the Father, because Christians rightly worshiped the Spirit and God alone should be the object of cultic or liturgical worship.

In AD 325, the Council of Nicaea produced a creed that affirmed that the Son was "God from God," "of the being [*ousia*] of the Father," and "consubstantial [*homoousion*] with the Father." The term "consubstantial"

---

52. Athanasius, *Orations against the Arians* 2.28–29.
53. Gregory of Nyssa, *On the Holy Spirit against the Followers of Macedonius*, 325.
54. Ambrose, *On the Holy Spirit* 1.5.76–80.
55. Ambrose, *On the Holy Spirit* 2.8.71.
56. Ambrose, *On the Holy Spirit* 3.11–12.
57. Basil, *On the Holy Spirit*.

(*homoousios*) was controversial not only because it was not a scriptural term but also because it had been previously condemned as used by Paul of Samosata, who likely claimed that the Father and Son were consubstantial in the sense of "a single, undifferentiated being."[58] That this is not what was meant at Nicaea reveals one of the major challenges of the word "consubstantiality," that it can mean at least four things: (1) Consubstantiality could mean, as in Paul of Samosata, that two so-called distinct things were actually one and the same reality, the distinction between them being merely an illusion.[59] (2) It could also mean that two things were made of the same matter, in the way that two glasses of water have the same molecular composition.[60] (3) Two beings could be consubstantial if they were "aspects, parts, or expressions" of a single individual essence or **substance**.[61] (4) Finally, two beings might also be consubstantial if they belonged to the same **genus**, even if they were not identical in matter. Angels, for example, were considered immaterial yet consubstantial with one another.[62] This ambiguity meant that Nicaea's affirmation of consubstantiality initially did little to resolve the trinitarian debates. A second ecumenical council at Constantinople (381) provided some clarification, including the affirmation that the Holy Spirit was "worshipped and glorified" together with the Father and Son. However, ambiguity remains even in the present day, which is why the affirmation of consubstantiality alone does not constitute a complete doctrine of the Trinity. I would like to note one particularly modern interpretation of the idea of consubstantiality before providing further dogmatic clarification.

Often, contemporary analytic theologians understand consubstantiality in terms of a principle made famous by G. W. Leibniz: the **indiscernibility of identicals**.[63] According to this principle, two **identicals** have no distinctive properties, and they must have all properties in common if they are truly identical. If the claim of consubstantiality is understood in the sense of being Leibnizian identicals, it creates an intractable problem: How can Father, Son, and Spirit be consubstantial yet distinct? This would mean that they are both identical and not identical, a logical impossibility. To resolve this problem, some analytic philosophers, such as Keith Yandell, abandon the notion of a single divine essence, instead claiming that there are three property bearers who have the properties necessary to be God and that these three property

---

58. Kelly, *Early Christian Creeds*, 248.
59. Stead, *Divine Substance*, 246.
60. Kelly, *Early Christian Creeds*, 244.
61. Stead, *Divine Substance*, 246–47.
62. Stead, *Divine Substance*, 247.
63. E.g., see Hasker, *Metaphysics and the Tri-personal*, 36–37, 59, 187.

bearers are composite and necessarily conjoined.[64] It is difficult to see how this remains monotheism instead of **tritheism**. Other analytic theologians, such as Thomas McCall, treat the claim "The Father is *homoousios* with the Son and Spirit" as a claim that the Father and Son are identicals, having no disparate properties.[65] Though McCall is not consistent on this point, it is difficult to see how such an account would preserve a genuine distinction of persons. Clearly the doctrine of consubstantiality needs further clarification. I turn now to three examples in an attempt to clarify the doctrine: Basil of Caesarea, Thomas Aquinas, and Christian debates with Muslims on the Trinity.

Three Historical Explanations of Consubstantiality

Basil of Caesarea

Basil of Caesarea's theology provides a starting point for considering what it means to say that Father, Son, and Holy Spirit are all *homoousios*, or consubstantial. He is credited with developing and promoting the terminology that serves as the basic trinitarian grammar: Father, Son, and Holy Spirit are different hypostases but the same being.[66] At various times in church history, different terms, often derived from different languages and in the context of different debates, have been used as equivalent: Father, Son, and Spirit are also different persons, eternal modes of existence, and subsistences, but they are the same in nature, essence, and substance. The last of these words makes its way into the English "consubstantial," which I am using as an approximate translation for *homoousios*.[67] At a more technical level, there are subtle distinctions between many of these terms. Some differences will be addressed shortly; others will be addressed in later chapters. For the moment, however,

64. Yandell, "How Many Times," 165–67.

65. McCall, *Whose Monotheism?*, 179–80, 200. This is evident in McCall's objections both to John Zizioulas's principle of the Father alone having aseity (since the Son and Spirit are from the Father) and to evangelical claims of the eternal submission of the Son. McCall objects to both claims on the basis that attributing such properties to one person but not the other would undermine consubstantiality.

66. Basil was not the first to make such a distinction. It is likely that he drew the terms from George of Laodicaea, though he did develop and defend the notion more extensively than his contemporaries (Behr, *Formation of Christian Theology* II/2, 296n90).

67. At a very technical level, "substance" risks a more material interpretation than *ousia* ("being") and carries a little more baggage, given the widespread criticism of substance metaphysics in much modern theology, though the concept of being does not escape these critiques either. The prefix "con-" ("with") also may inadvertently hint at a class of objects, where "homo-" ("same") suggests a little more clearly the sharing of the same single being, nature, and essence. These differences are minute, and in my opinion, they are not serious enough to preclude the use of "consubstantial" as an English equivalent of *homoousios*.

they can be treated as roughly interchangeable. Exploring Basil's terminological distinction will help us begin to understand the consubstantiality of the Father, Son, and Holy Spirit.

Though he took some time to arrive at this point, Basil eventually settled on the terminology of the Father, Son, and Holy Spirit being distinct hypostases but a singular being (*ousia*, which forms part of the term *homoousios*), an affirmation of consubstantiality. To simplify greatly a complex matter, the Greek word **hypostasis** can mean either "that which underlies," in the sense of the matter that makes a thing concrete, or "that which gives support/resistance." The former meaning treats *hypostasis* as a synonym for "substance" or "being," and the original Nicene Creed (325) actually uses these words interchangeably.[68] Basil rejects this first meaning when he insists on "the non-identity of hypostasis and ousia."[69] In trinitarian theology, the term "hypostasis" does not mean that which makes a thing concrete, as in its matter or substance. The second meaning of hypostasis, "that which gives support/resistance," could refer to a law according to which something functions or to whatever makes a given thing real.[70] According to Basil, the divine nature truly exists as three realities. God is only real because God is Father, Son, and Holy Spirit. Conversely, there is no reality to God that is not Father, Son, and Holy Spirit.

Basil treats being (*ousia*) as that which is common and abstract, whereas hypostasis refers to what is particular and individuated.[71] Basil writes, "Ousia has the same relation to hypostasis as the common has to the particular."[72] John Behr summarizes, "Whatever properties are held to characterize divinity constitute 'the principle of the essence.'"[73] As we have seen in our exegetical study of mediatorial figures in the New Testament, to be God is to be characterized as the object of worship. Therefore, since Father, Son, and Holy Spirit are all the object of worship, and since only God is characterized as the object of right liturgical worship in the canon, there is justification for affirming consubstantiality. It is generally true that anything rightly worshiped is God, so the Son and Holy Spirit must share the divine being. Let us return to Basil's distinction between being and hypostasis. Lewis Ayres explains that he sees being as "undifferentiated substrate."[74] In other words, when we think only about being, we think in abstraction about what would count as an example

---

68. Somewhat embarrassingly, it anathematizes those who say the Father and Son are a different hypostasis.

69. Basil, *Letters* 214.4.

70. See the helpful discussion in Prestige, *God in Patristic Thought*, 163–73.

71. There are smaller variations between Basil and other pro-Nicenes.

72. Basil, *Letters* 214.4.

73. Behr, *Formation of Christian Theology* II/2, 294.

74. Ayres, *Nicaea and Its Legacy*, 200. Ayres traces this to a Stoic origin.

of that being. The being of humanity, for example, would include the ability to be conscious.[75] This is only an abstraction; any given human either will or will not be conscious at any given moment. Still, anything that would count as human must, at some point, be capable of consciousness. This abstract being is concrete and particular; it is differentiated from other possible humans only at the level of hypostasis, a particular exemplar of humankind. A specific human being, such as a boxer in the ring, either is or is not conscious at a given moment during a fight. A boxer who has been knocked out still counts as a human being, for he is capable of consciousness at some point in his life. However, this boxer particularizes this attribute as a possibility, not a reality, at that given moment when he hits the mat. This is the level of hypostasis, a particularization in a specific form of what is generally true of something. So, Basil writes, being "has no standing" or "circumscription" until it is given "standing" and "circumscription" in a hypostasis.[76]

Unfortunately, though Basil provides the basic terminology of "being" and "hypostasis," he does not go very far in clarifying how these terms explain consubstantiality in a manner that fully resolves the philosophical problem of how God can be both one and three. Jaroslav Pelikan speaks of Basil's "puzzling, indeed frustrating, combination of philosophical terminology for the relation of One and Three with a refusal to go all the way toward a genuinely speculative solution."[77] Though Basil's acceptance of *homoousios* grew over time, he also continued to speak of the Father, Son, and Spirit as merely similar (*homoios*).[78] Apparently, Basil partly understands consubstantiality as a notion confirming the likeness of Father, Son, and Spirit, for all three have the attributes necessary for them to be counted as divine. He has strong scriptural foundation for affirming such likeness, particularly between the Father and the Son (e.g., John 14:9; Col. 1:15). Basil argues that the Holy Spirit must be God because the Spirit is said to have, by nature, many attributes proper only to the divine essence, such as incorruptibility, goodness, and holiness.[79] More will be said about this likeness in the next chapter. For now, one should note that this aspect of Basil's thought has led to a considerable debate concerning how

75. I highlight the ability to be conscious here because if someone is knocked unconscious, they do not thereby lose their humanity.

76. Basil, *Letters* 38.3. This letter is classically attributed to Basil but may actually have been written by his brother Gregory of Nyssa. Elsewhere, Basil distinguishes between, on the one hand, the being of God as what God is and, on the other hand, the unbegottenness of the Father as how the Father is as God or what the Father's Godhood is like. See Basil, *Against Eunomius* 1.15.

77. Pelikan, *Christian Tradition*, 1:223.

78. See the helpful discussion in Hildebrand, *Trinitarian Theology of Basil of Caesarea*, 76–82.

79. Basil, *Letters* 189.5.

Father, Son, and Holy Spirit are *homoousios*. Some **social trinitarians** tend to argue that Basil understands the three hypostases as distinct exemplars of a common nature in a fashion similar to how three humans exemplify a common nature. Father, Son, and Spirit are three conscious divine things, according to such accounts.[80] Admittedly, there is some basis for this interpretation in the writing of Basil, Gregory of Nyssa, and Gregory of Nazianzus (collectively called the Cappadocians) when they compare Father, Son, and Spirit to three human persons who share the same nature. However, I am not convinced that they intend such a direct correspondence in this analogy. When we treat the doctrine of simplicity, we will see specifically why this interpretation is unsatisfactory such that three hypostases do not require three distinct exemplars of a common nature. This debate does clarify that the distinction between being and hypostasis, coupled with the affirmation of the consubstantiality of the Father, Son, and Spirit, is not enough, on its own, to make up the doctrine of the Trinity. This is partly because the term *homoousios* in itself can have many meanings, as addressed above.

Basil has helped us set one parameter around the idea of consubstantiality: each possesses the fullness of the divine attributes. To say that the Father, Son, and Spirit are consubstantial is to say that each has all attributes that are necessary to count as God and that each has them in a full manner.[81] Any divine attribute found in Scripture must therefore apply to all three persons. At the same time, consubstantiality allows for an affirmation of plurality. As Vladimir Lossky remarks, consubstantiality "united [three] persons irreducibly different, without absorbing them in their very unity."[82]

Basil begins to help us identify how the analytic interpretation of consubstantiality as the indiscernibility of identicals misses the mark. The distinction between being and hypostasis tells us that at the level of being, the Father, the Son, and the Spirit are the same, but at another level, that of hypostasis, they are different. This means that confessing that the Father, Son, and Spirit are *homoousios* is not to confess them as identicals in the sense meant by Leibniz's principle of the indiscernibility of identicals.[83] In order to clarify my claim

80. E.g., see Hasker, *Metaphysics and the Tri-personal God*, 35. Hasker's account is stronger than some, given that he recognizes that modern social trinitarianism is present in Cappadocian theology only inchoately. Even here, I think he goes too far.

81. "For after saying that the Son was light of light, and begotten of the substance of the Father, [the representatives at Nicaea] went on to add the homoousion, thereby showing that whatever proportion of light any one would attribute in the case of the Father will obtain also in that of the Son" (Basil, *Letters* 52.2).

82. Lossky, *Dogmatic Theology*, 39.

83. As we develop additional doctrines, particularly divine simplicity, there will be more to say on this subject.

regarding the significance of Basil, consider an argument by J. P. Moreland and William Lane Craig on the challenge of trinitarian theology: "Suppose that two things x and y could be the same N but could not be the same P. In such a case x could not fail to be the same P as x itself, but y could. Therefore, x and y are discernible and so cannot be the same thing. But then it follows that they cannot be the same N, since they cannot be the same anything."[84] Moreland and Craig apply this argument to claim that Father, Son, and Spirit are not identical in nature, but are rather three parts of God that, when combined, make up the Trinity, which as a whole is "properly God."[85] A possible counterexample is as follows: Moreland can be the same species as Craig without being the same person as Craig, so Moreland and Craig can be the same S but not the same P.[86] Of course, this counterexample leads us to the same ambiguity in Basil addressed above, where Father, Son, and Spirit are compared with three human persons, a position ultimately quite similar to that of Craig and Moreland and one that is not clearly monotheistic. We might point to other possible ways in which something may be the same N but a different P. Moreland and Craig consider the example of a couch being the same color as a chair, noting that "neither piece of furniture is literally a color; rather, they have the same color as a property."[87] This example does not clearly apply to the distinct hypostases of the Father, Son, and Holy Spirit, which are not merely properties. In order to see how Father, Son, and Spirit can be consubstantial yet distinct persons, we need to do considerably more than develop a terminological distinction. Toward that end, I will return to the question of the indiscernibility of identicals and to the fact that the nature of the persons is not a property and is not analogous to three persons in community. First, I must lay some groundwork through the theology of Thomas Aquinas.

Thomas Aquinas

Writing nearly a millennium after Basil of Caesarea, Thomas Aquinas, the exemplary Catholic theologian of the doctrine of the Trinity, provides greater

84. Moreland and Craig, *Philosophical Foundations for a Christian Worldview*, 592.

85. Moreland and Craig, *Philosophical Foundations for a Christian Worldview*, 589. They name this view "Trinity monotheism."

86. G. W. Leibniz, often credited with developing the principle of the indiscernibility of identicals, admits as much: "It is certain that two leaves, two eggs, two bodies, although of the same species, are never perfectly alike, and all these infinite variations, which we could never comprehend under one notion, make up different individuals, but not different species" (Leibniz, "Leibniz's Comments," 239).

87. Moreland and Craig, *Philosophical Foundations for a Christian Worldview*, 592.

terminological clarity and thus furthers our understanding of the doctrine of consubstantiality. I will attend to his philosophical ideas in particular, only briefly referencing his analysis of Scripture, though this should not lead the reader to conclude that his theology was not deeply rooted in Scripture. This mischaracterization of medieval trinitarianism in general and Aquinas in particular has been aptly addressed elsewhere.[88] I will expand on Aquinas by using a broader philosophical tradition known as Thomism, which has fundamental continuity with his ideas but which has provided terminological clarity even beyond Aquinas's significant achievement. The unfortunate downside of these philosophical distinctions is that this section may be one of the most complicated in the book. For those who struggle with what follows, the content on Basil and Muslim-Christian dialogue should still serve as a serviceable foundation for understanding consubstantiality.

In order to grasp Aquinas's concept of consubstantiality, we must begin with a brief text from Aristotle known as the *Categories*. This text, which systematically lays out various logical distinctions, has had tremendous influence in theology and philosophy, including on Thomas Aquinas and his successors. Aristotle identifies ten categories of statements about a thing: substance, quantity, quality, relation, place, time, position, state, action, and affection.[89] These ten categories can be divided into smaller subcategories. For any given claim of the form "X is Y," the term Y must fit into one of these categories. In the sentence "I am human," the word "human" would fit into the category of substance. Similarly, in the sentence "I am sitting," the word "sitting" would fit in the category of action. Aristotle argues that the category of substance can be used as a predicate (the Y), as "human" is in the "I am human" example. This use of substance is known as **secondary substance. Primary substance** refers to the use of substance as the subject of a sentence, the X. For example, in the sentence "That human is alive," "human" is a primary substance. Primary substances are "the entities which underlie everything else."[90] Aristotle argues that all categories except substances are derivative of substance and exist only by virtue of dependence on these substances.[91]

In many respects, Aquinas stands in continuity with Aristotle. Like his predecessor, he assumes that in the created order only primary substance

88. See in particular Emery, *Trinitarian Theology of St. Thomas Aquinas*, 18–22; Long, *Perfectly Simple Triune God*, 67–69.

89. Aristotle, *Categoriae* §4.

90. Aristotle, *Categoriae* §5.

91. It should be noted, however, that Aristotle is not always consistent with his use of the word "substance." As Stead notes, "substance" indicates *ti esti kai tode ti* ("literally, 'what-it-is and this so-and-so'"), yet *tode ti* "by no means always means, as one might suppose, a particular individual object; it can mean a particular shape or form or character" (*Divine Substance*, 69).

fully has being in itself. (Below I will show how Aquinas modifies this with respect to God.) At the most basic level, being refers to *what is*. As I have discussed above, there is ambiguity in the concept of being. Not all categories have being in the same way. For example, categories like privations (a variety of quality) refer to a lack of existence and therefore have only what might be called propositional or true being—such statements *are* only in the sense that they *are true*. A privation does not refer to an underlying thing that exists.[92] Different categories of movement, such as generation or corruption, lead to the existence or corruption of primary substances. Though they are not substances themselves, they do inhere in, or genuinely exist within, a primary substance.[93] This claim may seem peculiar to many modern readers, but it makes more sense when we remember that Aquinas "thinks of [being] as a kind of act. It is an act embracing all perfections, including life, goodness, power, and wisdom."[94] As John Wippel remarks, motion as a change in act then would have "a fragile degree of being."[95] However, nonsubstance categories have an existence that depends on something else. Corruption must be corruption of some-*thing*.[96] The nine categories beyond substance are classified as "**accidents**"—this word has a very different meaning in Aristotelian philosophy than it does in common speech—and we can understand substance, in some sense, to be their cause.[97]

In the centuries between Basil and Thomas, theologians spent considerable effort clarifying their trinitarian terminology. As a result of this work, and in dialogue with Thomists in particular, I can now further distinguish between being, essence, nature, and substance.[98] Essence establishes the distinctive characteristics of a thing in hierarchical relation to others. Anything with real being, as opposed to a propositional being, has an essence that makes that real being specifically what it is.[99] As Aquinas states, "Essence . . . is that which is

92. See the discussion in Bobik, *Aquinas on Being and Essence*, 31–38. Aquinas's own thoughts are in §4.

93. Wippel, "Metaphysics," 91.

94. Bradshaw, *Aristotle East and West*, 244.

95. Wippel, "Metaphysics," 91.

96. To speak more technically, all categories have a particular *ratio*, and since the *ratio* of the accidental categories pertains to substance, it depends on substance for its existence. Henninger gives the following example: "If *a* is an accidental form of quantity, by its very *ratio a* is the measure of a substance, and so its very *ratio* implies that it can only exist in a substance" (*Relations*, 16).

97. Aquinas, *On Being and Essence* §§103–7. See also Meyer, *Philosophy of St. Thomas Aquinas*, 105.

98. Though I supplement with other texts, the broad contours of the following distinctions are based on the helpful schema given in Hugon, *Le mystère de la Très Ste Trinité*, 309.

99. Aquinas, *On Being and Essence* §§5–7. See also Feser, *Scholastic Metaphysics*, 211–12.

signified by the definition."[100] Substance, which I have already discussed above, refers to the fundamental reality that bears different categories of properties. In scholastic metaphysics like Aquinas's, all substances are thought to be oriented toward a particular end.[101] Nature refers to the same reality as essence and substance, except typically in terms of actions or **operations** performed by a thing; a thing acts according to its nature due to a characteristic power that nature possesses. I will discuss the relation between act and nature more fully in chapter 7. Aquinas continues to affirm what Basil has established: the divine substance has its concrete existence only in the divine hypostases, though Aquinas uses the preferred Latin term *personae*, "persons."[102] What, then, does Aquinas mean when he affirms that Father, Son, and Spirit are consubstantial? Since being relates to essence, substance, and nature, we can answer with respect to all three.

We can begin to understand Aquinas's treatment of consubstantiality by looking at his understanding of essence. As mentioned above, contemporary analytic theology understands consubstantiality to entail the indiscernibility of identicals. According to this way of thinking, if Father, Son, and Spirit are the same being, they must have identical properties to the point of being indiscernible. Put another way, if the Father and the Son were to have different properties, this would, some say, entail different essences.[103] This formulation of consubstantiality assumes that essence simply is a bundle of properties. Such an approach certainly poses a challenge for trinitarian theology, as we can clearly discern between Father, Son, and Spirit but still claim they are the same essence. When we carefully consider what Aquinas means by essence, we see that the indiscernibility of identicals does not apply. As Edward Feser remarks, "The essence of a thing, as Scholastics understand it, is *not* a property or cluster of properties [as analytic theologians assume]. It is rather that *from which* a thing's properties *flow*, that which *explains* the properties."[104] In other words, to say that Father, Son, and Spirit have the same essence is not to say that all properties attributed to them must be identical but rather

---

100. Aquinas, *On Being and Essence* §100.

101. Feser, *Scholastic Metaphysics*, 175. Modern philosophy since John Locke has tended to see substance as static, but the Thomist notion is far more dynamic. This is evident in part through this teleological substance, which is what it is when in act toward its end. See Clarke, *The One and the Many*, 128–29. The reader should note that twentieth-century Roman Catholic theology spent considerable time debating precisely the nature of the ends of created being.

102. Arguably, Aquinas's theory for the individuation of created being corresponds with Basil's notion of hypostases as *tropos hyparxeos*, or "modes of being," though this is debated. See Dewan, *Form and Being*, 238–47.

103. E.g., McCall, *Whose Monotheism?*, 179–80.

104. Feser, *Scholastic Metaphysics*, 230.

to say that there is a single reality that explains all that is Father, Son, and Spirit.[105] For example, in the *Summa contra Gentiles*, Aquinas can write, "Whatever God has in Himself is His essence, as was shown in Book I. But, all things the Father has are the Son's." Aquinas cites John 16:15 and 17:10, adding, "The essence and nature, then, of the Father and Son is the very same. Therefore, the Son is not a creature."[106] In affirming consubstantiality, Aquinas means that the Father has given to the Son and the Spirit all that is his, so that whatever reality explains or defines the Father's divinity explains the Son's and the Spirit's too. In any event, the patristic and medieval theologians do not have the logical framework of the indiscernibility of identicals, and if they did, it is unlikely they would appeal to it, given that each divine person has a unique **personal property**.[107]

Gilbert of Poitiers, a brilliant predecessor of Aquinas whose system was condemned at a council in Rheims (1148), provides a contrast that helpfully illuminates Aquinas's thought. When simplified, as it likely was by his contemporaries, Gilbert's position involves three things: (1) associating persons with the accidental category of relations, (2) following Aristotle in treating relations as externally affixed to a substance, and (3) claiming that the persons are divine by participating in or instantiating a common essence.[108] Gilbert's contemporaries, with some accuracy, feared that this led to four Gods: the divine essence and three persons who were divine by participating in that essence to which they were externally attached. In this interpretation, Gilbert could be interpreted as treating divinity like a secondary substance or like a common genus.

Decades after Gilbert's theology was denounced, Aquinas explicitly rejected Gilbert's position.[109] Aquinas is quite clear in saying that the essence

---

105. Though, as we shall see, the doctrine of simplicity further complicates this issue.
106. Aquinas, *Summa contra Gentiles* 4.7.11.
107. Baber, *The Trinity*, 14, 110.
108. This is not an entirely accurate representation of Gilbert's position. According to Gilbert himself, the persons are distinct by virtue of their properties. The persons are "unities" and not substances, because they accompany their properties. In Gilbert's metaphysics, a substance does not accompany an accident (i.e., a contingent property); rather, an accident accompanies a substance. Therefore, the three persons are one substance, one *quod est* (roughly, "that which it is"), because they are derived from one divinity, one *quo est* (roughly, "that from which it is"), but they are still distinct because they each accompany a unique property. This property functions as a sort of "form" for the persons, some *extrinsecus affixae res* (extrinsically connected thing). Gilbert worries that eliminating the distinction between *quod est* and *quo est* would require one to predicate everything about the persons to divinity itself, thereby resulting in the dissolution of the personal distinctions. See Thom, *Logic of the Trinity*, 78–93; Gemeinhardt, "Logic, Tradition and Ecumenics," 37–43.
109. Aquinas, *Summa Theologica* I, Q. 28, A. 2.

is numerically the same between Father, Son, and Spirit.[110] In other words, Father, Son, and Spirit are one primary substance, not members of a common genus or participants in the same secondary substance. How, then, are they different? Aquinas corrects Gilbert's purported error by modifying Aristotle's categories. Aristotle treats relations as accidents that "are explained by reference to [another] thing."[111] As accidents, these relations do not completely have real being like primary substance does. Aquinas also treats real relations in created beings as accidents that inhere in a substance and are oriented outward, but he argues that there are no accidents in God. "Whatever has an accidental existence in creatures, when considered as transferred to God, has a substantial existence."[112] Here Aquinas appeals to the doctrine of simplicity, which I will discuss in chapter 3. What this means is that in God, the relations do not inhere in the substance; they are the substance. Aquinas treats the persons as relations that persist and **subsist**.

At this point, some readers may be justifiably confused, because I have claimed that there is one primary substance, that there are three persons, and that each of the three persons is the one substance. Unraveling this claim will require several more chapters of work, but I can make a few comments now to begin addressing the puzzle. First, we can note that the problem is partly one of language. As will be explained more in the next chapter, words cannot perfectly correspond to the divine reality they describe. Our words for primary substance and essence, three and one, create an inconsistency when we claim that the single primary substance simply is Father, Son, and Holy Spirit, but that inconsistency could be a byproduct of inadequate language. As Gilles Emery remarks, "Our words cannot do any better than this."[113] Second, we might think of the problem in terms of metaphysics. Karl Rahner admits, "We must grant the fact that when two absolute realities (*esse in*) are identical with a third, they are also identical with one another." He adds, "The case is different, however, when two opposed relations are given." Relations, by definition, require an opposite or correlate, meaning that to which a relation is related, in order to be what they are in themselves, such that any primary substance that simply is a relation must thereby include plurality, an "intelligibility" that does not "simply and altogether" let them identify with the substance that they are. Rahner admits that this cannot be empirically

---

110. "The form of the begetter and begotten is numerically the same" (Aquinas, *Summa Theologica* I, Q. 33, A. 2).

111. Aristotle, *Categoriae* §7.

112. Aquinas, *Summa Theologica* I, Q. 28, A. 2. See the clarifying discussion in Emery, *Trinitarian Theology of Thomas Aquinas*, 90–93.

113. Emery, *Trinitarian Theology of Thomas Aquinas*, 146–47.

demonstrated in the created world, for God is one of a kind.[114] It is precisely in the doctrine of relations that we say the consubstantiality of the Father, Son, and Spirit must be normed by their genuine plurality and relationality.

Aquinas appeals to two common Aristotelian aspects of relations that will conclude our discussion: relations are simultaneous, and they include understanding of a **correlative**. Emery explains simultaneity as follows: "The subjects, considered in themselves, are not necessarily simultaneous by nature (a father, *as a human being*, exists before his son), but the *relations* themselves are by nature simultaneous. . . . Relations allow [Aquinas] to show that the divine persons are *co-eternal*, in response to Arianism that could not accept the eternity of the Son's generation."[115] In other words, if God eternally is Father, then the Son and Spirit must also be eternal. And if only God is eternal, then Father, Son, and Spirit must be God. The correlative aspect of relations can also lead us to consubstantiality. As we have seen, the trinitarian nature of worship and liturgy both as historically preserved in the New Testament and as derived from the New Testament canon by practicing Christians today makes it difficult to worship the Father, Son, or Spirit in isolation from one another. Doing so would violate the common baptismal form, the structure of benedictions and doxologies, the mode of singing hymns in the Spirit, and the proclamation of the gospel through preaching. To know God as Father is to know God in relation to Son and Spirit. In the Jewish tradition, the essence of God, that which is fundamentally distinctive of God, is that God is the only reality worthy of worship, though I have discussed above debates about what forms of worship are reserved for God. As soon as we identify God as the eternal Father, knowing that Father is a relative term demanding a correlative or correlatives, then we are driven to worship the Father in terms of his relation to the Son and Spirit, with the result that all worship takes a triune form. If worship takes this form, then Son and Spirit are thereby known as consubstantial with the Father. This dogmatic statement should stand as a challenge to the many local congregations whose Sunday worship is filled with prayers, hymns, liturgy, and rites that are directed to one divine person and do not reference the others. This is a tacit rejection of the consubstantiality of Father, Son, and Holy Spirit as correlatives, subsistent relations that simply are the divine substance.

Christian-Muslim Dialogue

One final case study should help us understand the doctrine of consubstantiality: trinitarian theology and apologetics in a Muslim context. Islam emphasizes

---

114. Rahner, *The Trinity*, 71.
115. Emery, "Central Aristotelian Themes in Aquinas's Trinitarian Theology," 14.

the **oneness** and uniqueness of God (*tawhid*) as a central belief. At times, this belief has taken on the form of a challenge to Christian trinitarianism on the grounds that it is not properly monotheistic. For example, the likely anti-Christian Sūrat al-Ikhlās reads as follows:

> Say, "He, God, is one,
> God the eternal refuge,
> He begetteth not, nor is he begotten,
> And none is like unto Him."[116]

Prompted by such challenges from Muslims, Christian theologians in predominately Muslim contexts have, for centuries, tried to explain how Father, Son, and Spirit can be consubstantial, and one typical pattern of explanation is illuminating. Najib Awad notes that the problem behind the Christian doctrine of the Trinity is often presented as a question of unity. The answer to this question typically involves an exploration of how there can be distinctions between Father, Son, and Spirit without division of the Godhead. In contrast, Christian apologists in majority Muslim contexts face the problem of explaining how God can be meaningfully one in a manner that would appeal to a Muslim audience and also agree with such Old Testament affirmations as the Shema in Deuteronomy 6:4.[117]

Several important early Arabic-speaking Christian apologists offer a helpful insight into consubstantiality and the oneness of God. For example, 'Ḥabīb ibn Khidma Abū Rā'iṭa al-Takrītī distinguishes between types of oneness in his *Risāla al-ūlā*. In this text, Abū Rā'iṭa asks his imaginary Muslim dialogue partner what sort of oneness Islam affirms: Is God one in number, genus, or species?[118] We must deny God is one in genus, for that would make a number of different species God,[119] and that would surely be a form of polytheism. If we say God is one in number, Abū Rā'iṭa argues, God must be part of a series and thus not one of a kind, which is contrary to both Muslim teaching and Orthodox Christian assumptions of Abū Rā'iṭa's time. Therefore, God must be one in species.[120] Abū Rā'iṭa then challenges his Muslim reader with

---

116. Translated in Siddiqui, *Christians, Muslims, and Jesus*, 71.

117. Awad, *Orthodoxy in Arabic Terms*, 184.

118. Abū Rā'iṭa al-Takrītī, *First* Risālah *on the Holy Trinity* §7.

119. "Genus" as used by Abū Rā'iṭa must include several distinct things by definition.

120. Abū Rā'iṭa al-Takrītī, *First* Risālah *on the Holy Trinity* §8. Sara Husseini notes that Muslim philosopher al-Kindī would deny that God's oneness is numerical, while other Muslim scholars like al-Warrāq would argue that the Christians who affirm the Trinity could not deny that this would make God plural in number and thus not one at all. The latter argument assumes that God's unity is at least in number (Husseini, *Early Christian-Muslim Debate*, 123,

a puzzle: "If the meaning of your teaching is that 'one in species' is 'one in number,' and you do not define what 'one in species' is and how it is, then you return to your first statement, that [God] is 'one in number.'"[121] He concludes that instead of identifying being one in species with being one in number, we must define oneness in species in terms of sharing one *ousia*; that is to say, we must define it in terms of consubstantiality.[122] A similar argument is made by Abū Rā'iṭa's contemporary 'Ammār al-Baṣrī.[123] In modern times, Coptic Patriarch Shenuda III has denied that God can be counted as three, in response to the Qur'an 5:73, which claims that Christians say "God is the Third of Three."[124] This line of argumentation helps us see that consubstantiality is a claim not about the absolute numerical oneness of God but about the proper singular referent of worship and the singular explanation of all that exists.[125]

The uncountability of God is a puzzling argument at first glance, but I see two possible ways of interpreting Abū Rā'iṭa and others so that the argument may work. The first is to argue that God's infinite nature is uncountable. Certain infinite sets are considered uncountable by mathematicians,[126] though God is not a set, so the parallel is somewhat tenuous. A second possibility can be explained through the notion that God is beyond kinds. Recently, Kathryn Tanner has argued for what she calls the "non-contrastive transcendence" of God, which demands that "a God who genuinely transcends the world must not be characterized . . . by a direct contrast with it."[127] In other words, we ought not think of God's transcendence as "up" in comparison to creation being "down." Such a view of transcendence is not radical enough, for it would place both God and creation in a common kind: "things in space." As Tanner argues elsewhere, treating God as beyond kinds, a form of transcendence, results in a simultaneous radical immanence, because "God is not a kind of

---

178). Al-Kindī therefore did not allow plurality in God, arguing that all multiplicity depends on an ultimate unity (see Siddiqui, *Christians, Muslims, and Jesus*, 87).

121. Abū Rā'iṭa al-Takrītī, First *Risālah* on the Holy Trinity §9.

122. Abū Rā'iṭa al-Takrītī, First *Risālah* on the Holy Trinity §10.

123. Husseini, *Early Christian-Muslim Debate*, 123.

124. Shenuda III, *Trinity and Unity*, 5. God is "certainly not in three" (2).

125. This may fit with the intent behind first-century Jewish affirmations of monotheism, which were apparently not a numerical claim. See Wright, *New Testament and the People of God*, 249–50.

126. Today, mathematicians speak of countable and uncountable infinites. A countable infinite would require counting forever, but it would be possible to reach a given number within that infinite set in a finite amount of time. An uncountable infinite, on the other hand, would never allow one to count and reach a given number in a finite amount of time. An uncountable infinite set would include "all real numbers," where one could count an infinite amount of numbers before ever reaching the number one, for example.

127. Tanner, *God and Creation in Christian Theology*, 46.

thing whose nature needs to be protected from compromise and corruption when coming into close contact with things of an opposed nature—the way, say, fire needs to be kept from corruption, the loss of its own nature, through contact with water."[128] In other words, because God is not similar to anything, he can be radically close to all things without undermining the inner integrity of the nature of anything. How does this relate to the question of the countability of the Trinity? We can imagine many unique things that are countable. There is only one Mount Rushmore, but we can still count it. However, Mount Rushmore is part of the kind "mountains," so we can say it is one mountain and Kilimanjaro is a second. Mount Rushmore is clearly circumscribed in comparison with another object, helping us identify it as one, as this particular thing but not that particular thing. Even if I found an object of an unknown kind, so that I could not point to any other object of the same type, the object would still be in space, so I could count it as one by saying it was here in this space and other things were not here but there. If God is beyond kinds, then we cannot delineate God in any of these manners. Even saying God is countable would put God in the kind "things that are countable." An uncircumscribed God beyond kinds is thus uncountable. If we interpret "series" as "kind," then I believe Tanner helpfully illuminates Abū Rā'iṭa.

The context of Muslim debates has alternatingly caused a diminished and an increased emphasis on plurality in the Godhead. The former we see in the case of the ninth-century bishop Theodore Abū Qurrah, who often uses the terminology of God having three "faces" (*wujūh*), even though this risks **modalism**, an ancient heresy that denied real and eternal plurality in God.[129] An example of an *increased* emphasis on plurality in the Godhead is found in the work of contemporary Jordanian evangelical theologian Imad Shehadeh. Shehadeh argues that there is a difference between the "absolute oneness" (*tawhid*) of Islam and "oneness in Trinity."[130] First John 4:7–21 clearly states that "God is love." Shehadeh argues that God cannot have love as an essential attribute without an essence that is relational. He asks, "How can the attributes of God be active eternally apart from the existence of creation without God existing in relationship?"[131] In chapters 4 and 6, I will argue that Christians answer this question by positing that God's relations to the

---

128. Tanner, "Is God in Charge?," 121.

129. Admittedly, the frequency with which he uses this term may be amplified by later compilers or editors. See Awad, *Orthodoxy in Arabic Terms*, 205–6, 217–21. Awad argues that Abū Qurrah still is "eclectically orthodox" (191). Modalism will be discussed in greater detail in chap. 4.

130. Shehadeh, *God with Us*, 1:43–45.

131. Shehadeh, *God with Us*, 1:110.

created order derive from the eternal **divine relations**. If God is absolutely one, Shehadeh argues, there is no equivalent answer. Using the example of the Mu'tazilites and Ash'arites, two Muslim schools of thought, Shehadeh argues that absolute oneness leads to a number of metaphysical problems.[132] Evaluating his specific arguments is beyond the scope of the book, but we should note that Shehadeh's trinitarianism tends toward social trinitarianism, emphasizing plurality. Such Christian theologians writing in a Muslim context reveal that the Christian affirmation of consubstantiality is not an absolute oneness but a oneness normed by the relations between Father, Son, and Spirit. While these writers differently characterize the difference between Christian trinitarianism and Muslim absolute unity, all reveal that consubstantiality is not unqualified oneness (*tawhid*).

The Dogmatic Meaning of Consubstantiality

After this survey, I can now conclude with a brief dogmatic explanation of consubstantiality. To say that Father, Son, and Spirit are consubstantial is to affirm that each has what is necessary to count as fully and equally divine. They are not identicals, nor are they an absolute numerical unity, for at the level of person, hypostasis, and relation, they are distinct. Plurality must always norm consubstantiality in this way. Nevertheless, the persons are not divided into distinct substances. Consubstantiality does not mean that the persons are fully distinct, individual instantiations of the same secondary substance or of a common genus. The consubstantiality of the Father, Son, and Spirit is a dogmatic presupposition of the claim that the Son and Holy Spirit are the self-revelation of the Father, mediators unlike any others. Consubstantiality also follows from the trinitarian nature of Christian worship, since only God is worthy of worship but recognition and worship of God as Father requires worship of the correlative Son and Holy Spirit. Here again, consubstantiality is normed by divine plurality, for the definition of God, what it means to be God, is to be Father, Son, and Holy Spirit. There is no God the Father apart from the Spirit and Son, no God without his breath and reason. We must regulate the unity we affirm in proclaiming divine consubstantiality through an equal affirmation that this unity is not one that destroys the distinction in hypostases. In other words, plurality in the Godhead regulates our initial affirmation of unity, just as the unity of the divine nature will help us clarify our initial steps toward speaking of divine plurality, as we will see in the next chapter. A denial of consubstantiality is a denial of the Trinity, but

132. Shehadeh, *God with Us*, 1:113–34.

an affirmation of the consubstantiality of the Father, Son, and Holy Spirit is not yet a full affirmation of the doctrine of the Trinity. Much more should be said, so we turn now to additional dogmatic claims concerning the triune God.

FOR FURTHER READING

Christological Monotheism

Hurtado, Larry W. *One God, One Lord: Early Christian Devotion and Ancient Jewish Monotheism*. Philadelphia: Fortress, 1988.

> Hurtado's text is the definitive starting point for contemporary discussions of the veneration of Christ in the Bible as the basis for a high Christology.

McGrath, James F. *The Only True God: Early Christian Monotheism in Its Jewish Context*. Urbana: University of Illinois Press, 2009.

> McGrath is one of the leading critics of Hurtado, arguing that the dividing line between God and creature is sacrifice, not cultic worship.

Stuckenbruck, Loren T. *Angel Veneration and Christology: A Study in Early Judaism and in the Christology of the Apocalypse of John*. 1995. Reprint, Waco: Baylor University Press, 2017.

> This text is a robust treatment of angelomorphic Christology that I have found to be particularly illuminating.

On the Concept of Consubstantiality

Hanson, R. P. C. *The Search for the Christian Doctrine of God: The Arian Controversy 318–381*. Grand Rapids: Baker, 1988.

> This work was considered the standard treatment of the Nicene debates until the publication of Ayres's *Nicaea and Its Legacy*. It offers valuable context for the doctrine of consubstantiality.

Stead, Christopher. *Divine Substance*. Oxford: Oxford University Press, 1977.

> Stead demonstrates that the term *homoousios* could have implied identity, membership in a common genus, or a relationship of two parts to a whole, meaning that confusion following the Council of Nicaea was inevitable.

Secondary Literature on Major Historical Figures Discussed

Emery, Gilles. *The Trinitarian Theology of St. Thomas Aquinas*. Translated by Francesca Aran Murphy. Oxford: Oxford University Press, 2010.

> There are countless strong treatments of Aquinas's trinitarian thought, but I find Emery's particularly clear, insightful, and enjoyable to read.

Hildebrand, Stephen. *The Trinitarian Theology of Basil of Caesarea: A Synthesis of Greek Thought and Biblical Truth.* Washington, DC: Catholic University of America Press, 2007.

> Hildebrand's exploration of Basil's thought is helpful for its attention to his exegesis, something survey treatments tend to neglect.

Husseini, Sara Leila. *Early Christian-Muslim Debate on the Unity of God: Three Christian Scholars and Their Engagement with Islamic Thought (9th Century C.E.).* Leiden: Brill, 2014.

> Husseini's text is the best introduction to major figures like Abū Rā'iṭa whose treatments of the Trinity receive far less attention than they deserve.

Analytic Theology and the Trinity

Baber, H. E. *The Trinity: A Philosophical Investigation.* London: SCM, 2019.

> Baber offers the most compelling philosophical critique of social trinitarianism of which I am aware. She also recognizes that the doctrine of the Trinity does not map onto questions of identity in modern philosophy in the way that much modern analytic theology assumes.

Hasker, William. *Metaphysics and the Tri-personal God.* Oxford: Oxford University Press, 2013.

> Hasker's defense of social trinitarianism through a retrieval of pro-social elements in patristic thought is one of the strongest of this perspective of which I am aware, though in the end I find his reading of the tradition and his dogmatic reasoning problematic.

McCall, Thomas. *Whose Monotheism? Which Trinity? Philosophical and Systematic Theologians on the Metaphysics of Trinitarian Theology.* Grand Rapids: Eerdmans, 2010.

> McCall's work is helpful both as a survey of analytic thinking on the Trinity and as an example of the productive use of analytic methods when examining theologians like John Zizioulas and Robert Jenson.

CHAPTER 2

Processions and Personal Properties

We turn now to an initial effort to distinguish the Father, Son, and Spirit in a manner that does not undermine their consubstantiality. Traditionally, theologians have distinguished the Father, Son, and Spirt by eternal processions within the Godhead. Catholic and Protestant theologians use the word "procession" to refer to the eternal origin of the Son and Spirit from the Father. Orthodox theologians tend to restrict the word "procession" to its use as a technical term describing the Spirit's origin in the Father. There is significant disagreement between these traditions regarding how the Spirit's procession relates to the Son, a topic I will address in chapter 4. Most theologians in all three of these historic varieties of Christianity agree in their use of the term "eternal generation" to refer to the Son's eternal origin in the Father.

Historically, most theologians relied on a common nexus of biblical texts when explaining the eternal generation of the Son. Athanasius of Alexandria is typical in his *Defense of the Nicene Definition* when he appeals to two key texts to argue that the Son is eternally begotten by the Father: "You are my Son, and today I have begotten you" (Ps. 2:7), and "Before all the hills, I was brought forth" (Prov. 8:25). In each passage in the Septuagint, the key verb is *gennaō*, signifying begetting or generation. Acts 13:33, along with Hebrews 1:5 and 5:5, cites Psalm 2:7 and applies it to Jesus Christ, so Athanasius follows this biblical precedent in applying the term *gennaō* to the Son, though the Bible does not openly use this passage to speak of the inner life of the Trinity. Proverbs 8:25 is spoken by the personification of Wisdom, and Christ is called the Wisdom of God in 1 Corinthians 1:30, so Athanasius makes a connection, common for his time, between Proverbs 8 and Jesus Christ, a connection already explored in chapter 1. Pro-Nicene figures also frequently cited Wisdom 7:25 and Sirach 24:3 to make a similar point.[1] Based on this language of generation, Athanasius concludes that the Father did not create the Son. "If then son, therefore not creature; if creature, not son."[2]

Athanasius situates this exegetical foundation within a larger theological framework. Two arguments are again typical. First, Athanasius appeals to what Michel Barnes calls the "X from X" formula.[3] Christ is the "radiance of the glory of God" (Heb. 1:3 ESV), but "who is capable of separating the radiance from the sun?" So, too, we cannot separate the Son from his eternal Father.[4] Generation, then, describes the eternal procession in God that is analogous to the procession of light from the sun. Second, Athanasius argues that it is not possible for us to exalt the Son to the status of a partially divine mediator. Either the Son was begotten by nature, or he is no different than we are, for the Bible also speaks of human beings as God's children (Athanasius here cites Isa. 1:2).[5] Athanasius explains that there are only two ways to be a child of God: by adoption and by nature through generation. Humans are adopted as sons and daughters of God, but Christ is the eternal Son of God by nature. He "alone is acknowledged by the Father to be from him, saying, 'This is my beloved Son, in whom I am well pleased' (Matt. 3:17)."[6] Christ alone is the Word who was with God in the beginning (John 1:1) and through whom God created all things (Col. 1:16). It is in the context of such arguments that Athanasius appeals to Psalm 2:7 and Proverbs 8:25 to defend the idea that the Son was eternally generated by the Father, as "light from light" and "very God of very God," to use the Nicene terminology. The Son is uniquely and eternally related to the Father by way of generation.

Athanasius's position on eternal generation was long the default manner of distinguishing the Father and Son, though this has recently been subject to a number of challenges. In particular, many have questioned the exegetical

---

1. Wisdom 7:25 describes Wisdom as "a certain pure emanation of the glory of the almighty God" (Douay-Rheims). Sirach 24:3 depicts Wisdom saying, "I, wisdom, came forth from the mouth of the Most High, the first-born before all creatures" (Douay-Rheims). "First-born before all creatures" is preserved in the Vulgate but may not have been original to the text, leading many translations to offer different wording here.

2. Athanasius, *Defense of the Nicene Definition* 3.14.

3. The formula has been clarified by Barnes, *Power of God*, 108–9, 120. It typically involves not only likeness but a similar power.

4. Athanasius, *Defense of the Nicene Definition* 3.12.

5. Athanasius, *Defense of the Nicene Definition* 3.10. Athanasius's point is somewhat stronger in the LXX of Isaiah 1:2, which uses the verb *egennēsa* of human beings.

6. Athanasius, *Defense of the Nicene Definition* 3.11.

foundations for eternal generation and for eternal **spiration**, a term often used by Catholic and Protestant theologians to describe the eternal procession of the Spirit. Any treatment of the processions as the basis for differentiating the divine persons must engage these objections head-on. Therefore, this chapter will respond to exegetical objections by using a precise theological method long present in the tradition. When speaking of eternal generation, theologians must deny, by **way of negation**, many features of generation found in the created world. The divine attributes are particularly helpful in clarifying what must be denied during this process. The remaining dimensions of generation provide a conceptually clear meaning for the term that fits the biblical evidence, thereby rebutting the typical exegetical objections. I will begin this chapter by briefly introducing the typical objections before proceeding, in dialogue with Origen of Alexandria and Thomas Aquinas, to establish the dogmatic meaning of the divine processions. I can then conclude with an exegetical justification and an introduction to the resulting personal properties.

Recent Challenges to Eternal Generation

By the middle of the twentieth century, certain strands of North American theology in particular began to question the validity of the idea of eternal generation.[7] J. Oliver Buswell's treatment of Psalm 2:7 is an early and typical representative of such moves. To the original authors, Buswell argues, Psalm 2:7 refers to the coronation of a king, not literal generation. When used in Acts 13:32–33, it references a declaration of sonship as evidenced by the resurrection. When cited in Hebrews 1:5 and 5:4–6, it is part of a declaration of uniqueness not attached "to any particular event."[8] Buswell concludes, "We are thus justified in saying that the 'begetting' of the Son referred to in Psalm 2:7, as interpreted in the New Testament, is not a literal generation of His being in any sense of the word, but is a reference to God's declaratory revelation of the eternal divine Sonship, particularly in Christ's resurrection from the dead."[9] This conclusion led Buswell to question the very legitimacy of the doctrine of eternal generation.[10]

---

7. Similar arguments may be found to a lesser extent in European theologians who held that the metaphysical system of Origen, in which eternal generation emerged, represents a decisive point in the decline of Christianity into a Hellenistic form that bears little resemblance to the religion of Jesus. Notably, see Harnack, *History of Dogma*, 2:332–61.

8. Buswell, *Systematic Theology of the Christian Religion*, 1:107–9.

9. Buswell, *Systematic Theology of the Christian Religion*, 1:109.

10. "I do believe that the 'eternal generation' doctrine should be dropped" (Buswell, *Systematic Theology of the Christian Religion*, 1:112).

Much of the modern debate on eternal generation centers on the meaning of *monogenēs*, traditionally translated as "only begotten" and applied to the Son in John 1:14, 18; 3:16, 18; and 1 John 4:9. A number of modern scholars argue that the word derives from *genos*, rather than *gennaō*, which means "to beget." If *genos* is taken to mean "kind," *monogenēs* would mean that the Son is one of a kind, or unique.[11] On the other hand, *genos* occasionally means "derivation," in which case *monogenēs* could mean "of sole descent" or perhaps, in a metaphorical sense, "unique," in which case the term would have roughly the same meaning as "only begotten."[12] This debate over the meaning of *monogenēs* partly relates to the meaning of similar compounds.[13] Three examples will illustrate the problem. The word *homo-genēs* ("of the same kind") suggests the meaning "kind" for the *genes* root. The word *eu-genēs* ("of noble origin") appears to signify derivation but not literal birth, suggesting that the *genos* root here carries the sense of derivation. Words like *proterē-genēs* ("firstborn") and *patro-genēs* ("born of the father") have a meaning more literally connected to birth, suggesting *gennaō* ("beget") as a root. This aspect of the debate depends on a complex analysis of the origin of Greek words, and there is, in my estimation, no definitive position. The entire pursuit is questionable, given that the root of a word often does not dictate its meaning.[14]

Modern debates extend into lexical usage, contextual clues, and textual criticism, though results are equally unclear. Lexical usage does show that *monogenēs* does not always refer to offspring.[15] However, it can take this sense, even in the Gospels (Luke 7:12; 8:42; 9:38). Contextual clues in the Gospels are conflicting. On the one hand, Johannine literature rarely uses *gennaō* of Jesus (but see John 18:37; 1 John 5:18).[16] On the other hand, it uses *monogenēs* twice in the context of a discussion of the word *gennaō*, as in John 3:16, where the context is the conversation about being born again (John

---

11. See Warden, "God's Only Son," 218; Moody, "God's Only Son," 213–19.

12. Büchsel, "μονογενής [*monogenēs*]," 739–40.

13. For discussion of etymologically related words, see Pendrick, "*Monogenēs*," 587; Büchsel, "μονογενής [*monogenēs*]," 738; Irons, "Lexical Defense," 104–5.

14. This mistake is often known as the root fallacy, which seeks to derive the meaning of a word from its components. D. A. Carson uses the example of *monogenēs* as a classic illustration in his explanation of the root fallacy. He ultimately sides with interpreting *monogenēs* to mean "unique," but not for etymological reasons. See Carson, *Exegetical Fallacies*, 28–33.

15. Pendrick, "*Monogenēs*," 588. Pendrick points to Theophrastus, who calls the beech, yew, and alder trees *monogenēs*, the only ones of their genus, in contrast with the elm, which has several varieties in the genus. Pendrick grants that the notion of *monogenēs* may have "occasionally" referred to birth, but if this were the norm, such classical examples as those cited here would not be comprehensible (592).

16. *New International Dictionary*, s.v. "Monos."

3:3). The limited sample size here precludes the drawing of any firm conclusion. A broader study shows that, in Greek literature, the word is frequently used in the context of *gennaō*,[17] but not always. Nor does textual criticism lead to a decisive resolution. Some Old Latin texts translate *monogenēs* as *unicus* (unique).[18] This has led to the accusation that the "only begotten" interpretation was a late development that arose in response to Arianism.[19] This claim is, in my opinion, unpersuasive, since all parties in the pre-Nicene debates appeared to adopt a version of eternal generation.[20] Furthermore, Tertullian renders *monogenēs* as *unigenitus* ("only begotten") well before the Arian debates.[21] *Monogenēs* was certainly understood to refer to generation by at least some figures prior to the resolution or even emergence of the Arian debates. Though I lean toward understanding *monogenēs* in the sense of "only begotten," the evidence is mixed. While those biblical scholars who prefer to translate *monogenēs* in the Johannine writings as "one and only Son" generally do not intend to deny the doctrine of eternal generation, they are certainly interpreted by some theologians as having undermined its exegetical foundations.[22]

The exegetical debates surrounding eternal generation do raise significant questions concerning how to think about plurality in the Godhead, but a theologian committed to the tradition still has good reason to affirm the classical notion of divine processions. Not only is eternal generation explicitly affirmed in the **Niceano-Constantinopolitan Creed**, which describes the Son as "begotten [*gennēthenta*] of the Father before all worlds, . . . begotten [*gennēthenta*], not made," there is also widespread support for the doctrine of the divine processions in most major theological figures in history and in many creeds and catechisms as well. One may be tempted to conclude that the processions themselves are rooted in tradition but not Scripture, leaving even the first step toward understanding plurality in the Godhead unmoored from any exegetical basis. I do not believe this to be the case, but before I can fully explain why the divine processions are biblical through and through, I must turn to consider what the terms themselves have meant in Christian tradition.

17. Irons, "Lexical Defense," 106–7.
18. Warden, "God's Only Son," 220.
19. An early source of this claim (tracing to 1883) is Westcott, *Epistles of St. John*, 171.
20. Dahms, "Johannine Use of *Monogenēs*," 226. Dahms notes the important fact that many of the theologians involved in the Arian debates were well trained in classical Greek. Given that the debates focused on the technical meaning of various words, it is unlikely that they would suddenly invent a connection with begetting were that meaning not already accepted for the word.
21. Irons, "Lexical Defense," 102.
22. On these points, see Giles, *Eternal Generation of the Son*, 30, 65.

Eternal Generation in Christian Tradition

Theologians consistently affirmed the divine processions even before the Arian debates of the fourth century. Indeed, both Arius and his opponents affirmed some version of this doctrine, with important differences.[23] Though the doctrine is certainly ancient, it did grow in clarity over time as successive generations deployed a consistent methodology to clarify the meaning of such terms as "generation" and "procession." The development largely depended on reflection on eternal generation rather than eternal spiration for two reasons: the fourth-century christological debates emerged before debates about the divinity of the Holy Spirit, and God has chosen to reveal less about the eternal procession of the Spirit than about the eternal generation of the Son. Even eternal generation is not directly the subject of an extended treatment in Scripture. The entire debate would certainly be far less complicated if one could simply turn to a chapter in Romans and read Paul's extended treatment of the subject, but there is no such passage in the Bible. This lack makes it surprising that the divine processions are so consistently affirmed in history and may tempt us to posit a wooden traditionalism behind the consistency. I believe this would be a mistake, for the persistence of the divine processions is actually rooted in a sound methodological approach present since the first formulation of the doctrine.

Since the time of Origen of Alexandria, theologians have used the relatively rare biblical language of the Son's "generation" (Ps. 2:7 in Acts 13:33; Heb. 1:5; 5:5, etc.) to speak of the eternal differentiation of the Son from the Father. However, there is a wide range of possible definitions for the term. Arius, for example, could use the idea of generation to claim that there once was a time when the Son was not. The pro-Nicenes could argue the opposite. Christian tradition found a solution in qualifying the meaning of "generation" using the divine attributes, a subject on which the Bible speaks much more frequently and clearly. The doctrine of analogy requires that when theologians describe God with a term that usually applies to created reality, they negate some aspects of the usual meaning of the term but affirm and purify other aspects. The divine attributes help identify which aspects of the terms "generation" and "procession" or "spiration" in their created sense do not apply to the Godhead. This methodology has been consistently deployed throughout the history of trinitarian thought, providing increasing clarity concerning the divine processions, especially as early, implicit use of the doctrine of analogy was replaced by a conscious awareness of the doctrine in all its complexities.

23. Arius affirms that the Son is begotten, but he treats this generation as in time: "Before he was begotten . . . he was not" (Arius, *Letter of Arius to Eusebius of Nicomedia*, 330).

When restricted in accordance with this method, the meaning of "generation" provides a reason to affirm the pro-Nicene position over alternatives such as those found in Arius.

I will illustrate this development in the doctrine of the divine processions by focusing on two theologians. Origen of Alexandria is notable because he is the first to develop a thorough doctrine of eternal generation, using the basic elements of the classical methodology. By the time of Thomas Aquinas, we can see a full-fledged doctrine of analogy in place as well as a more robust deployment of the divine attributes to clarify the meaning of eternal generation. Attending to Aquinas's theology provides the added benefit of connecting an approach to plurality in the Godhead with his explanation of unity addressed in chapter 1. One could easily argue the same point using a wide range of theologians who are also committed to the doctrine of the processions and to the method of analogically norming the processions with the divine attributes. After discussing Aquinas, I will briefly summarize the findings of this wider tradition before returning again, at the end of the chapter, to the question of the exegetical foundations of the eternal processions.

Origen of Alexandria

Origen is credited with being the first to develop the doctrine of eternal generation. In his book *On First Principles*, he cites common texts to develop his thought on the Son's generation: Proverbs 8:22–25; Colossians 1:15; and Wisdom 7. Origen's treatment of the Son follows a similar trajectory to that of Hellenistic Judaism's mediatorial figures, but it combines this traditional motif with a keen investigation of the doctrine of God, though his speculative investigations ultimately make his version of the doctrine of generation both confused and inadequate. Origen is also the first to use the divine attributes to determine in what sense the Son is generated by the Father, asserting that any such generation must be compatible with the divine nature.

Origen's method is most clear in his treatment of eternal generation in light of divine **immutability** (changelessness) and eternality (timelessness). When interpreting John 1:1, "In the beginning was the Word," Origen negates several possible meanings of "in the beginning." He writes, "It is clear that we are not to understand it in its meaning related to change, . . . and we should certainly not take it in its meaning related to creation."[24] In Origen's thought, the Word is not brought into being with creation through a change in God, for the Father cannot become Father. Note two important features

---

24. Origen, *Commentary on the Gospel according to John* 1.109.

of this denial: first, Origen draws on divine immutability to deny that generation results in divine change, and second, Origen treats God's fatherhood as fundamental to God, meaning that the Father is defined in relation to the eternal Son.[25] Both claims are significant. For Origen, the divine attributes clarify the Trinity, and the triune relations clarify the divine attributes. Origen also makes the point exegetically. If the Word was in the beginning (John 1:1), he is "clearly older than what was made in the beginning,"[26] though this does not prevent Origen from speaking of the Son elsewhere as a creation of God.[27] In part, this is no doubt due to the language, in Proverbs 8:22, of the creation of Wisdom, a scriptural claim that caused trouble for many generations of theologians who identified Christ with Wisdom. Origen's tendency to think of the Son as a creature is also present partially because, though it would be inaccurate to label Origen a **subordinationist**,[28] he still elevates the Father above the Son, for the Father is "the true God," while the Son is "the archetypal image" that participates in divinity.[29] The Son is not, however, a creation in time. Origen remarks in *On First Principles* that the Son "was born of [the Father], and derives from him what he is, but without any beginning, not only as may be measured by any division in time, but even that which the mind alone can contemplate within itself, or so to speak, with the naked powers of understanding."[30] Unfortunately, the connection between the generation of the Son and creation in *On First Principles* also pushes Origen to speculate about the eternal existence of creation, a position ultimately and

25. See Ayres, "At the Origins of Eternal Generation," 153. Ayres remarks, "The eternity of the relationship reveals to us something about the nature of God as such—God is eternally generative."

26. Origen, *Commentary on the Gospel according to John* 2.36.

27. Such phrasing can be seen as clear subordinationism; see Giles, *Eternal Generation of the Son*, 100. It may also be seen as "a conscious concession to the usage of Prov. 8:22" that "should not be pressed" (Kelly, *Early Christian Doctrines*, 130).

28. Ayres remarks that any theologian like Origen, who "spends considerable effort showing how the Son can be said to possess some of the Father's attributes or to image those attributes because of the manner in which the Son is uniquely generated," cannot rightly be said to intend subordinationism. Such an accusation "directs our attention away from the concern to emphasize the continuity between the two" (Ayres, *Nicaea and Its Legacy*, 21). Though there are ways in which Origen depicts the Son as inferior to the Father, Crouzel notes that there are also elements in Origen that seem to point toward equality between the Father and the Son, a fact that leads some to posit an internal contradiction in Origen or else an evolution of his thought. Crouzel is perhaps more accurate when he concludes that Origen posits subordination not in a dogmatic manner (*façon dogmatique*) but, rather, as a result of the rudimentary nature of trinitarian theology in his time (Crouzel, *Théologie de l'image de Dieu chez Origène*, 112–13, 120–21).

29. Origen, *Commentary on the Gospel according to John* 2.18. Origen will also, at times, speak of the Son as *deuteros theos*—"second God."

30. Origen, *On First Principles* 2.1.2; cf. Origen, *Commentary on the Gospel according to John* 1.204, where Origen denies both a beginning and an end to generation.

rightly rejected in the Christian tradition.[31] Origen has not worked out a clear distinction between Creator and creature, and his ideas on time and creation are obscure. Yet, he has laid an important foundation.

We see in Origen a pattern that continues throughout the centuries in trinitarian thought. Origen denies a number of ideas about the Son, which Lewis Ayres aptly calls "transgressive thoughts," as inappropriate to use of the Son because of the divine attributes.[32] Origen then affirms some restricted meaning of "generation." I have already noted Origen's negation of change in "generation" due to immutability. Origen also negates the claim that the hypostasis of the Son has distinct bodily characteristics from the Father,[33] for "it is impious and shocking to regard God the Father in the begetting of his only-begotten Son . . . as being similar to any human being or other animal in the act of begetting."[34] This may be one reason why Origen frequently uses the analogy of will emerging from mind to explain generation: this is not a material procession.[35] There can be no physical division in an incorporeal being like God.[36] The generated Son is united to the Father, but not in a unity of flesh, as when husband and wife are one (Gen. 2:24), nor in a unity of Spirit, as in Christians' union with Christ (1 Cor. 6:17). This is a unity as God.[37] What, then, is generation? To say that the Son is generated is to say that he "draws his being" from God, "as brightness is begotten from light."[38] Here he is alluding to the description in Hebrews of the Son as the "radiance of God's glory" (Heb. 1:3). The Son is "akin to the Father."[39] To summarize, then, generation implies distinction between the Father and Son, likeness, unity in nature, and derivation of the Son from the Father. Generation does not imply change, bodily division, unity by composition (as with a husband and wife in procreation, for example), or the creation of the Son in time.

---

31. "We cannot even call God almighty if there are none over whom he can exercise his power. Accordingly, to prove that God is almighty, we must assume the existence of the universe" (Origen, *On First Principles* 1.2.10). See also Anatolios, *Retrieving Nicaea*, 16–17. Anatolios convincingly argues that the connection between eternal generation and the eternal nature of creation in Origen led subsequent generations to conceive of generation of the Son *ex nihilo*, setting the stage for the trinitarian debates of the fourth century, which often centered on generation.

32. Ayres, "At the Origins of Eternal Generation," 152.

33. Origen, *On First Principles* 1.2.2.

34. Origen, *On First Principles* 1.2.4.

35. Stead, *Divine Substance*, 129–30.

36. Origen, *On First Principles* 1.2.6.

37. Origen, *Dialogue with Heraclides*, 439. For more on the distinction between triune unity and our union with Christ in the Spirit, see chap. 5.

38. Origen, *On First Principles* 1.2.2; 1.1.4.

39. Origen, *Dialogue with Heraclides*, 440.

Origen is a complex historical figure. His ideas were influential on pro-Nicene orthodoxy,[40] but some of them were debated in the so-called Origenist controversies, which were centered on Evagrius Pontus, who was indebted to Origen. The disputes culminated in a series of condemnations at the Second Council of Constantinople (553) that focused on the proper distinction between God and the world in creation and incarnation.[41] Despite his contested legacy, a survey of Christian tradition reveals that his basic insight into and method with eternal generation carried the day, as is evident, for example, in the theology of Thomas Aquinas.

Thomas Aquinas

Thomas Aquinas's treatment of the eternal processions improves on the foundation laid by Origen, which is to be expected, given the tremendous developments in dogmatic theology, conciliar decisions, and even philosophical method in the centuries between the two theologians. Aquinas is better able to distinguish generation from creation, though some elements of his thought can be seen emerging in Origen.[42] He can also deploy a more robust doctrine of God, the fruit of several generations of scholarship at newly founded European universities. Despite these differences, the basic method of clarifying the divine processions by using the divine attributes remains.

The doctrine of analogy helps Aquinas more clearly differentiate generation from creation by clarifying the relationship between God and the world. Aquinas recognizes that when humans use words to speak of God, they use words they have learned "as they are in creatures." These creatures have attributes as they have received them from God, their cause. One implication is that, properly speaking, these attributes most fully belong to God and only secondarily to creatures, who have these attributes by participation.[43] However, in our theological language, the terms primarily signify created realities perceived by the human mind and signify God only in a second-

40. See Ramelli, "Origen's Anti-subordinationism," 21–49; Anatolios, *Retrieving Nicaea*, 39–41; Ayres, *Nicaea and Its Legacy*, 20–30.

41. The anathemas concerning creation rightly target the historical Origen, while the anathemas concerning the incarnation likely trace back to Evagrius Pontus or Didymus the Blind instead of Origen, with whom they were often associated. See Davis, *First Seven Ecumenical Councils*, 246–47; Meyendorff, *Byzantine Theology*, 25–27.

42. See Crouzel, *Théologie de l'image de Dieu chez Origène*, 84–85. Particularly helpful here is Aquinas's clarification on the inward procession of the Word, a concept that is not clearly articulated in Origen, though Origen's treatment of the Son as glory from a light source, or as will from a mind, does imply a generation immanent to the Godhead. There is nothing quite so explicit as Aquinas's inward procession in Origen, who often blurs the lines between the Son and creatures.

43. Aquinas, *Summa Theologica* I, Q. 13, A. 3.

ary and analogical sense.[44] To give an example, God is more properly good than humans (Luke 18:19), but when I use the word "good," I have in mind various experiences from the created realm, so my meaning is incomplete and inaccurate in certain respects when I apply the word to God. This does not mean that any word signifying a created reality has its complete analogical fulfillment in God; here Copleston helpfully explains Aquinas's point by noting that God is a rock only in a metaphorical sense (as in, e.g., Ps. 18:2). The perfection of what it means to be a rock is proper to finite things, but the divine perfections, like goodness, are proper to God.[45] Analogy does not tell us which words to use of God, but once the right words are determined, the doctrine of analogy helps us to use these words precisely. As Brian Davies summarizes, "Any talk of procession in God must be understood in a way that prevents us from attributing to him anything essentially creaturely."[46]

Aquinas uses the Bible to identify which words to use to distinguish the Father, Son, and Spirit, though theologians who restrict themselves to the *Summa Theologica* may miss this fact.[47] In the *Summa contra Gentiles*, he begins with the texts one expects in a defense of eternal generation, including Psalm 2:7 and Proverbs 8:24–25, as well as John 1:14, drawing on the Latin description of the Son as *unigenitus* ("only-begotten").[48] When Aquinas desires to speak of the divine processions in the *Summa Theologica*, he does not turn to the texts one expects in an argument for the language of the "generation" of the Son, but he does affirm that "divine Scripture uses, in relation to God, names which signify procession." Here he cites the Vulgate of John 7:42, *Ego ex Dei processi*, or "From God I proceeded." Aquinas then argues that where there is an outward procession or act, there must be a corresponding inward procession or act.[49] In the *Summa Theologica*, he derives the divine processions from the divine **missions**, a strategy I will explore further below.

Once Aquinas has determined to use the word "generation" to speak of the Son, he clarifies the meaning of this term analogically through use of the divine attributes. Because the being of God is of a higher mode than created

---

44. Aquinas, *Summa contra Gentiles* 1.34.6.

45. Copleston, *Aquinas*, 129–30.

46. B. Davies, *Thought of Thomas Aquinas*, 195.

47. Holmes aptly summarizes, "The [*Summa Theologica*] presentation is no doubt an attempt to aid conceptual clarity, but it is in danger of obscuring the exegetical basis of Thomas's doctrine if it is read in abstraction from the other treatments" (*Quest for the Trinity*, 156–57).

48. Aquinas, *Summa contra Gentiles* 4.2.5. Aquinas also appeals to Ps. 2:7 in *Summa Theologica* I, Q. 27, A. 2.

49. Aquinas, *Summa Theologica* I, Q. 27, A. 1.

bodies, we cannot understand the divine processions "from what it is in bodies, either according to local movement, or by way of a cause proceeding forth to its exterior effect."[50] We can affirm the meaning of divine "generation" common with created generation: a procession by way of likeness.[51] However, we must further deny specific features of various creaturely forms of generation. Aquinas makes this most clear in the *Summa contra Gentiles*. We cannot imagine the generation of the Son as like the generation of fire by way of adding some characteristic to matter, for God is immaterial. Eternal generation is also not like reproduction in plants and animals, for this requires parts, and God is simple (see chap. 3). The generation cannot be in the form of the generation of sense experiences by an outside stimulant, the way rays of light generate human perception of color, for God is the prime agent and is not acted upon. He is impassible. The best analogy that Aquinas can produce is that eternal generation is similar to an intellectual emanation in which there is no division, change, material component, or external cause.[52] This analogy does have a scriptural sensibility about it, as the intellectual emanation he considers is the production of a word in the mind, and the Son is the Word of God (John 1:1). However, the negations and affirmations made through the use of the divine attributes are, in my opinion, more strongly warranted.

Where Origen does not have a thorough understanding of the Holy Spirit, Aquinas puts forward a clear theology of eternal spiration. He contrasts the analogy of the Word proceeding by way of intellectual emanation with that of an internal emanation by the will. The Spirit proceeds as love, and Aquinas understands this truth to require that love somehow be in the lover. Here again we are speaking of an internal procession that does not divide God into parts, change God, or move outside of God, for God is simple, immutable, and uncircumscribed. Aquinas is clear, though, that procession by way of love is distinct from procession by way of likeness, so generation is not spiration.[53] We must admit that even Aquinas's results here are modest. To use the phrasing of Matthew Levering, they give us merely "a glimpse into the Trinitarian mystery, rooted in the testimony of Scripture and illuminated by the analogy of the interior processions."[54] This glimpse is, nevertheless, a glimpse into the true beauty of the eternal Trinity.

50. Aquinas, *Summa Theologica* I, Q. 17, A. 1.
51. Aquinas, *Summa Theologica* I, Q. 17, A. 2.
52. Aquinas, *Summa contra Gentiles* 4.11.8.
53. Aquinas, *Summa contra Gentiles* 4.19.
54. Levering, *Engaging the Doctrine of the Holy Spirit*, 107.

Other Theologians

The use of analogy and the divine attributes to explain the divine processions is prevalent across various eras and methodologies. In fact, theologians have even used different language for the generation of the Son, including light emanating from light or the Father speaking a Word.[55] Differences in selected images, the era an author writes in, or the author's broader theological methodology typically do not cause them to abandon Origen's basic approach. For example, in the medieval period, William of Auvergne's rationalist *The Trinity, or the First Principles* uses the divine attributes to clarify the analogical meaning of generation in a largely speculative and philosophical manner. The Son's generation results in likeness that is "ultimate and complete," whereas creation or other forms of causation prohibit such likeness.[56] This is in part, William argues, because human procreation unites two natures, but God is simple. Unlike human procreation, generation in God is without change, for God is immutable.[57] Generation implies receiving one's nature, but not in "the literal intentions to which we are accustomed," for God is eternal, but only in "that intention in which it means 'to have from another.'"[58] William makes his argument with rarely an explicit mention of Scripture or tradition. In Wilhelmus à Brakel, a seventeenth- and eighteenth-century Dutch Protestant theologian who relies heavily on exegesis in his polemic against the Socinians, the appeal to the divine attributes is largely implicit. À Brakel explains, "We must therefore remove any notion of human generation from our minds as we ascend to divine generation,"[59] for we are "conveying spiritual matters by using vocabulary relating to aspects of human existence."[60] One must read his resulting exegesis closely to see that à Brakel's treatment of the preexistence of the Son against the Socinians assumes the eternality of the divine nature, to consider only a single example.[61] The Socinians, much like modern exegetes, read passages like Psalm 2:7 as referencing a temporal begetting in the incarnation, but à Brakel insists on the unique likeness between Father and Son indicated in the *homoousion*, which requires that we understand generation as an eternal act.[62] Be they medieval

---

55. While Galot makes a good case that Jesus never self-identifies as Word and that the theme of light is more prevalent, I see no reason to restrict analogies for eternal generation to a single biblical motif. See Galot, "La generation éternelle du Fils," 657–78.

56. William of Auvergne, *The Trinity* §14.

57. William of Auvergne, *The Trinity* §33.

58. William of Auvergne, *The Trinity* §34.

59. À Brakel, *Christian's Reasonable Service*, 1:148.

60. À Brakel, *Christian's Reasonable Service*, 1:149.

61. À Brakel, *Christian's Reasonable Service*, 1:150–55.

62. À Brakel, *Christian's Reasonable Service*, 1:149.

or post-Reformation, speculative or exegetical, explicit or implicit, historical treatments of eternal generation rely on some conception of analogy as
qualified by the divine attributes.

A reader well steeped in the trinitarian theology of the late twentieth century may be tempted to summon the ghost of once-cherished arguments and
accuse me of a prototypical Western approach to the Trinity. For a time, many
theologians feared that paying attention to the divine attributes and God's
oneness in this way would lead to the elimination of the divine threeness.
One might accuse me, to use Rahner's words, of using "the Augustinian-
Western conception of the Trinity, as contrasted with the Greek conception."
One might argue that I begin with "the one divine essence as a whole, and
only *afterwards* . . . see God as three in persons."[63] Here a response must
be limited to three points. First, the late twentieth-century emphasis on so-
called Eastern and Western versions of trinitarianism stems from an earlier
study by Theodore de Régnon, who actually posited a distinction between
patristic and medieval approaches, rather imprecisely called Greek and Latin,
respectively.[64] Much of the distorted transmission of de Régnon's hypothesis
has been seriously challenged for its lack of historical merit. It is not clear
that the West actually subordinates the persons to the divine nature.[65] Second, my book will proceed dialectically. Just as God's oneness as expressed
in the divine attributes must be used to norm plurality as understood in the
processions, so, for example, plurality in the Godhead must be used to norm
God's unity through divine simplicity, the subject of chapter 3. Every effort
will be made to provide balance. Third, though there is legitimate disagreement between East and West concerning the processions, this has primarily
been manifested in questions concerning whether the Spirit proceeds from
the Father *and* the Son (the *filioque* controversy) and in debates surrounding whether processions are from the divine nature or the divine persons.
I will address these differences in chapter 4. Despite these differences, the
basic method of using divine attributes to norm the eternal processions is
present in Eastern and Western theologians, as is evident in the citations in
the subsequent section.

63. So Rahner, *The Trinity*, 17.
64. See de Régnon, *Études de théologie positive*, 1:252, 257–60. The Western/Eastern dicho-
tomy breaks down because figures like Tertullian and Hilary of Poitiers, who wrote in Latin and
were Western figures, are counted as representatives of the "Greek" approach. De Régnon does
lay much of the blame at the feet of Augustine, though he argues that Gregory of Nazianzus
partly leads to the scholastic development because he begins to speak of the triune nature in
itself. This certainly stands in stark contrast with the late twentieth-century tendency to exalt
the Cappadocians.
65. I offer my own treatment in Butner, "For and against de Régnon," 399–412.

The Dogmatic Meaning of Eternal Generation and Eternal Procession

I turn now to a summary of the dogmatic meaning of the divine processions. When speaking of something so mysterious as this, we must be cautious, so I will classify negations and affirmations into those that appear to have wide agreement and those that we can trust with a lesser degree of confidence. A thorough survey of the tradition on these claims could easily fill an entire book, so I will summarize the tradition from my own perspective and provide representative sources only in a footnote here, except where a specific debate may require further information.[66]

When speaking of the divine processions, we can with great confidence deny that the processions began or ended in time or required change in God, for this would conflict with divine immutability. We can negate any division of the divine nature into parts, for this would conflict with divine simplicity. We can deny any bodily or spatial separation between the Father and Son, as is experienced in human generation, for God is uncircumscribed, infinite, and immaterial. The processions are not a response to any lack in God, for divine **aseity** shows that God has no need. We can negate any imperfection in the processions, for God is perfect. Generation and spiration are not to be confused with the acts of creation or, rather obviously, with human sexual reproduction.[67] To speak in an Aristotelian idiom, generation does not involve a move from potency to act, for God is *actus purus*, and such a change would conflict with divine immutability anyway. Finally, generation and spiration pertain not to the essence but to the persons, or hypostases.

With greater hesitation, we can still reasonably deny that generation is an operation of personal power, for power is classically proper to the divine nature. The fact that the Son does not generate, nor the Spirit generate or spirate, does not indicate that they are less powerful than the Father, for they possess the same divine essence and power.[68] However, we must also clarify that natures only exist as persons, so if the Son is generated and the Spirit

66. Athanasius, *Defense of the Nicene Definition* 3.11; Bonaventure, *Disputed Questions on the Mystery of the Trinity*, Q. 6, A. 2; Calvin, *Institutes of the Christian Religion* 1.13.8; Gregory of Nazianzus, *Theological Orations* 3.13; John of Damascus, *Exposition of the Orthodox Faith* §7; Palamas, *Topics of Natural and Theological Science* §96–98.

67. A transposition of biological processes into the theological realm can result in many of the meanings negated above, especially the generation of one essence from another, which divides the divine essence. See Helmer, *The Trinity and Martin Luther*, 120–21.

68. Lombard, *Sentences*, book 1, 7.1.1. Given that Lombard's text was a standard introduction to theology for generations, his argument would have considerable influence in the Middle Ages.

spirated by the power of the divine nature, it is by that nature as it belongs personally to the Father. We can also deny with some degree of confidence that procession is an operation of the will, at least in the sense that the divine decrees are an expression of the will. The Son and Spirit are equally causes of the decrees, so their processions cannot depend on the decrees. The fact that the processions are also not by compulsion renders this conclusion less clear than those negations listed above.[69]

When speaking of the processions, we can, with great confidence, affirm an order or *taxis* to the processions: the Father begets and breathes, the Son is begotten, and the Spirit is breathed. The specifics of the relational order between Son and Spirit, however, are far more contested, a controversy that will be treated in chapter 4. We can also confidently affirm that the divine processions uphold the consubstantiality of Father, Son, and Spirit while also maintaining a clear differentiation. Father, Son, and Spirit have the fullness of Godhead, but they are not identicals. The processions suggest intimacy between Father, Son, and Spirit, with a uniqueness with regard to how this intimacy is expressed. Eternal generation in particular also entails that the Son is not Son due to the incarnation or resurrection but is eternally so and is therefore best known by this title.

With lesser confidence, we can affirm that the Son and Spirit have their hypostatic existence from the Father, a claim commonly affirmed in the tradition, yet one also debated due to divine aseity. It may seem that the Father, Son, and Spirit are not consubstantial if only the Father has aseity. John Calvin, most notably, has shown concern, arguing that the Son is of himself (*a se*) when considered essentially but that in his person the Father is also the *principium* (principle) of the Son.[70] At times, affirming that the Spirit and Son receive their existence from the Father has prompted subordinationist tendencies.[71] Despite this, the notion of the processions as a communication of the divine essence was traditionally affirmed. Even Reformed theologians

---

69. For a helpful survey of what Reformed thinkers have said about this claim, see Heppe, *Reformed Dogmatics*, 120–21.

70. Calvin, *Institutes of the Christian Religion* 1.13.19. This argument led to several challenges against Calvin's trinitarian orthodoxy. See the helpful historical analysis in Ellis, *Calvin*. For similar concerns about the Father as cause of the Son and Spirit in an Eastern Orthodox perspective, see Papanikolaou, *Being with God*, 150–51.

71. William Burt Pope represents many of his era when he defends a form of subordination of the Son and Spirit to the Father on the basis of the divine processions: "The same divines, however, who laid stress on the numerical unity of the Divine essence, zealously maintained the eternal derivation of the Son, quoad Son, from the Father: thus teaching a subordination of relation" (Pope, *Compendium of Christian Theology*, 1:278). Pope does reject "Arian and Semi-Arian" positions as well as extreme views of some Dutch Remonstrants that suggested a subordination of being or an inequality (282–83). Ultimately, this language of relational

usually affirm, despite Calvin's hesitation, that generation entails a certain "fromness" by way of procession. Francis Turretin offers a helpful insight here when he notes that the Son does not derive his existence from the Father, which might seem to jeopardize aseity, but his mode of subsisting is determined by and derived from the Father.[72] Zacharias Ursinus adds that since this communication is not by grace, there is no resulting inequality.[73] We can also confidently affirm that generation and spiration are different, meaning that Son and Spirit cannot be confused. However, the specifics of how these processions are different are less clear. Using a **psychological analogy**, Aquinas is willing to claim that generation is procession as image by way of likeness, while spiration is procession as gift by way of imprint. Less precisely, Gregory of Nazianzus compares the different ways that Eve and Seth proceeded from Adam, the former by removal of a rib (Gen. 2:21), the latter by generation.[74] Many other theologians have tended to be more cautious, treating the mode of procession as beyond human comprehension.

The Exegetical Foundations for the Divine Processions

Among those Christians who particularly value tradition, the doctrines of eternal generation and procession remain in high regard despite questions among biblical scholars concerning the classical exegetical arguments for the doctrines. Some may be content to affirm the divine processions whether or not there is sound exegetical basis for them because of their inclusion in the Niceano-Constantinopolitan Creed and the so-called Athanasian Creed[75] and their acceptance by most major theologians until the modern era. However, in more biblicist-leaning theological landscapes, particularly evangelical ones, the tendency has been to offer exegetical defenses of eternal generation and procession or else to offer theological alternatives for distinguishing among the persons. Our analysis of the eternal processions in light of the doctrine of analogy and the divine attributes allows an alternative exegetical path for such defenses. It also provides a means of evaluating alternative proposals for eternally differentiating the divine persons.

---

subordination is a less precise way of speaking of the eternal *taxis* between Father, Son, and Spirit, one that, in some circles, has led to problematic conclusions and is best left behind.

72. Turretin, *Institutes of Elenctic Theology* 3.29.21.

73. Ursinus, *Commentary on the Heidelberg Catechism*, 195.

74. Gregory of Nazianzus, *Theological Orations* 5.11.

75. The creed's Athanasian authorship has largely been rejected by modern scholarship.

Current Exegetical Strategies for Defending the Divine Processions

There are two common strategies for defending the exegetical basis for the eternal processions: the first is an appeal to the "**economy**" of redemption as revelatory of divine processions, and the second is a defense of the classical hermeneutical methods that led to a scripturally based affirmation of the eternal processions. The first strategy is evident in Fred Sanders, who advocates a canonical approach[76] that derives the processions exegetically from the divine missions: "The revelation of the Trinity occurred primarily in the historical event of the arrival of the persons of the Son and the Holy Spirit."[77] This is not to say that there are not key verses of Scripture that improve our understanding of the Trinity; it is to insist that isolated biblical statements most clearly reveal the Trinity when read in light of the canonical story in which God sends his Son and Spirit to redeem humankind.[78] Here Sanders points to Galatians 4:4 and 6: "But when the fullness of time had come, God sent forth his Son. . . . And because you are sons, God has sent the Spirit of his Son into our hearts, crying 'Abba! Father!'" (ESV).[79] If the entire narrative of salvation involves God's self-revelation and redemptive action through the sending of the Son and Spirit, then, Sanders argues, we can deduce some eternal relationship between the Father, Son, and Spirit that is the basis of this sending. (I will explore this argument further in "Divine Missions and the Divinity of the Son and Spirit" in chap. 6.)

Katherine Sonderegger has recently argued for the divine processions on the basis of the economic work of God in the Old Testament, which she believes reveals "the Deep Descent that is Inwardness in the Life of God."[80] Sonderegger focuses her explanation of the economic revelation of the inner processions on Isaiah 53:8, a passage often cited in patristic treatments of the divine processions. The text asks of the suffering servant, "Who shall declare his generation?" (KJV).[81] Seeing the suffering servant as a type of Christ and

---

76. Brevard Childs is the famous advocate of a canonical approach, which "studies the canonical text in detailed exegesis, and seeks to do justice to the witness of both testaments in light of its subject matter who is Jesus Christ" (Childs, *Biblical Theology*, 78–79). Sanders directly appeals to Childs in his argument. From Sanders's perspective (and Childs's), much of modern scholarship has undermined the exegetical basis for the Trinity by being too fragmented, dividing theology from biblical studies, the historical Jesus from the religion of the apostles, and the Old Testament from the New Testament (F. Sanders, *Triune God*, 98–101 [note esp. 98n16], 168–71).

77. F. Sanders, *Triune God*, 124.

78. F. Sanders, *Triune God*, 70–72.

79. F. Sanders, *Triune God*, 240.

80. Sonderegger, *Systematic Theology*, 2:340.

81. Sonderegger, *Systematic Theology*, 2:255–352.

therefore applying this ineffable generation to the Son might seem like a stretch if we consider only 53:8, but Sonderegger sees the general movement of the suffering servant from prestige to humble self-sacrifice as a reflection of the entire Old Testament prophetic witness to Christ—a descending movement out from the Father.[82] Sonderegger insists that the eternal procession is not identical with the servant's sufferings but that it must be compatible with it. There must, then, be eternal "descent," to speak metaphorically, that corresponds with the historical suffering of the servant.[83] The movement of consuming fire outward from God to consume the sacrifice (e.g., Lev. 9:24) and the pleasing aroma that ascends back to God reflect the dynamism of a God who is the Giver and the Gift,[84] says Sonderegger, as do the dynamic, consuming flames that burn up Aaron's sons Nadab and Abihu for their rebellion, flames that are the glory of the Lord (Lev. 10:1–2).[85] Sonderegger's theological reading does much to show hints of the immanent processions in the economic acts of God in the Old Testament, though I suspect that fully grounding the processions requires further engagement with New Testament texts (and I look forward to reading her work in this area in the next volume of her systematic theology).

The second common strategy for defending the eternal processions defends the ancient hermeneutical methods that derived them. Eternal generation comes from passages such as Proverbs 8:25 and Psalm 2:7, which use the word *gennaō* ("beget") and are applied to Christ in the New Testament in such passages as Acts 13:33, Hebrews 1:5, and 5:5. Language of the Spirit being breathed out fits with the language of Job 33:4 or Ezekiel 37:4–14, which speak of the breath of God, or God's appearance through a breeze or wind in 1 Kings 19 and Acts 2.[86] As we have seen, ancient authors cited such passages in defense of the notion of eternal generation, but many modern scholars are unconvinced. Kevin Giles is exemplary of the second strategy when he acknowledges that "Psalm 2:7 *read critically and historically* does not speak of *the eternal begetting of the Son of God*."[87] Giles also admits that when Psalm 2:7 is cited in Acts 13:33, it is interpreted as having been fulfilled in the resurrection of Christ, while the citations of Psalm 2:7 in Hebrews 1:5 and 5:5 are interpreted as having been fulfilled "in the Son of God's exaltation."[88] Nevertheless, Giles defends

82. Sonderegger, *Systematic Theology*, 2:305.
83. Sonderegger, *Systematic Theology*, 2:313, 316.
84. Sonderegger, *Systematic Theology*, 2:465.
85. Sonderegger, *Systematic Theology*, 2:390–92, 413.
86. Slotemaker, *Anselm of Canterbury*, 40.
87. Giles, *Eternal Generation of the Son*, 79; italics original.
88. Giles, *Eternal Generation of the Son*, 79.

patristic exegesis against modern critical hermeneutics. He explores how such patristic methods build on the apostolic christological reading of Psalm 2:7 by extending generation into eternity, precisely because patristic christological reading is an extension of the sort of exegesis already found in Acts and Hebrews. New Testament authors extend the Old Testament meaning beyond its original historical referent by reading christologically, so perhaps early patristic authors are warranted in moving beyond the literal historical New Testament meaning. Giles sees this as a superior alternative to "a historical and critical approach to the reading of the Scriptures" that "ignores or denies the prophetic and christological implications of Old Testament texts."[89] Simply put, "the historical meaning of a biblical text does not exhaust the meaning of a text."[90] The two strategies present in Sonderegger, Sanders, and Giles do give some warrant to the divine processions, but attending to the dogmatic meaning of procession developed above provides a third venue.

Exegetical Warrant by Way of Analogy

If theologians affirming the doctrine of analogy use the divine attributes to negate certain concepts associated with processions and to affirm others, then a new exegetical strategy for justifying the divine processions is possible. Where this approach has provided greater specificity to terms like "generation" and "spiration," it is possible to provide exegetical warrant for many specified aspects of each procession. This approach has a biblical sensibility to it insofar as the divine attributes used in Scripture themselves have biblical support, a claim that I admit is challenged today.[91] A full treatment of debates surrounding the divine attributes would require a complete work on the doctrine of God, so for now I simply note that there are others whose defense of traditional views of the divine attributes I find compelling.[92]

If we turn to the affirmations we can make about the meaning of eternal generation, we find a wide range of exegetical support for the claim that generation is a procession resulting in a unique likeness between Father and

89. Giles, *Eternal Generation of the Son*, 56.
90. Giles, *Eternal Generation of the Son*, 56.
91. There have been challenges to doctrines like immutability, simplicity, and eternality from many quarters, drawing on philosophical, pragmatic, and exegetical arguments. Since the question at hand concerns the biblical warrant for the divine processions, I will simply note two texts whose emphasis is particularly exegetical, though even these texts would diverge from one another considerably in method, conclusion, and scope: Keller, *Face of the Deep*; J. Sanders, *God Who Risks*.
92. A brief treatment is available in Dolezal, *All That Is in God*. Others will be referenced in the discussion of the doctrine of simplicity in the next chapter.

Son. A clearer definition of the doctrine of eternal generation reveals that the debates over the word *monogenēs* in John 1:14, 18; 3:16, 18; and 1 John 4:9 have little impact on the doctrine of eternal generation. Even if we translate *monogenēs* as "unique" or "one and only," we have warrant for saying eternal generation signifies likeness. *Monogenēs* understood to mean uniqueness also would require that the Father-Son relationship differ from the Father-Spirit relationship, so the term provides some support for using a different word of the Spirit's procession. If *monogenēs* means "unique" or "one of a kind," there is explicit endorsement of the Son as unique in relation to the Father. Of course, if *monogenēs* explicitly means "only begotten," we also have affirmation of an eternal derivation.

The unique relation between the Son and the Father is demonstrable from other scriptural texts. In Romans 8:32, Paul argues that God did not spare (*ouk epheisato*) his own Son, which parallels the language used in the Septuagint of Genesis 22:16, where Abraham does not withhold (*ouk epheisato*) Isaac, the unique son of the promise. This suggests a similar unique status of Jesus Christ before the Father.[93] Jesus is frequently presented as the unique Son of God throughout the New Testament narrative. He alone has no physical father listed in Matthew's genealogical list (Matt. 1:16),[94] and though he is a descendant and son of David, in the Synoptic Gospels Jesus stumps his interlocutors by asking how David may call the Messiah "my Lord" if the Messiah is David's son (Mark 12:37 and pars.). When Hebrews 1:5 and 5:4–6 cite Psalm 2:7, "You are my Son, today I have begotten you" (ESV), they do so to establish the uniqueness of the Son, using the language of generation.[95] The Son is "much superior to angels" (Heb. 1:4 ESV). He is the unique priest in the order of Melchizedek (Heb. 5:1–10). Even in this uniqueness, the Son differs from the Spirit, who does not assume a priestly role and does not serve as the final and unrepeatable sacrifice.

The unique status of the Son also suggests a certain intimacy and likeness with the Father. This is evident at the baptism of Christ, where the Father

93. Dunn notes the difference between Paul speaking of God's own (*idou*) Son and the Septuagint's use of "beloved" (*agapētou*), but he argues that "Paul may have wanted to avoid any confusion of his assertion of Christ's elder brotherhood (vv. 14–17, 29), which *agapētos* . . . might cause" (Dunn, *Romans 1–8*, 501). Even if the parallel does not stand, the emphasis on Jesus as God's *own* Son has long been used by theologians wishing to affirm the Son's uniqueness as eternal Son. E.g., see à Brakel, *Christian's Reasonable Service*, 1:149.

94. Crowe, "The Trinity and the Gospel of Matthew," 30.

95. Hebrews 1 is arguably an example of *synkrisis*, a genre of persuasive comparison that typically begins with origin narratives. See Pierce, *Divine Discourse*, 38–39, 41–43. Pierce notes that "today" (*sēmeron*) is used elsewhere in the book of Hebrews to refer to an ongoing period of time.

calls the Son beloved (*agapētos*; Matt. 3:17 and pars.), and in Matthew's account of the transfiguration, where the same term is used (Matt. 17:5). The Holy Spirit shares this intimacy, for it searches the depths of God (1 Cor. 2:10). This intimacy is based on a likeness, for the Son is "the radiance of [the Father's] glory and the exact representation of his nature" (Heb. 1:3 NASB). The Greek *apaugasma* may be translated "radiance or effulgence," suggesting a procession, or as "reflection," which would suggest relationality.[96] It is an obscure term, possibly intended to link the coming of the Son with the coming of Wisdom in Wisdom 7:25.[97] Commentators on this text come to differing conclusions. George Buchanan argues that the Son is a representation of the Father in a *legal* sense but that the Father is still greater in nature.[98] Luke Timothy Johnson notes that *hypostaseōs* (here translated as "nature") means in "its basic etymological sense . . . 'that which stands under.'" He adds that *charaktēr* (here "representation") is used in some sources to denote a similarity in nature. Therefore, the phrase must "bear its most metaphysical sense."[99] I note here the disagreement but merely intend to demonstrate a unique likeness rooted in nature and glory. I will sidestep the exegetical question now and will return to texts in which the Son is directly called God when I treat divine simplicity, providing a dogmatic answer to the dispute over whether there can be gradation in the Godhead.

Despite the fact that there is a clear similarity between the procession of the Spirit and the Son in that they are both shown to have an intimate connection with the Father, the New Testament clearly distinguishes between the coming of the Son and of the Spirit in the divine economy of redemption. This is particularly clear in the Upper-Room Discourse in John 14–16, where Jesus promises the sending of another *paraklēton* (John 14:16). The term *paraklēton* is at times translated "comforter" (as in the KJV, ERV, and YLT), but this translation does not fit John 14:16. The fact that the Spirit is *another* Paraclete suggests that the Son is one, too, but whose departure had Jesus come to comfort the disciples about? For this reason, it is better to identify the *paraklēton* as an intercessor or advocate, as this fits both the circumstances of the Son as an advocate and the common meaning of the term in rabbinic and Hellenistic contexts.[100] The role of intercession implies a connection between the mission of the Spirit in the economy of redemption

96. See Johnson, *Hebrews*, 69.
97. Lane, *Hebrews 1–8*, 13.
98. Here I take Buchanan's claim that the Father is greater "physically" as using that word not in a crude material way but in the sense of nature (as *physis*) (Buchanan, *To the Hebrews*, 7).
99. Johnson, *Hebrews*, 69–70; cf. Bruce, *Epistle to the Hebrews*, 47–48.
100. Keener, *Gospel of John*, 2:954–61.

and the relation between the Father and Spirit in the heavens. This intercessory role is different than that of the Son—the Spirit is "another" *paraklēton*—though in each of the five texts about the Spirit coming or being sent in the Upper-Room Discourse, there is a clear relationality between the Son and Spirit, what Sergius Bulgakov calls a "dyadic union."[101] If the economic mission of the Spirit and Son is part of the evidence for the eternal processions, then the Upper-Room Discourse provides warrant for distinguishing and yet relating the eternal generation of the Son and procession of the Spirit. Here, too, there is warrant for a differentiation between Son and Spirit beyond that which is evident in the economy.

The Bible also clearly depicts a fundamental relationality between Father, Son, and Holy Spirit. When the Gospels are read in their probable order of composition, there appears to be, within these documents, a growing awareness of the threefold nature of God, made evident in duplex and **triplex formulas**. So, for example, in Matthew 11:25–27, Jesus praises the Father and says, "All things have been handed over to me by my Father, and no one knows the Son except the Father, and no one knows the Father except the Son and anyone to whom the Son chooses to reveal him" (11:27 ESV). Here we see the intimacy posited by eternal generation as well as a relationality between Father and Son. The parallel Luke 10:21–22 includes the same exclamation but adds, in 10:21, that Jesus rejoices "in the Holy Spirt" when making this claim. This triplex formula suggests a Lukan development in the awareness of a threefold relationality in God's redemptive and revelatory action.[102] In the Pauline Epistles, this relationality is particularly clear in passages where God is identified as the God who raised Jesus from the dead (Rom. 4:24; 8:11a, 11b; Gal 1:1).[103] We should not go very far with this claim. God identifies himself as the God of Abraham, Isaac, and Jacob (e.g., Exod. 3:6), and this identification alone would not lead us to posit the divinity of Abraham. Such

101. Bulgakov, *The Comforter*, 167–68. Bulgakov notes that the Spirit is another Advocate (John 14:16), distinguishing Son and Spirit. Christ says the Spirit is sent "in my name" (John 14:26), by the Son from the Father (John 15:26), and as a result of the Son's departure (John 16:7). Finally, the Spirit will receive from what is Christ's to show the disciples those things that the Son has spoken (John 16:13–15). In each of these cases, the procession of the Spirit in the economy "attests that dyadic interrelation of the Son and the Spirit in the self-revelation of the Father" (168).

102. Schelkle, *Theology of the New Testament*, 2:298. A related development may be present in the birth narratives in Matthew and Luke. Matthew is clear that Mary is with child through the power of the Holy Spirit (Matt. 1:18), but Luke provides an explanation in a clearer threefold form: "The Holy Spirit will come upon you, and the power of the Most High will overshadow you; therefore the child to be born will be called holy—the Son of God" (1:35 ESV). In general, Luke–Acts has a more prevalent pneumatology than Matthew.

103. See discussion in Hill, *Paul and the Trinity*, 52–71.

relationality on its own does not demonstrate the full deity of Christ or the doctrine of the Trinity.[104] Yet, the New Testament does suggest a priority of the Son over even Abraham—"Before Abraham was, I am" (John 8:58)—and many of the other actions that define God in the New Testament are christologically based.[105] While the New Testament does not explain precisely the significance of these triplex formulas or explicitly explain how they relate to the divine being, it does orient systematic theology toward an exploration of how such relationality exists for God.[106]

The Bible presents Son and Spirit as having unique, intimate, ordered, and differentiated relations with the Father since before they appeared in the redemptive-historical acts that are central to the biblical narrative. The economic sending of the Son and Spirit implies a certain "fromness" that precedes the incarnation and Pentecost. This scriptural data naturally leads to theological questions, such as "Are the Son and Spirit also somehow from the Father in an eternal sense?" and "What terms should we use to speak of these unique, intimate, ordered, and differentiated relations?" Here the tradition wisely draws on terminology from the biblical record itself in speaking of the eternal generation of the Son, even if the original human authors of Psalm 2:7 or Proverbs 8:25 did not intend to apply this generation literally to the Father and Son in an eternal sense. Faced with even sparser scriptural guidance concerning what to call the relation of the Spirit and Father (and Son?), theologians have developed and often used conservative terms such as "spiration" and "breathing," terms drawn from the ambivalent dual mean-

---

104. Here Robert Jenson goes too far in linking events and the divine nature. He argues, "Were God identified by Israel's Exodus or Jesus' Resurrection, without being identified *with* them, the identification would be a revelation ontologically other than God himself. . . . And this, of course, is the normal pattern of religion: where deity reveals itself is not where it is. At Delphi, one hears Apollo's voice but does not meet him" (Jenson, *Systematic Theology*, 1:59). Jenson has too low a view of transcendence, upholding a contrastive view that cannot imagine the possibility that God is truly transcendent to the act of the exodus (meaning that God is not the exodus) while simultaneously being fully present in it (meaning that God is identified with it). A corrective noncontrastive view of transcendence is clearly outlined in Tanner, *God and Creation in Christian Theology*.

105. Hill points to Rom. 4:5 and 17, which identify the Father by the acts of justifying the ungodly and giving life to the dead, respectively. Both acts are christologically determined. In the Old Testament, we see statements that God did not justify the ungodly (see, e.g., Exod. 23:7), though he did count the faith of individuals like Abraham as righteousness. In the New Testament, the standard is for God to justify the ungodly. What has changed? Christ has died for the ungodly (Rom. 5:6). Why does God give life to the dead? Because Jesus was raised as the firstfruits of the resurrection (1 Cor. 15). So, these God-identifying acts in Rom. 4 are subordinate to Rom. 4:24's identification of God as the one who raised Jesus from the dead. Hill, *Paul and the Trinity*, 53–61.

106. For more detail, see Kaye, "New Testament," 21.

ing of the Hebrew *ruach* and Greek *pneuma*. Others have simply made the term "procession" a technical designation for the Spirit alone. When we are pressed to define these terms, a careful use of the way of negation and the divine attributes leads to a definition of the processions that is so restricted that its intended meaning can be closely mapped onto the scriptural patterns discussed above. So, when exploring the best means of discussing the difference between the Father, Son, and Spirit in the Godhead, we can do no better, from a scriptural standpoint, than to begin by affirming the two eternal divine processions.

The Personal Properties

The processions lead to an additional means of distinguishing the persons: their personal properties (Greek *idiōmata* or *idiotētes*, Latin *proprium*). In English these may be also called "relative properties," "personal characteristics," "peculiarities," or even "**incommunicable properties.**" I will continue to speak of "personal properties." A personal property is that which is proper to the persons due to the processions. Basil of Caesarea was instrumental in developing the distinction between person and essence, which is fundamental to the understanding of consubstantiality put forward in chapter 1. In Basil, this development is more about how we know God than about metaphysics. Basil insists that there are certain particularities proper to Father, Son, and Spirit—namely, being unbegotten, being begotten, and proceeding, respectively—that are a means of knowing the modes in which God eternally exists.[107] However, Basil's theory is not fully developed, and he speaks in epistemological terms more than ontological ones: "That which is spoken of in a special and peculiar manner is indicated by the name hypostasis."[108] In short, a hypostasis is known by a unique personal property.

The later definition of Richard of St. Victor is somewhat more precise, though it creates problems of its own: "Yet, with no doubt, in that Trinity we must have as many personal properties as the number of persons. Now,

---

107. Commenting on Basil's development of the distinction in *Contra Eunomium*, Ayres remarks, "One of Basil's main concerns is to demonstrate how this division helps us articulate what we come to know of God and speak appropriately of both identity and difference between Father and Son. The concern is as much epistemological as strictly ontological. We might even say that Basil's point implies a metaphysics (or at least an analogy with the metaphysics of creation), but the metaphysical distinction he makes is only vaguely defined in comparison with the precise epistemology which drives the clarity of the distinction" (Ayres, *Nicaea and Its Legacy*, 199).

108. Basil, *Letters* 38.3.

certainly, the personal property is incommunicable. The personal property is that which gives to each [person] that which he is. We define 'personal property' as the thing by which each one is unique, distinct from everyone else."[109] Richard's definition does cause a certain conundrum for the doctrine of the divine processions, which claims a communication of the divine nature from Father to Son and Spirit. If personal properties are incommunicable, it could seem that the processions are impossible. Some fine distinctions may help here. The Father communicates the divine essence to the Son by generation but does not communicate the personal property of being generated to the Son, for that is eternally the Son's incommunicable property. Similarly, the Father (and the Son?) communicates the divine nature to the Spirit by spiration but does not communicate the property of being spirated, for that is eternally the Spirit's incommunicable property. Because a hypostasis is a subsistence of a nature and is nothing without that nature, we can still say that the subsistences of the Son and Spirit are derived from the communication of the nature by the Father, even if the personal property and **mode of those subsistences** are incommunicable and unique.

At the very least, then, we can now say that the Father is unbegotten, meaning that the Father is God in a mode of subsistence that communicates the divine nature eternally without change, imperfection, beginning, or end to establish unique, ordered, eternal relations that allow for differentiation and likeness. The Son and Spirit, then, are God in a mode of subsistence that receives the divine nature eternally by generation and spiration, respectively, without change, imperfection, beginning, or end. This development gives us the initial sense of how we can speak of diversity in the Godhead, but much work remains for further chapters. At this stage, consubstantiality and the eternal divine processions have merely laid the groundwork.

FOR FURTHER READING

Recent Defenses of Eternal Generation

Giles, Kevin. *The Eternal Generation of the Son: Maintaining Orthodoxy in Trinitarian Theology*. Downers Grove, IL: IVP Academic, 2012.

> Kevin Giles has written the first accessible English book-length treatment of the doctrine of eternal generation, defending the doctrine largely on dogmatic and patristic grounds.

109. Richard of St. Victor, *On the Trinity* 4.17.

Sanders, Fred, and Scott R. Swain, eds. *Retrieving Eternal Generation*. Grand Rapids: Zondervan, 2017.

> This collection of essays considers how major historical figures explore eternal generation, exegetes key texts, and considers the dogmatic significance of eternal generation.

Helpful Explorations of Procession

Bulgakov, Sergius. *The Comforter*. Translated by Boris Jakim. Grand Rapids: Eerdmans, 2004.

> Bulgakov's work covers much important content on the Holy Spirit, but I place it here because of his fascinating insistence that procession and generation cannot be reduced to matters of origin.

Congar, Yves. *I Believe in the Holy Spirit*. Vol. 3, *The River of Life Flows in the East and in the West*. Translated by David Smith. New York: Seabury, 1983.

> Congar's treatment of the Holy Spirit is detailed, insightful, and ecumenically oriented. While it covers much ground, like the Buglakov text, a central question is the procession of the Holy Spirit.

CHAPTER 3

Simplicity

The consubstantiality of the Father, Son, and Holy Spirit, which leads to our worship of the three as one God, is an important foundation for the doctrine of the Trinity, but on its own it does not sufficiently specify what it means to say that Father, Son, and Holy Spirit are one. More must be said regarding the divine unity. This brings us to the doctrine of divine simplicity, the belief that God is not composed of parts. Simplicity is affirmed by many of the earliest Christian theologians of the postapostolic age. For example, Athenagoras writes, "Socrates, indeed, was compounded and divided into parts, for the very reason that he was created and perishable. But God is uncreated, impassible, and indivisible. He does not, therefore, consist of parts."[1] Notice that Athenagoras distinguishes between composite creatures and a simple God, and for good reason. Anything that is composite requires an explanation for why its parts are composed in this particular manner or in any manner at all. Since God is the absolute explanation for everything, God certainly cannot have parts that require his being explained by an outside cause.

As theology advanced through the centuries, increasingly complex explanations of divine simplicity emerged. Not only was God thought to have no material parts, but many also denied that God was composed of matter and form, that God's existence and essence were distinct, and even that any real distinction existed between God's attributes. It is evident that simplicity was central to patristic, medieval, and Reformation scholastic accounts of the Trinity. Despite this fact, many modern accounts of the Trinity have lost a clear vision of simplicity's dogmatic role in the doctrine of the Trinity. I

---

1. Athenagoras, *Plea regarding Christians*, §8.

remember once sitting in a lecture by a deservedly renowned philosopher of religion when he taught that early Christians merely affirmed simplicity to make sure that God did not fall apart. While it is true that a being without parts can neither fall apart nor be divided, a closer reading reveals far more important purposes for simplicity. It not only preserves the absolute nature of the divine essence but also is a lynchpin in explaining the doctrine of the Trinity. Without simplicity, the classical doctrine of the Trinity must be dramatically modified.

Today, there are many philosophers and theologians who would prefer to challenge and reject divine simplicity. While much of the debate remains both quite technical and better treated in a book on the doctrine of the divine attributes, two common major objections will be treated at length in this chapter. A large number believe, in Richard Plantinga, Thomas Thompson, and Matthew Lundburg's words, that simplicity has "no real biblical basis and has in fact worked to defeat the resources of a full-fledged trinitarianism."[2] I will argue for the contrary. Not only is divine simplicity dogmatically indispensable for the doctrine of the Trinity, but it also finds indirect yet sufficient support in the Bible to warrant its acceptance.

While I have already introduced the basic meaning of the doctrine of simplicity, several important details remain to be discussed. First, I will address several versions of the doctrine, each with its own position on how to think of a simple God having distinct properties like power and goodness. In particular, we must ask how God can have distinct attributes if there are no parts in God. After all, aren't attributes like power and goodness different, suggesting that God's power and goodness refer to different parts of his nature? Then I will explain the dogmatic role of simplicity in the Trinity. Finally, I will respond to objections against simplicity that claim the doctrine is unbiblical and antitrinitarian.

Versions of Simplicity and the Divine Attributes

There are four common approaches to divine simplicity that explain how the doctrine is compatible with the many divine attributes Christians rightly affirm. The first three posit a kind of distinction between the divine attributes: a conceptual distinction, a **virtual distinction**, or a formal distinction. Each of these approaches attempts to provide an explanation of how the diverse divine attributes are one in God. A fourth approach is **apophatic**, refusing such an explanatory approach.

2. Plantinga, Thompson, and Lundberg, *Introduction to Christian Theology*, 104.

Simplicity and a Conceptual Distinction between Divine Attributes

During the fourth-century disputes on the Trinity, the doctrine of divine simplicity increasingly became a component of debates over the consubstantiality
of the Father, Son, and Spirit. This shift was prompted by the theology of
Eunomius of Cyzicus, who argued partly on the basis of divine simplicity that
the Son could not have received the essence of the Father through generation.
The confession of Eunomius acknowledged God as "not divided in the *ousia*
in which he exists nor distributed into more."[3] Since a simple essence could
not be divided through generation or procession and bestowed in part to the
Son or the Spirit, Eunomius concluded that the Son was unlike (*anomoios*)
the Father in essence. Because God's attributes were his essence, Eunomius
reasoned that the divine attributes must have been identical with one another.
He therefore concluded from the fact that the Father is unbegotten (*agenētos*)
that the Son, who is begotten (*genētos*), could not have the same essence, for
to have the divine essence and to be unbegotten were the same thing.[4]

Both Basil of Caesarea and Gregory of Nyssa responded directly to Eunomius's arguments. One dimension of their response was an appeal to Basil's
distinction between hypostasis and *ousia*, addressed in chapter 1. However,
each also appealed to a different theory of theological language to challenge
Eunomius. As Khaled Anatolios summarizes, "Eunomius's doctrine of God
had its immovable foundation in the premise that the word-sign 'unbegotten/
unoriginate' renders the divine essence immediately present to the mind."[5]
On this account, to know a divine attribute is to know the divine essence.
This theory of theological language compelled Eunomius to reduce the divine
essence to the single attribute of being unbegotten. Basil and Gregory argued
that the divine names and attributes were not identical to one another yet
all identified the same simple essence. To make sense of this claim, the two
Cappadocians developed an alternative theory of theological language: the
words used to describe the divine attributes "conceptualize[d]" the essence
as presented to people but the words do not properly signify the essence as
it is in itself.[6] "To be, and to be called are not convertible terms," Gregory of
Nyssa insisted, adding, "God is by his nature what he is, but he is called by
us by such names as the poverty of our nature will allow us to make use of."[7]

---

3. Eunomius adds that "the glory of the almighty cannot be communicated" and cites Isa. 42:8:
"My glory I will not give to another." The confession is reconstructed by R. P. C. Hanson from
its citations in Gregory of Nyssa (Hanson, *Search for the Christian Doctrine of God*, 619–20).
4. See the discussion in Radde-Gallwitz, *Basil of Caesarea*, 105.
5. Anatolios, *Retrieving Nicaea*, 159.
6. Behr, *Formation of Christian Theology* II/2, 286.
7. Gregory of Nyssa, *Against Eunomius*, 266.

To the objection of some contemporary theologians that divine simplicity makes properties like omnipotence and goodness identical in meaning, when they clearly differ,[8] Gregory and Basil might respond that these terms are conceptually distinct only in the human mind. This distinction is, according to them, a byproduct of our knowledge of God as he presents himself to us in revelation and divine action. By contrast, the divine essence that presents these attributes remains simple. This defense illuminates a nontrinitarian role of the doctrine of simplicity: securing a necessary degree of mystery concerning the essence of the God whom we currently know only "through a glass, darkly" (1 Cor. 13:12 KJV). Our knowledge of the simple God is true, but it is also human knowledge that does not grasp the infinite essence of God as Eunomius ambitiously attempted to do.[9] Therefore, we inevitably describe God as possessing complex attributes even though he is truly simple, but such description remains true of God's work and revelation.

Simplicity, Analogy, and the Virtual Distinction between Attributes

Thomas Aquinas gives a particularly robust explanation of divine simplicity that involves the denial of various kinds of composition. There is no composition of act and potency in God, which means that God cannot change. There is no bodily or corporeal composition in God, who is spirit (John 4:24). There is no composition of matter and form in God, for this would make God a creature of whatever had imposed the form on matter. There is no composition of genus and species in God, for God is not a particularized instantiation of a more universal divine nature. There is no composition of essence and existence in God, for this would require (*per impossibile*) that something gave existence to God, who is the cause of all existence and who is being itself.[10] Aquinas's explanation of divine simplicity leads to subsequent affirmations of divine perfection, immutability, infinity, eternity, and unity, which follow logically from divine simplicity. As Steve Long notes, the perfections qualify one another, so God's immutability does not deny the "necessary motions that the operations of knowledge and will entail." Similarly, "it is insufficient to argue 'God is simple' if it does not contribute to God's unitary essence manifested in the real distinctions of the three persons."[11] The attributes must qualify one

---

8. See Moreland and Craig, *Philosophical Foundations for a Christian Worldview*, 524; Hughes, *On a Complex Theory*, 60–63.

9. See Radde-Gallwitz, *Basil of Caesarea*, 117.

10. For Aquinas's full presentation of divine simplicity, see Aquinas, *Summa Theologica* I, Q. 3. A thorough explanation of this definition of simplicity is found in Dolezal, *God without Parts*, 31–66.

11. Long, *Perfectly Simple Triune God*, 23.

another, and divine triunity must qualify divine simplicity, in part because of the analogical nature of all theological language. God is not immutable in the way that we think of immobile created things, nor does God know or will in the manner that creatures know or will. How, then, does Aquinas think of the distinction between the divine attributes?

Though it shares some features with the Cappadocian explanation of divine simplicity, Aquinas's theology offers a different explanation of the distinction between the attributes given divine simplicity. Aquinas argues that we attribute "perfections found in other things" to God "in the same way as effects are found in their equivocal causes." Here Aquinas uses the analogy of the sun, which is called hot because it produces heat, "because the power through which it does this has some likeness to heat." Similarly, "God is called wise not only in so far as He produces wisdom, but also because, in so far as we are wise, we imitate to some extent the power by which He makes us wise."[12] Given this, the distinction between the divine attributes can be described as a virtual distinction. A virtual distinction differs from a conceptual distinction in that it specifies that the basis for the mental distinction between attributes lies in God. There is something real about the divine essence that makes it capable of being the cause of differing created effects that lead us to call God strong or wise.[13] Some Thomists clarify that there is a *minor* virtual distinction in God, meaning that the distinction between the attributes is based on the reality of God's nature but is not due to different potencies in God, because God is pure act.[14]

Simplicity and Formal Distinctions

John Duns Scotus provides yet another version of divine simplicity that allows for more robust distinctions between the divine attributes. Scotus accepts **univocity**, the theory of theological language that says that at least some words used of God and creatures have the same lexical meaning. Univocity prevents Scotus from explaining simplicity in the way that Thomas Aquinas does, and it may appear to undermine simplicity. After all, if goodness and justice mean the same thing in God and humans, and if goodness and justice in humans are different things, composite parts of a given human nature, then apparently goodness and justice are different things in God, composite parts of a complex divine nature.

Scotus avoids univocity's challenge to divine simplicity by appealing to the notion of modes or modalities of being. As Richard Cross summarizes,

12. Aquinas, *Summa contra Gentiles* 1.31.2.
13. See the discussion in Dolezal, *All That Is in God*, 133–34.
14. Garrigou-Lagrange, *The Trinity and God the Creator*, 119–20.

a modality of being is something that "determines the way in which that attribute is instantiated." Cross gives the example of the shade of a color, which is a mode that determines the precise way in which that color is manifest.[15] Scotus thinks that if God is perfect, he must have all perfections infinitely. If univocal theories of theological language are true, then these perfections must be distinct in God.[16] Scotus believes that if infinity is the modality of all divine attributes, we can still have a simple being. For creatures, if we distinguish the form of goodness and justice, we find two limited, distinct, and delineated finite realities, since goodness and justice are finite in creatures. Yet, these perfections are infinite and limitless in God, so if we distinguish the form of goodness and justice, we do not thereby find two distinct realities in God. Goodness and justice remain infinite in God and therefore cannot be distinct, limited, and delineated from one another at the level of being. The properties are the same infinite being at the level of identity, though they are formally distinct.[17] Because the properties are instantiated in the mode of infinite being, of which there can be only one, these formally distinct properties remain one simple being. In other words, there can be only one infinite being (two would limit one another). Therefore, infinite properties of this single infinite being cannot be distinct things or beings, since there cannot be two infinite beings. Therefore, the distinctions must be distinctions of form rather than divisions of essence.

There is some disagreement regarding the meaning of the formal distinction in Scotus. Réginald Garrigou-Lagrange summarizes Scotus's formal distinction as "not between one thing and another but between two formalities of the same thing."[18] On this reading, Scotus is attempting to have a distinction somewhere between a notional and real distinction. Garrigou-Lagrange denies this is possible: "This formal actual distinction . . . either antecedes the consideration of our minds and then, however small, it is real; or it does not antecede the consideration of our minds, and then it is a distinction of reason . . . or a virtual distinction."[19] Some interpreters believe that both the virtual distinction and the formal distinction are attempting to make the same point: God's attributes are distinguished by our minds, but the distinction is based in God. However, where Aquinas's virtual distinction emphasizes the way the

---

15. Cross, *Duns Scotus*, 42.

16. Gilson, *John Duns Scotus*, 188.

17. Gilson, *John Duns Scotus*, 191. Gilson summarizes, "Thus, it is still true to say with St. Augustine that God's wisdom *is* his justice, but it is no less true to say with Duns Scotus that *what is* God's wisdom is not what is his justice, because God's justice is not formally identical with his wisdom" (191).

18. Garrigou-Lagrange, *The Trinity and God the Creator*, 120.

19. Garrigou-Lagrange, *The Trinity and God the Creator*, 120.

difference is rooted in the mind, Scotus's formal distinction emphasizes the way the difference is rooted in God. Others would argue that Scotus's formal distinction is quite different from the virtual distinction in that it is objective, suggesting a real distinction in God, but a distinction in mode, not in simple essence or nature.[20]

It is widely held that Scotus's concept of simplicity is weaker than other versions.[21] Scotus himself would admit that unity of what is simple (*unitas simplicitas*) is a lesser unity than the *formal identity* of things, which is not present in the divine attributes.[22] Many of the most significant objections to Scotus's account of formal distinctions in the divine nature arise in the doctrine of the divine attributes or concerning univocity as a theory of theological language.[23] In my estimation, other theories of divine simplicity are preferable.

Gregory Palamas, Simplicity, and the Uncreated Divine Energies

The Eastern Orthodox position on simplicity is complicated somewhat by the Byzantine distinction between the divine essence and **energies**, popularized particularly by Gregory Palamas. To put the matter briefly, Palamas agrees with the position discussed in chapter 1 that of Aristotle's categories, substance and relation can both be used of God as referring to ontological aspects of the Trinity, but he adds that energy, which is sometimes translated as "activity" or "operation," applies as well. Thus, when we think of God, we must discuss not only persons and essence but also uncreated divine energies.[24] Because of this distinction, Gregory Akindynos accused Palamas of undermining divine simplicity, a charge that has continued into the present.[25] It is clear, however, that Palamas intends to uphold the doctrine of divine simplicity, which he openly affirms: "We worship one true and perfect God in three true and perfect hypostases—not, certainly, a threefold God but one who is simple."[26] What is less clear to modern scholars is how Palamas understands the distinction between essence and energies in light of divine simplicity.[27]

---

20. Vogt, "Note on the 'Formal Distinction' in Scotus," 40–41.
21. E.g., Dolezal, *All That Is in God*, 133; Cross, *Duns Scotus*, 43.
22. Gilson, *John Duns Scotus*, 187.
23. These are important discussions, though they remain beyond the scope of this work.
24. Palamas, *Topics of Natural and Theological Science* §134.
25. Plested, "St. Gregory Palamas on the Divine Simplicity," 512.
26. Palamas, *Topics of Natural and Theological Science* §37.
27. This is due to many factors, including the relatively limited number of Palamas's texts that have been translated into English and the fact that his texts do not take the form of scholastic manuals like the writings of Aquinas or Scotus, with whom theologians are prone to compare him.

Several features of Palamas's treatment of this distinction help us map his understanding of divine simplicity. First, when discussing the distinction, he has a tendency to appeal to Basil of Caesarea in his dispute with Eunomius,[28] thereby making the point that we can use words with distinct meanings when speaking of God without undermining simplicity.[29] Second, Palamas takes the additional step of consistently arguing that if we allow a real distinction between the divine persons without questioning simplicity, we can also allow for a distinction among the divine energies and between the energies and essence without undermining simplicity.[30] This has led many commentators to believe that Palamas affirms a real distinction between the essence and energies, which would raise considerable questions regarding how God is not complex.[31] Others avoid using the terminology of a real distinction and summarize Palamas to mean, in the words of Marcus Plested, that "the energies are precisely the essence revealed."[32] On this account, simplicity could perhaps be something closer to a virtual distinction, though to my knowledge Palamas does not use this terminology. The ambiguity here is partly a byproduct of Palamas shifting the balance in theology more heavily toward apophatic thought than such Western figures as Duns Scotus and Aquinas. This apophatic tendency is a fourth possible approach to understanding the distinction between divine attributes: perhaps we can affirm distinct energies whereby we know distinct attributes while affirming divine simplicity, all without exhaustive explanation.[33]

The Dogmatic Function of Divine Simplicity in the Doctrine of the Trinity

Stephen Holmes remarks, "From Gregory of Nyssa . . . to Francis Turretin . . . there was an assumption on all sides that to believe in divine simplicity was to

28. See Palamas, *Topics of Natural and Theological Science* §§125–26; Palamas, *Dialogue between an Orthodox and a Barlaamite* §§3, 14, 40–41. I have discussed this point more extensively in Butner, "Communion with God," 33–36.

29. It does not appear to me that Palamas uses the fully developed notion of conceptualization we find in Basil and in Gregory of Nyssa, though further specialized study is warranted.

30. See the discussion in Plested, "St. Gregory Palamas on the Divine Simplicity," 513–14.

31. For an example of an interpreter who thinks there is a real distinction in Palamas between essence and energies, see Meyendorff, *Byzantine Theology*, 186.

32. Plested, "St. Gregory Palamas on the Divine Simplicity," 519.

33. Palamas may have preferred a counterattack against a cataphatic explanation of the energies and divine simplicity. Against Akindynos, he argued that rejecting eternal energies in God does not preserve simplicity but ensures a nonexistent God. See Mantzaridis, *Deification of Man*, 106.

be an orthodox trinitarian, and to deny simplicity was to attack the doctrine of the Trinity."[34] This is a point that is often missed in modern discussions of simplicity, which tend to treat the doctrine of the Trinity as incompatible with divine simplicity.[35] I have already briefly discussed divine simplicity in the context of eternal generation but will now expand the significance of simplicity for trinitarian doctrine, illustrating four key dogmatic functions for simplicity, primarily with reference to Athanasius of Alexandria.

The first important role for the doctrine of simplicity in pro-Nicene debates was rejecting any notion of a hierarchy of divinity. Arius himself seemed to affirm that the Son was greater than other creatures, a god of sorts, but not true God. Some modern scholars have speculated that there may have been a fear among early Arians that consubstantiality would lead to a diminishment of the Father, who gave up what was his to give it to the Son. On this account the Father might lose some divinity in giving it to the Son or Spirit.[36] Whatever the motive, various fourth-century groups sought to situate the Son and Spirit at different levels of proximity to the full deity of the Father. Divine simplicity does not allow any such sliding scale. The divine essence is indivisible, so other beings are either completely unlike the Father or are fully identical in nature to the Father. The Father could not give up part of his divinity to the Son, for a simple being is indivisible and immutable. Nor could the Son receive only a part of the divine nature and be less than fully God, for the divine nature cannot be partitioned. Athanasius tends to explain this by frequent appeal to a contrast between those who participate in the divine nature (2 Pet. 1:4) by grace and the Father, Son, and Spirit, who share the identically same nature essentially.

Athanasius would also appeal to simplicity to help explain how there is only one God. This is an important second function of simplicity for the Trinity. The Son is not related to the Father as if God is one thing divided into two parts, for the Son is not another God, nor are there many Gods. The divine essence of the Son is identical to the essence of the Father.[37] The same argument can be made of the Holy Spirit in relation to the Father and Son. At first glance, trinitarians could easily be accused of polytheism, which is clearly contrary to the Bible's insistence that there is one God (Deut. 32:39; Isa. 43:10; 1 Tim. 1:17). Simplicity defends the singularity of the divine nature by insisting that Father, Son, and Spirit are neither distinct members of a genus nor parts of a larger whole. The single divine essence eternally and

34. Holmes, "Attributes of God," 65.
35. E.g., see Hughes, *On a Complex Theory*, 153–240.
36. Gregg and Groh, *Early Arianism*, 104.
37. Athanasius, *Orations against the Arians* 3.4.

fully exists concurrently in the three divine persons. Without simplicity, it is not immediately clear how one could believe in a single God while maintaining a distinction between Father, Son, and Holy Spirit.[38]

As noted in chapter 2, divine simplicity plays an important role in clarifying eternal generation. Here Athanasius is influenced by Origen of Alexandria, who relied on simplicity to qualify the notion of eternal generation.[39] Whereas Arius seems to fear that consubstantiality and generation taken together entail that there are two Gods, Athanasius can appeal to the Origenistic tradition to insist that generation does not multiply or divide the divine essence.[40] Several decades into the Arian debates, Athanasius is still making the same point in *On the Councils of Ariminum and Seleuca*. In this work, Athanasius challenges anomians like Eunomius because they accept generation and divine simplicity but argue that the Son is unlike the Father. Athanasius points out that if generation is different from creation *ex nihilo*, it must differ in that generation is from the Father. If it is not from the Father's essence, as anomians insist, then it must be from accidental properties of the Father, which is impossible according to simplicity. Therefore, if the Son is generated from the Father, it must be from the Father's essence, for all that is in God is the essence and is God.[41] In the same work, Athanasius implicitly draws on simplicity when he insists that eternal generation is impassible and occurs without division of the divine nature; one God remains, even given generation.[42] Simplicity, then, allows Athanasius simultaneously to uphold eternal generation, consubstantiality, and a strong monotheistic affirmation of one singular divine essence.

A fourth role of divine simplicity in trinitarian doctrine concerns the divine economy, since simplicity ensures that God is truly revealed in Christ. This is a surprising role for simplicity, given that modern sensibilities are prone to suspect that simplicity undermines the very possibility of divine self-revelation. For example, Barth sets up his discussion of the doctrine of simplicity in the context of the problem of the knowledge of God. If, due to divine simplicity, the distinction between God's attributes is simply a subjective one in our minds, can we say we know God at all?[43] This "nominalist" problem leads to Barth's conflicted relationship with divine simplicity, which he seems to fear can lead us to deny that God is "wholly revealed and wholly

---

38. See the discussion in Duby, *Divine Simplicity*, 102, 158; Dolezal, *All That Is in God*, 106.

39. Hinlicky, *Divine Complexity*, 180; Hanson, *Search for the Christian Doctrine of God*, 425.

40. Weinandy, *Athanasius*, 54.

41. Athanasius, *On the Councils of Ariminum and Seleuca* §§34–36.

42. Athanasius, *On the Councils of Ariminum and Seleuca* §41.

43. Barth, *Church Dogmatics* II/1, 322–37.

concealed."[44] Similarly, Isaak Dorner believes that most historical versions of divine simplicity—here Dorner admits as an exception the formal distinction of Duns Scotus—risk making it such that we do not truly know God, for the attributes are merely subjective while the essence of God remains unknown.[45]

Pro-Nicene theology, in contrast, understands divine simplicity to ensure God's self-revelation. R. P. C. Hanson remarks that "Arian theology tended to see the Son as a safeguard against God the Father coming into dangerously close contact with the world."[46] The fact that, in Arianism, God and the Son are similar yet different in nature ensures that God can be revealed through a mediator while kept distant from the sinful, corruptible world. This is hardly a *self*-revelation, and if theologians like Barth are correct in saying that creatures cannot reach knowledge of God by their own capabilities, then it is hard to see how this is any revelation at all. Athanasius of Alexandria, by contrast, believes that the Son is not divisible from the Father and that "the Father's Godhead" is therefore in the Son in such a manner that those who have seen the Son have seen the Father (John 14:9).[47] Here simplicity safeguards the possibility of true knowledge of the Father through the Son, since the Son is not separated from the essence of the Father. The partial knowledge of God that simplicity requires also guarantees truthful knowledge of God, contrary to modern fears.[48]

In summary, the doctrine of simplicity is essential to trinitarian theology because it clarifies both the doctrine of the processions and the doctrine of consubstantiality. The Father, Son, and Spirit share the same simple primary substance without any hierarchy of divinity, and neither eternal generation nor eternal spiration in any way divides this essence or allows a merely partial transmission of God's nature through a procession. Because eternal generation and eternal spiration communicate the full divine essence due to simplicity, the divine missions, which are the manifestation of the processions in the created realm, truly reveal God.

The Biblical Case for Divine Simplicity

Though the doctrine of simplicity has historically been a major component of trinitarian thought, there are many today who doubt that it is a biblical

44. Barth, *Church Dogmatics* II/1, 341.
45. Dorner, *System of Christian Religion*, 1:195–96.
46. Hanson, *Search for the Christian Doctrine of God*, 426.
47. Athanasius, *On the Councils of Ariminum and Seleuca* §52.
48. One could also argue that Barth fundamentally misunderstands the virtual distinction in Aquinas. Knowledge of God is *human* knowledge and hence incomplete knowledge, yet it remains true knowledge.

doctrine. I will add two specifically trinitarian defenses of the biblical warrant for simplicity to the typical defenses that tend to focus more directly on the doctrine of simplicity itself. When we attend to the biblical manner of speaking of the Son as God, we see that he is fully the Son without separating the singularity of the Godhead and without permitting a hierarchy of divinity. These biblical emphases are support for the dogmatic function of divine simplicity.

Jesus as God without a Hierarchy of Divinity

The New Testament depicts worship of the Son and Holy Spirit in a manner that suggests they are consubstantial with the Father. This conclusion is further supported by the fact that there are several passages in which the word "god" (*theos*) is applied to Jesus and the Spirit (for examples beyond those discussed below, see John 20:28; Acts 5:3–4; Titus 2:13; 2 Pet. 1:1).[49] As discussed above, one dogmatic function of the doctrine of divine simplicity is to regulate the sense in which Jesus can be God. Since God is simple, neither the Son nor the Spirit can have only part of the divine nature, which means that they cannot be situated on a spectrum of divinity, being somewhat divine but less divine than the Father. Moreover, since an implication of the doctrine of simplicity is that the divine nature cannot be divided into parts, both the Son and the Spirit must share the entirety of the same primary substance of the Father. One initial step that we can take in exploring the biblical case for divine simplicity is to ask whether those rare occasions in which the word "god" (*theos*) is applied to the Son fit with this theory of shared simple divinity.

Though Romans 9:5 is more contested than other passages, many interpret it to be a doxology to Christ as God. Paul's doxology may be translated, as in the CSB, as "The ancestors are theirs, and from them, by physical descent, came the Christ, who is God over all [*ho ōn epi pantōn theos*], praised forever." Other interpreters argue that the articular participle (*ho ōn*) is better translated as the subject of a new clause: "From them, by physical descent, came the Christ. May God be blessed over all!"[50] Several grammatical features of the verse suggest that the former translation is preferred. First, a properly declined antecedent for *ho ōn* is found immediately prior in "the Christ"

49. I intentionally choose to translate the Greek *theos* with a lowercase "god" at this early stage of my argument because I have not yet established that this word's use of Christ entails his association with the only true God.

50. Others may prefer a descriptive doxology: "From them, by physical descent, came the Christ. God is blessed over all!" Both translations share the common feature of Christ not being identified with God.

(*ho Christos*), so a subject change is unlikely without a clear new nomina-tive.[51] The natural reading of the phrase understands Christ as the one who is praised. Second, as Oscar Cullman summarizes, "Independent doxologies are differently constructed. They begin with the predicate nominative *eulogetos* (cf. 2 Cor. 1:3; Eph. 1:3; 1 Pet. 1:3), whereas in Rom. 9:5 the subject stands at the beginning—as is always the case wherever we find not a true indepen-dent doxology but a doxological apposition, which follows an immediately preceding relative pronoun."[52] While it is possible for Paul to use an atypical doxological formula here,[53] the fact that this formulation, when found else-where, typically follows an antecedent that is praised provides some evidence that Christ is the one being praised as God. Though grammatical features are not decisive here, on balance they favor the identification of Christ as God.

In addition to the grammatical features of the verse, several contextual clues suggest that Paul is here identifying Christ as God. The claim that Christ came from the Israelites "by physical descent" (*kata sarka*; 9:5) implies the need for a contrast, which would be provided by the subsequent identification of Christ as God.[54] Paul uses this exact phrasing in Romans 1:3–4, where Jesus is said to be a "descendent of David according to the flesh [*kata sarka*]" but "Son of God according to the Spirit [*kata pneuma*]." It may be that a similar contrast between Christ as descendant of Israel and Christ as God is at play here in Romans 9:5.[55] Second, the language of God "over all" (*epi pantōn*) finds parallels in the description of Christ as "before all things" (*pros pantōn*) in Colossians 1:17 and having ascended "to fill all things" (*plerōsē ta panta*) in Ephesians 4:10.[56] Third and finally, later, in Romans 9:33, Paul cites a conflation of Isaiah 28:16 and 8:14 to describe the Israelites tripping over the stumbling stone: "As it is written, 'Look, I am putting a stone in Zion to stumble over . . . , and the one who believes on him will not be put to shame.'" In the original Isaianic references, tripping refers to the Israelites not trusting God, the stumbling stone, but in Romans, Christ is the stumbling stone, the One who is not trusted. This is apparent from the fact that Romans 10:9–11

51. Harris, *Jesus as God*, 159. Wainwright says the participle *ho ōn* is completely superflu-ous if it does not point back to "Christ" (Wainwright, *The Trinity in the New Testament*, 52).

52. Cullman, *Christology of the New Testament*, 312–13.

53. James Dunn suggests that Paul may have used an atypical formula to center God being over all, since the context is the unity of Jew and gentile in the "embrace" of God (Dunn, *Romans 1–8*, 535–36).

54. Longenecker, *Epistle to the Romans*, 791.

55. This is a classical theological interpretation of the passage. See, e.g., C. Hodge, *Com-mentary on the Epistle to the Romans*, 301.

56. These parallels might be less compelling to some, given that some scholars dispute the Pauline authorship of these epistles.

references the conflated citation to suggest that the one who affirms "Jesus is Lord" will "believe on him." It is also evident from the fact that Paul elsewhere treats Christ as a stumbling stone (1 Cor. 1:23).[57] Paul's citation of these Isaianic texts provides two further reasons to interpret Romans 9:5's doxology as identifying Jesus as "God over all": Paul here applies an Old Testament text about God to Jesus, and Paul understands Jesus to be a stumbling stone. Why a stumbling stone? Contextually, the claim that Jesus is "God over all" would provide a clear occasion for stumbling and would explain the larger question of Romans 9–11, which is the general failure of Israel to believe the gospel.[58] These contextual clues, when combined with the grammatical features noted above, strongly suggest that Paul is here identifying Jesus with "God over all."

We can contrast the language in Romans 9:5 of Jesus being "God over all" with other Jewish texts that begin to elevate mediatorial figures. For example, 3 Enoch, likely written several centuries after the New Testament, describes Metatron as the "Lesser YHWH" (3 Enoch, *Synopse* §§15, 73, 76), granting certain similarities between the divine presence and the mediator but denying full equality.[59] Similarly, in the Dead Sea Scrolls, angels "appear frequently as *elim* ('gods')" (e.g., 1QM [War Scroll] I, 10–11) and are therefore seemingly distinct from the one true God.[60] The New Testament, in contrast, will name the Son as "KING OF KINGS AND LORD OF LORDS" (Rev. 19:16), a title applied to God in the Old Testament (Deut. 10:17; Ps. 136:3; Dan. 2:47) and other ancient Jewish literature (2 Macc. 13:4; 1 Enoch 9:4; 1QM XIV, 16). This title suggests no inferiority of the Son.[61] Similarly, Colossians 2:9 can describe the Son as having "the entire fullness of God's nature." Coupled with Romans' language of the Son being God over all, this language helps us see the manner in which the New Testament (occasionally) calls the Son *theos*. The Son is not God in a hierarchy of divinity, but as one who is fully divine. A similar interpretation is warranted by the fact that Jesus and the Spirit are significantly incorporated into first-century Christian cultic worship, as discussed in chapter 1. These scriptural patterns provide exegetical backing for simplicity, whose dogmatic function includes rejecting a hierarchy of divinity. In other words, the doctrine of simplicity can be seen as a reasonable inference from

57. Carraway, *Christ Is God over All*, 132–43.

58. George Carraway explains, "Merely the fact that Jesus was crucified would not need extensive explanation were it not for the claim of who he is. Many in Jesus' time must have been crucified without it giving an offense" (*Christ Is God over All*, 143).

59. Orlov, *Enoch-Metatron Tradition*, 143–44.

60. Fletcher-Louis, *Jesus Monotheism*, 1:298.

61. Ian Paul notes that this title is usurped by other figures in the Old Testament (see Ezek. 26:7; Dan. 2:37; Ezra 7:12), but there is no sign of usurpation here ("Trinitarian Dynamic of the Book of Revelation," 91).

the way in which the New Testament depicts the divinity of the Son while rejecting the hierarchy of divinity.

Here many readers might push back against these claims by noting scriptural imagery that does suggest some form of subordination of the Son. Often, accounts of the Son being seated at the Father's right hand are treated as evidence of such hierarchy (e.g., Matt. 26:64 and pars.). However, language of one figure being at the right hand of another does not require that the first figure be subordinate. In the Old Testament, for example, God is at times depicted as at the right hand of a king, but obviously this should not be taken to mean that God is subordinate to these earthly figures (Pss. 16:8; 110:5; 121:5; Isa. 41:13; 45:1). It may be that when Jesus is described as being at the right hand of God, the image is meant to convey authority, intimacy, and cooperation, but not subordination. Further support of this hypothesis is found in the fact that Acts 2:25 interprets Psalm 16, through **prosopological** exegesis, as the Son speaking to the Father, meaning that the Father is at the Son's right hand. Other exegetes point to 1 Corinthians 15:28, seeing subordination when the passage speaks of the Son being "subject to the one who subjected everything to him, so that God may be all in all."[62] While many interpret this passage as evidence of an eternal hierarchy within the Godhead, contextual clues suggest that Paul has Christ's role as the second Adam in view in this passage, in which case it cannot tell us anything of the eternal relationship between the Father and Christ as God.[63]

Jesus as God without Eliminating Divine Singularity

When the New Testament describes Jesus as God, it does so in a manner that suggests there is no hierarchy of divinity. It also describes Jesus as God in a manner that suggests that there is still only a singular God. This is perhaps most clearly depicted in John 1:1's statement that "in the beginning was the Word, and the Word was with God, and the Word was God." Ancient interpreters take this passage to mean that Jesus was fully God in such a manner that there was only one God but that he was personally distinguished from the Father.[64] In the modern era, this passage has been heavily disputed.

---

62. E.g., James Dunn uses 1 Cor. 15:24–28 as evidence against the claim that Rom. 9:5 could be describing Christ as "God over all" (Dunn, *Romans 9–16*, 535–36).

63. I have made the exegetical case for this claim extensively in Butner, *Son Who Learned Obedience*, 162–72.

64. Gregory of Nazianzus, e.g., treats John 1:1 as part of a collection of texts (including John 1:18; 1 Cor. 1:24; Heb. 1:3; Rev. 1:8) that prove consubstantiality and personal distinction (*Theological Orations* 3.17).

Though John 1:1 is a relatively straightforward affirmation of the Son's divinity in English translations of the Bible, features of the underlying Greek make this verse less clear to some interpreters. The most significant issue is the lack of an article before *theos* in 1:1c, "and the Word was God" (*kai theos ēn ho logos*). Whereas English has a definite article ("the") and an indefinite article ("a"/"an"), in Greek there is only a definite article. Nouns without an article are therefore often translated into English with the addition of an indefinite article. Accordingly, 1:1c could be rendered, "and the Word was a god." Obviously, this translation would suggest that there was more than one God, and it would bring into question whether Jesus was fully divine or only a lesser god.

There are a number of reasons to doubt this translation. I will begin with the most technical discussions of Greek grammar, which also happen to be the least persuasive. For nearly a century, it has been customary to appeal to what is known as **Colwell's Rule** to explain the lack of an article in John 1:1c. Colwell's Rule states that definite predicate nouns that come before the verb typically lack the article for the purpose of identifying that they are the predicate. According to this rule, if the subject of 1:1c were "the Word" but John moved "God" (*theos*) to the beginning of the sentence for emphasis, then he would leave out the article on "God" even if he intended a definite meaning for "God" (not "*a* god," but "*the* God" or just "God"). The absence of the article would indicate that "the Word" was the subject ("the Word was God"), not "God" ("God was the Word").[65] However, in Raymond Brown's words, "the absoluteness of the rule is debatable."[66] For example, it may also be that **anarthrous** predicates, which are descriptive nouns coming before the verb that lack an article, may be intended to convey a qualitative meaning.[67] If that is the case, then 1:1c is best rendered "the Word was divine." Considering the Gospel of John more widely, I do not believe that the presence or absence of an article can bear much weight in the interpretation of this clause. For example, Jesus can be called both the articular "Son of God" (*ho huios tou theou*) in John 1:34; 5:25; 11:4, and other passages and the anarthrous "Son of God" (*huios theou*) in John 19:7, suggesting that John does not intend a distinction in hierarchy between articular and anarthrous titles.[68] Similarly, John 1 uses the anarthrous "God" (*theos*) elsewhere to refer to the Father

---

65. Colwell, "Definite Rule," 12–21. For an appeal to this rule, see Keener, *Gospel of John*, 1:373; Harris, *Jesus as God*, 61, though Harris prefers theological explanations.

66. Brown, *Introduction to New Testament Christology*, 187.

67. Harner, "Qualitative Anarthrous Predicate Nouns," 75–87. Harner notes that forty of fifty-three anarthrous predicate nominatives before the noun in John fit this classification (83).

68. Harris, *Jesus as God*, 53.

(1:6, 12, 13, 18a).[69] We cannot conclude by the absence of an article in John 1:1c that John intended to depict Jesus as "a god" or "divine" but not the one true God.[70]

Contextual clues provide stronger evidence that John 1:1c is correctly translated as "the Word was God." First, the Gospel's conclusion involves a dramatic postresurrection appearance of Christ to Thomas, who replies by calling Jesus his Lord and God (John 20:28), both affirmations being articular. It is likely that these affirmations and the prologue serve as an inclusio, setting apart a central theme in John at the beginning and end of the work. Second, John 1:18, at the end of the prologue, also appears to call Jesus the "only begotten God," though textual variants make this passage debatable.[71] Third, John 1:1 begins with the phrase "In the beginning," which likely is meant to draw on the imagery of Genesis 1:1.[72] C. K. Barrett notes that the continuous or ongoing tense of "was" (*ēn*) stands in contrast with the "punctiliar" time of creation (1:3), the appearance of John the Baptist (1:6), and the incarnation (1:14). He concludes, "It indicates that by ['beginning'] is meant not the first point in a temporal sequence but that which lies beyond time."[73] Jesus is not a created lesser deity, but has eternal and atemporal preexistence with the Father (see also John 8:58). Fourth and finally, Jesus's opponents in the Gospel of John repeatedly accuse him of making himself "equal to God" (5:18), a charge Jesus does not deny.[74] Instead, as we will see in chapter 7, Jesus shows that he does the same works as his Father. John 1:1 in context can be reasonably translated as "the Word was God," meaning that he was the coeternal Lord and God, equal to the Father.

Taken theologically, John 1:1 stands as a strong defense of divine simplicity's dogmatic role in the doctrine of the Trinity. The Word (i.e., the Son) was with God, suggesting a personal differentiation. We have already seen how this differentiation is explained dogmatically in terms of eternal generation,

---

69. Bauckham, "The Trinity and the Gospel of John," 95.

70. As Arthur Wainwright notes, "If an adjective had been wanted, the word θεῖος, [*theios*] which occurs three times in the New Testament (Acts 17:29; 2 Pet. 1:3, 4), could have been used" (Wainwright, *The Trinity in the New Testament*, 60).

71. See the discussion in Harris, *Jesus as God*, 73–103.

72. Schnackenburg, *Gospel according to St. John*, 1:232–33.

73. Barrett, *Gospel according to St. John*, 152.

74. James McGrath interprets this passage to mean that Jesus was only "functionally" equal to God, and this only because he was "subordinate and obedient." Likewise, McGrath believes Jesus classifies himself as only among the "gods" when citing Ps. 82:6 in John 10:33–34 (*Only True God*, 57–59, 68–69). Contextually, this interpretation is not persuasive, given that the Jews plan to stone Jesus for blasphemy (10:33) and that the New Testament regularly understands blasphemy to refer to violating God's person, name, word, or law. See Beyer, "Βλασφημία [*blasphēmia*]," 622–23.

drawing on language seen in John 1:18, for example. However, the fact that Jesus remains God despite this differentiation is part of the broader biblical emphasis on the singularity of God. Simplicity is intended to safeguard dogmatically the singularity of God, preventing the divine nature from being divided. Some biblical commentators reach the same conclusion regarding John 1:1. Thus, Rudolf Schnackenburg writes, "*Theos* is not a genus, but signifies the nature proper to God and the Logos in common."[75] Simplicity as a doctrine is generally taken to deny genus and species in God, for the divine nature is not a common nature that can be divided between members of a genus. Steven Duby summarizes, "The denial of genus-species composition in God [due to simplicity] centers on his uniqueness."[76] Craig Keener says that John presents the Word as "fully deity but not the Father."[77] Again, simplicity is also the dogmatic safeguard against the hierarchy of divinity; Jesus is either fully divine or not divine. Simplicity preserves the meaning of John 1:1, since, as Murray Harris notes, the emphasis on the Word being God in the beginning "denies that the Logos was ever elevated to divine status."[78] Finally, divine simplicity is the safeguard to the dogmatic notion of immutability: a being without parts cannot change, so the Son could never have *become* divine. In summary, we see in John 1:1 exegetical warrant for accepting divine simplicity as the dogmatic basis for affirming Jesus as fully God, indivisibly and eternally one with the Father.

John 1:1 cannot alone bear the weight of divine simplicity, not even when supplemented by an appeal to verses like Romans 9:5, Colossians 2:9, and Revelation 19:16, which challenge the hierarchy of divinity. However, there are further New Testament texts that provide evidence for the assertion that Jesus is divine in a manner that does not undermine divine singularity. We can classify these texts into several categories. First, there are texts where the Son and/or Spirit is said to share the divine name (Matt. 28:19; John 17:11; Eph. 1:21; Phil. 2:9; Heb. 1:4). The absolute "I am" statements in John may also be linked to the divine name (John 4:26; 6:20; 8:28, 58; 18:5, 6, 8).[79] Noncanonical literature includes instances of mediators sharing the divine name—for example, in 1 Enoch 61:15 and 3 Enoch 12:5.[80] However, similar instances are far more rare in the canon (see chiefly Exod. 23:21), especially in comparison with the frequency with which the Son is said to have the divine

75. Schnackenburg, *Gospel according to St. John*, 1:234.
76. Duby, *Divine Simplicity*, 85.
77. Keener, *Gospel of John*, 1:374.
78. Harris, *Jesus as God*, 71.
79. Bauckham, "The Trinity in the Gospel of John," 106.
80. See the discussion in Gieschen, *Angelomorphic Christology*, 76–78.

name. Sometimes examples of angelic mediators with the name are used to argue that sharing in the divine name does not imply divinity, but it may also be the case that New Testament texts reinterpret angels with the divine name to be Christ.[81] Second, there are texts that suggest the Son shares in the appearance of the Lord. For example, in Ezekiel 1:26–27 the anthropomorphized manifestation of the glory of the Lord is described as having a torso of gleaming metal surrounded by something like fire or a rainbow.[82] Similarly, Daniel 7:9–10 describes the Ancient of Days as having a throne of flames, white robes, and hair like wool. In Revelation 1:13–16, Jesus appears, dressed in long robes, with a bronze body, hair like wool, and a face shining brightly light like the sun. The visual overlap is significant. Third, the New Testament uses an assortment of terms to explain the unity of the Father and Son. The Son is in the form (*morphē*) of God (Phil. 2:6) and is the exact expression of his substance (*karaktēr tēs hypostaseōs*) (Heb. 1:3). He is the dwelling place of the fullness (*plerōma*) of God (Col. 1:19). Fourth and finally, there are instances where the Father, Son, and Spirit are identified as doing the same action, a topic discussed in further detail in chapter 7.

Taken together, each of these patterns reveals a consistent New Testament concern of showing the unity of Father, Son, and Spirit, who share the same name, form, actions, appearance, character of substance, fullness, and glory. When the relevant passages are read in light of John 1:1, it is apparent that the passages ought to be interpreted in their canonical context as speaking of the triune unity of Father, Son, and Spirit, a singularity of the divine nature that is precisely what the doctrine of divine simplicity is attempting to defend. When we examine the ways that the New Testament describes the Son as God, it is clear that he is depicted as a person sharing the one divine nature without any inferiority or any hierarchy of divinity.

Other Scriptural Defenses of Divine Simplicity

Thus far, my analysis of whether the doctrine of simplicity is biblical has depended on a close examination of the manner in which the New Testament describes Jesus as God, arguing that it does so in a way that affirms divine singularity, denies any hierarchy of divinity, and yet still can affirm divinity of the Son and Spirit. This is indirect biblical evidence for the simplicity of

81. Angelomorphic Christology rooted in the divine name is certainly widely present in New Testament and early patristic texts, but the intent of authors with respect to earlier Jewish traditions is rarely clear. See the survey in Gieschen, "Divine Name in Ante-Nicene Christology," 115–58.

82. Rowland, *Open Heaven*, 96–97. Rowland notes a distinction here between God and the hypostatized glory of God that could be read as a predecessor to trinitarian distinctions.

God, given that simplicity safeguards divine singularity and denies any possible hierarchy of divinity. To these biblical evidences for simplicity, I should also add a number of the more classical arguments for divine simplicity. I will highlight two: first, scriptural patterns that appear to describe God's attributes as his essence and, second, scriptural affirmation of divine properties like aseity, immutability, and spirituality, from which divine simplicity logically follows.

Several patterns of Scripture have traditionally led Christians to affirm divine simplicity. The first is the tendency of Scripture to identify God with such properties as light (1 John 1:5), truth, life (John 14:6), wisdom (1 Cor. 1:30), and love (1 John 4:8). The Bible does not say just that God is loving, for example, but that he is love. Theologians from Thomas Aquinas to Herman Bavinck have pointed to such passages to argue that God is his attributes, which is consistent with divine simplicity.[83] Admittedly, it is possible to interpret such statements as being merely metaphorical, like many instances where God is called a rock (e.g., 2 Sam. 23:3) or his name a strong tower (Prov. 18:10), but this pattern is still compatible with the doctrine of simplicity. It also may be possible to strengthen this argument with what Scripture does not say. As Karl Barth summarizes, "While in Holy Scripture God has quite definite attributes and an abundance of perfections, we are never concerned merely with these attributes or perfections as such, but with them as his, and therefore always directly with himself."[84] A second, more significant scriptural pattern indirectly identifies God with his attributes. God swears by himself (Heb. 6:13) yet swears by his holiness (Amos 4:3). He creates by himself (Isa. 44:24) yet creates by his power (Rom. 1:20). This has led some to believe that God's attributes are God himself, which again would be a consequence of divine simplicity.[85]

Divine simplicity finds stronger theological warrant when it is derived from other divine attributes that find more direct exegetical support. For example, the fact that God is spirit (John 4:24) would mean that there is no material composition in God. Few would deny this, though some would stop here and offer a reduced form of simplicity that allows for other forms of composition.[86] After all, angels and human spirits are also immaterial. This would be a mistake, however, for it does not recognize the analogical nature of God's

83. Steve Long notes, e.g., how regularly Aquinas appeals to John 14:6, where Jesus claims to be life, at key points in his arguments for divine simplicity (Long, *Perfectly Simple Triune God*, 77–78).

84. Barth, *Church Dogmatics* II/1, 326.

85. Boston, *Illustration of the Doctrines of the Christian Religion*, 1:80.

86. See, e.g., Frame, *Systematic Theology*, 428–33.

spirituality.[87] God's infinite nature (1 Kings 8:27; Job 11:7; Isa. 48:12; Rev. 1:8) also provides support for divine simplicity, since, as James Dolezal notes, "whatever is perfectly infinite in being cannot be built up from that which is finite in being."[88] Similarly, divine aseity leads to the conclusion that God is simple, for any composite being depends both on its parts and on whatever cause is responsible for assembling the parts. Even if essence and existence were treated as distinct in God, some explanation outside of God for the existence of the divine essence would still be required.[89] But God does not depend on anything, as is evident both from the direct teaching of Scripture (Acts 17:25; Rom. 11:35; Job 35:7–8; 41:11) and from a comparison of Genesis with other ancient Near Eastern creation accounts, which depict divine needs as a motive for creation, a theme conspicuously absent in Genesis.

Perhaps the divine attribute that most compellingly supports divine simplicity is immutability. To argue that God cannot change requires that God is utterly simple, for any composition allows for the possibility of change, as the parts can reconfigure. More than the other attributes linked to simplicity, though, the biblical grounds for divine immutability are heavily disputed. The dispute arises from the close proximity of claims that seem to support immutability juxtaposed with claims to the contrary. For instance, Scriptures teach that God cannot repent (Num. 23:19; 1 Sam. 15:29) but claims that God has, in fact, repented (Num. 14:11–25; 1 Sam. 15:11). Some point to clear teaching such as this to insist that God can and does change.[90] Those who defend immutability argue that biblical language regarding God repenting (Gen. 6:6; Amos 7:3), changing his purpose (Exod. 32:10–14; Jon. 3:10), or experiencing emotions like anger (Num. 11:1) are anthropopathisms that are nonliteral, much like biblical descriptions of God's eyes (Ps. 11:4), ears (Ps. 34:15), nose (Deut. 33:10), or mouth (Deut. 8:3).[91] Why treat language of change as anthropopathic? In part, close exegesis of proximate, seemingly conflicted passages like Numbers 14:11–25 and 23:19 leads toward treating change in God as metaphorical rather than allowing for some nonhuman means of change in God. After all, if we interpret the teaching in Numbers 23:19 that "God is not a man, that he might lie, or a son of man, that he might change his mind" to allow some means of God changing his mind, parallelism would suggest we also allow some means of God lying. This would be

---

87. See the discussions in van Mastricht, *Theoretical-Practical Theology*, 2:1.2.6; Aquinas, *On Being and Essence* §76.

88. Dolezal, *All That Is in God*, 48.

89. Dolezal, *All That Is in God*, 47.

90. E.g., see Boyd, *God of the Possible*, 79, 158.

91. See Calvin, *Institutes of the Christian Religion* 1.17.13–14.

contrary to divine goodness.[92] Moreover, narrative works like 1 Samuel and Numbers are ambiguous in seeming to support divine immutability beside divine change, but there are no passages in didactic works like the Epistles that are equivalent to the strong statement found in James 1:17, which teaches that God "does not change like shifting shadows." The balance of evidence is in favor of divine immutability, which further reinforces the exegetical case for divine simplicity: only a simple God is truly above change.

If we accept the Reformation principle of *sola scriptura*, then philosophical objections to simplicity, though important, must yield to scriptural teachings that warrant our adoption of this doctrine. Simplicity is the dogmatic safeguard of the unity of God despite generation and spiration, of the full deity of the Spirit and Son, and of the denial of any hierarchy of divinity. Each of these dogmatic functions is scripturally warranted. When combined with further aspects of Scripture that provide more direct scriptural support for the doctrine of simplicity, the biblical case for simplicity turns out to be far stronger than critics often suppose.

The Logical Problem of the Trinity and Simplicity

I now finally turn to the problem of the Trinity and simplicity. Can a simple God also be triune? One may be tempted here to follow the path of theologians like Johann Gerhard, who writes, "Articles of faith must not be set against each other. Both the simplicity of the divine essence and the trinity of persons are set before us in the Word. Therefore, both must be accepted with the obedience of faith."[93] In the end, divine simplicity certainly fosters a degree of mystery, as it demonstrates that the nature of God is unlike any nature we have experienced, for a simple nature has no composition and is therefore immutable, eternal, impassible, and independent. One function of divine simplicity is certainly to restrain those who would seek exhaustive comprehension of the Trinity through an appeal to some formal syllogism. Yet, if Christians wish to avoid accusations of being irrational, it does seem that more must be said in defense of the compatibility of simplicity and triunity, even if complete explanation is not possible. Here a faithful theologian must take steps to preserve and protect divine plurality in the context of this strong affirmation of divine unity.

To begin, theologians might follow the example of Bonaventure in explaining how other divine attributes help us understand trinitarian simplicity. Bonaventure argues that God has the highest perfection by nature, while any

92. Duby, *Divine Simplicity*, 137.
93. Gerhard, *Commonplace III* §133.

created perfections arise from God's gracious gifts to creatures of analogical participation in the higher perfections of God.[94] Because the created perfection of simplicity exists in spirits and angels, for example, there must be a higher simplicity in God. However, the created perfections of plurality, communication, and production also exist, so we must attribute such things to God through the divine processions and persons.[95] We must be careful to clarify what sort of plurality and production occur in God. Appealing to divine immateriality and infinity, Bonaventure can conclude, "Where there is neither matter nor position in space, there can be no separation. Therefore, a production that prescinds from matter and place does not imply any separation."[96] Production of this sort may imply not division but merely distinction. Bonaventure further clarifies divine plurality by distinguishing between a plurality that adds something and a plurality that adds nothing.[97] An example of a plurality that adds something would be a pile of rocks, where each additional rock adds mass and volume, among other things, to the pile. Plurality in God is not a plurality that adds accidental properties like quantities and qualities to the divine substance. This is because the divine persons are not parts: "Every whole involves something more than a part thereof," but "no property is greater in the three persons than in one."[98] Each person has the entirety of the undivided divine essence fully and without separation, so the procession of the Spirit, for example, does not add to that essence. Bonaventure compares the plurality of the Trinity to a plurality of a point. A point can be a beginning and an end in relation to other lines, but does not thereby lose its simplicity.[99] Such arguments help us begin to see how the Trinity can remain simple in essence.

A final approach to defending the compatibility of simplicity with the Trinity turns to a philosophical understanding of the persons themselves in an appeal to **relational opposition**. As discussed in chapter 1, the trinitarian persons have long been associated with the Aristotelian category of relations, but it was not until the Middle Ages that more sophisticated appeals to relation resulted in a technical doctrine. Anselm of Canterbury, for example, argues that due to simplicity, whatever we say of the essence of God is said of the Father, Son, and Spirit together, except where there is relational opposition. In the relation of the Father and Son, the pair of terms "Father" and "Son" are set in opposition to one another in such a manner that Father and Son are

---

94. This distinction between having a perfection by nature and having a perfection by participation also featured prominently in pro-Nicene debates.

95. Bonaventure, *Disputed Questions on the Mystery of the Trinity*, Q. 3, A. 2, arg. 6–7.

96. Bonaventure, *Disputed Questions on the Mystery of the Trinity*, Q. 3, A. 2, arg. 10.

97. Bonaventure, *Commentary on the Sentences* 1.8.2, Q. 1, resp. 3.

98. Bonaventure, *Disputed Questions on the Mystery of the Trinity*, Q. 3, A. 2, resp. 6.

99. Bonaventure, *Commentary on the Sentences* 1.8.2, Q. 1, resp.4.

what they are in relation to one another but also in such a manner that the
Father and Son must be distinct from one another. Without this distinction
and opposition, there is no relation and hence no Father and Son.[100] Simplicity
requires the identity of all aspects of the Godhead, except for those relations
whose formal character is an opposition of one to another.[101]

Are oppositional relations composed? Several arguments are typically used to
answer that such relations are not composite. First, due to the simplicity of the
divine substance, the processions cannot be understood as acts of one thing or
object upon another, as if there are two things in God.[102] Rather, the relations
are two modes of a single thing in opposition to one another.[103] There are not,
therefore, two substances in God. The Trinity is not a compound of several
instantiations of a genus or kind. Second, theologians have been careful to define
the relations in such a way that they are neither material nor accidental in the
Aristotelian sense. If material, they would introduce material composition into
the Godhead. If accidental, then there would be a composition of substance
and accident.[104] The relations are "subsistent relations," to use the terminology of Aquinas.[105] There is no essence apart from the three hypostases, and the
hypostases simply are relations. The Godhead is one perfect, simple, threefold
relationality. Relations require real distinctions, but simplicity denies only a
particular kind of distinction: composition. These arguments attempt to show,
to the best of human ability, that divine plurality does not require composition.

Conclusion

Though many modern critics view the doctrine of simplicity as a threat to
genuine trinitarianism, it has historically been understood as being the dogmatic safeguard to divine unity and consubstantiality by requiring a necessary
rejection of any hierarchy of divinity and by qualifying the nature of eternal
generation. Furthermore, simplicity ensures that through the incarnation the
Son reveals the fullness of God. I have argued that there is biblical warrant for
accepting the doctrine of divine simplicity. While there is some variety in how
people understand simplicity to be compatible with multiple divine attributes,
the doctrine as a whole is compatible with classical accounts of the Trinity

100. Anselm, *On the Procession of the Holy Spirit* §1.
101. This point is clear in Thomistic theology. See Emery, *Trinitarian Theology of Thomas
Aquinas*, 97.
102. Dolezal, "Trinity," 92.
103. Duby, *Divine Simplicity*, 227–28.
104. Dolezal, "Trinity," 85–86.
105. Aquinas, *Summa Theologica* I, Q. 29, A. 4.

through precise clarifications of the nature of the relations and persons. These clarifications are not themselves above dispute, particularly between Eastern and Western Christians, a subject I will treat at greater length in chapter 4.

FOR FURTHER READING

Dogmatic Treatments of Divine Simplicity

Dolezal, James E. *God without Parts: Divine Simplicity and the Metaphysics of God's Absoluteness*. Eugene, OR: Pickwick, 2011.

> Drawing on Thomistic and Reformed-scholastic sources, Dolezal argues that the doctrine of divine simplicity is necessary for the preservation of God's absoluteness. It is an excellent, yet technical, treatment.

Duby, Steven J. *Divine Simplicity: A Dogmatic Account*. New York: Bloomsbury T&T Clark, 2016.

> Duby's greatest contribution is an extended exegetical defense of God's immutability, aseity, singularity, infinity, and creation of the universe *ex nihilo*, coupled with dogmatic arguments for why such biblical doctrines compel us to accept the doctrine of divine simplicity.

Historical Treatments of Simplicity

Long, D. Stephen. *The Perfectly Simple Triune God: Aquinas and His Legacy*. Minneapolis: Fortress, 2013.

> Long introduces us to the theology of Thomas Aquinas as it relates to his prominent appeal to simplicity. He then provides a survey of those who have followed Aquinas and those who have critiqued his reliance on simplicity.

Radde-Gallwitz, Andrew. *Basil of Caesarea, Gregory of Nyssa, and the Transformation of Divine Simplicity*. Oxford: Oxford University Press, 2009.

> This text is especially helpful for seeing the significant role that divine simplicity had in debates following the Council of Nicaea. It gives special attention to the connection between simplicity and our human thoughts/language about God.

Explorations of Theos *Used of the Son*

Harris, Murray J. *Jesus as God: The New Testament Use of* Theos *in Reference to Jesus*. Grand Rapids: Baker, 1992.

> Harris's treatment of key texts is thorough, balanced, and insightful. Though the book is growing a little dated, as debates about the Trinity in Scripture have shifted toward other concerns, I am unaware of a more recent text that has surpassed Harris's on this question.

CHAPTER 4

Persons and Relations

Chapter 2 introduced the divine processions as the means of differentiating the divine persons, but in so doing, it avoided several important questions, perhaps most significantly the question, What is a divine person? The answer to this question is not as obvious as one might think, and even as notable a theologian as Augustine of Hippo could admit to using "persons" to speak of what is relational in God simply as a means of avoiding being silent.[1] Though the divine persons must remain veiled in mystery, surely we can make some minimal progress toward understanding the preferred vocabulary of the Christian tradition. Another important question that was avoided in chapter 2 concerns a dispute regarding the procession of the Spirit: Does the Spirit proceed from the Father, or from the Father and the Son? The latter option is known as the *filioque*, a Latin word that means "and the Son." This word was inserted into the Niceano-Constantinopolitan Creed in the West and is now widely accepted among Catholics and Protestants, but the insertion remains heavily criticized by Orthodox theologians in the East. As I will show, the question of the *filioque* and the definition of divine personhood are closely connected, as each of these subjects is linked with the notion of relations in the Godhead. Therefore, the goal of this chapter is to provide some dogmatic common ground for these oft-contested theological topics.

The *Filioque* Controversy: Processions, Relations, and Persons

The *filioque* was first made prominent in Western theology at the **Third Council of Toledo (589)**, where King Reccard of the Visigoths converted

1. Augustine, *On the Holy Trinity* 5.9.

from Arianism to Catholic Christianity by affirming, with his priests and
subjects, the Niceano-Constantinopolitan Creed. The version of the creed
they confessed included the affirmation that the Spirit proceeded from the
Father "and the Son" (Latin *filioque*), a novel development, though those in
attendance likely believed the *filioque* was original.[2] The Eastern church had
limited engagement with the *filioque* for centuries,[3] and by the time they began
to address it, considerable social and political baggage was attached, as the
Greek-speaking Byzantine church and the Latin-speaking Roman church had
already diverged politically, culturally, and ecclesiastically.

The first substantive critique of the *filioque* was penned in the ninth century by Patriarch Photius of Constantinople. He learned of the *filioque*
when Byzantine missionaries to Bulgaria returned to Constantinople and
reported on Latin-speaking Frankish missionaries' use of the word in the
creed. Photius responded with an encyclical letter to his churches and a
more extensive work titled *The Mystagogy of the Holy Spirit*.[4] Three arguments from the *Mystagogy* warrant mention here. First, Photius appeals to
simplicity, arguing that if the Spirit proceeds from the double cause of the
Son and the Father, he must be composite and not simple, receiving some of
his being from the Father, some from the Son.[5] Since the divine persons are
simple, the *filioque* must be false. Second, Photius accuses the *filioque* of
undermining the distinctions between the divine persons, since it applies a
personal property of the Father to the Son in saying that the Spirit proceeds
from both.[6] Several contemporary Latin theologians, like Alcuin of York
and Theodulf of Orléans, attributed divine attributes like "first principle"
and "procession" to the divine nature, not to a single person.[7] Perhaps being
aware of this, Photius makes a third argument, that the *filioque* eliminates
a "personal source" within the Godhead, replacing the **monarchy** of the
Father with the priority of the divine essence.[8] Photius's third argument
reveals a feature of ninth-century polemic that has often been extrapolated

2. Richard Haugh points out that the council's eleventh anathema rejected modification
of the creed and the canons twice speak of the need to profess the faith of the Eastern church
(Haugh, *Photius and the Carolingians*, 27–29).

3. A notable exception is Maximus the Confessor, who did briefly treat the subject. Yet, we
do not see extensive treatment of the *filioque*, nor the *filoque*'s emergence as a central point of
contention, until Photius of Constantinople.

4. Some dispute whether Photius is the author, but typically the text is attributed to him.

5. Photius, *Mystagogy of the Holy Spirit* 1.4.

6. Photius, *Mystagogy of the Holy Spirit* 1.10.

7. Siecienski, *Filioque*, 95–98. Alcuin specifically attributed "first principle" to the divine
nature, while Theodulf of Orléans taught that the Spirit did not proceed from the person of
the Father or Son, but from the divine nature. Alcuin, *Commentary on the Gospel of John*, 43.

8. Photius, *Mystagogy of the Holy Spirit* 1.18.

to the entire history of Greek and Latin trinitarian thought, leading to the idea that, as is popularly thought, the West begins with the divine unity and attempts to distinguish the persons, while the East begins with the persons and seeks to establish divine unity. This summary does little justice to Eastern or Western trinitarian thought outside of the ninth century. Photius's conclusion from these arguments and others is that the Spirit proceeds from the Father alone (*ek monou tou Patros*), a phrase that is itself innovative, yet less egregiously so than the *filioque*, given that Photius does not insert it into the Niceano-Constantinopolitan Creed itself.[9]

Many Western theologians have written defenses of the *filioque*, but I find that the most helpful for comparison with Photius's *Mystagogy of the Holy Spirit* is Anselm of Canterbury's *On the Procession of the Holy Spirit*. Like Photius, Anselm appeals to simplicity, but he reaches the opposite conclusion. Anselm appeals to the notion of relational opposition, discussed in chapter 3, to argue that the simple divine unity "should never lose its consequences except when a relational opposition stands in the way."[10] In other words, the Father and Son remain distinct persons despite simplicity because the unbegotten Father begets the Son, and this procession is the basis for a relation of opposition: that which is begotten and unbegotten cannot logically be the same. This same principle, insists Anselm, requires that either the Son is from the Spirit or the Spirit is from the Son, for without a procession and the resulting oppositional relation, there would be no distinction between Spirit and Son.[11] Furthermore, Anselm is clear that only a procession can be the basis for such relational opposition, because if it is not in the "origins" of the Spirit that we find distinction, the Spirit is not eternally distinct from the Son.[12]

A comparison between Anselm and Photius reveals considerable overlap in their dogmatic objectives. Both seek to maintain the unity of the simple divine nature, Anselm by recourse to relational opposition and Photius by a rejection of compound causation for fear that it leads to composition in the Spirit. Both are concerned to maintain clear distinctions between the divine persons. Photius believes that affirming the *filioque* blurs the distinction between Father and Son, while Anselm believes that denying the *filioque* eliminates the distinction between Son and Spirit. The concerns on both

9. Interestingly, though, later Western authors accuse some Greek theologians of adding the word alone (*monou*) to the Athanasian Creed's "from the Father alone." See Turretin, *Institutes of Elenctic Theology* 3.31.4.

10. Anselm, *On the Procession of the Holy Spirit* §1.

11. Anselm, *On the Procession of the Holy Spirit* §1.

12. Anselm, *On the Procession of the Holy Spirit* §2.

sides have validity to them. Some modern Orthodox historians and theologians recognize that Photius's theology leaves unanswered the question of the relation (and hence distinction) between the Son and Spirit.[13] The initial introduction of the *filioque* into Latin confessional practice prior to the Council of Toledo was likely an attempt to demonstrate the divinity of Christ by pointing to a commonality that the Father has with the Son—the procession of the Spirit. It is noteworthy that this commonality is lacking in the Spirit, which could be taken to blur the distinction between Father and Son by suggesting that they have a greater commonality with each other than with the Spirit.[14] How, then, do we determine what doctrinal formulation is preferable?

Unfortunately, Scripture provides limited support for resolving the *filioque* dispute. Western theologians like Anselm would appeal to the scriptural language of the "Spirit of Christ" (Rom. 8:9) and "the Spirit of his Son" (Gal. 4:6) to argue that the Spirit proceeds from the Son too.[15] However, as Edward Siecienski points out, "The Greek phrase *pneuma Christou* can be interpreted several ways, to be understood as an objective genitive (the Spirit that brings us to Christ), possessive genitive (the Spirit that belongs to Christ), a genitive of origin (the Spirit that comes from Christ), or a genitive of identity (the Spirit who is Christ)."[16] The phrase on its own is not sufficiently clear to resolve the dispute. Eastern Orthodox theologians tend to point to the Greek word *ekporeuomai* ("to proceed"), used of the Spirit proceeding from the Father in John 15:26, as a technical term designating the procession. Though the New Testament speaks of both the Father and the Son sending (*pempō*) the Spirit (John 14:26; 15:26)—a fact Latin theologians note in defense of the *filioque*—the word *ekporeuomai* is used of the Spirit only in relation to the Father. Eastern theologians have sought to use this as a refutation of the *filioque*. It is doubtful that the historical authors intended this word to have any technical sense. The doctrine of the procession of the Spirit is best derived from the larger scriptural and theological data concerning the Son's relation

13. So, Aristeides Papadakis calls Photius's language of procession from the Father alone "unfortunate, since the view that the Spirit proceeds from the Father only had the result of blocking any discussion of the eternal relationship existing between Son and Spirit as divine hypostases" (Papadakis, *Crisis in Byzantium*, 114; cf. Bulgakov, *The Comforter*, 99).

14. This blurred distinction is evident much later in the Latin tradition. Here is Richard of St. Victor: "Possessing the fullness of divinity is common to all persons in the Trinity. But possessing the fullness of divinity and not giving is the particular property of the Holy Spirit. However, both possessing *and giving* the fullness of divinity is common to the Father and the Son" (Richard of St. Victor, *On the Trinity* 6.18; italics added).

15. Anselm, *On the Procession of the Holy Spirit* §12.

16. Siecienski, *Filioque*, 28.

to the Spirit, which is precisely what is in question here. Scriptural prooftexts do not resolve the dispute.

Several key issues in the *filioque* debate pertain to the question of divine personhood, indicating that the most fruitful approach to clarifying the procession of the Spirit will examine the *filioque* in light of a theological understanding of the divine persons. I have already noted that Photius and Anselm are both concerned that the wrong position on the *filioque* undermines personal distinctions. Modern theologians raise a number of additional connections between the *filioque* and divine personhood. John Zizioulas argues that having the Father as the personal principle of the Son and Spirit rather than having the shared substance of the Father and Son as the principle ensures that God is ultimately free and loving and hence that creation and salvation are ultimately gratuitous.[17] Sergius Bulgakov argues that the fundamental problem with the *filioque* debate is that Western theologians reduced the distinction of persons to a matter of origin and Eastern theologians like Photius bought completely into the Western problematic.[18] Western theologians at least tend to insist that origin is a significant component in the distinguishing of the persons; sometimes they reduce personhood to origin alone.[19] This dispute raises the important question of whether anything of conceptual substance is added by speaking of "persons" in addition to processions or relations. Such questions compel us to consider the nature of divine personhood before further engaging the complicated question of the *filioque*.

Defining Divine Personhood

Theologians have disagreed significantly on the meaning of divine personhood, to the point that the usefulness of the term "person" itself has been disputed. In a robust word study, Ángel Cordovilla Pérez explains that the Latin *persona* (from which the English "person" is derived) could refer to a "role in theater," "the person of the verb in grammar," or an "individual in a social sense." *Prosopon*, the Greek theological equivalent, could signify "face," "to gaze," or "that which is seen."[20] In its original historical context, the terms were somewhat ambiguous, and there is evidence that early Christian theologians deployed the words in a technical sense that was absent in

---

17. Zizioulas, *Being as Communion*, 40–49.
18. Bulgakov, *The Comforter*, 95–97.
19. As evidence of the former, see Matthew Levering's extended pushback against Sergius Bulgakov: Levering, *Engaging the Doctrine of the Holy Spirit*, 113–68. The latter is evident in Holmes, *Quest for the Trinity*, 200.
20. Cordovilla Pérez, "Trinitarian Concept of Person," 109.

or modified from their typical ancient usage.[21] Nevertheless, Cordovilla Pérez concludes that, at minimum, the word *prosopon* augments *hypostasis*: the latter signifies a concrete subsistence, while the former highlights the manner in which that subsistence presents itself.[22] Therefore, in addressing the question of personhood, we are asking what sort of subsistence the Father, Son, and Spirit have toward one another and toward us. This is a worthwhile question, so the term "person" remains worthy of consideration.

Given the importance of the question and the range of technical definitions for the term "person" that have historically been provided, it is necessary to identify certain parameters within which any definition must fit. These theological parameters will help us evaluate which meaning or meanings might be doctrinally sound and which might be problematic. I will explain six criteria that must be met in any satisfactory definition of divine personhood: rationality, dissimilarity, christological compatibility, relationality, unity, and uniqueness.

The Rationality Criterion

One of the more influential definitions of the word "person" in the history of Western theology comes from Boethius: a person is "an individual substance of a rational nature."[23] This definition is helpful in clarifying that not just any hypostasis counts as a person; only a rational being can be a person. An emphasis on persons as rational may also help us highlight the freedom associated with persons as opposed to nonrational beings.[24] Furthermore, person specifies that which is particular. However, the definition is marred with several problems, making it insufficient as a theological definition of the trinitarian persons. First, Boethius so closely associates persons and natures/substances that it seems as if three persons in the Godhead would imply three divine substances.[25] Boethius himself goes so far as to identify the Latin

21. John Zizioulas, e.g., argues that early Christians developed the notion of personhood in the process of developing their trinitarian theology by identifying the person and the hypostasis (see Zizioulas, *Being as Communion*, 27–48). Though Lucian Turcescu disagrees with Zizioulas's interpretation of the Cappadocian concept of persons (more on this below), Turcescu believes that there is no ancient equivalent to the Cappadocian idea of personhood. For a survey of his critiques of arguments to the contrary, see Turcescu, *Gregory of Nyssa*, 7–23.

22. Cordovilla Pérez, "Trinitarian Concept of Person," 113. Nearly a century before, Prestige reached the same conclusion: "[*Prosopon*] comes to express the external being or individual self as presented to an onlooker" (Prestige, *God in Patristic Thought*, 157).

23. Boethius, *Contra Eutychen* §3.

24. Such an emphasis was likely not in Boethius but has been particularly important in modern Orthodox trinitarianism. See the summary in Papanikolaou, "From Sophia to Personhood," 1–20.

25. Boethius writes, "Person cannot exist apart from nature," then denies that person may be accidental in nature, concluding that "it therefore remains that Person is properly applied to substance" (*Contra Eutychen* §1).

substantia ("substance") with the Greek *hypostasis*.[26] Second, Boethius's definition emphasizes the particularity of persons but does not suitably explain how this particularity is established in relation to others,[27] as is the case with the divine persons, which are distinguished by the processions. (I have noted, with respect to the *filioque*, the debate regarding whether they are distinguished *only* by the processions.)[28] Boethius's definition is insufficient, but it is a helpful starting point nonetheless.

Occasionally, theologians—and, more frequently, Christians in the pews—have understood the Holy Spirit to be something less than rational, more akin to a force or power than a rational person. This is a somewhat understandable mistake: often the Spirit is depicted with the impersonal images of fire and wind (Acts 2:2–3), as a seal or down payment (Eph. 1:13–14), or in the form of a dove (Mark 1:10 and pars.). In fact, even the Hebrew *ruach* and the Greek *pneuma* are both ambiguous in that they can be translated with impersonal terms like "breath" or "wind" in addition to the term "spirit." Such patterns tempt some to conclude that the Holy Spirit is less than rational and hence not personal.

Against this denial of what is often called the **personality** of the Holy Spirit, three forms of arguments can be raised. The first and perhaps most common variety of argument notes the various descriptions of the Spirit that imply rational or intentional action. In the Gospel of John, the Spirit teaches (14:16), bears witness (15:26–27), and guides the disciples by speaking what he hears (16:13). Paul uses some similar language, speaking of the mind of the Spirit (Rom. 8:27) and warning Christians not to grieve the Holy Spirit (Eph. 4:30; cf. Isa. 63:10), in each case suggesting that the Spirit is personal in nature.[29] Though such language does provide some evidence of the personality of the

---

26. Boethius, *Contra Eutychen* §3.

27. Boethius does not include relation in his definition of personhood, but he does include the notion of relation in personhood elsewhere. For instance, he insists, "If Father and Son are predicates of relation . . . and if relation is not asserted of . . . substantial quality, it will affect no real difference in its subject, but in a phrase which aims at interpreting what we can hardly understand, a difference of persons" (Boethius, *De Trinitate* §5).

28. It is clear that Boethius's intended meaning of the word "individual" is "particular, specific, or unique," as is evident, e.g., in his placing "individual" in parallel with "particular" immediately before he provides his definition: "Person cannot in any case be applied to universals, but only to particulars and individuals" (Boethius, *Contra Eutychen* §2). Some modern theologians have emphasized a contrast between "person" and "individual," treating an individual as particular through a uniqueness established in community, while defining "person" by its uniqueness preserved in community. E.g., see Zizioulas, *Being as Communion*, 164–65. Boethius likely does not intend to deny a relational component to personhood, but his failure to mention it does produce certain problems.

29. A robust example of this approach is found in Cole, *He Who Gives Life*, 65–69.

Spirit, some New Testament scholars are convinced this is not the dominant perspective in the New Testament, and they suggest that a majority of texts understand the Spirit as an impersonal force.[30] Of course, if we commit to the canon in its entirety, even an infrequent affirmation of the personality of the Spirit warrants its theological acceptance. One risk in accepting the position that there is minimal scriptural affirmation of the personality of the Spirit is that it allows us to address the vast majority of New Testament pneumatology without reference to the Trinity, separating the pneumatological dimension of God's acts in history nearly entirely from the reality of who God is eternally. Another risk is that so minimizing the personality of the Spirit in the New Testament divides systematic and biblical theology. Therefore, a broader defense of the personality of the Holy Spirit is needed.

A second, supplementary argument places the work of the Holy Spirit and the work of Satan and demons in parallel, reasoning, from the personality of demons, that there must be a comparable personality of the Spirit, who combats these demons. This approach is taken by Leonard Hodgson, for example, who points to the role of the Spirit in exorcism accounts in the Synoptic Gospels as implying the personality of the Spirit vying against personal demons.[31] Certainly, this contrast is clear in John, where the Spirit's title as Paraclete is likely a legal term contrasted with the accuser (*katēgōr*, used of Satan in Rev. 12:10).[32] A similar case can be made for the Synoptic Gospels. In the Gospel of Mark, for example, the word *pneuma* is used six times of the Holy Spirit (Mark 1:8, 10, 12; 3:29; 12:36; 13:11) and fourteen times of "unclean spirits" (Mark 1:23, 26, 27; 3:11, 30; 5:2, 8, 13; 6:7; 7:25; 9:17, 20, 25 [2x]), constituting a considerable majority of the Markan instances of the word.[33] Mark appears to be setting up a contrast between evil personal spirits,

---

30. Rudolf Bultmann, e.g., argues that there is a personal "animistic" pneumatology and an impersonal "dynamistic" pneumatology and that "the dynamistic conception is the usual one." Bultmann appeals to the prevalence of language describing the Spirit as a "gift" or as being "poured out" into all new believers (Bultmann, *Theology of the New Testament*, 1:156). George Montague reaches a similar conclusion when he argues that only with the Gospel of John do we see the development of a fully personal Holy Spirit through the deployment of angelomorphic pneumatology of the Spirit as Paraclete (*Holy Spirit*, 357). Montague is admittedly inconsistent in this position, at times admitting a Pauline "understanding of the Spirit akin to the Johannine paraclete" (*Holy Spirit*, 211) and at times minimizing the personality of the Spirit outside of John as something "other New Testament texts only at best imply" (357).

31. Hodgson, *Doctrine of the Trinity*, 81.

32. Keener, *Gospel of John*, 2:956–57. Keener notes that popular Jewish literature from the same period often opposes Michael the paraclete with Samma'el, the angelic accuser of Israel (e.g., Rabbah Exodus 18:5; Rabbah Deuteronomy 5:12).

33. *Pneuma* is also used in an anthropological sense to refer to the spiritual part of an individual's makeup in Mark 2:8; 8:12; 14:38.

which we might call demons, and the good and personal Holy Spirit. This is particularly clear when, recognizing the parallel in terms of the personal nature of the agency behind Christ's miracles, some misdiagnose Jesus's work as a product of Satan's agency instead of the Holy Spirit's (Mark 3:20–30). This contrast between Satan and the Holy Spirit provides further warrant for accepting the personality of the Spirit.

I should briefly mention a third and final argument, which will be explored in greater detail below in terms of the relational criterion: at times, the Holy Spirit is associated with the Father and Son in a manner that would be peculiar were the Spirit not also personal. Thus, John Owen writes that the Spirit "is placed in the same rank and order, without any note of difference or distinction as to a distinct interest in the divine nature (that is, as we shall see, personality) with the other divine persons."[34] The Spirit is often placed as one of three coordinate names with Father and Son in reference to divine agency and identity in a manner that leads us to affirm the personality of the Spirit or else risk implying an impersonal Father and Son. The cumulative case warrants retaining rationality as a necessary component of divine personhood.

The Dissimilarity Criterion

Two of the most notable European trinitarian theologians of the twentieth century challenge the very viability of the word "person" in trinitarian theology. Karl Rahner points to a twofold problem with the word "person." First, "we never discover in our experience a case where [person] can be thought of as multiplied without a multiplication of natures."[35] Second, when we use the term "person" in modern language, "we think almost necessarily . . . of several spiritual centers of activity, or several subjectivities and liberties."[36] For reasons discussed below, we cannot affirm three subjectivities in God. Rahner therefore prefers the term "distinct manner of subsisting" (*subsistenzweisen*). Writing before Rahner, Karl Barth argues that there is no argument but tradition to support the use of "person" and that our context leads to much confusion with the word. He prefers instead to speak of three "modes of being" (*seinsweisen*) based on the earlier Greek *tropos hyparxeōs*, which he thinks avoids the Boethian implication of tritheism by highlighting the manner in which "God is God three times in another way."[37]

---

34. Owen, *Brief Declaration and Vindication*, 401.
35. Rahner, *The Trinity*, 105.
36. Rahner, *The Trinity*, 106.
37. Barth, *Church Dogmatics* I/1, 412–14.

It should be clear from the chapter title that I consider the term "person" worth retaining, not least because of the Boethian insight that the term "person" pertains to that which is rational,[38] whereas the terms "mode of being" or "distinct manner of subsistence," though appropriately used of the hypostases, could apply to any number of impersonal realities, from the created mode of being of an individual tree to the distinct manner of subsistence of antimatter in comparison with matter.[39] Nevertheless, Barth and Rahner both reveal important challenges to the undiscriminating use of words like "person." The question of distinct subjectivities is complicated and cannot be explained fully until we discuss the christological-compatibility criterion below, but there are other obvious ways in which the term "person" applied to God cannot mean what it means in the created realm. Most obviously, I am distinct from another human person because I have a different body, but God is incorporeal and immaterial, so we ought not to consider the three divine persons to be three bodies. We can draw from Barth and Rahner the necessity of affirming the dissimilarity between the divine persons and human persons. Recognizing this dissimilarity is merely extending our analogical analysis of the procession of the Spirit and the generation of the Son into our consideration of the Father, Son, and Spirit in their hypostatic uniqueness as persons.

One modern theological movement that has pushed theology to recognize this need for analogical clarification of the persons has been feminist theology, with its analysis of the notion of divine fatherhood. Feminist theology has raised the concern that calling God "Father" construes God as male, which may lead to harmful social consequences for women. In response, feminist theologians like Elizabeth Johnson have endeavored to depict God as metaphorically feminine and masculine by pointing, for example, to texts that depict God as a mother in labor (e.g., Deut. 32:18; Isa. 42:14) or describe God's people as born from God (John 1:13). Johnson insists that this should not lead us to conclude that God is literally female. "The mystery of God is properly understood as neither male nor female but transcends both in an unimaginable way."[40] God is immaterial, lacking a body, and thus God has no

---

38. Boethius, *Contra Eutychen* §1.

39. A number of additional criticisms should be raised to Barth's and Rahner's preferred terminology. Alan J. Torrance notes that Barth fails to explore fully the eternally interrelated nature of the *seinsweisen*. The language of "person" implies such relationality historically, if not always today, whereas "mode of being" has never clearly required relationality (*Persons in Communion*, 251–52). Catherine Mowry LaCugna's critique is far more practical: these technical terms "are unintelligible for nonspecialists and unsuitable for preaching" (LaCugna, "Trinitarian Mystery of God," 179).

40. E. A. Johnson, *She Who Is*, 55. See also Johnson, *She Who Is*, 45; Janet Martin Soskice: "God is not a human being, and *a forteriori* not a male human being" (*Kindness of God*, 69);

sex. Though this should be obvious, my own teaching experience suggests that it may be overlooked at the lay level. Most agree with Johnson's rejection of sex in God, but many feminist theologians have adopted approaches that differ from Johnson's language of God as Father and Mother, some going so far as to reject personal language for God altogether.[41] The proposed language of "Creator, Redeemer, Sustainer" that is intended to replace personal, gendered titles is problematic because it does not easily fit with inseparable operations (see chapter 7) and it obscures the internal relations of the Godhead.[42]

Feminist concerns prompt us to speak carefully and wisely of God. While affirming biblical usage of masculine and feminine imagery of God, sound theology must insist that we clarify such imagery by denying real gender in God. Here we can supplement God's immateriality by pointing to contrasts between the Bible and ancient Near Eastern religions whose pantheons included literal masculinity and femininity, often manifest in sexual pairings.[43] This countercultural feature of the Bible suggests the biblical authors are intending to convey something different in their depictions of God, something asexual, beyond male and female. Language of God as Father is predominant but must be normed by the doctrine of analogy in a manner that precludes our envisioning God as a bearded man hiding in the sky.

Just as any theological explanation of a specific divine person must be careful and precise, so too must any theological explanation of the idea of "personhood" in general. Barth and Rahner recognize this much, even if their proposed alternative vocabulary is insufficient. Thus, any definition of "person" in trinitarian theology must meet a criterion of dissimilarity, explaining how the term is used differently of God than of the created order. But how do we know what dissimilarity exists? To begin to answer this question, we turn to the christological-compatibility criterion.

The Christological-Compatibility Criterion

It is important that the doctrine of the Trinity be coordinated with Christology to ensure that theological affirmations in one theological locus do not contradict affirmations in another. Conceivably, certain theological positions

---

Catherine Mowry LaCugna: "We must acknowledge that God is unlike a father because God is neither male nor female. Theological feminism is in part a critique of the propensity to literalize metaphors for God and to forget the dissimilarity of every analogy" ("Trinitarian Mystery of God," 181). Maria Bingemer emphasizes the Eleventh Council of Toledo (675), which spoke of the Son being born from the Father's womb (*da utero Patris*) (*Face for God*, 162–63).

41. See the brief list of possible options listed in Soskice, *Kindness of God*, 73.

42. LaCugna, "Trinitarian Mystery of God," 182.

43. Sonderegger, *Systematic Theology*, 1:385.

in Christology could undermine certain foundations of trinitarian thought. Similarly, mistakes in the doctrine of the Trinity could undermine sound understandings of the person and work of Christ. This is perhaps most obvious when we seek to define terms like "person" and "nature," given that both words are used in a technical sense in both Christology and the doctrine of the Trinity. Therefore, considering which aspects of definitions for these terms are necessary for Christology will establish guidelines for sufficient definitions in trinitarian thought. This christological-compatibility criterion uses God's self-revelation of Christ as one means of understanding the eternal relations of the **immanent** Trinity.

As discussed in chapter 1, the worshiped Christ is revealed as consubstantial with the Father, but now we must add that he is also revealed as fully human. Suffice it to say, in lieu of a lengthy scriptural proof of this point, that what is affirmed of Christ (John 1:14; Gal. 4:4; Heb. 2:14) and what is denied (1 John 4:2–3) both entail his full humanity, as do numerous christological titles like "Son of David" (Matt. 1:1) and "last Adam" (1 Cor. 15:45). The Council of Chalcedon (451) provides the standard metaphysical explanation of Christ's joint humanity and divinity. Christ is two natures in one person and hypostasis, each nature united "unconfusedly, unchangeably, indivisibly, inseparably." This denial is meant to preserve divine simplicity (among other things): the simple divine nature cannot mix with a human nature. It also cannot undergo change through the process of the incarnation. God's radical transcendence is preserved by the insistence that Christ's human and divine natures remain distinct, much like how nondivine humans have two distinct natures in a single person—the nature of a soul and of a body.[44]

One important way that the work of Christ is connected with the Chalcedonian definition is summarized in Gregory of Nazianzus's famous dictum: "That which [the Son] has not assumed he has not healed; but that which is united to his Godhead is also saved."[45] Gregory rightly believes that human nature has been purified from sin because the Holy Spirit transformed our humanity into the sort of humanity that Christ had.[46] Later Protestant, Orthodox, and Catholic theologians affirm a similar perspective, believing that our union with Christ's human nature enables our transformation and

---

44. In this case, the Son takes on a full human nature that includes body and soul, so the analogy should not be taken to imply that the divinity of Christ replaces the human soul.

45. Gregory of Nazianzus, *To Cledonius against Apollinaris*, 218.

46. See Gregory of Nazianzus, *Second Letter to Cledonius against Apollinaris*, 226. See also the helpful summary of Gregory of Nazianzus on theosis in Russell, *Doctrine of Deification*, 220–23.

purification.[47] In keeping with this idea, we see scriptural teaching that "we have the mind of Christ" (1 Cor. 2:16), that we ought to have the attitude of Christ (Phil. 2:5), that Christ "dwells in our hearts" (Eph. 3:17), indeed that our very bodies will become spiritual bodies like Christ's, bearing his image (1 Cor. 15:40–49). We can take all of this to mean that our sanctification and glorification are rooted in a deeper union with Christ,[48] because we are "clothed with Christ" (Gal. 3:27) as our nature is joined by the Holy Spirit to his, with the result that Christ himself is our sanctification (1 Cor. 1:30). We must insist, however, that our unity is with Christ's humanity, not his divine essence.[49] As Chalcedon affirmed, the union between the human and divine natures in Christ occurs without mixture or change.[50] This, in turn, means that if Christ does not have a human mind, will, body, or heart, we cannot be expected to have his mind, attitude, heart, or spiritual body. That which he has not assumed, he has not redeemed.

Since, according to Chalcedon, Christ has only assumed a human nature and not a preexisting human person, this must mean that things like mind, will, and body are all proper to nature, not person. In other words, because he has two natures, Christ has a human mind, will, and body through the human nature, and a divine will and mind (but no body—God is immaterial) through the divine nature. Indeed, there are early christological heresies that denied various aspects of Christ's human nature: Appollinarianism denied Christ a human mind and soul, monothelitism denied a human will, and docetism denied a human body and nature altogether. In response to such heresies, later councils made the logic of Chalcedon explicit: "Each nature wills and works what is proper to it" such that there are "two natural wills and operations."[51] Attributing mind and will to nature also provides a metaphysical means of explaining such puzzling questions as how Christ could be tempted (Mark 1:12–13 and pars.; Heb. 4:15) even though God cannot

47. See, e.g., the discussion of John Calvin on this point in Billings, *Calvin, Participation, and the Gift*, 55–64. A. N. Williams describes Gregory Palamas's theology as follows: "The fact that union denotes both the relation between divine and human nature in Christ and between God and human persons in deification indicates a similarity between the two and points onward to the authenticity of the contact with the divine in deification" (*Ground of Union*, 136).

48. For further information on the subject of union, see chap. 5, but for now, suffice it to say that its New Testament roots are deep.

49. Many Orthodox theologians would complexify the matter by appealing to the divine energies, in which Christians are said to participate and which are proper to God, though they are distinct from the divine essence itself.

50. This later technical language is distinct from that typically used by Gregory of Nazianzus, who often likes to speak of the "mingling" of humanity and divinity in Christ. His less precise language here can be read in a manner compatible with the later definition of Chalcedon.

51. "Statement of Faith of the Third Council of Constantinople," 384.

be tempted (James 1:13): Christ was tempted in his human nature with his human will.[52] Because the terms "person" and "nature" are used with the same meaning in Christology and the doctrine of the Trinity—it is the Second Person of the Trinity, the Son, who assumes flesh in the incarnation—we must define the word "person" in trinitarian thought in a manner informed by these christological conclusions.

The christological-compatibility criterion leads us to identify one manner in which the triune persons are dissimilar to human persons: to say that God subsists as three persons is not meant to indicate three distinct minds, wills, or streams of consciousness. The Christian tradition has overwhelmingly affirmed a singular mind and will in God.[53] However, this tradition runs contrary to much modern theology. For example, many evangelicals have adopted the position that part of the distinction between the Father and the Son is that the Son eternally submits to the Father.[54] Variously called **Eternal Functional Subordination (EFS)**, Eternal Relations of Authority and Submission (ERAS), or the Eternal Submission of the Son (ESS), this theological perspective clearly associates will with person, not nature.[55] The logical conclusion of this, when coupled with the Chalcedonian insistence that there is only a human nature, not person, in the incarnation, is a denial of the human will of Christ. The christological ramifications of this theology are significant and problematic.[56]

Social trinitarianism is another theological perspective that deviates from the traditional association of will and mind with nature or essence, thus running afoul of the christological-compatibility criterion. William Hasker, one proponent of social trinitarianism, insists that persons are distinct centers of consciousness, will, love, and action.[57] While he concedes that it would be inappropriate to "describe any ancient or medieval thinker as a Social Trinitarian"—after all, much modern philosophy must be assumed of the

---

52. I have elaborated on this Christology extensively in Butner, *Son Who Learned Obedience*, 62–94.

53. For a few representative texts, see Ames, *Marrow of Theology* 1.4.58; Anselm, *On the Incarnation of the Word*, 241; Augustine, *On the Holy Trinity* 2.5; Gregory of Nazianzus, *Theological Orations* 4.12; Palamas, *Topics of Natural and Theological Science* §112; John of Damascus, *Exposition of the Orthodox Faith* 1.8.

54. Two early works that led to the popularizing of this perspective are Ware, *Father, Son and Holy Spirit*; Grudem, *Systematic Theology*. More recent works have attempted to defend against criticism of this position. See, e.g., Routley, *Eternal Submission*.

55. To cite one example, see Bruce Ware, who calls submission "strictly and only a personal property," and who explains submission in terms of one will yielding to another ("Does Affirming," 244).

56. For my full refutation of this position, see Butner, *Son Who Learned Obedience*.

57. This is a common modern position. Another oft-discussed example is found in Plantinga, "The Threeness/Oneness Problem of the Trinity," 37–53.

social trinitarian perspective of personhood—Hasker still believes he has an ally in Gregory of Nyssa, who may be described as "pro-Social."[58] Hasker points to the analogy between three men and the three divine persons in Gregory's *Answer to Ablabius*[59] in order to suggest that Gregory must have accepted this as a viable comparison. Noting examples of patristic figures like Athanasius who did not develop a clear human psychology as part of the human nature, Hasker can conclude that Gregory is a pro-social theologian, not developing a clear notion of persons as centers of consciousness but setting a trajectory that can be reasonably fulfilled by that conclusion due to modern developments in biblical studies and philosophy.[60]

The social account of the Trinity, as exemplified in Hasker's extensive treatment, undermines the fundamentals of Chalcedonian Christology as developed in subsequent councils.[61] If consciousness and will are proper to the persons rather than natures, then Christ lacks a proper human consciousness and will and is not fully human. Moreover, this account poorly represents the pro-Nicene tradition. Writing years before Hasker, Sarah Coakley anticipates his perspective in her response to other social trinitarians' use of Gregory of Nyssa. Coakley shows that Gregory's anti-Eunomian texts typically emphasize unity of will, not plurality, and that his emphasis on communion (*koinōnia*) is distinct from community. The term is meant as a balance to distinction and is not intended to imply distinct minds or centers of consciousness.[62] Moreover, Coakley points out the "strongly apophatic sensibility" of Gregory that dissuades him from formulating too confident a description of the divine essence.[63] To this we might easily add a caution against attempting to understand fully the divine mind and what consciousness must be like in God.

One might object to these conclusions by pointing to recent exegetical work in exploring what is known as prosopological or prosopographic exegesis. Prosopological exegesis refers to the early Christian (i.e., New Testament and patristic) practice of interpreting passages of Scripture as if they

58. Hasker, *Metaphysics and the Tri-personal God*, 24–25.
59. Gregory of Nyssa, *Answer to Ablabius*, 256–57.
60. Hasker, *Metaphysics and the Tri-personal God*, 31–35, 168–69, 195.
61. Some social trinitarians would openly reject dyothelitism (the idea that Christ has two wills, one human and one divine) in favor of monothelitism (the idea that Christ has one will). Thus, William Lane Craig and J. P. Moreland admit their Christology "implies monothelitism," but they do not see this as problematic, "since dyothelitism, despite its conciliar support, finds no warrant in Scripture" (Moreland and Craig, *Philosophical Foundations for a Christian Worldview*, 611).
62. Coakley, "'Persons' in the 'Social' Doctrine," 133–34. Chapter 8 will develop the notion of communion in fuller detail.
63. Coakley, "'Persons' in the 'Social' Doctrine," 135.

were dialogues between the Father and the Son.[64] There is a long tradition in Christian theology of supposing there were preincarnate conversations between the Father, Son, and Spirit. For example, early Christians could point to God's statements at creation, such as "Let there be light" (Gen. 1:3), and suppose that God was speaking to the Son.[65] Even after the Reformation, the Lutheran Johan Gerhard interpreted Isaiah 6:8's question—"Whom shall I send? Who will go for us?"—as a discussion among the three persons of the Trinity.[66] This prosopological exegesis may imply that Father, Son, and Spirit have distinct minds and wills and that they deliberate and communicate with one another about their distinct thoughts. For example, where Arians point to Hebrews 1:4 to argue that the Son only *became* superior to angels at some point in history, pro-Nicene theologians look at the context in Hebrews 1:5–13 and interpret the passage as a preincarnate conversation between Father and Son, suggesting the Son's eternal superiority to angels.[67] Such conversations might imply three eternal streams of consciousness. This variety of exegesis finds its modern counterpart in certain trinitarian theologies that speak of an eternal dialogue or colloquy within the Godhead, as does Brahmabandhab Upadhyay, for example.[68]

We can best explore the question of whether prosopological exegesis supports an identification of each divine person with a consciousness, mind, and will by considering a particular passage. In this case, I have chosen Hebrews 1:8–9. The entirety of Hebrews is a series of comparisons between the old and new covenants intended to demonstrate the Son's authority, beginning with a comparison between the Son and angels as heavenly mediators (1:1–14; 2:5–18) but moving to a comparison between earthly "covenant inaugurators" (3:1–6) and the priestly acts and roles of each covenant (5:1–10; 7:1–10:18).[69] It is within the first stage of this comparison, where the author is establishing the Son as a higher mediator than angels, that we see a particularly interesting piece of prosopological exegesis:

> But to the Son [he says]:
>   "Your throne, O God,
>   is forever and ever,
>   and the scepter of your kingdom
>   is a scepter of justice.

64. See Pierce, *Divine Discourse*, 6–22.
65. E.g., Origen, *On First Principles* 1.109.
66. Gerhard, *Commonplace III* §154.
67. Sieben, "Herméneutique de l'exégèse dogmatique d'Athanase," 204–5.
68. Joseph, *Indian Trinitarian Theology*, 189.
69. Pierce, *Divine Discourse*, 56.

> You have loved righteousness
> and hated lawlessness;
> this is why God, your God,
> has anointed you
> with the oil of joy
> beyond your companions." (1:8–9)

Psalm 44:7–8, quoted from the Septuagint, is interpreted by the author of Hebrews as a conversation between multiple figures. The speaker addresses an enthroned figure as "God" (1:8)[70] and mentions a second figure, "God, your God," who anointed the first. We can reasonably conclude that the reference to the enthroned God is a clear example of the Son being called God. The author of Hebrews interprets Psalm 44 as spoken to the Son, but not to angels, thus providing part of the evidence of the Son's superior mediatorship.[71] The God who has anointed the enthroned God must be the Father. Note, however, that the speaker addresses these two divine figures in the third person, suggesting a different voice for the speaker. This third voice may well be the Holy Spirit, an identification found in early Christians like Justin Martyr.[72] It is worth noting that elsewhere in Hebrews (3:7 and 10:15) the Spirit is explicitly said to speak, giving further credence to this possible interpretation.[73]

This passage illustrates several reasons why prosopological exegesis should not necessarily compel us to think of three centers of consciousness in the Godhead. First, though I am convinced that prosopological readings are found throughout the New Testament, these are often contested. For example, in

70. This is contested, for the Greek *ho theos* here could be in the nominative, in which case the verse could be translated as "God is your throne." There are several compelling arguments against such a translation. E.g., the phrase *pros de ton huion* in 1:8 is linked with the earlier verb "to say" (*legein*; 1:7). In the vast majority of New Testament uses of this verb-preposition combination, the verb means "says to" or "says for/against." It rarely ever means "says about," as would be needed if we were to translate 1:8 as referring to God being the Son's throne. Second, the metaphor of God being someone's throne is never attested in the Old Testament or elsewhere in the New Testament. Further, in v. 10a, we see a second-person addressee in a passage that is implied to continue the action of the verb *legein* in 1:7. The parallel structure here would suggest that there is a second-person addressee in 1:8, justifying the vocative translation. The LXX of Psalm 44:7 has an address to God in the vocative in verses 4 and 6. Note that verse six immediately precedes the verse in question. Parallelism in Hebrew poetry suggests that this verse should therefore be translated in the vocative. Finally, the inclusion of "forever and ever" as a descriptor of the Son implies eternality and immutability, providing further evidence that the text depicts him as divine. See Harris, *Jesus as God*, 214–18; Brown, *Introduction to New Testament Christology*, 185–87; Lane, *Hebrews 1–8*, 29.

71. Arthur Wainwright suggests that this interpretation of Ps. 44 would be rooted in its use in Christian worship (*The Trinity in the New Testament*, 60).

72. See Justin Martyr, *Dialogue with Trypho* 56.14–15.

73. See the discussion in Bates, *Birth of the Trinity*, 163–65.

this passage it is not as clear that the Spirit is the speaker as it is that the Father addresses the Son as a distinct divine person, and even the latter can be contested. I am convinced that prosopological exegesis is common, but others might disagree. Second, and more importantly, the theological intent behind these passages is never to explain the inner workings of the Trinity. Rather, the motif of dialogue is put at the service of other theological goals—in this passage, for example, the goal of illustrating the Son's preincarnate superiority to angelic mediators. This suggests that though prosopological exegesis reinforces the divinity of the three persons, we ought not to put too much weight on such passages' ability to explain the inner life of the Trinity. Third, the divine attributes make it quite probable that these passages are partially anthropomorphic. This passage gestures to divine eternality—the Son's throne is "forever and ever" (1:8)—but classical explanations of eternality deny any succession of moments. How could actual conversation occur eternally? More than that, why would one omniscient person need to speak audibly to another? Such questions imply that passages deploying prosopological exegesis are attempting to illustrate key theological truths in an anthropomorphic manner that is often explained as accommodation or *synkatabasis*.[74] The passages do not compel us to posit three centers of consciousness in God, and they certainly do not compel us to overturn the christological-compatibility criterion rooted in the Council of Chalcedon. The divine persons do not each have their own mind, consciousness, or will. On the other hand, we should avoid being too forceful with our negations, as if prosopological exegesis is *merely* anthropomorphic. Taken analogically, this language conveys some form of relationality and communication (by procession, perhaps) between the persons, one best expressed anthropomorphically but whose true form is beyond human comprehension.

The Relationality Criterion

The christological-compatibility criterion shows us that we cannot import our typical association between personhood and consciousness or will into our understanding of the Trinity, but there are further dissimilarities in the word "person" when used of God and the word when used of humans. Another, more central dissimilarity is that we cannot associate divine personhood with autonomy and individuality in the manner that is typical in modern Western philosophy. Colin Gunton, for example, traces the dominant modern Western conception of personhood to René Descartes, who understood persons

---

74. The former term is common among the Reformed, the latter among the Orthodox.

to be discrete thinking things and whose method of skepticism questioned the reality of the rest of the world. Descartes's method required him first to establish the reliability of an individual person's thought (in this case, himself) before considering the person's relation with the world; personhood is established with reference to the individual as the basis for then exploring relationality.[75] Gunton prefers an "alternative tradition" in which "a person . . . can be defined only in terms of his or her relations with other persons."[76] This relational emphasis is necessary for any sound theological definition of divine personhood.

Paying attention to how other cultures understand the notion of personhood reveals the manner in which Western culture has often diminished the relational nature of the term. Nozomu Miyahira illustrates this fact by pointing to the term *ningen*, which originally meant "community" in Chinese characters but came to mean "human" in Japanese. *Hito*, one of the characters composing *ningen*, can still mean "self" or "people in a community."[77] Etymologically, this demonstrates that the notion of relationality is included in and even prior to the notion of individuality.[78] Miyahira contrasts the Japanese tendency of tailoring behavior to the needs of others with the common Western emphasis on being true to one's own individual values, suggesting that there is a Japanese cultural assumption that personhood is relational. Having highlighted these themes, Miyahira suggests that Japanese Christians would be particularly able to understand the notion of God being three persons as meaning three "betweennesses" (*aida*).[79] Miyahira admits that all cultures fall short of univocally understanding divine personhood but says that where many Westerners are prone to interpret the divine persons without reference to relations, in Japan the risk runs in a different direction.[80]

There is biblical warrant for understanding the persons to be what they are because they are in relation to one another. For example, we see clear relational implications in Paul's language about the Father and Son. On the one hand, Christ is often the one in and through whom God works for salvation or to establish the church (e.g., Rom. 5:21; 1 Cor. 1:4; Phil. 3:14).[81] On the other hand, God is often identified by this action in and through Christ—he is the

---

75. Gunton, *Promise of Trinitarian Theology*, 87–88.

76. Gunton, *Promise of Trinitarian Theology*, 98. Gunton's insight here is sound, though at times he overcorrects too much, as when his theology appears to require three wills or consciousnesses.

77. Miyahira, *Towards a Theology*, 114.

78. Miyahira, *Towards a Theology*, 117.

79. Miyahira, *Towards a Theology*, 118, 143.

80. Miyahira, *Towards a Theology*, 136.

81. N. Richardson, *Paul's Language about God*, 266–67.

one who raised Christ from the dead (Rom. 4:24; 8:11; 2 Cor. 4:14; Gal. 1:1). Wesley Hill argues that this identification of God is central to Paul's entire doctrine of God. When Paul identifies God as the one who raised Christ in Galatians 1:1, he assumes that God was always this God, as is evident in Paul's appeal to Genesis 13:15 and God's promised "seed" as a prediction of Christ. The God of the promise was the God who promised Christ, and God fulfills this promise by raising Christ. These acts determine for Paul the very identity of God.[82] In fact, one basic Pauline confession of faith requires faith that God acted on Christ—a fundamentally relational profession.[83] In other words, Paul understands God to be the one who has worked through Christ (and who has always planned this), while Christ is the one in and through whom God works. God is "the God and Father of the Lord Jesus" (2 Cor. 11:31); Jesus is the Son and image of God (2 Cor. 4:4).

Similar conclusions can be drawn about Paul's theology of the Holy Spirit. Consider 1 Corinthians 12:3, where Paul claims that no one can affirm Jesus as Lord without the Spirit. James D. G. Dunn remarks, "In Paul's view the Spirit has been limited or has limited himself in accord with the yardstick of Jesus. The power of God has become determined by its relation to Jesus."[84] Hill points to Galatians 4:6b—"God sent the Spirit of his Son"—as an example of Paul "opening up" the mutual identification of Father and Son through coordinate action to include the Holy Spirit.[85] Similarly, Romans 8:11 links the identifications of the Spirit *of God* with the identification of God as the one who raised Jesus from the dead. This text, along with Romans 1:3–4, may indicate the Spirit's role in the resurrection of Jesus, integrally linking the agency of the Spirit to the mutual determination of the identity of the Father and the Son.[86]

The scriptural patterns discussed here pertain to the divine economy, showing how God is identified through his work in the Son or how the Spirit's work in the believer is fundamentally and relationally oriented toward the Son. One historical misinterpretation of this data has been modalism, which understands these relations and the distinctions between the three persons to

---

82. Hill, *Paul and the Trinity*, 68–69. Hill makes a similar point about Rom. 4. God is identified as the one who raised Christ (4:24), and this explanation clarifies why Paul understands God to be the one who justifies the ungodly (4:5). The very nature and character of God are revealed in the relationship between God and Christ in the resurrection (Hill, *Paul and the Trinity*, 59–61).

83. Werner Kramer identifies a "pistis-formula"—*pistis* means "faith"—where "God is the subject; the verb is aorist; the verb is qualified by the expression 'from the dead'" (*Christ, Lord, Son of God*, 26; see Rom. 7:4; 8:11a; 10:9b; 1 Cor. 15:20; Eph. 1:20; Col. 2:12).

84. Dunn, *Jesus and the Spirit*, 319.

85. Hill, *Paul and the Trinity*, 142–43.

86. Hill, *Paul and the Trinity*, 154–63.

be a mere manifestation of God in history, not realities that were eternally in God prior to creation. This heresy, often called **Sabellianism**, after an early advocate of the position named Sabellius, apparently seeks to preserve the unity of the Godhead by interpreting the Son and Spirit as economic operations of the Godhead.[87] Several arguments refute this position. First, the Bible teaches that Christ has revealed God to us (John 1:18; 14:9; Matt. 11:27), but if God is not eternally Father, Son, and Spirit, then the Son has not actually revealed God's eternal nature and identity. Second, the New Testament describes all three persons simultaneously at the baptism of Christ (Mark 1:9–11 and pars.). This simultaneous manifestation undermines any simplistic modalism that would treat Father, Son, and Spirit as a singular person under different forms at different times. Third, the prosopological exegesis discussed above suggests a threefold relationality between Father, Son, and Spirit prior to creation and the incarnation.

Relationality is thought to be fundamental to the Godhead, to the point that Thomas Aquinas can even define persons as "subsistent relations."[88] The persons are who they are in relation to one another. This aspect of divine personhood has been jeopardized by some Orthodox responses to the *filioque*. For example, it is widely recognized today that Photius neglected to develop any relation between the Son and Spirit,[89] a shortcoming that was overcome by Gregory of Cyprus at the Orthodox Council of **Blachernae** (1285), which opposed the reconciliation between East and West attempted at **Lyons** (1274), a reconciliation predicated on acceptance of the *filioque*. Gregory's *Tomus*, which summarized the conclusions of Blachernae, claimed that "the very Paraclete shines forth and is manifest eternally through the Son, in the same way that light shines forth and is manifest through the intermediary of the sun's rays; it further denotes the bestowing, giving, and sending of the Spirit to us. It does not, however, mean that it subsists through the Son and from the Son, and that it receives its being through him and from him."[90] Those who interpret Gregory favorably claim that he is making a distinction between the Spirit existing through the Son, which is affirmed, and the Spirit *having existence* through the Son, which is denied.[91] Put another way, Gregory may be distinguishing between procession, mission, and manifestation.[92] The Spirit does not proceed from the Son, meaning that he does not have the Son as a

87. For a classic discussion, see Kelly, *Early Christian Doctrines*, 119–23.
88. Aquinas, *Summa Theologica* I, Q. 29, A. 4.
89. E.g., see Papadakis, *Crisis in Byzantium*, 113–14.
90. Gregory of Cyprus, *Exposition of the Tomus of Faith*, anathema 4.
91. Papadakis, *Crisis in Byzantium*, 123.
92. Alexopoulos, "Eternal Manifestation of the Spirit," 77.

principle or cause of his existence. However, the Spirit's relation with the Son is not merely missional—that is, in history and in the created realm. There is an eternal relation between Son and Spirit that differs from procession. Some Orthodox critics dismiss Gregory's proposal as "empty phraseology,"[93] but it is perhaps best seen as an effort to secure the eternal distinction between Son and Spirit through a real relation while denying that this relation is due to one person being the source of another. Any lack of clarity here is no more serious than that faced by those who attempt to distinguish procession and generation.

The West has an argument ready at hand to challenge the idea of **eternal manifestation**. In the words of Richard of St. Victor, "Existence can be differentiated either according to the nature alone of a being or according to the origin alone of a being, or according to a concurrence of both."[94] Clearly, the Son and Spirit do not differ from each other in terms of nature, so the widely held belief is that they must differ in origin.[95] This line of reasoning requires an affirmation of the *filioque*, which pertains to the origin of the Spirit, and denial of eternal manifestation, which does not pertain to origin. I am unconvinced by arguments that the only conceivable relations within the Godhead pertain to origin.[96] Given that the word "origin" is already used in a quite different manner for God than for created reality, it strikes me as overreaching to insist that origin alone, and not some other concept like eternal manifestation, can apply analogically to the relation between Son and Spirit, especially given the limited scriptural guidance here. Indeed, even in the medieval Latin West, some theologians held that the Son and Spirit must be distinguished by a relation of opposition rooted in origin, while others, notably John Duns Scotus, allowed for disparate relations without requiring a difference between Son and Spirit rooted one's originating from the other.[97] Therefore, I consider the concept of eternal manifestation a viable Orthodox

93. Bulgakov, *The Comforter*, 105.
94. Richard of St. Victor, *On the Trinity* 4.13.
95. Besides Richard of St. Victor, see chiefly Aquinas, *Summa Theologica* I, Q. 36, A. 2.
96. E.g., Thomas Aquinas appeals to Aristotle to reach this conclusion. Aristotle claims that every relation is based on quantity or action. There is no quantity in God, Aquinas claims, and the only actions in the Godhead are the processions. Here Aquinas appeals to a psychological analogy, which compares the procession of knowledge and of love to generation and spiration, respectively. This seems to move the psychological analogy from a tool used to clarify the distinction between generation and procession to a controlling concept that restricts possible actions between Father and Son. I do not find sufficient warrant for moving the psychological analogy from a clarifying to a restrictive role. See Aquinas, *Summa Theologica* I, Q. 28, A. 4.
97. Slotemaker, *Anselm of Canterbury*, 76–78. The affirmation of disparate relations does not go so far as to posit a relation beyond origin like eternal manifestation.

alternative to the *filioque* in that it preserves the central dogmatic concern of the relationality criterion.

The Unity Criterion

Typically, when we think of human persons, speaking of three persons would entail admitting the existence of three things or three different beings. The affirmation that Father, Son, and Spirit are consubstantial pushes us to recognize one final and crucial dissimilarity between divine and human personhood— divine personhood cannot be defined in a manner that undermines divine unity. Here again, the unity of the Godhead must norm our understanding of divine plurality, just as divine plurality qualifies and norms any exploration of divine unity.

In both Eastern and Western traditions, certain key figures have violated the unity criterion, developing explanations of the Trinity that are clearly tritheistic. In the sixth century in the East, John Philoponus (sometimes known as John the Grammarian) applied Aristotelian logic to claim that each divine hypostasis must have its own individual substance, since all substances are particular, not shared. Philoponus saw the three divine persons as one substance only in the sense of a secondary substance—a mere conceptual reality whereby we can associate the three together due to common traits.[98] Writing four centuries later in the Latin West, Roscelin of Compiègne likely assumed a linguistic theory that all words must point to a particular thing (*res*) when he argued that unless the Father, Son, and Spirit were different things, the Father was incarnate with the Son.[99] It may also be the case that Roscelin adopted a similar particularist metaphysic to that of Philoponus.[100] Whatever his reasoning, Roscelin reached similar conclusions to Philoponus—there must be three things that are God.

Both of these examples reveal the serious risk that the distinctions between the persons may become so pronounced that they overcome the unity of the divine being. Both East and West, however, have striven to avoid this risk by insisting on the simplicity of God. We see this, for example, in the *filioque* debate, where both Photius and Anselm argue that their position is more

---

98. As Christophe Erismann summarizes, "According to Philoponus, everything that is, is particular, including nature and substances." This philosophical commitment leads to the conclusion that there are three particular deities (Erismann, "The Trinity, Universals, and Particular Substances," 288).

99. For a brief summary of Roscelin's theology in historical context, see Nielson, "Trinitarian Theology from Alcuin to Anselm," 162–67; Gemeinhardt, "Logic, Tradition and Ecumenics," 15–16.

100. Erismann, "The Trinity, Universals, and Particular Substances," 297–98.

clearly compatible with divine simplicity than their opponents'. It is important to note that the persons, too, are simple. This is true for two reasons. First, because the persons are particular existences of the divine essence, they each have the properties of that essence, including simplicity. Second, if the persons were composite, then they would fall subject to the concerns of chapter 3: the composite persons would be mutable and less than absolute. When we discuss how the Father both eternally spirates and generates, we are not suggesting that part of the Father spirates and another part generates. Rather, the Father communicates the fullness of divinity in a unique manner to the Son and to the Spirit, and this communication entails a relation between the fullness of the Father and the fullness of the Son and Spirit but no division of the divine nature. Admittedly, such concepts strain the limits of human understanding.

The Uniqueness Criterion

The previous five criteria lead us to conclude that divine persons are the modes of existence of a rational nature, though Christology prevents us from attributing a distinct mind, will, or consciousness to each person. Divine persons are distinguished by relations, but these relations ought not be understood in such a manner that each person entails a distinct being, nature, or thing—divine unity must be preserved. One final and significant criterion remains to be explored: that of uniqueness.

A number of biblical arguments can be cited to defend the uniqueness of the divine persons. In chapter 2, I explored the description of the Son as *monogenēs*, which could mean "unique" or "only begotten." Either definition would support the notion that the Son is a unique divine person with a relation to the Father distinct from the Spirit's. A similar conclusion can be drawn from the fact that all of Paul's seventeen references to the divine Son use either the definite article ("*the* Son," as in Rom. 1:4; 1 Cor. 15:28; 2 Cor. 1:9; Gal. 2:20; Eph. 4:13) or a possessive pronoun ("*his* Son," as in Rom. 1:3, 9; 5:10; 8:3, 29, 32; 1 Cor. 1:9; Gal. 1:16; 4:4, 6; Col. 1:13; 1 Thess. 1:10).[101] When the *tropikoi* of the fourth century denied the divinity of the Holy Spirit by pointing to passages that spoke of created spirit (e.g., Amos 4:12–13),[102] Athanasius of Alexandria developed a similar hermeneutical principle concerning the Holy Spirit. Where the Old and New Testaments speak of spirit without an article, they typically do not refer to the Holy Spirit. Exceptions are found where we see "Spirit of God" (e.g., 2 Cor. 3:3) or "his Spirit" (e.g., 1 John 4:13). When

---

101. Toon, *Our Triune God*, 164.
102. Athanasius would be reading the Greek Septuagint, but "spirit" in the Hebrew is also indefinite here.

the Bible speaks of the Holy Spirit, Athanasius argues, it uses the article—"*the* Holy Spirit"—indicating his unique status.[103]

It is widely agreed in the theological tradition that each divine person is unique in comparison with the others. This is evident in various significant historical definitions of personhood, like Richard of St. Victor's: "A divine person is an incommunicable existence of a divine nature."[104] Richard traces the etymology of "existence" back to the Latin word "to be" (*sistere*) and the prefix "from" (*ex-*).[105] He claims that specific existences can generally be distinguished by nature or origin, but since Father, Son, and Spirit are consubstantial, the uniqueness of each person is rooted in the processions and explained in the personal properties: the Father is unbegotten, the Son begotten, and the Holy Spirit spirated.[106] While the Father eternally shares and communicates his entire nature through the generation of the Son and the procession of the Spirit, he does not and cannot share or communicate his unique, personal, unbegotten mode of existence.

The medieval Richard of St. Victor's scholastic Catholic definition of "person" bears some resemblance to the theology of contemporary Orthodox systematician John Zizioulas. Zizioulas insists that "difference is a natural or moral category; uniqueness belongs to the level of personhood."[107] In other words, we do not distinguish persons by recognizing how they possess different attributes than others; this is an appeal to nature. Rather, we recognize that each person is irreducibly unique. A person "simply *is* and *is himself* or *herself* and not someone else."[108] Persons are "concrete, unique, and unrepeatable" entities.[109] Aspects of Zizioulas's theology of personhood are contentious, not the least of which is his understanding of persons as distinct subjects, but his fundamental insight on uniqueness, and particularity of each person, is both defensible and helpful.[110] In the end, we can qualify some of Zizioulas's

103. Athanasius, *Letters to Serapion on the Holy Spirit* 1.4.
104. Richard of St. Victor, *On the Trinity* 4.22.
105. Richard of St. Victor, *On the Trinity* 4.12.
106. Richard of St. Victor, *On the Trinity* 4.17.
107. Zizioulas, *Communion and Otherness*, 69. These sorts of statements by Zizioulas are often attributed to his being influenced by the modern philosophy of personalism. In point of fact, similar statements are found earlier in the tradition. E.g., the Lutheran scholastic Johann Gerhard writes, "'Difference' is the characteristic of things that differ essentially" (Gerhard, *Commonplace III* §46).
108. Zizioulas, *Communion and Otherness*, 111; italics original.
109. Zizioulas, *Being as Communion*, 46.
110. Much of the debate centers on whether Zizioulas's definition results in three distinct volitional subjects and centers of consciousness. Critics often argue that Zizioulas's emphasis of personhood and freedom implies three wills in God and treats divine and human personhood univocally. Defenders of Zizioulas argue that while Zizioulas is intentionally dialoguing

statements by emphasizing the apophatic dimension of his thought, which acknowledges some limitations in naming precisely what persons are: "We cannot give a *positive qualitative content* to a hypostasis or person."[111]

What I am calling the uniqueness criterion is what concerned the Orthodox patriarch Photius about the *filioque*. He fears that the "Spirit's unique characterizing procession" is "confused" by the *filioque*, and he worries further that such a move may lead to making "common to all three persons what uniquely characterizes" only one person.[112] Eventually, the West implicitly acknowledged this difficulty, which was found in early formulations of the *filioque*. Major Western theologians had to develop a conceptual framework that would allow the procession of the Holy Spirit through the Father and Son to be explained in a manner that preserved the uniqueness of each. Several strategies were deployed. Sometimes we see claims that the Father and Son share the power of spiration but possess this power in a different manner—the Father having it from himself and the Son having it from the Father.[113] Sometimes we see the claim that while spiration is numerically one, there are two unique spirators.[114] Others insist that while the power of spiration is shared between Father and Son, it is also true that in some sense the Father spirates through the mediation of the Son.[115] The Son is the principle, but the Father the "principle without principle."[116] Such attempts show a clear effort by the West to preserve the uniqueness of the persons while affirming the *filioque*.

Though some of these Western solutions were developed after Photius lived and wrote, I suspect that he would not be convinced by them. Photius's emphasis on the uniqueness of the persons is rooted in the basic principle of Basil of Caesarea discussed in chapter 1: hypostasis pertains to what is unique, and *ousia* pertains to what is common. If there is a common trait shared between the persons, such as spiration, then that trait should be shared among all three persons. "For reason demands equality for each person so that each person exchanges the grace of causality indistinguishably," unless, of course, causality is a unique property of the Father with respect to the

---

with personalism, he consciously distances himself from personalist approaches that define personhood in terms of consciousness. For a brief and lucid critique, see Holmes, *Quest for the Trinity*, 13–15. For an able defense of Zizioulas, see Papanikolaou, "Is John Zizioulas an Existentialist," 601–7.

111. Zizioulas, *Communion and Otherness*, 112.
112. Photius, *Mystagogy of the Holy Spirit* 1.9–10.
113. Pohle, *Divine Trinity*, 235.
114. William of Auvergne, *The Trinity* §43.
115. Henry of Ghent, *Summa of Ordinary Questions*, A. 54, Q. 7, §15.
116. Emery, *The Trinity*, 146–47.

processions.[117] Photius's argument prompts greater clarity in our analysis of Western attempts to preserve the uniqueness of each divine person. Surely, language of "two spirators" suggests a commonality between Father and Son that is denied the Spirit, risking a subordinationism that denies the Spirit full consubstantiality. On the other hand, language of the Father spirating mediately, through the Son, and of the Son spirating immediately preserves uniqueness—the Father and Son do not have mediate spiration in common. The same is true, though somewhat less clearly, of distinctions between the Son as principle with a principle and the Father as principle without principle. While it must be admitted that such solutions to the problem of divine uniqueness leave a considerable degree of ambiguity, this ambiguity is no worse than that which Orthodox Christians face in explaining the precise meaning of eternal manifestation as an alternative to the *filioque*. In the end, full comprehension is eclipsed by apophatic mystery.

Definition of Divine Persons

With the five criteria in place, I can now define the term "person" as used in trinitarian theology. A divine person is a unique subsistence of the singular and rational divine nature that is distinguished from yet inseparably united with the other divine persons by the divine relations. The divine persons do not possess different natures, bodies, or material forms from one another, nor are they distinct centers of consciousness, willing, or knowledge. Rather, the fullness of the divine nature is hypostatized in its entirety in each person, indivisibly without splitting the divine nature into parts and irreducibly in a threefold relation.

Divine relations refer to the fact that each divine person is a unique subsistence that is determined entirely by how that person eternally is ordered toward the other persons by the divine processions. Traditionally, the Father is distinguished by the relations of **paternity** to the Son and active spiration to the Spirit, the Son by **filiation** to the Father, and the Spirit by **passive spiration** to the Father. Beyond this, the relations are contested. According to the Latin West, the Son shares the Father's relation of active spiration to the Spirit, and the Spirit is related to the Son by passive spiration. According to Gregory of Cyprus and some Orthodox ever since, the relation is explained in terms of manifestation: the Son is manifest by the Spirit, and the Spirit manifests the Son. The primary difference between these conceptions seems to be vocabulary and the fact that the West treats the Son as the cause of the

117. Photius, *Mystagogy of the Holy Spirit* 1.3.

Spirit while the East limits all causation within the processions to the Father, resulting in a greater emphasis on divine monarchy.

The *Filioque*, Persons, and Relations

Disputes over the *filioque* include reciprocating accusations that either the acceptance of the *filioque* or its rejection leads to theological problems in distinguishing the divine persons. The six criteria proposed above (rationality, dissimilarity, christological compatibility, relationality, unity, and uniqueness) reveal the necessary theological components for speaking of divine persons and help us to identify theologies that fail to explore adequately the notion of divine personhood. In addition to various problematic theologies like social trinitarianism, improper understanding of the divine persons can lead to more significant heresies like modalism and tritheism. Furthermore, some defenses of the *filioque* and some criticisms of it can result in deficient explanations of the divine persons, yet both East and West have made concerted efforts to overcome these deficiencies in their own ways. Given that Scripture does not clearly adjudicate between the two views, what options might the church pursue in order to foster unity? While it seems clear that unilateral modification of the Niceano-Constantinopolitan Creed by the West, even if unintentional, was a problem, is it nevertheless theologically necessary to affirm the *filioque*?

Theologians have proposed numerous compromise explanations of the Son's relationship to the Spirit, ranging from proposals that have little hope of leading to agreement to those that for a time seemed to have potential yet ultimately failed to bring unity. Some proposals offer constructive and novel theological language as a possible solution, such as Leonardo Boff's argument that we should balance the *filioque* with the claim that the Son is generated *ex Patre Spirituque*—from the Father and the Spirit. Boff believes that this addition will balance the creed, and he claims it is based in the biblical account of the Spirit bringing about the virginal conception.[118] Boff's position lacks any warrant in the tradition, so it is unlikely that either side would adopt this formula. If the *filioque* risks blurring the uniqueness of the persons, adding a *spirituque* clause merely amplifies the problem. The innovation also leads Boff to some strange conclusions about Mary, including that the Holy Spirit "took on human form in her."[119] For all of these reasons, Boff's proposal should gain no traction.

---

118. Boff, *Trinity and Society*, 205–7.
119. Boff, *Trinity and Society*, 210. For a critique of Boff on this point, see Kärkkäinen, *The Trinity*, 289.

A common Eastern Orthodox tactic has been to try to propose alternative language for the relation between the Son and Spirit that does not require the Son to share in the Father's procession of the Spirit. This approach's most frequent language is found in John of Damascus, who speaks of the Spirit's procession from the Father through the Son (*dia huiou*).[120] John's language here has often been used by theologians to describe the Son not as a cause of the Spirit—this is reserved for the Father alone—but as the power of God the Father through whom the Father causes all things.[121] Unfortunately, at the Council of Lyons (1274), which sought to unite East and West, John Beccus, the key Orthodox unionist, interpreted John's language as synonymous with the *filioque*, which leads many contemporary Orthodox figures to be skeptical that the phrase may be helpful as a compromise alternative.[122] Gregory of Cyprus's language of the Spirit eternally manifesting the Son has found some support among some contemporary Western theologians. Kathryn Tanner, for example, believes that the Spirit's involvement in the virginal conception in the Son's mission may suggest an eternal manifestation while complicating claims of a double procession.[123] At the Council of Florence (1438–45) Gennadius Scholarius proposed that the church say the Spirit "gushed forth" from the Son and "flowed forth" from Father and Son, a view many Orthodox delegates accepted at the time, but one rejected by Latin participants as too imprecise and unclear.[124] No alternative language has found anything near a consensus between East and West.

What, then, must we say dogmatically of the *filioque*? Scripture does not clearly resolve the matter, and tradition is deeply divided. The dogmatic function of the processions is to ensure the eternal distinction between, and consubstantiality of, Father, Son, and Spirit. Both East and West strive to explain the procession of the Spirit in a manner that preserves three unique persons without dividing the one simple divine essence. This means that though acceptance or rejection of the *filioque* can jeopardize these dogmatic goals, as discussed above, neither the *filioque*'s acceptance nor its rejection *necessarily* results in these problems. As long as theologians insist that the

---

120. "He is the Spirit of the Son, not as being from Him, but as proceeding through Him from the Father—for the Father alone is cause" (John of Damascus, *Exposition of the Orthodox Faith* 1.12).

121. See the helpful summary in Grégoire, "Relation éternelle," 713–55.

122. Papadakis, *Crisis in Byzantium*, 24–25; Bobrinskoy, *Mystery of the Trinity*, 303. As a unionist, Beccus is often viewed as a traitor to the Orthodox cause.

123. Tanner, "Beyond the East/West Divide," 202.

124. For a concise summary of Scholarius's involvement at Ferrara-Florence, see Turner, "George-Gannadius Scholarius," 84–86.

Father and Son are unique persons with their own personal properties and
modes of existence, and as long as there is some eternal relation between
the Son and the Holy Spirit, whatever it is named (whether the *filioque*; or
procession through the Son, which suggests the Son's involvement in spiration; or eternal manifestation, which does not), then the necessary dogmatic
objectives can be obtained. For this reason, I would side with major twentieth-
century theologians on both sides to suggest that the *filioque* dispute will
likely never be resolved[125] and that acceptance or rejection of the *filioque* may
be confessionally binding but not dogmatically so.[126] This position preserves
the necessary dogmatic affirmations while allowing an ecumenical spirit that
is in service of the important goal of Christian unity, so that Christians may
be one as Father and Son are one (John 17:22), even if it remains unclear
whether the Father and Son's oneness includes sharing in the procession of
the Spirit.

FOR FURTHER READING

Theological Treatments of Divine Personhood

Miyahira, Nozomu. *Towards a Theology of the Concord of God: A Japanese Perspective on the Trinity*. Carlisle, UK: Paternoster, 2000.

Among Miyahira's many contributions is a detailed analysis of how to express
the idea of a tripersonal God in a Japanese context. His constructive proposal
helpfully illustrates that divine personhood need not require a violation of what
I call the christological-compatibility criterion.

Torrance, Alan J. *Persons in Communion: Trinitarian Description and Human Participation*. Edinburgh: T&T Clark, 1996.

Torrance's exploration of the theology of divine personhood is particularly helpful as a guide for reflecting on Barth's and Rahner's rejections of the concept's
viability in the modern world.

Zizioulas, John D. *Communion and Otherness: Further Studies in Personhood and
the Church*. New York: T&T Clark, 2006.

In this text, Zizioulas gives his most extensive explanation of how he understands
personhood. The book will therefore help the reader understand this theological
figure, who is central to discussions of personhood. For Zizioulas, persons are
unique others in communion, are free, and are ecstatically creative.

125. Yves Congar argues that "we may say quite unambiguously that this is not the goal to
be pursued" (*I Believe in the Holy Spirit*, 3:201).
126. Such was the position of V. V. Bolotov (see Bobrinskoy, *Mystery of the Trinity*, 291).

Historical Analysis of the Filioque Debate

Papadakis, Aristeides. *Crisis in Byzantium: The Filioque Controversy in the Patriarchate of Gregory II of Cyprus (1283–1289)*. Rev. ed. Crestwood, NY: St. Vladimir's Seminary Press, 1997.

> One of the more significant trinitarian debates in history concerns the *filioque*, one major reason for the split between Christians East and West. Papadakis adeptly introduces the reader to an important chapter in these debates, and he includes a translation of Gregory of Cyprus's *Tomus*.

Siecienski, A. Edward. *The Filioque: History of a Doctrinal Controversy*. Oxford: Oxford University Press, 2010.

> Siecienski's text is the definitive historical treatment of the development of the *filioque* debates. It is a must-read for anyone interested in the discussion.

CHAPTER 5

Perichoresis

In John 10:38, Jesus says, "The Father is in me and I in the Father." From this quite basic statement and others like it (John 14:10; 17:21, 23), early Christians developed the doctrine of **perichoresis** as another means of speaking of the unity of Father, Son, and Spirit. Perichoresis has been much discussed in modern theology, some finding it "a major advance in terminological clarification"[1] and others describing it as "fundamentally a placeholder" for something "wondrously beyond our understanding"[2] or even as a "black box" whose contents have been ignored.[3] It is certainly the case that much modern theology has appealed to perichoresis without substantive analysis of its meaning, and the problem is further amplified by the fact that the same passages in John that speak of the Father being in the Son and the Son in the Father speak also of believers being in the Father and the Son and of the Son being in them (John 17:21–23). Noting this feature of the text, modern theologians have explored the implications of perichoresis for salvation and a wide range of other subjects in a manner that amplifies confusion about perichoresis by overextending its use.

This chapter will introduce the dogmatic significance of perichoresis—namely, helping to explain the unity of the Godhead by clarifying the notion of consubstantiality and of the divine processions, showing that the divine persons are both contained within and moving within one another.[4] As we

---

1. Twombly, *Perichoresis and Personhood*, 105.
2. Treier, *Introducing Evangelical Theology*, 86.
3. This helpful turn of phrase is from Woznicki, "Dancing around the Black Box," 103–21.
4. Durand, *La périchorèse des personnes divines*, 33.

will see, perichoresis also goes a step further than this to clarify the nature of the divine personhood. I will begin the chapter by exploring three common metaphors used to explain perichoresis, situating these metaphors in the context of the historical and lexical development of the term. I will then move to summarize perichoresis's role in trinitarian dogmatics before exploring the significance of perichoresis for salvation by dialoguing with Jürgen Moltmann and recent studies of the theme of union in Paul's Epistles.

Conceptions of Perichoresis

Perhaps one reason that perichoresis is viewed as inscrutable by certain modern commentators is that it is often explained in terms of metaphors of motion, space, and mind, seemingly leaving the metaphysical details of the doctrine unexplored. To further complicate matters, perichoresis was historically applied to both the Trinity and Christology, and in modern theology it has extended to such areas as soteriology, ecclesiology, the doctrine of creation, and eschatology.[5] Despite this broad and often metaphorical use, it remains true that the application of perichoresis to the Trinity and Christology did serve to clarify the union of three persons in the Trinity and of two natures in Christ. Fundamentally, this is because, in Ralph Del Colle's words, "perichoresis prevents distinction from becoming separation or division."[6] I turn now to an exploration of three metaphors for perichoresis and their dogmatic deployment.

Perichoresis and Mutually Interpenetrative Motion

One of the more common modern metaphors for perichoresis is that of a dance. For example, Karen Baker-Fletcher speaks of the Greek tradition of perichoresis as indicating a "dance of the Trinity," a metaphorical "way of describing the dynamic relational nature of divine creativity."[7] Baker-Fletcher is well aware that an incorporeal God does not literally dance in an embodied way, yet she thinks that we can meaningfully speak of "the dynamic, ongoing movement of God," and she believes that the word *perichōrēsis* is literally translated "to dance around" or "to envelope."[8] She creatively draws on the imagery of God as a whirlwind to illustrate the idea biblically (Job 38:1;

---

5. Indeed, some explorations of the term "perichoresis" insist on three dimensions of the word's definition: christological, trinitarian, and soteriological/eschatological. See K. A. Richardson, "Uncreated and Created Perichoretic Relations," 81.
6. Del Colle, "Triune God," 130.
7. Baker-Fletcher, *Dancing with God*, 25.
8. Baker-Fletcher, *Dancing with God*, 45.

40:6)[9] and extends the dance of God, as many modern theologians do, into God's "ongoing movement" in creation, including the divine invitation for humans to join this dance.[10]

Unfortunately, the common understanding of *perichōrēsis* as meaning "to dance around" is rooted in an etymological mistake. The Greek *perichōrein* is derived from *chōrein*, meaning "both 'to go' and 'to make room for' or 'to contain,'" rather than from *choreuein*, which refers to dancing in a chorus.[11] The metaphor of three individuals dancing also distinguishes between the agency of the Father, Son, and Spirit in a manner that risks tritheism and is contrary to the doctrine of inseparable operations, which will be explored in chapter 7. Nevertheless, the metaphor does highlight a dynamic meaning for perichoresis found in early Christian theology, for which Baker-Fletcher's gesture to the whirlwind in Job provides an interesting biblical foundation. We first see the idea of perichoresis in Gregory of Nyssa, with his frequent use of imagery of circular motion. For example, he refers to the "revolving circle of the glory moving around [*periphero*] from like to like [person]," since each person glorifies the others.[12] Gregory uses the verb form of *perichōrēsis* (*perichōrein*) four times to speak of the cooperation of the human and divine natures in Christ, and he draws on several related terms (e.g., *periphero* in the quotation above). He probably understands *perichōrein* to refer to "passing reciprocally."[13] Images of circular motion persist throughout the tradition in less technical form—for example, in Jan van Ruusbroec's mystical theology of God as a "fathomless eddy or bottomless whirlpool."[14]

While Gregory of Nyssa did not have a developed doctrine of perichoresis, his use of the term paved the way for such a doctrine, first in Christology and then in the doctrine of the Trinity. In the seventh century, Christians (especially Byzantines in the East) debated monoenergism, the idea that there was a single operation in Christ, and monothelitism, the idea that there was a single will in Christ. Maximus the Confessor notably argued against each perspective on a number of grounds, including that combining the divine wills and operations/energies jeopardized the full humanity of Christ by inappropriately uniting humanity and divinity.[15] His critics worried that speaking of two wills

9. Baker-Fletcher, *Dancing with God*, 57.
10. Baker-Fletcher, *Dancing with God*, 45–48.
11. T. F. Torrance, *Christian Doctrine of God*, 170n8.
12. Gregory of Nyssa, *On the Holy Spirit against the Followers of Macedonius*, 323.
13. Harrison, "Perichoresis in the Greek Fathers," 54, 56; Stramara, "Gregory of Nyssa's Terminology," 258–60.
14. Hunt, *Trinity: Nexus of the Mysteries*, 30.
15. Maximus was also concerned that if Christ lacked a full human will, the salvation of full human nature was impossible. Gregory of Nazianzus's rule, discussed in chap. 4, helpfully

and two operations risked the unity of Christ.[16] What was needed was a term for speaking of the operations and wills of Christ that allowed for unity in diversity, in parallel to Chalcedon's affirmation of united natures in Christ without mixture or confusion. Maximus's solution was, in part, to appeal to the idea of perichoresis, a term fundamentally meant to speak of identity and difference, or "union without absorption."[17] Perichoresis allowed for a clearer unity of the person of Christ because the actions of the human and divine natures permeated one another and reciprocated in such a manner that there was a single subject, the eternal Son of God, without eliminating the distinct human and divine natures.[18]

While Maximus did not directly apply the idea of perichoresis to the Trinity, successive Orthodox theologians did. A tractate titled *On the Trinity* and wrongly attributed to Cyril of Alexandria was the first to use the term *perichōrēsis* of the Trinity,[19] but John of Damascus was the first theologian to center this idea in his explanation of the Trinity. John recognized the parallels between Christology and the Trinity: "Just as the three persons of the Holy Trinity are united without confusion and are distinct without separation and have number without causing division, or separation, or estrangement, or severance among them, . . . so in the same way the natures of Christ, although united, are united without confusion, and although mutually immanent [*perichōrousin*], do not suffer any change or transformation of one into the other."[20] John consistently deploys perichoresis in his trinitarian thought to explain the possibility of the divine persons being united without "confusion," "blending," "mixture," or "change," using concepts similar to Chalcedon's definition of the hypostatic union, though with slightly different vocabulary in the Greek.[21]

As explored so far, the analogy of interpenetrating movement illustrates one dogmatic function of the doctrine of perichoresis: perichoresis serves to clarify the nature of the doctrine of consubstantiality. Whereas simplicity clarified this doctrine by explaining the indivisibility, lack of composition, and immutability of the single divine essence, perichoresis sets the

---

clarifies what was at stake here: "That which [the Son] has not assumed he has not healed; but that which is united to his Godhead is also saved" (*To Cledonius against Apollinaris*, 218).

16. It is interesting that in Maximus's *Disputation with Pyrrhus*, the first objection raised by Pyrrhus to dyothelitism is "Is Christ one or not?" (Maximus the Confessor, *Disputation with Pyrrhus* §8).

17. Twombly, *Perichoresis and Personhood*, 9, 42.

18. See Prestige, "ΠΕΡΙΧΩΡΕΩ and ΠΕΡΙΧΩΡΗΣΙΣ in the Fathers," 243.

19. Pseudo-Cyril of Alexandria, *De Trinitate* 10, Patrologia graeca 77.1144B.

20. John of Damascus, *Exposition of the Orthodox Faith* 3.8.

21. John of Damascus, *Exposition of the Orthodox Faith* 1.14.

stage for the insistence of a single operation *ad extra*[22] as deriving from the single essence and being performed by all three divine persons, who interpenetrate one another. As John Meyendorff explains, human persons, though consubstantial, often act in isolation or in conflict: "In God, however, the *perichōrēsis* expresses the perfect love, and, therefore, the perfect unity of 'energy,' of the three hypostases, without, however, any mingling or coalescence."[23] The doctrine of inseparable operations, the subject of chapter 7, is therefore, at least in part, the external manifestation of the divine perichoresis.[24]

Perichoresis and Mutual Indwelling

Though the concept of the mutual indwelling of the divine persons was present from the patristic era thanks to such verses as John 10:38, the Greek term *perichōrēsis* only made its way into Latin theology through Burgundio of Pisa's Latin twelfth-century translation of John of Damascus's *The Orthodox Faith*.[25] Eventually, Latin-speaking Christians would offer two Latin terms to translate the Greek *perichōrēsis*. *Circumincessio*, drawing on the root *incedere* ("to march," "to extend," etc.), refers to the movement of mutual interpenetration, but *circuminsessio*, from the root *insidere* ("to sit down," "to occupy"), refers more properly to mutual indwelling, coinherence, or inexistence (the state of existing in).[26] This variety of perichoresis can be understood in terms of "reciprocally contain[ing] one another."[27] This meaning may have been central to John of Damascus, who may have understood the root *chōrein* to apply in the sense of "holding" or "containing."[28] Others believe that it may have been present in the earliest usage in Gregory of Nyssa.[29] The Greek root *peri-* can refer to movement into something or to the encircling of something, so a degree of ambiguity is always present, and it is perhaps best to

---

22. As explained in detail in chapter 7, all works of the Father, Son, and Holy Spirit toward creation are called *ad extra* works and are thought to be the indivisible work of all three persons together.

23. Meyendorff, *Byzantine Theology*, 186.

24. Durand, *La périchorèse des personnes divines*, 163. Durand shows how Bonaventure reaches a similar conclusion. This is sometimes recognized in modern systematic theology. See, e.g., Jüngel, *Doctrine of the Trinity*, 35.

25. Durand, *La périchorèse des personnes divines*, 151.

26. Stamatović, "Meaning of Perichoresis," 306.

27. T. F. Torrance, *Christian Doctrine of God*, 170.

28. Prestige, "ΠΕΡΙΧΩΡΕΩ and ΠΕΡΙΧΩΡΗΣΙΣ in the Fathers," 243–44.

29. Harrison, "Perichoresis in the Greek Fathers," 54. The concept of the Spirit containing the Father and Son, an expansion of John's language of the mutual Father-Son indwelling, can be traced back at least as far as Athenagoras, *Plea regarding Christians* §10.

understand perichoresis as a "metaphor of spatial motion."[30] Regardless, the spatial metaphor is certainly evident in the basic Johannine language of the Father being in the Son and vice versa.

When perichoresis is understood in terms of coinherence or reciprocal containing, it serves to clarify further the doctrine of the divine processions. Recall that in chapter 2 I introduced the idea of an internal procession. Aquinas, for example, made the analogy between eternal generation and the procession of a thought that remains in the mind. Christians have consistently maintained that the procession of the Spirit and the generation of the Son are internal to the Godhead. The spatial aspect of perichoresis helps reinforce this claim. Since the processions are internal, the persons coinhere within one another eternally.[31] Furthermore, since perichoresis ensures no separation through the processions, but merely distinction, many have argued that it "overcame the last vestiges of subordinationism."[32] The generated Son and the spirated Holy Spirit are within the Father's being, glory, power, and life, and the Father in theirs, such that there is no possible subordination.

Perichoresis and Unity of Love, Consciousness, and Will

A third metaphor commonly used to explain perichoresis is that of a unity of love, consciousness, and will. For example, Charles Hodge explains perichoresis by appealing to 1 Corinthians 2:10–11, which says that the Spirit searches "the depths of God," which Paul explains by noting, "Who knows a person's thoughts except his spirit within him?"[33] Besides attesting to the divinity of the Spirit, this passage's language of the Spirit being "in" God suggests perichoresis, much like the indwelling language of John 17. The idea of the Spirit being within the mind of God finds parallels in various places. I have already explored the wisdom Christology that treats Jesus as the very Wisdom of God (1 Cor. 1:30). The unique mutual knowledge of the Son and the Father in recognizing one another's identities may evoke a similar shared mind (Matt. 11:27; Luke 10:22). Hodge describes perichoresis as meaning "what the one knows, the others know," noting that "a common knowledge implies a common consciousness."[34] Writing centuries earlier, John of Damascus sometimes juxtaposes the idea of perichoresis with "existence in one another" and unity of "will, operation, virtue, power, and, so to speak, motion," at least once in the

---

30. Gunton, *Promise of Trinitarian Theology*, 137.
31. Durand, *La périchorèse des personnes divines*, 323.
32. Del Colle, "Triune God," 132.
33. C. Hodge, *Systematic Theology*, 1:461.
34. C. Hodge, *Systematic Theology*, 1:461.

context of discussing John 14:11: "I am in the Father and the Father is in me."[35] It is also noteworthy that Jesus's high-priestly prayer, from which perichoresis derives, focuses on eternal life as knowing God (John 17:3), suggesting a faint parallel between being in God and knowing him. The same passage also links God being in the faithful with the love of God being in them (17:26).

The concept of perichoresis as a unity of mind, consciousness, and love is historically most evident in the Thomist theological tradition, which explains the divine processions as analogous to the procession of a thought and of love within a mind. In this analogy, the Son is the reason of God, and the Spirit is the love between Father and Son. The Father is the mind within which this love and reason occurs. The analogy suggests that the Son and Spirit are in the Father and that the Father's acts of loving and knowing are in the Son, capturing aspects of both the spatial metaphor and the movement metaphor for perichoresis. It adds some clarification regarding the divine persons that is not immediately evident in the other metaphors. Because of the mutual indwelling and interpenetration of perichoresis, the Father, Son, and Spirit are a single mind, consciousness, and love, fitting the christological-compatibility criterion of divine personhood. Yet, we cannot go as far as to say that this perichoresis reduces God to a single subject, meaning that this mind is simultaneously and equally the mind of Father, Son, and Spirit, three who act in one operation.[36] Perichoresis also allows us to affirm two patterns of prayer. One pattern emphasizes the tripersonality of God and addresses each divine person without denying a single deity. The other pattern of prayer addresses God as a single listner but intends to pray to all three.[37] While human finitude prevents us from knowing how God experiences such things as mind, consciousness, and knowledge—and my use of the word "experience" of God is so limited that it has minimal meaning here—perichoresis does reduce any anxiety that may have been produced by denying that each person is a distinct center of consciousness. It is not that there is only a single subject who is God, but that the three subjects so perfectly coinhere that they share a singular consciousness, mind, will, and love.

Perichoresis in Modern Theology

Our three metaphors allow us to begin to understand the doctrine of perichoresis, but a turn to modern theology will further clarify the matter. Though

---

35. John of Damascus, *Exposition of the Orthodox Faith* 1.8.
36. See the discussion in Bourassa, *Questions de théologie trinitaire*, 168–73.
37. C. Hodge, *Systematic Theology*, 1:262.

the doctrine of perichoresis played a specific and limited function in Byzantine and medieval Latin theology, its role in modern theology has, at times, grown more expansive. This is perhaps most evident in the work of Jürgen Moltmann, who has used the concept as a centerpiece of much of his theology. For this reason, it will be helpful to focus on his work, beginning with his exposition of the doctrine of the Trinity in *The Trinity and the Kingdom*, his most extensive treatment of the subject. Moltmann considers three possible approaches to divine unity. He fears that a unity-of-substance approach to the Trinity faces two related risks. First, unity of substance risks eliminating the distinctions between the divine persons, since any difference in properties appears to entail a difference in substance. Moltmann here assumes something similar to the idea of the indiscernibility of identicals discussed in chapter 1, though without explicit appeal to the concept. Second, theologians seeking to avoid the elimination of personal distinction may instead think of Father, Son, and Spirit as three substances that were only later united. Here Moltmann's worry fits the theology of Roscelin of Compiègne discussed in chapter 4, which treats each divine person as a discrete thing. In summary, Moltmann rightly recognizes certain misapplications of the unity of the divine substance but responds by rejecting an emphasis on substance altogether.[38]

The second possible approach to divine unity is that of the single divine subject, which Moltmann attributes to Karl Barth and Karl Rahner. As we saw in chapter 4, both theologians are concerned by the fact that much modern Christianity has adopted the notion of personhood as distinct centers of consciousness, which violates what I have called the christological-compatibility criterion. Moltmann is concerned that the reduction of God to a single divine subject risks modalism, since there is only one subject who thinks but who is manifest in a threefold form.[39] Moltmann prefers a social model of the Trinity and considers divine persons as engaged in I-Thou relationships by which they are fundamentally determined.[40] In order to explain the unity of these three persons, Moltmann says the "uniting at-oneness" of the Trinity "lies in the eternal perichoresis of the Father, the Son, and the Spirit."[41] Perichoresis serves as an alternative to unity of substance and unity of subject, and through perichoresis the Father, Son, and Spirit "form their own unity by themselves in the circulation of the divine life."[42] It is perichoresis that maintains divine personhood against the risk of three isolated divine

---

38. Moltmann, *The Trinity and the Kingdom*, 10–12, 149.
39. Moltmann, *The Trinity and the Kingdom*, 141, 144.
40. Moltmann, *The Trinity and the Kingdom*, 145, 157, 172, 224.
41. Moltmann, *The Trinity and the Kingdom*, 157.
42. Moltmann, *The Trinity and the Kingdom*, 175.

individuals.[43] As Moltmann explains in a later work, "Each Person actively dwells in the two others and passively cedes space for the two others—that is to say, at once gives and receives the others. God's Being is personal being-there (*Da-sein*), social being-with (*mit-sein*) and, perichoretically understood, being-in (*in-sein*)."[44]

Having given perichoresis a central role in trinitarian doctrine in *The Trinity and the Kingdom*, Moltmann explores its other possible uses throughout his corpus. Scripture speaks of the world being in God (Acts 17:28) and God filling the world (Jer. 23:24). It speaks of an eschatological hope of God being "all in all" (1 Cor. 15:28). Through salvation, Paul teaches that we are "clothed with Christ" (Gal. 3:27) and that Christ lives in us (Gal. 2:20). Led by such imagery, Moltmann deploys the idea of perichoresis to a wide range of doctrines. In the doctrine of creation, Moltmann endorses panentheism[45] and an evolution of creation by the Spirit that yields "mutual perichoreses."[46] In terms similar to the spatial imagery of perichoresis, Moltmann wonders where God can have space for his creation, a problem he resolves by appeal to the Jewish notion of *zimsum*, which explains how God can dwell in a finite location like the temple without having a body. Moltmann says that according to the idea of *zimsum*, which renders God in space, God can withdraw into himself, restricting his presence to allow for a space that is other. Nevertheless, creation still dwells within the space of the infinite God.[47] If creation is perichoretically in God and vice versa, and if God is somehow actually in space, not merely metaphorically so, then it seems that God and creation begin to be taken on similar terms. If, on the other hand, the notion of creation being in the space of God is merely metaphorical, then perichoresis as applied to the Trinity risks being mere metaphor, leaving us with a minimal understanding of God's unity.

The blurred lines between creation and God are most evident in the eschatological consummation of creation. As previously noted, Moltmann speaks of a perichoretic relationship between the Spirit and the evolution of creation, but at times, in his later work, he mingles these processes in ways that jeopardize the unity of the Godhead. For example, he writes, "Eschatologically, therefore, the unity of God is bound up with the salvation of creation, just as glory is bound up with his glorification through everything that lives. Just

43. Moltmann, *The Trinity and the Kingdom*, 199.
44. Moltmann, *Experiences in Theology*, 319.
45. Moltmann suggests that "this is a concept which can really only be thought and described in trinitarian terms" (*God in Creation*, 98).
46. Moltmann, *God in Creation*, 100.
47. Moltmann, *God in Creation*, 86–89.

as his glory is offered to him out of the world by the Holy Spirit, so his unity too is presented to him through the unification of the world with himself in the Holy Spirit."[48] Such statements not only undermine divine aseity (and with aseity also simplicity and immutability), a fact that Moltmann does not mind, but also threaten to undermine the present unity of the Trinity. If God's perichoretic unity is because of the world and he is perichoretically in the world, then it is difficult to see how God is distinct from the process of the world by which he is a unity of perichoresis.

As his theology develops, Moltmann is seemingly aware of the problem, attempting, with increasing clarity, to explain the distinction between creational perichoresis and trinitarian perichoresis. In his early work, he writes that "God does not manifest himself to an equal degree in everything."[49] In his later work, Moltmann distinguishes between perichoresis of the Trinity, which is between those "of the same kind" through "homologous love," and perichoresis between those "of a different kind" "by virtue of heterologous love," which is presumably the perichoresis involved in the *imago Dei* and the hypostatic union of Christ's humanity and divinity.[50] This distinction is an improvement, but it still lacks sufficient clarity. Some argue that Moltmann is able to maintain a distinction between God and the world because Moltmann insists that at the eschaton, God will be judge over the world.[51] Though there is some merit to this suggestion, a distinction based on final judgment is far less robust than that offered through something like the doctrine of analogy and the appeal to the simple essence of God.

Moltmann's appeal to perichoresis is at least partly rooted in social ethics. Moltmann is concerned that religious monotheism translates into political absolutism, concentrating power in the hands of a singular figure who is a reflection of the singular God.[52] Perichoresis and social trinitarianism, on the other hand, constitute both the church and the state in nonhierarchical manners by distributing power and emphasizing community.[53] Moltmann's thinking on this point is but one example of many modern attempts to appeal to the Trinity as a pattern that can be applied to social issues. To give another example, Leonardo Boff argues that the "perichoretic-communion" model of the Trinity serves as an example for ideal political, economic, and

---

48. Moltmann, *Future of Creation*, 92. See also the similar yet less developed ideas in Moltmann, *The Trinity and the Kingdom*, 149, 161.

49. Moltmann, *God in Creation*, 103.

50. Moltmann, *Experiences in Theology*, 319, 323.

51. Grenz, *Rediscovering the Triune God*, 87.

52. Moltmann, *The Trinity and the Kingdom*, 195–97.

53. Moltmann, *The Trinity and the Kingdom*, 202.

ecclesial structures.[54] Unfortunately, such appeals tend to produce a wide range of incompatible political and social solutions, likely because there are few clear scriptural connections between the Trinity and social life, the teaching in John 17 about perichoresis and the church being the most notable exception.

Our exploration of Moltmann's use of perichoresis reveals that perichoresis alone cannot establish the divine unity, for several reasons. First, the scriptural foundations for perichoresis in the Gospel of John are not enough on their own to ensure the divinity of the Son, especially given the fact that Jesus prays for the disciples to receive the same unity. This fact was not lost on fourth-century Arians, and it has resulted in periodic trinitarian problems over the centuries.[55] For example, in the thirteenth century, Joachim of Fiore noted Jesus's prayer that the disciples and church be one "just as" (*kathōs*) the Father and Son are one (John 17:11, 20) when he argued for the Trinity as a mere collective.[56] Second, there is some exegetical evidence that John uses the imagery of mutual indwelling to clarify his claims about the Father and Son being one. As Richard Bauckham notes, "It is significant that this uniquely Johannine formulation [that of mutual indwelling] occurs first in 10:38, following the remarkable version of the Shema in 10:30."[57] Third, perichoresis serves to clarify unity in distinction, but it assumes prior ontological categories that describe the unity and the distinction. In Christology, two distinct natures and one united hypostasis are assumed. In the Trinity, one being and three hypostases are assumed. Without these prior categories, it is not obvious what perichoresis serves to clarify.[58] This is why Moltmann must ultimately also appeal to the monarchy of the Father and to the divine processions in order to explain the unity of the Trinity.[59] Fourth, because of the imagery of God and the created world indwelling each other, overreliance on perichoresis can blur the lines between God and creation.[60]

Furthermore, Moltmann's use of perichoresis for social ends demonstrates the risks of social objectives guiding theological conclusions too extensively. Karen Kilby notes that there is a significant risk in explaining complex terms like "perichoresis." The problem, Kilby suggests, comes from the fact that

54. Boff, *Trinity and Society*, 150.

55. Durand, *La périchorèse des personnes divines*, 284. This is evident, e.g., in the theology of Asterius, who interpreted the Johannine passages of the oneness and mutual indwelling of the Father and Son in terms of a unity of will and action. See Anatolios, *Retrieving Nicaea*, 55.

56. Durand, *La périchorèse des personnes divines*, 285.

57. Bauckham, "The Trinity and the Gospel of John," 112.

58. Otto, "Use and Abuse of Perichoresis," 366, 368, 376–77.

59. Moltmann, *The Trinity and the Kingdom*, 165, 177. See commentary in Durand, *La périchorèse des personnes divines*, 60.

60. McCall, *Whose Monotheism?*, 156–74.

the kind of unity we are seeking here, where three persons are one God, is atypical for the sorts of persons that we normally encounter. We have to label this unity somehow, so we appeal to the term "perichoresis." Then, to explain perichoresis, "the social theorist points to those things which do to some degree bind human persons together, into couples or families or communities—interrelatedness, love, empathy, mutual accord, mutual giving, and so on."[61] Then this analogy is used as an ideal for humanity, which makes projection all the more likely.[62]

Moltmann has served as a helpful case study in modern theology and has raised several questions. First, what is the dogmatic function of perichoresis? It is clear that the doctrine on its own cannot explain the unity of the Godhead. I have introduced some functions of the doctrine in exploring three metaphors above, but it would be helpful at this juncture to state clearly and succinctly the doctrine's role. Second, Moltmann rightly identifies patterns in Scripture that imply mutual indwelling in creational, eschatological, soteriological, and ecclesial contexts, but he fails to explain properly the distinctions between trinitarian perichoresis and these patterns of speech. This is a question that has been neglected in some areas of the tradition. For example, Francis Turretin simply dismisses the connection between perichoresis and union: "And if believers are said to dwell in God and he in them (1 John 3:24; John 14:23) on account of the intimate presence of the Spirit (who is the strictest bond of their communion with God), does it not follow that such an *emperichōrēsis* can be attributed to them? There is the widest difference between the mystical union of believers with God and the divine union of the persons of the Trinity in nature, or of the human and divine natures in the person of Christ."[63]

Surely, something more must be said to clarify the relation between union and perichoresis. So, we must ask, How does trinitarian perichoresis relate to such doctrines as union with Christ, ecclesiology, and eschatology? The remainder of this chapter will seek to answer these two questions.

The Dogmatic Function of Perichoresis

The doctrine of trinitarian perichoresis builds on the Johannine language of the Father and Son reciprocally being within one another (John 10:38; 14:10; 17:21, 23) and on Paul's language of the Spirit within God searching his depths (1 Cor. 2:10–11) to clarify the nature of divine consubstantiality,

---

61. Kilby, "Perichoresis and Projection," 441.
62. Kilby, "Perichoresis and Projection," 442.
63. Turretin, *Institutes of Elenctic Theology* 3.23.13.

procession, action, and personhood. Perichoresis, at its simplest level, is a way of affirming distinction without separation. The doctrine is meant to qualify divine unity to preserve distinction, while qualifying divine plurality to preserve unity. In the Trinity, perichoresis clarifies consubstantiality by implying a spatial coinherence and mutual indwelling. Consubstantiality can thus speak of one substance in three modes of existence because these three modes are within the substance and within one another. Perichoresis also clarifies the divine processions by showing that spiration and generation occur within the Father, such that the Son and Spirit mutually indwell one another. As Amos Yong notes, this means that perichoresis can be a particularly important response to Oneness Pentecostals who accuse trinitarians of tritheism. The accusation does not hold, because perichoresis demonstrates that the persons are not "outside or alongside" one another.[64] The mutual indwelling and interpenetration of the divine persons also sets up one metaphysical precondition for the inseparability of the actions of the Father, Son, and Spirit in creation, discussed in chapter 7. Finally, the doctrine of perichoresis serves to clarify the idea of divine personhood. Though there is one mind, will, and love proper to the single divine nature, the coinherence of the Father, Son, and Holy Spirit allows us to speak of three persons who perfectly share the singular mind, will, and love.

Perichoresis and Salvation

Though Moltmann's reliance on perichoresis in explaining the divine unity is problematic, he does have legitimate insights when he connects the doctrine of perichoresis to God's salvific work of creation, though we must modify his account with certain dogmatic corrections. The New Testament is filled with language that describes the relationship between Christ and the faithful in a way that parallels the perichoretic language found in John 10:38; 14:10; and 17:21–23. I have already noted the rather obvious example of the parallel between the unity of the Father and Son and the unity of the Son and the church, found in John 17:21–23. A more extensive example is found in Paul's frequent use of the language of union with Christ. On eighty-three occasions the Pauline corpus uses language of "in Christ," with an additional forty-seven instances of "in the Lord."[65] Paul's meaning for such phrases is

64. Yong, *Renewing Christian Theology*, 301.
65. Dunn, *Theology of Paul the Apostle*, 396–97. Similar concepts are found in the Johannine corpus, and occasionally the phrase itself or its equivalents are seen in other New Testament literature. See Acts 4:2; 1 Pet. 3:16; 5:10, 14; Jude 1; Rev. 1:9; 14:13.

widely discussed and quite complex, but it is generally agreed that Christians being "in Christ" entails objective aspects and subjective aspects.[66] The objective aspects include both the spatial imagery of a "mutual indwelling," involving a state where Christ and the church "co-inhere in one another,"[67] and the active imagery of Christians participating in the key operations or movements of Christ's life, such as his death and resurrection.[68] The latter aspect is particularly evidenced in the *syn-* compounds found throughout the letters, where Paul adds the prefix *syn-*, meaning "with," to describe various events in a Christian's life. For example, a Christian has been "crucified with him," "died with [him]," and been "buried with him," all so that we may "live with him" (Rom. 6:4–8).[69] The subjective aspects include having the "mind of Christ" (1 Cor. 2:16) and being aware of the ongoing presence of Christ in our lives.[70] There is clear conceptual overlap between the doctrine of union with Christ and perichoresis.

We can add to this conceptual overlap the fact that union with Christ is clearly trinitarian in Paul. Though he may lack the full metaphysical explanation of the Trinity that we have been exploring in this work, seventeen of the eighty-three uses of "in Christ" coordinate the phrase with the work of another divine person (Rom. 8:2, 39; 1 Cor. 1:4, 30; 2 Cor. 5:19; Gal. 3:14, 26; Eph. 1:3; 2:6–7, 10; 3:21; 4:32; Phil. 3:14; 4:7, 19; 1 Thess. 5:18), and the number is even higher if we include Paul's language of "in him," "into Christ," and "in the Lord."[71] This coordination can involve the Father's work in and through the Son (1 Cor. 1:4; Eph. 1:4), our being brought into the Father's presence in Christ (Eph. 2:6), and the fullness of the Father's presence dwelling in Christ (Col. 1:19). The examples given may suggest a binitarian theology, but the work of the Holy Spirit is also integral to union with Christ. First, Paul's language of the Spirit's presence in Christians (Rom. 8:9, 11; 1 Cor. 3:16; 6:19) and Christians' presence "in the Spirit" (Rom. 8:9) parallels his concept of union with Christ. Christians are both "part of Christ's body" (1 Cor. 6:15) and a "temple of the Holy Spirit" (1 Cor. 6:19), and the two are apparently recognized by Paul as parallel concepts with parallel ethical implications. By the way, the fact that this indwelling presence of the Spirit makes us a temple, God's dwelling on earth, is further evidence for the divinity of

66. Dunn, *Theology of Paul the Apostle*, 397–98. Some scholars prefer to emphasize the objective dimensions; see Ridderbos, *Paul*, 59.
67. Campbell, *Paul and Union with Christ*, 410.
68. Campbell, *Paul and Union with Christ*, 408. Cf. Dunn, *Theology of Paul the Apostle*, 401–2.
69. Note that in the original Greek, the English phrases "crucified with him," "buried with him," and "live with him" are each a single word with the prefix *syn-*, meaning "with-."
70. Dunn, *Theology of Paul the Apostle*, 400.
71. Campbell, *Paul and Union with Christ*, 126–41.

the Holy Spirit.[72] Second, there is evidence that Paul understands our union with Christ to be linked to the work of the Holy Spirit. This is evident, for example, in Romans 8, where the "Spirit of life in Christ Jesus" is the one who has freed us from the law to live in Christ (8:2). This same Spirit is both the "Spirit of God" and the "Spirit of Christ" (8:9), a fact that could either be taken dogmatically as explaining the processions, in which case it would endorse the *filioque*, or be interpreted as a gesture to perichoresis, with the mutual interpenetration of the two meaning that the work of the Spirit necessarily draws the believer into the work of Christ.[73] The same is true in John 17, which Köstenberger and Swain explain as follows: "Though the Spirit remains 'anonymous,' literally unnamed, in Jesus' high-priestly prayer, his *characteristic mode of activity* cannot be missed. Indeed, there is a real sense in which the Holy Spirit is both the basis of and the answer to every one of Jesus' petitions."[74] Union with Christ is therefore linked both to indwelling by the Spirit and to the coinherent operations of Son and Spirit.

Dogmatically, we can join perichoresis to the doctrine of salvation by insisting that as we are united to Christ by the Spirit, we are also united to the Father in whom the Son and Spirit coinhere. As James Steward once wrote, "The more any man comes to be 'in Christ,' the more he is 'in God.'"[75] This is why Paul can write that we are "hidden with Christ in God" (Col. 3:3). This pattern makes it entirely appropriate to say with Marcus Peter Johnson that "by virtue of being incorporated into the life of Jesus Christ, we participate in the life, love, and fellowship of the Trinity."[76] What is less clear is how to distinguish this union with Christ from perichoresis.

Though the exegetical parallels between union and perichoresis are clear, the metaphysical distinctions between the two concepts are not always clearly expressed. To distinguish properly between trinitarian perichoresis and believers' union with Christ, four differences must be maintained. I will briefly outline each before concluding the chapter.

Duration and Change of Sharing

One simple difference between the perichoretic relationships of Father, Son, and Spirit and believers' union with Christ is that of duration. Paul's language of "in Christ" is paired with imagery, especially baptismal imagery, of "into

72. See the discussion in R. N. Davies, *Doctrine of the Trinity*, 222.
73. Part of this content is explained in greater detail in Ray, "Was Paul a Trinitarian?," 340–43.
74. Köstenberger and Swain, *Father, Son and Spirit*, 176.
75. J. S. Steward, *A Man in Christ*, 170.
76. M. P. Johnson, *One with Christ*, 42.

Christ," suggesting a "definite beginning."[77] For example, Romans 6 begins by explaining that Christians have been baptized into Christ (6:3) before moving to insist that this was "in order that, just as Christ was raised from the dead by the glory of the Father, so we too may walk in newness of life" (6:4). Because of baptism, we were crucified with Christ (6:6), we died with him (6:8), and now we are "alive to God in Christ Jesus" (6:11). Baptism into Christ initiates this process of union. In John 17, Jesus claims a preexistence and unity with the Father that was "before the world existed" (17:5) and "before the world's foundation" (17:24). The disciples, however, receive unity with the Father, Son, and Holy Spirit in time. This fact suggests that union is changeable and can be received and even developed—we "grow in every way into him who is the head" (Eph. 4:15). Perichoresis, by contrast, does not begin or change.[78] Trinitarian perichoresis is eternal and immutable. In Christology, the claim that the human nature was enhypostatic but never anhypostatic, meaning that Christ's humanity only ever existed in the divine person of the Son, shows that there was never a point when a preexisting, autonomous human nature was brought into a perichoretic relationship with Christ's divinity by newly being assumed by the person of the Son. While union with Christ allows Christians to begin to share in the triune life, that life has eternally been common to Father, Son, and Spirit.

Extent of Sharing

Traditionally, theologians have distinguished between the **communicable attributes** that God graciously allows creatures to participate in and the **incommunicable attributes** that he reserves for himself. For example, God bestows his holiness on us, but humans never receive simplicity or aseity. In the context of John 17, we see several communicable attributes: as Jesus has God's glory (17:5), so the church has God's glory (17:22); and both Jesus and the disciples are sanctified (17:19). We do not, however, see that John attributes being creator to humans as he does to the Word (1:3). Union allows Christians to share in certain divine attributes, but trinitarian perichoresis is a complete and perfect sharing between Father, Son, and Holy Spirit.[79] As Gregory Palamas notes, we participate in Christ and the divine nature (2 Pet. 1:4), and "that

---

77. Dunn, *Theology of Paul the Apostle*, 410.

78. Twombly, *Perichoresis and Personhood*, 100.

79. There may be a difference between trinitarian and christological perichoresis here. E.g., Kathryn Tanner raises the following concern: "Unlike the case of the trinitarian Persons, the natures that interpenetrate are different, and it is unlikely the co-inherence is fully mutual. (Jesus' humanity may be fully suffused with the divine; but the Word's being fully suffused with the human is a much more controversial claim, involving a denial of a Logos apart from Jesus. Even the former case is problematic, encouraging insistence on something like Christ's resurrected

which is said to participate in something possesses a part of that in which it participates; for if it participates not in part but in the whole, then strictly speaking it does not participate in but possesses that whole."[80] Union reveals that our salvation includes the analogical reception of certain divine attributes proper to the Trinity, but we never become God.

The Ontological Basis for Sharing

Though there are divine attributes that are communicable, it is important to recognize that humans possess these attributes "not in the same mode nor with the same meaning."[81] This claim may appear to contradict John's teaching that we are one "just as" (*kathōs*) the Father and Son are one (John 17:11, 21). Aware of Arian interpretations of this Johannine language, which reduced the Son to a creature participating in the divine nature just as created humans do, pro-Nicene theology interpreted the phrase "just as" to indicate an imitation, not an ontological equivalence.[82] We participate in God by grace, whereas the unity between Father, Son, and Spirit is by nature of their consubstantiality. The Son's coinherence in the Father (John 10:38) is introduced in the context of his consubstantiality (10:30).[83] Because God is simple, we do not possess the divine attributes in the same manner that God does.[84] Rather, we analogically share in them by virtue of God's grace. The overlap between the concepts of union and perichoresis shows the trinitarian shape of salvation. We are adopted as sons and daughters (Eph. 1:5), sharing in the filial status of the Son, to whom we are united. Yet, we remain *adopted* by grace through the work of the indwelling Spirit (Rom. 8:14–15). We are not sons and daughters by nature. Christ remains the only begotten Son.

Symmetry in Perichoresis and Union

Father, Son, and Spirit are fully in one another and fully defined by their relations with one another. To be God the Father is simply to be the one who begets the Son and spirates the Spirit. This unity amid distinction is constitutive of the life of the Father. By contrast, though in a real sense the Christian's life is

---

life—the glorified humanity of Christ—before the crucifixion.)" (*Jesus, Humanity and the Trinity*, 23). Full treatment of this question must be reserved for a work focusing on Christology.

80. Palamas, *Topics of Natural and Theological Science* §110. The concept used by Palamas and by Peter is the Greek *koinonia*. Note that the word "part" here must not be taken to be a denial of divine simplicity.

81. Ames, *Marrow of Theology* 1.4.30.

82. Durand, *La périchorèse des personnes divines*, 286.

83. Aquinas, *Commentary on the Gospel of John* §2214.

84. Palamas, *Topics of Natural and Theological Science* §109.

constituted by their relation to the Father though the power of the indwelling Spirit that unites us to Christ our mediator, this is not a reciprocal relation. The Father, Son, and Spirit's identities and life are not constituted by the believer with whom they abide. Thus, there is a fundamental asymmetry in union with Christ that is not found in trinitarian perichoresis. This point may not apply to all varieties of perichoresis. Notably, many theologians have argued that christological perichoresis cannot be entirely symmetric, for Christ's divine nature permeates the human in ways that his human cannot permeate the divine.[85] Even here, the asymmetry is less than that seen in union with Christ.

These four points of difference between perichoresis and union are enough to ensure a distinction between God and creation, but we ought not to emphasize this distinction to the point that the genuine parallels between perichoresis and union with Christ are lost. The perichoretic divine life of the Trinity is one that is graciously bestowed in time to those who are united to Christ, that they may asymmetrically share in part of the divine life that is communicated to them by God. Though they do not become additional divine persons who share the simple divine essence, Christians do have their natures restored to be in the image of God through Christ, who is the very image itself (2 Cor. 3:18). We remain creatures, yet creatures who are adopted as sons and daughters, having a relationship to the Father that parallels the Son's relationship because we are in him and he in us. Perichoresis therefore reveals the fundamentally trinitarian shape of salvation.

A Concluding Ecclesiological and Eschatological Note

While this chapter has focused on the dogmatic function of perichoresis in the doctrine of the Trinity, as well as this doctrine's implications for salvation when properly distinguished from union with Christ, more could be said in describing the relationship between perichoresis, ecclesiology, and eschatology. I want to conclude the chapter by briefly exploring these connections. First, we should note that the basic biblical imagery of mutual indwelling applies to the entire creation eschatologically, with the hope that "God may be all in all" (1 Cor. 15:28). When Scripture speaks of a Christian's union with Christ, it is also clear that there are corporate aspects of this union. The one who is joined with Christ is part of a body with many members (1 Cor. 12:12–14), and union with Christ brings about a unity between Jews and gentiles in which they form a corporate whole (Eph. 2:11–22). Within this context Paul

---

85. K. A. Richardson, "Uncreated and Created Perichoretic Relations," 91; Tanner, *Jesus, Humanity and Trinity*, 23; Harrison, "Perichoresis in the Greek Fathers," 63.

speaks of the entire church as a temple (Eph. 2:21), and elsewhere he says that individuals are temples too (1 Cor. 6:19). Second, while John of Damascus never uses perichoresis to describe the relationship between God and the created world or between Christ and the believer,[86] perichoresis may play some role in Maximus the Confessor's vision of cosmic redemption.[87] This would be an atypical pattern of use, but not one entirely beyond the bounds of the Christian tradition. Can we therefore speak, with Constantine Scouteris, of the church "filled with the Holy Trinity" in a manner that is related to perichoresis without confusing the distinction between God and creation?[88]

My answer to this question is a qualified yes. I have attempted to show the structural parallels of union with Christ and perichoresis in order to demonstrate that salvation is fundamentally trinitarian in nature, with the result that Christians in some sense share in the life of the Trinity. Yet, I have also insisted that this sharing in the divine life is distinct from the perichoresis of which it is an image. In contrast with perichoresis, union is not eternal, is incomplete, is by grace and not by nature, and is asymmetric. Since Christian conversion initiates a process that terminates in our eschatological glorification, we should expect eschatology to be trinitarian in its contours, just as conversion is. Since union with Christ entails union with those who are also joined with him—that is, the church—we should expect parallels between ecclesiology and trinitarian perichoresis. Perichoresis illustrates aspects of ecclesiology and eschatology, yet the eschatological dwelling of the Father in this world and the indwelling of the church by the Trinity must be carefully distinguished from perichoresis, just as eschatology and ecclesiology must be carefully distinguished from the doctrine of union itself. Though there is much left to say about the relationship between perichoresis, ecclesiology, and eschatology, I hope that naming the need to explore how Father, Son, and Spirit mutually indwell one another in a manner that spills into other doctrines dispels any idea that the doctrine of the Trinity is detached from the gospel and the ministry of the church.

FOR FURTHER READING

Historical and Biblical Studies of Perichoresis

Köstenberger, Andreas J., and Scott R. Swain. *Father, Son and Spirit: The Trinity and John's Gospel.* Downers Grove, IL: InterVarsity, 2008.

86. Twombly, *Perichoresis and Personhood*, 93.
87. Harrison, "Perichoresis in the Greek Fathers," 65.
88. Scouteris, *Ecclesial Being*, 28–43.

Offering a close theological reading of John, this text explores, in a manner informed by both theology and biblical studies, many of the passages that are fundamental to an understanding of perichoresis.

Twombly, Charles C. *Perichoresis and Personhood: God, Christ, and Salvation in John of Damascus*. Eugene, OR: Pickwick, 2015.

Twombly provides extensive analysis of John of Damascus's treatment of the doctrine of perichoresis in its christological, trinitarian, and soteriological dimensions. This work is one of the few book-length treatments of perichoresis in historical and systematic perspective in the English language.

Perichoresis in Systematic Theology

Baker-Fletcher, Karen. *Dancing with God: The Trinity from a Womanist Perspective*. St. Louis: Chalice, 2006.

Baker-Fletcher relies heavily on perichoresis, deploying several creative and clarifying exegetical moves to explore the doctrine, and uses social trinitarianism to explore questions in spirituality and ethics. This work represents many modern trends in trinitarianism.

Moltmann, Jürgen. *The Trinity and the Kingdom*. Translated by Margaret Kohl. San Francisco: Harper & Row, 1981.

Moltmann's widely influential treatment of the Trinity helped place perichoresis in the center of modern discussions of the doctrine of the Trinity, though often in problematic ways, as explored in this chapter.

CHAPTER 6

Missions

The first five chapters of this book focused on the inner life of God *in se*. This is not to say that doctrines like consubstantiality or perichoresis do not spill over into the work of God in history. As explored already in this work, consubstantiality has significant ramifications for the structure of Christian worship, and perichoresis is the foundation for the broad contours of the salvation of Christians in union with Christ, to cite only two examples. Yet, had God chosen not to create worshiping humans (or angels) who were foreknown to need salvation, the Father, Son, and Holy Spirit would eternally remain consubstantial, eternally interpenetrating and indwelling one another. By contrast, the final three chapters of this book focus on the acts of the Trinity in the economy, acts that the Christian tradition has long considered contingent. This chapter will begin to address the contingent acts of God by introducing the doctrine of the divine missions. A divine mission is a voluntary extension of the divine processions into creation through the assumption of a created term, a concept explained later in this chapter. The missions are concisely summarized in Galatians 4:4–6: "When the time came to completion, God sent his Son, born of a woman, born under the law, to redeem those under the law, so that we might receive adoption as sons. And because you are sons, God sent the Spirit of his Son into our hearts crying, 'Abba, Father!'"

A theology of the divine missions was developed in its basic contours well before any extensive dogmatic explanation of such concepts as divine personhood, the processions, or consubstantiality. Consider Irenaeus of Lyons, a second-century Christian theologian, who frequently speaks of the Son and

Holy Spirit as the two hands of God.[1] Though Irenaeus generally uses this language with respect to creation—the Son and Spirit are those to whom God said, "Let us make man in our image" (Gen. 1:26), and through these hands God fashioned humankind—he also uses this language to speak of the assumption of Enoch and of Elijah (Gen. 5:24; 2 Kings 2:11).[2] God's hands play a role in making humanity and in returning humanity to the presence of God. Irenaeus's metaphor of the Son and Spirit as God's hands finds a dogmatic foundation in the clear distinction that Irenaeus draws between God's economy and the inner being of God.[3] Though Irenaeus writes before the development of the doctrine of consubstantiality, he is clear that Son and Spirit are within the inner life of God. In the economy, Irenaeus explains, the Son's incarnation revealed the Father, for God is invisible and therefore cannot be known to humans, who know and learn through the physical senses.[4] For this reason the Son took on flesh to become visible and reveal the Father.[5]

Irenaeus's concept of the divine missions raises a number of issues that this chapter will explore. I will begin with an analysis of the biblical basis for divine missions, considering both what evidence there is that the saving work of the Son and Holy Spirit is rooted in their antecedent eternal being with the Father and also what the divine missions contribute to the exegetical case for the divinity of the Son and Holy Spirit. Having explored these exegetical topics, I will next consider metaphysical issues, of which there are two. First, Irenaeus distinguishes between the economy and inner life of God, but this distinction requires a clear dogmatic formulation of the connection between economy and triune life *in se*, a topic much explored in twentieth- and twenty-first-century theology. Second, since the account of God's life *in se* explored in the first five chapters insisted that God is simple and immutable, the possibility of contingent divine missions requires clarification: How can a simple being perform acts that could be otherwise? After treating these metaphysical questions, I will conclude the chapter with a brief summary of the ways that the divine missions shape other doctrines.

1. Irenaeus, *Against Heresies* 4.20.1–2; 5.1.3; 5.55.1; 5.28.4; etc. Some believe that Irenaeus's imagery here may derive from Theophilus of Antioch (see Lashier, *Irenaeus on the Trinity*, 213n78). I will focus on Irenaeus because he arguably had a more robust account of the divine missions than Theophilus.

2. Irenaeus, *Against Heresies* 4.5.1. Lashier notes that every time Irenaeus uses the imagery of God's hands, he does so in the context of citing Gen. 1:26 (*Irenaeus on the Trinity*, 214).

3. Kelly, *Early Christian Doctrines*, 104.

4. Irenaeus, *Against Heresies* 4.6.6.

5. Michel Barnes notes, "The Son's visibility, which for Irenaeus is the same as his materiality, is the necessary means for making the invisible known to the visible, the immaterial known to the material, for humans know and learn through material senses" ("Irenaeus's Trinitarian Theology," 88).

Scripture and the Divine Missions

The biblical roots of the divine missions are found throughout the Old Testament. For example, the prophets promise a coming Messiah, and God repeatedly sends the Holy Spirit to accomplish divine purposes (e.g., Exod. 31:3; Num. 11:17, 29; Joel 2:28–29).[6] Occasionally, this sending may even take on a trinitarian structure, Isaiah 48 being a notable yet debated case. Verses 12–16a involve God speaking as one who "founded the earth" as the "first and last" (48:13), the one who called the servant (48:15). In historical context, the servant refers to Cyrus the Great, the Persian leader who had introduced policies allowing the Israelites to return from exile and restore worship in the temple. When, in Isaiah 48:16b, the speaker shifts away from God, it is somewhat unclear who is saying, "And now the LORD God has sent me and his Spirit." Modern interpreters look at the historical context and conclude either that the original human author understands Cyrus himself to speak here[7] or that perhaps Isaiah inserts his own voice.[8] However, early Christian interpreters, who recognize that Isaiah's servant (the subject of this section of the book of Isaiah) is a type of Christ and who believe that the inspiration of the prophets allows for meaning beyond what was intelligible to the historical authors, prefer a trinitarian reading. For example, Origen, Ambrose, Athanasius, and Didymus the Blind all interpret this passage through prosopological exegesis, though there is some disagreement in terms of how to read the verse: Does the Son speak of the Father sending him and the Spirit to accomplish the divine plan, or does the Son speak of being sent by the Father and Spirit?[9] Either interpretation is decidedly trinitarian. The former would highlight how the missions are rooted in the processions, the latter the inseparable operations of the Trinity.

In the New Testament, we see more extensive treatment of the Father sending the Son and Spirit (e.g., John 14:16; Gal. 4:4), of the Son sending the Spirit (e.g., John 15:26; 16:7; Acts 2:33), and of the Spirit empowering the coming of the Son (e.g., Luke 1:35; 4:17–19). The broader theology of the New Testament helps us grasp a deeper understanding of the divine missions and establish an exegetical foundation for a full dogmatic account.

---

6. Note, however, that the more common formula speaks of the Holy Spirit actively coming upon certain individuals, a fact that further affirms the personality of the Holy Spirit. See, e.g., Judg. 3:10; 11:29; 1 Sam. 10:10; 16:13; 2 Chron. 15:1.

7. The case is extensively argued in Wegner, "Isaiah 48:16," 233–44.

8. Oswalt, *Book of Isaiah*, 278.

9. See Origen, *Commentary on the Gospel according to John* 2.81; Athanasius, *Letters to Serapion on the Holy Spirit* 1.13.3; Didymus the Blind, *On the Holy Spirit* §117; Ambrose, *Of the Christian Faith* 2.9.

Preexistence

One central component of the divine missions is the preexistence of the Son and Spirit, who are sent. The term "preexistence" needs further clarification, as it can possess several meanings. First, we must distinguish between **ideal preexistence**, where a being exists in the mind of God in potency prior to its creation, and **actual preexistence**, where a being exists in act prior to a specific time.[10] Ideal preexistence is often criticized as a weak concept, given that omniscience means all beings would have ideal preexistence.[11] Within the category of actual preexistence, several further distinctions are necessary. Protological preexistence refers to a being existing prior to creation, and eschatological preexistence refers to a being existing before its future eschatological manifestation.[12] There is also a sort of preexistence we might call heavenly—this variety is apparently given a technical name less frequently—which refers to a being that did not exist prior to creation but that did exist prior to some past manifestation. This term would apply to created angels revealed in Old Testament manifestations. The theology of the divine missions holds to the protological preexistence of both the Son and Spirit.

The protological preexistence of the Holy Spirit has, understandably, not been the subject of much debate.[13] The case for it is fairly straightforward for those who accept that the Spirit is a distinct hypostasis (and this hypostatic distinction is the focal point of much modern debate). Not only is the Holy Spirit seen in Genesis 1:2 "hovering over the surface of the waters," but we also see language of the "eternal Spirit" in Hebrews 9:14, to cite only two examples.[14] The protological preexistence of the Son is the subject of wider disagreement. While his personality is obvious in Scripture, his preexistence is not as evident to all interpreters as one might think. For example, James Dunn argues that a clear concept of real preexistence is only found in the Gospel of John.[15] Karl-Josef Kuschel goes a step further to argue that Matthew and

---

10. The basic distinction was extensively developed in the work of Harnack, who saw ideal preexistence as a distinctively Jewish idea and real preexistence as Hellenistic (Harnack, *History of Dogma*, 1:318–34). Such sharp dichotomies are not tenable, given the mixture of Hellenistic and Jewish culture in the first century.

11. Gathercole, *Preexistent Son*, 12; McCready, *He Came Down from Heaven*, 17.

12. Hamerton-Kelly, *Pre-existence*, 21.

13. This becomes evident when one compares how frequently works of theology and biblical studies refer to the preexistence of Christ with how frequently they refer to the preexistence of the Spirit. The preexistence of the Spirit is so settled that the subject is rarely even included in the index of most relevant works of theology.

14. Despite some scholarly debate, Hebrews' exclusive prior use of *pneuma* thus far for the Holy Spirit, combined with common Jewish notions of Spirit-enabled sacrifice, compels me to see a reference to the Holy Spirit. See Pierce, *Divine Discourse*, 230n47, for a survey of opinions.

15. Dunn, *Christology in the Making*, 259.

Luke's theology of the virginal conception and the idea of real preexistence are "logically exclusive," suggesting that Matthew and Luke intentionally avoid speaking in terms of preexistence in order to center a different and contradictory theological motif.[16] He claims that virginal conception clearly implies that Jesus was begotten at the time of conception and that Matthew and Luke deploy this concept to avoid a possible docetism that would downplay or deny the real humanity of Christ.[17]

The preexistence of the Son in the New Testament can be established by appeal to several sets of evidence. First, the Synoptic Gospels have numerous statements that combine "I have come" or "the Son of man came" (or a variant) with a purpose statement.[18] For example, in Luke 19:10, Jesus says, "The Son of Man has come to seek and to save the lost." Besides being a sweeping purpose statement for the entire incarnate life of Jesus, this statement mirrors God's responsibility to seek and save his lost flock of sheep (Ezek. 34:10–22).[19] While some have explained these statements as referring to Jesus's prophetic role or his geographic migration, such explanations are not compelling.[20] Jesus identifies his reason for coming with a sweeping purpose statement that characterizes his entire life and ministry. Furthermore, the Gospel of John explicitly deploys similar statements in terms of coming from heaven (6:38, 42) or coming into the world (9:39; 12:46; 16:28; 18:37),[21] as does the noncanonical Nag Hamadi text Sophia of Jesus Christ.[22] This evidence, dating from shortly after the composition of the Synoptics, suggests that Christians understood the Synoptic statements as indicating the real preexistence of the Son who came into the world. It is also significant that when we survey textual precedents for the Synoptic formula, the best analogues are the purpose statements of angels, who are also examples of real (but not protological) preexistence.[23]

Real preexistence is also evident when Paul explains that though Christ Jesus existed "in the form [morphē] of God, [he] did not consider equality

16. Kuschel, Born before All Time?, 318.

17. Kuschel, Born before All Time?, 323–26.

18. Simon Gathercole notes three forms of the statement in the Synoptics: passages where demons ask why Jesus came (Mark 1:24 // Luke 4:34; Matt. 8:29); statements where Jesus says "I have come" and adds a purpose statement (Mark 1:38; Mark 2:17 // Matt. 9:13; Luke 5:32; Matt. 5:17; Luke 12:49; Matt 10:34 // Luke 12:51; Matt. 10:35); and statements that include "the Son of Man came" with an infinitive statement (Mark 10:45 // Luke 12:51; Luke 19:10) (Gathercole, Preexistent Son, 84).

19. Gathercole, Preexistent Son, 168–69.

20. See the treatment in Gathercole, Preexistent Son, 95–109.

21. Gathercole, Preexistent Son, 83.

22. See Sophia of Jesus Christ 3.96.19–21; 3.106.6–9; 3.118.15–19 (Gathercole, Preexistent Son, 86).

23. See Gathercole, Preexistent Son, 92–147.

with God as something to be exploited. Instead he emptied himself, taking the form of a servant, taking on the likeness of humanity" (Phil. 2:6–7). This passage has been heavily debated, with some arguing that it does not prove the Son's codivinity with the Father and others denying that it suggests preexistence. In an early writing, James Dunn argues that this passage refers to Jesus having the image of God as Adam did but, unlike Adam, not grasping for equality with God, instead living in a humble manner.[24] However, several features of the text persuade me that Paul has the real preexistence of the Son in mind. First, Paul places the claim that Christ "assumed the form of a servant" in parallel with his "taking on the likeness of humanity," suggesting a contrast between the "form of God" that Christ already possessed and the "likeness of humanity" that he took on and implying that verse 6 refers to Christ's status before assuming this form of humanity. "The form of God" in verse 6, then, does not refer to the image of God, which is already a human possession. Second, Paul would have the language of God's image at hand to use if it was intended, so his reference to the "form" (*morphē*) of God (2:6) likely indicates that he has something else in mind: possessing the characteristics that God manifests.[25] Third, Paul writes of two successive steps: Christ "emptied himself" in taking the form of a servant (2:7), then he "humbled himself" to the point of dying on a cross (2:8). As Michael Gorman summarizes, "The divine one emptied himself by becoming a slave, becoming human. So, too, the human one humbled himself by becoming obedient to death."[26] Fourth, Paul presents the narrative of Christ as a moral example for the believers (2:3, 5). Jesus behaving in a way opposite to Adam in not seeking to elevate himself could serve as a moral example; however, Paul's emphasis on humility (2:3) and his appeal elsewhere to Jesus giving up riches for poverty (2 Cor. 8:9) suggest that a move from preexistent glory to humility is in mind.[27] Fifth and finally, the language of the Son "emptying himself" attributes preexistent agency to the Son, suggesting something more than ideal preexistence.[28]

For further evidence of Pauline belief in preexistence, we turn to Colossians 1:15–16, which teaches that Christ is "the firstborn over all creation"

24. Dunn, *Christology in the Making*, 114–21. See a concise, helpful survey of both positions in McCready, *He Came Down from Heaven*, 77–79. Dunn has since softened his position on the matter, though it is not clear he would accept full protological, real preexistence (see Dunn, "Christ, Adam, and Preexistence," 74–83).

25. In any event, it is not clear that *morphē* and *eikon* have identical meaning (see Steenburg, "Case against the Synonymity").

26. Gorman, *Inhabiting the Cruciform God*, 22.

27. See Hamerton-Kelly, *Pre-existence*, 167, 194.

28. Harnack, *History of Dogma*, 3:327.

but also insists that "everything was created by him, in heaven and on earth" and that "all things have been created through him and for him."[29] Some modern exegetes suggest that Christ's title "firstborn over all creation" may imply that Jesus was the first creature and therefore had preexistence from the moment of creation.[30] This conclusion follows a common trend in the anti-Nicene exegesis of Asterius and Arius as well as the so-called dedication creed from Antioch, arguably non-Nicene in emphasis.[31] Against this kind of reasoning, the common pro-Nicene argument is that Jesus must be eternal, for he created everything that was created (John 1:3; Col. 1:16).[32] As Gregory of Nyssa summarizes, "If the creation was by him, but he was not [created] by himself," which Gregory rightly concludes, given that nothing can cause itself, "plainly he is something outside of creation."[33]

Preexistence is most clearly evident in the Gospel of John, a fact rarely contested in the literature.[34] Jesus is the preexistent Word who was with God in the beginning (1:1) and through whom all creation was made (1:3). These claims clearly demonstrate real protological preexistence in John, a claim easily supported elsewhere in the Gospel (3:13; 8:26, 58; 16:28; 17:5). From a canonical perspective, then, John by itself provides sufficient grounds for holding to the protological preexistence of the Son. Given claims that other Gospels directly contradict preexistence, I have provided further evidence to support the real preexistence of the Son. This truth, taken together with the real preexistence of the Spirit, reveals that the divine missions involve divine hypostases already in existence becoming manifest and active in creation in new ways.

29. Of course, some interpreters would not take Colossians to be authentically Pauline, so they would not count this evidence as particularly decisive.

30. Raymond Brown considers this possibility in *Introduction to New Testament Christology*, 135–36. Dunn suggests Paul's thought is characterized by "ambivalence" here (Dunn, *Christology in the Making*, 189).

31. See Ayres, *Nicaea and Its Legacy*, 54, 118–21.

32. The argument is a favorite of Athanasius, found in *Orations against the Arians* 2.18–19, 21; *To the Bishops of Egypt* §15; *To the Bishops of Africa* §4. See also Hilary of Poitiers, *On the Trinity* 4.16.

33. Gregory of Nyssa, *Against Eunomius* 1.23. Nothing can cause itself, for it would have to exist to cause something, but would not exist prior to being caused. It would thus have to exist and not exist at the same time, violating the law of noncontradiction.

34. E.g., both Dunn and Kuschel, cited above as skeptics of preexistence in the Synoptics and Paul, grant preexistence in the Fourth Gospel (see Dunn, *Christology in the Making*, 249–50; Kuschel, *Born before All Time?*, 383–84). Dunn believes that John is the first to reconcile the theology of the personal eschatological figure of Christ and the impersonal preexistent Word or Wisdom. Kuschel admits preexistence but argues that this is a peripheral concern for John put in service of his larger concern: demonstrating the "origin of the revealer Jesus from God and the unity of Jesus with God" (384).

Missions as Theophanies

The New Testament provides further guidance in understanding the divine missions when it presents the Son as the manifestation of the Father. This is a recurring theme in the Gospel of John, where Jesus teaches that whoever has seen him has seen the Father (14:9), a point also clearly made in the prologue's insistence that "no one has ever seen God. The one and only Son, who is himself God and is at the Father's side—he has revealed him" (1:18). As T. F. Torrance remarks, "Since it is only through himself that God reveals himself, God himself is the personal content of his revelation to us embodied in Jesus Christ his incarnate Son."[35] The mission of the Son must be interpreted as a **theophany**, a manifestation of God in Jesus Christ, to use a central theme in much pro-Nicene theology.[36] Or to use the terminology of much modern theology, Christ is the self-revelation, self-communication, and self-disclosure of God.

More yet can be said on this subject, for God's self-revelation is triadic in nature. In a telling passage in the Gospel of Luke, Jesus unfolds an implicitly trinitarian theology of knowing God. He begins by rejoicing in the Holy Spirit, praising the Father for entrusting "all things" to the Son (10:21–22).[37] Jesus's prayer in the Spirit immediately follows the successful ministry of the seventy-two (10:17–20), foreshadowing the Spirit's role in the early church's missionary witness to Christ.[38] Jesus then explains, "No one knows who the Son is except the Father, and who the Father is except the Son, and anyone to whom the Son desires to reveal him" (10:22). Turning to his disciples, Jesus says, "Blessed are the eyes that see the things you see!" (10:23). The Son has the exclusive prerogative to reveal the Father, but only those who have eyes to see will receive this revelation. Throughout Luke-Acts, the Holy Spirit often plays the role of enabling true sight. At a physical level, the Spirit anoints Christ to restore sight to the blind (Luke 4:18), a proof of Jesus's messianic status (7:22). Similarly, physical sight is stripped from Paul at Christ's appearance on the road to Damascus (Acts 9:8) and is restored when he is filled with the Holy Spirit (9:17). Paul immediately responds in faith, being baptized (9:18). Throughout Luke-Acts these physical healings find a parallel in the Spirit's role in fostering conversion. The disciples must wait for the Spirit before being

35. T. F. Torrance, *Christian Doctrine of God*, 59.
36. E.g., the central biblical passages in Basil of Caesarea's polemical defense of the Trinity focus on how the Son reveals the Father: Matt. 11:27; John 14:9; 17:6. See Hildebrand, *Trinitarian Theology of Basil of Caesarea*, 161–70.
37. This passage itself is one of several implicitly trinitarian moments in the narrative of the Synoptics that could be used to deny modalism.
38. Hur, *Dynamic Reading of the Holy Spirit*, 217.

empowered to witness to the salvific work of Christ (Luke 24:49; Acts 1:4–8). Receiving the Holy Spirit is closely linked to conversion, either as conversion's immediate result (Acts 2:38), as an eventual but delayed consequence (Acts 8:15), or as its immediate antecedent (Acts 10:44). Such passages suggest that the Spirit has a role in preconversion illumination, regeneration unto saving faith, and postconversion charismatic experiences.[39] As the Spirit enables Stephen miraculously to see Christ at the right hand of God (Acts 7:55), so too the spiritual vision of all who believe is enabled by the Holy Spirit. The mission of the Son is a theophany, yet one contingent on our "having eyes to see," an ability itself contingent on the illuminating mission of the Holy Spirit, who reveals the Son as a theophany of the Father.

The scriptural tropes we have considered so far led to some of the earliest trinitarian developments in Christian tradition. Irenaeus's theology of the two hands of God, for example, is situated within a larger vision of the eternal protological preexistence of the Son and Spirit in the Father.[40] It includes the notion that key economic acts of God such as creation involved all three persons,[41] but it also suggests that the Son and Spirit are the means by which the Father accomplishes his work and revelation in creation. Yet, the incarnation of the Son does not separate him from the Father, in whose bosom he is found (John 1:18).[42] Moreover, Irenaeus has a clear sense of the simplicity of God, which would necessitate that the missions of the Son and Spirit, though distinct, necessarily cannot be divided from the other members of the Trinity or understood as indicating a hierarchy of divinity where the economic acts of Son and Spirit reveal the superior deity of the Father.[43] Here again, the unity of the Godhead norms the plurality of the missions, and one might speculate that the Spirit can bring awareness of the Son as the self-revelation of the Father precisely because the three are one simple essence, perichoretically indwelling one another.[44] These reflections move beyond the strict, literal meaning of the Scripture passages just explored, from which these doctrinal reflections are derived.

39. Dogmatic accounts of the Spirit's work regularly attribute illumination and regeneration to the Holy Spirit. E.g., John Owen attributes preparatory illumination and regeneration to the Spirit (*The Holy Spirit*, 138, 189–90).

40. Lashier, *Irenaeus on the Trinity*, 208–9.

41. Lashier, *Irenaeus on the Trinity*, 212–13.

42. Irenaeus, *Against Heresies* 3.11.6. In context, this argument is likely intended to have "anti-gnostic motivation" by ensuring that presence in creation does not "block the continuity between Father and Word-Son" (Barnes, "Irenaeus's Trinitarian Theology," 80).

43. Barnes, "Irenaeus's Trinitarian Theology," 74, 76. Irenaeus is writing precisely to counter these tendencies as found in second-century Gnosticism, though we should not read him anachronistically as if he were fully pro-Nicene.

44. This theme is also found in Irenaeus. See Barnes, "Irenaeus's Trinitarian Theology," 78–79.

Divine Missions and the Divinity of the Son and Spirit

At this juncture it is important to recognize the role that the divine missions play in demonstrating the divinity of the Son and Holy Spirit. Thus far we have already considered a number of biblical reasons for holding to the divinity of the Second and Third Persons of the Trinity. The fact that Father, Son, and Spirit are incorporated into New Testament cultic worship suggests that all three are equally God. There are a number of passages where the title "God" (*theos*) is directly attributed to the Son (John 1:1; 20:28; Rom. 9:5; Titus 2:13; 2 Pet. 1:1), and at least one where the title is attributed to the Spirit (Acts 5:3–4). Several passages also deny a hierarchy of divinity and reject any subordinate divine status of the Son (Rom. 9:5; Col. 1:19; 2:9; Rev. 19:16). Such passages help to make sense of the triplex formulas throughout the New Testament that coordinate the Father, Son, and Spirit in triadic relations such that each person is defined in relation to the others. Prosopological exegesis shows Father, Son, and Holy Spirit related to one another apart from creation and together willing and planning the history of redemption, thus suggesting equality and divinity. Our exploration of perichoresis found that the Holy Spirit knows the very mind of God (1 Cor. 2:10) and that the mutual indwelling of Father, Son, and Spirit is of a greater degree than the indwelling involved in union with Christ or baptism in the Spirit. We can now add preexistence to the biblical case for the doctrine of the Trinity, since the Son and Spirit's protological preexistence rules out any **adoptionist** or modalist interpretation of this data. Yet, the divine missions provide one further, more substantive argument for the doctrine of the Trinity, which we must now consider.

Much trinitarian theology since the turn of the twentieth century has made explicit what was often only implicit in the Christian tradition beforehand: the doctrine of the Trinity derives in large part from the biblical narrative of God's saving work through Christ and the Spirit.[45] To speak more precisely, there is a growing sense that it is the biblical narrative as a whole, not individual prooftexts, that provides the strongest biblical warrant for the Trinity.[46] Fred Sanders argues that, rightly understood, the missions can be interpreted as "the salvation-historical revelation of the triune depths of God."[47] These missions are communicative in that the Spirit inspires the writings of the biblical authors and in that Jesus teaches his disciples verbally.

45. See Jenson, *Systematic Theology*, 1:63–89; LaCugna, *God for Us*, 22, 223; Kasper, *God of Jesus Christ*, 243–49.
46. See F. Sanders, *Triune God*, 162–66 for a discussion of reasons why classical prooftexts have been undermined. See also Kasper, *God of Jesus Christ*, 244; Emery, *The Trinity*, 12.
47. F. Sanders, *Triune God*, 109.

Biblical propositions are part of the revelation of the Trinity.[48] Yet, the Bible is not merely a set of propositions but is also "the authoritative account of the coming of the Son and the Spirit, who themselves bring the revelation of the Trinity,"[49] an account that "came into existence to bear witness that the God of Israel sent his Son and poured out his Holy Spirit."[50]

One of the more noted advocates of this position is Robert Jenson, whose preference is to speak of the triune identity of God over some traditional formulas. Jenson argues that we are unable "to construe the biblical God's self-identity otherwise than by dramatic narrative" and that this narrative requires that the identity of the triune God be constituted at the cross and resurrection, the precise moment when it most appears that there are distinct and opposed divine agents.[51] God the Father is identified as the one who raised Jesus Christ from the dead (Rom. 4:24; 8:11; 1 Cor. 15:15; 2 Cor. 1:9; 1 Pet. 1:21), verifying God's identity as the God of the exodus.[52] The two events reveal the same identity, and the wider triplex structures of the New Testament confirm the centrality of this triune identity.[53] Jenson fears that historical affirmations of a timeless God render the economic manifestation of Father, Son, and Spirit in time a disclosure of something that is not truly God, which is effectively modalism.[54] Furthermore, Jenson fears that the missions may result in subordinationism, as the Son and Spirit who work in time are seen as less than the timeless Father.[55] In his strongest moments, Jenson recognizes that the doctrine of the Trinity is derived from the entire narrative of Scripture, which fundamentally identifies God. Yet, in these same moments, Jenson risks reducing God to this narrative.[56]

Though the role of narrative in establishing the doctrine of the Trinity is substantial, the larger contours of Jenson's project may lead to concerning conclusions. For example, Jenson does not merely claim God is identified by Christians through the economy. He adds that in various contexts God "can have no identity except as he meets the temporal end toward which creatures live,"[57] with the result that "temporal sequences" cannot be "unessential to

48. Though his focus is elsewhere, Fred Sanders never seems fully to reject what he calls the "piecemeal" approach to deriving the Trinity from the Bible (*Triune God*, 171–76).

49. F. Sanders, *Triune God*, 88.

50. F. Sanders, *Triune God*, 90.

51. Jenson, *Systematic Theology*, 1:65. See also Jenson, *Triune Identity*, 107: "It is by the temporal dynamic between Jesus and his Father and our Destiny, that the three are *God*."

52. Jenson, *Systematic Theology*, 1:45; Jenson, *Triune Identity*, 8–9.

53. Jenson, *Triune Identity*, 40–50.

54. Jenson, *Triune Identity*, 65; Jenson, *Systematic Theology*, 1:95–96.

55. Jenson, *Triune Identity*, 65, 77, 81–82.

56. See Jenson, *Systematic Theology*, 1:46.

57. Jenson, *Systematic Theology*, 1:65.

[God's] being."[58] This, as Francesca Murphy argues, is one major concern of the language of identities: the term "naturally slides, linguistically, toward the act in which someone else 'identifies' them."[59] Identity suggests dependence on an outside observer who recognizes or bestows identity. More than this, when narrative identity is allowed to define the triune persons, the persons may become known by their distinctive acts, which threatens trinitarian unity.[60] In this chapter and the next, we must perform a careful balancing act, not allowing the distinctiveness of the missions to undermine the unity of the Trinity and not allowing the inseparable operations of God to hide the persons. Relying too heavily on the derivation of trinitarian identity from narratives may risk tritheism if there is not sufficient eternal ontological unity to ground the apparently diverse acts.[61] Stranger still, Murphy argues, since in Jenson's thought the identities of the triune persons derive from contingent historical events that God could have freely determined to be otherwise, God in himself is a God of possibilities hidden to us. This hidden God of possibilities is revealed in modes that are not necessarily or eternally true of God. This is concerningly close to modalism.[62] Sound doctrine must more carefully explain God as he eternally is in relation to the divine missions. Further, it must allow us to use propositional ideas revealed in the narrative of Scripture to construct such accounts of the interiority of God.[63]

The Economic and Immanent Trinity

Critical engagement with Robert Jenson's work highlights how the doctrine of the Trinity derives at least in part from the sweeping redemptive work of God in history, yet God cannot be reduced to the identities revealed in this historical work. It is therefore necessary to explore in doctrinal terms how the triune God is truly revealed through redemptive history and to ask what distinction, if any, must be drawn between this self-revelation and the inner life of the Trinity. Such questions lead us inexorably to the most controversial axiom in modern trinitarian theology, **Rahner's Rule**, so named after Karl

58. Jenson, *Triune Identity*, 22.

59. Murphy, *God Is Not a Story*, 257, 268.

60. Murphy, *God Is Not a Story*, 260. Robert Jenson affirms as much: "The reality of God is repeatedly identified, and so has identity, without being defined by any one timelessly exemplified set of characteristics" (*Triune Identity*, 110).

61. See Hunsinger, "Robert Jenson's *Systematic Theology*," 161–200.

62. Murphy, *God Is Not a Story*, 266–67.

63. As Fred Sanders remarks, "The missions themselves are eloquent, conversational, and word-bearing" (*Triune God*, 70).

Rahner, who popularized the axiom in its modern form.[64] The rule states, "The '**economic**' Trinity is the 'immanent' Trinity and the 'immanent' Trinity is the 'economic' Trinity."[65] Here the term "economic Trinity" refers to the self-communication of the Father through the Son and Spirit in salvation history, while "immanent Trinity" refers to the immanent life of God—namely, the processions and relations between the three divine persons. Such terminology is contested. Speaking of the economic Trinity and immanent Trinity sets up a dualism that can prevent us from formulating clear ideas about the eternal Son who was revealed through the incarnation, for example.[66] At a lay level, it may also wrongly imply the existence of two trinities. Many theologians prefer the more ancient terminology of *theologia* and *oikonomia*. For example, Catherine Mowry LaCugna explains that *oikonomia* once meant "how God administers God's plan" (see usage in Eph. 1:10) but after the Nicene debates it began to refer to the "order of salvation," especially through Christ's humanity, in contrast with *theologia*, the sacred doctrine of God as Trinity.[67] With these alternative terms, LaCugna can affirm something akin to Rahner's Rule: "*Theologia* is fully revealed and bestowed in *oikonomia*, and *oikonomia* truly expresses the ineffable mystery of *theologia*."[68] Others prefer the language of God *ad intra* or *in se* to the immanent Trinity, because these phrases may more clearly convey relationality.[69] Setting aside these terminological debates for now, we can turn to an evaluation of Rahner's Rule, but first I should explain the reasons why Rahner deploys the axiom, reasons that also explain its rapid proliferation in modern trinitarian thought.

Several factors converge to lead Rahner to deploy his rule. First, he is concerned that much neoscholastic theology, which focuses on the immanent Trinity, results in abstractions that have little bearing on other doctrines. In short, if we cannot connect the divine processions with the missions, we are left with a doctrine of the Trinity in isolation.[70] Second, Rahner's Rule seems

64. The axiom was named Rahner's Rule sometime in the twentieth century, either by Ted Peters or Roger Olson, each of whom attribute the coining of the name to the other. See F. Sanders, *Image of the Immanent Trinity*, 3n10. Rahner himself admits that he does not know where the axiom first originated (see Rahner, "Oneness and Threefoldness," 114). The terminology of the immanent and the economic Trinity can be traced to Johann August Urlsperger (1728–1806) (F. Sanders, *Triune God*, 146). Walter Kasper traces the basic axiom to F. A. Staudenmaier (1800–1856) (Kasper, *God of Jesus Christ*, 274).

65. Rahner, *The Trinity*, 22.

66. F. Sanders, *Triune God*, 145.

67. LaCugna, *God for Us*, 24–25, 39.

68. LaCugna, *God for Us*, 221.

69. A. J. Torrance, *Persons in Communion*, 279.

70. To use Rahner's language, "We shall have to remember that this inner conception [of the processions] is indicated in Scripture only insofar as, in the economy of salvation, this

at least partly designed to help combat the lingering worry that the doctrine of the Trinity is not rooted in Scripture. Counter to this fear, Rahner insists that the narrative of the Bible, beginning with the Old Testament, asserts "the basic theme that God is the absolute mystery, whom nobody can see without dying, and . . . it is nevertheless this God *himself* who conversed with the Fathers through his actions in history. This revealing self-manifestation is, in the Old Testament, mediated mostly . . . by the 'Word,' which, while causing God to be present in power, also represents him; and by the 'Spirit,' who helps men to understand and to announce the Word."[71] Rahner insists that the economic Trinity of the missions of the Word and Spirit truly is a self-communication of the immanent Trinity of absolute mystery; if the economic Trinity is not the immanent Trinity, God remains remote.[72] This leads to Rahner's third reason for his axiom: if salvation is God's self-communication, then Rahner is convinced that the incarnation of the Son and the bestowal of grace by the Holy Spirit must communicate the immanent Trinity to believers in the economy.[73] According to Rahner, the fact that the identity of the immanent Trinity and economic Trinity flows from the record of salvation history in the Bible and from the dogmatic understanding of salvation as the self-communication of God returns the Trinity to central importance in all systematic theology by making it inseparable from soteriology.

Rahner's rule has faced much criticism, and the critiques require that we modify his axiom in two ways. First, we must say that the divine economy truly reveals who God is *in se* but does not exhaustively reveal God. The eschatological bent of both Testaments reveals a lingering hope for a fuller beatific vision of God in the new creation, a fact that prevents us from acknowledging an already-complete, exhaustive self-communication.[74] "We wait for the blessed hope, the appearing of the glory of our great God and Savior, Jesus Christ" (Titus 2:13). Even with the completion of God's self-communication at the eschaton, we must admit that the missions will not perfectly and exhaustively correlate with the processions and relations between the divine persons. A close reading of Scripture with Rahner's Rule in mind reveals that not every aspect of the economy can reflect the immanent Trinity without causing significant problems. Luke illustrates a new Father-Son relationship, in which the Son learns to be a wise, obedient human (Luke 2:52; 22:39–46),

---

intra-divine knowledge is seen as self-revealing, and this intra-divine love as self-communicating" (Rahner, *The Trinity*, 19).

71. Rahner, *The Trinity*, 41.
72. Rahner, *The Trinity*, 99–100.
73. See the discussion in F. Sanders, *Image of the Immanent Trinity*, 60–74.
74. Congar, *I Believe in the Holy Spirit*, 3:15.

and depicts the Son having new attributes such as limited knowledge (Luke 8:45–47). Furthermore, Luke depicts economic operations that do not mirror the inner life of the Trinity, such as the Son alone being able to reveal the Father (Luke 10:22), a fact that could suggest a kind of subordination of the Father to the Son.[75] The problem is particularly pointed where it concerns the *filioque* debate, because in the economy the Son is depicted as sending the Spirit (John 15:26), raising the question of whether the Spirit proceeds from the Father and Son. The exegetical issues have already been explored in chapter 4; here we must simply remember that the economy truly reveals the triune God, but not exhaustively.

Rahner is concerned primarily not with the revelation of God but with the self-communication of God, in which God communicates his own being instead of just revealing statements about himself.[76] It is only through the historical giving of the divine Son in the incarnation and the offer of the Holy Spirit that we receive and experience God as he is in himself.[77] Rahner's trinitarian theology progressively comes to recognize that if salvation is genuinely to result in a distinctive relation with each person of the Trinity, then salvation must communicate the immanent Trinity in the economy.[78] As explored in the discussion of perichoresis, salvation is fundamentally a participation in the life of God, yet if we are not careful in exploring the ways in which God is present and communicated in the economy, we can blur the distinction between God and the world. As it was with Moltmann, so too it may be with Rahner, or so many fear.[79] It is certainly the case that the immanent Trinity grounds the revelation of God in the missions of the Son and Spirit, but arguing the inverse, that the Son's and Spirit's missions ground the life of the immanent Trinity (i.e., that the economic Trinity exhaustively determines the immanent Trinity), eliminates divine aseity and immutability, undermining the gratuitousness of salvation. On this reading of Rahner, which is contestable,[80] God would need salvation history to be God and so must act to save. Rahner's impulse may be better defended using

---

75. Harrower, *Trinitarian Self and Salvation*, 88–90, 102–3, 109–12.

76. Rahner, *Foundations of Christian Faith*, 116–17.

77. Rahner, *Foundations of Christian Faith*, 136–37.

78. Rahner is concerned that the doctrine of inseparable operations will reduce these relations to appropriations, not genuinely distinct relations. For my treatment of this issue, see chap. 7. For a helpful analysis of Rahner in the context of salvation and grace, see Holzer, "Rahner, Balthasar, and Catholic Currents," 318–23.

79. Harrower, *Trinitarian Self and Salvation*, 46–49; Renczes, "Scope of Rahner's Fundamental Axiom," 256.

80. Stanley Grenz argues that Rahner "maintains the priority" of the immanent Trinity "as constituting the transcendent basis" for the economic Trinity, minimizing this risk (*Rediscovering the Triune God*, 66).

other language, like T. F. Torrance's: "What Jesus Christ does for us and to us, and what the Holy Spirit does in us, is what God himself does for us, to us and in us."[81]

What is the fruit of all this discussion? Certainly, we must say that God is truly revealed and truly communicated in the economy, meaning that God revealed in Jesus Christ and in the Holy Spirit is the true, eternal God, the Father who begat the Son and spirated the Holy Spirit. More than this, we can add that our knowledge of the divine processions follows, at least in part, from the divine missions. Yet, we cannot thereby claim that the missions exhaustively reveal God, who exceeds the missions that were freely and graciously undertaken. This leads us to acknowledge a fundamental difference between the missions and processions. The missions reveal God in and through creation and thus properly pertain to **cataphatic** theology, whereby we can speak positively of the work of God. The processions, as seen in chapter 2, are most properly understood apophatically, where the divine attributes negate aspects of human generation and procession, leaving us with a partial and largely negative understanding of the eternal origin of the Son and Spirit in the Father.[82]

A Dogmatic and Metaphysical Understanding of the Divine Missions

If we are to develop a dogmatic account of the divine missions, we must begin from a position of surprise, returning to the scandal and stumbling block of the salvific work of God (1 Cor. 1:23; 1 Pet. 2:8). This position of surprise is sometimes difficult to re-create in a Western context familiar with the idea that God has a Son whom he sent into the world. Perhaps considering other cultures can better express the point. For example, James Henry Owino Kombo notes that when the idea of the Trinity is presented in some modern African contexts, people's tendency to think of God as singular and unique may lead them to conceive of the Son and Spirit as belonging to a category of divinities and spirits that are subordinate to the highest ontological category, which is God.[83] (Admittedly, I suspect this is not uniquely African, given my experiences in grading undergraduate papers.) Saying that God sent his Son does not therefore convey the radical nature of the divine missions. In response, Kombo proposes that an enculturated doctrine of the Trinity

81. T. F. Torrance, *Christian Doctrine of God*, 95; italics omitted.
82. There is considerable patristic precedent for aligning cataphatic theology with the *oikonomia* and apophatic with *theologia*. See Renczes, "Scope of Rahner's Fundamental Axiom," 260–61.
83. Kombo, *Doctrine of God*, 234. Note exceptions on 178–79.

in some modern African contexts must present the Son and Spirit as *Nyase*, *Kiteme*, or *Muntu*, terms in various African cultures that denote the singular divine subject, which is transcendent over all other beings.[84] Fully equating Jesus with such terms creates a cultural shock—something akin to telling someone who is Jewish that Jesus is Yahweh.[85] Without this initial shock, we cannot properly proceed to develop a dogmatic account of the missions. The missions of the Son and Spirit do not belong to an ontological category lower than the transcendent Father, nor is the Father in the same plane of being as the mutable, time-bound, finite creations he has made. Rather, in the divine missions the fullness of the infinite, eternal, immutable, and simple God is manifest in the persons of the Son and Spirit within the finite, temporal, mutable, and composite created world. This paradoxical claim should foster shock and raise serious metaphysical questions. How are we to think of such a phenomenon?

To understand the divine missions, we must recognize that they are constituted by the processions but require a contingent created term.[86] I already laid the groundwork for this concept when I explored the preexistence of the Son and Spirit and argued that the economic work of both persons reveals something about the Trinity *ad intra*. The persons who come to us in the missions already exist as generated Son and spirated Spirit, and their temporal work is somehow rooted in their distinctive modes of origin. However, the point must be further clarified when we recognize how we can say anything contingent about God. Bernard Lonergan clarifies the matter immensely when he argues, "What is truly predicated contingently of the divine persons is constituted by the divine perfection itself, but it has a consequent condition in an appropriate external term."[87] When we say something true of God that could have been otherwise (i.e., something that is contingent), such as "God created the world" or "God raised Jesus Christ from the dead," the act itself is constituted—it is what it is—because of the divine perfections. These infinite perfections are sufficient in themselves to serve as the efficient cause of any of God's actions, and they render any supplemental explanations superfluous.[88] These acts are fully constituted and effectively caused by

---

84. Kombo, *Doctrine of God*, 235–36. Kombo frequently demonstrates that various African peoples acknowledge a singular deity who is either manifest by lesser divine personifications or supported by lower divinities and spirits. Properly speaking, Africa is generally monotheistic, affirming one God far above other levels of being (see Kombo, *Doctrine of God*, 171–72, 177–78, 188–91).

85. Kombo, *Doctrine of God*, 236.

86. Lonergan, *Triune God*, 457; Aquinas, *Summa Theologica* I, Q. 43, A. 2, r. 3.

87. Lonergan, *Triune God*, 439.

88. Longergan, *Triune God*, 441, 465.

God, for if they depended on creation, God's aseity and immutability would be jeopardized. Yet, any contingent truth also requires a contingent term, a component of a contingent statement that makes it true. This is because the immutable, eternal God is necessary and not subject to contingency. Consider the statement "God willed and created the universe." As Robert Doran helpfully explains, aseity demands that this willing and creating is constituted entirely by God, who does not need anything added to his agency to make the universe. However, for the statement to be true, the contingent term of creation must itself exist.[89] If creation itself did not exist, the statement "God willed and created the universe" would not be true. Returning to the missions, we can say with Bonaventure that mission "refers to nothing other than the emanation of one person from the other and the manifestation of this in a created effect," meaning that the only change is in the created effect, or, in Lonergan's vocabulary, a created term.[90] In the case of the incarnation, this created effect is the existence of the human nature of Christ, which exists only in and through the person of the Son.[91]

Perhaps an example from Scripture will illustrate this idea. We can theologically interpret Galatians 4:4–6 in the following manner. "God sent his Son," who was eternally Son by generation,[92] to be "born of a woman, born under the law" (4:4). The assumed human nature is the created, contingent term of the divine mission, and generation constitutes the mission as a sending *of the Son*. This occurs in the "fullness of time" (4:4 NRSV). It is an act fulfilling the merciful divine plan, a plan that is contingent on God's gracious decision to save. Thus, the truthfulness of the claim that God sent his Son requires the reality of the human nature involved in the virginal conception. Similarly, "God sent the Spirit of his Son" (4:6), meaning the Spirit who was with God in the beginning (Gen. 1:2), "into our hearts" (Gal. 4:6). Here the Spirit's coming is rooted in eternal procession but requires the created reality of the humans whom he indwells and on whom he bestows grace.

I can now give a dogmatic account of the divine missions. The missions are constituted by the processions, ensuring a connection between the Trinity *ad intra* and the divine economy, though we need not accept exhaustive

---

89. Doran, *The Trinity in History*, 1:42.

90. Bonaventure, *Disputed Questions on the Mystery of the Trinity*, Q. 4, A. 1, resp. 7–8.

91. Lonergan, *Triune God*, 471; cf. Doran, *The Trinity in History*, 49. Roman Catholic theology would explain the mission of the Holy Spirit in terms of "created grace," a subject that remains far more contentious in Protestant circles where grace is often understood as favor and in Eastern Orthodox circles that speak of uncreated energies.

92. Paul's theology of preexistence is explicit elsewhere but arguably implicit here. See DeSilva, *Letter to the Galatians*, 354–55; Burton, *Critical and Exegetical Commentary*, 216–17; McCready, *He Came Down from Heaven*, 93–94.

overlap.[93] Unlike the processions, the missions are contingent acts of the divine will, requiring a contingent, passive term in creation; as such, they are acts of grace, for the processions are "antecedently perfect without these works."[94] True change occurs only in the created terms, as the Father, Son, and Spirit remain immutable, eternal, and simple. God is not determined by the missions. Yet, because the missions are *constituted* by the processions, because they are what they are due to the processions, we cannot reduce the missions to merely human ways of thinking about God.[95] The missions truly are a self-revelation and self-communication of God. Here we must proceed with caution. Since the missions do not exhaustively disclose the Trinity, we should not read everything from the missions into the processions. For example, the Son submits to the Father in the divine economy (John 6:38), yet the processions themselves do not admit of any form of subordination. Aquinas helpfully notes that sending may occur by command, "as a master sends a servant"; by counsel, "as an advisor may be said to send the king to battle"; or by origin, "as a tree sends forth its flowers." Sending by command and counsel implies the one sent is subordinate in authority or wisdom, respectively. But sending by origin "is according to equality."[96] Only this form of sending applies to the Trinity.

The Missions and the Divine Economy

A full theology of the divine missions would now proceed to explain the salvation wrought and administered through the Son and Holy Spirit, yet such an account necessarily exceeds the capacity of this volume. However, just as it is important to show that analogical similarity between perichoresis and union with Christ determines the trinitarian shape of salvation, so too it is necessary to show that a robust theology of the divine missions reveals the trinitarian unfolding of salvation. This is why a pluralist like John Hick, who is seeking to demonstrate the functional equivalence of all religions,[97] must reduce Jesus Christ to a human being who was powerfully filled with God's Spirit, while insisting that other religious figures were equally filled with the

93. Emery, *Trinity in Aquinas*, 172.
94. Wittman, "On the Unity of the Trinity's External Works," 369.
95. See T. F. Torrance, *Divine Meaning*, 248. Torrance argues that this issue is central to the arguments of Athanasius, who defends consubstantiality in order to ensure that our thought about God is not mere human thought that cannot reach God. Here we see the dual influence of Barth and Athanasius on Torrance clearly displayed.
96. Aquinas, *Summa Theologica* I, Q. 43, A. 1.
97. Hick, "Trinity and Incarnation," 197.

Spirit.[98] Hick summarizes, "If God has revealed himself in the person of Jesus, all other revelations are thereby marginalized as inferior and secondary."[99] The missions are unique and definitive acts of God's self-revelation.

The New Testament frequently links the sending of the Son and Spirit with God's provision of salvation (e.g., John 3:17; 6:57; 16:8–9; Rom. 8:3–17; Gal. 4:4–7). Because of this link, rejecting the Son of God means rejecting the God who sent him (Luke 10:16), while receiving the Spirit who is sent leads to accepting the Son and his salvation (1 Cor. 12:3; cf. 1 John 2:3). Salvation is grounded in the divine missions, and this fact should challenge the church to better understand its own missionary activity. In the words of P. V. Joseph, "The Church is gathered into the trinitarian communion in worship and in sacrament—in the celebration of remembrance of that event which brought the Church into the Triune fellowship in the breaking of the bread and sharing of the cup—only to be sent again into the world."[100] Evangelization is therefore witnessing in all contexts to the activity of the triune God, pointing to the historic mission of the Son and the ongoing invisible and preparatory mission of the Holy Spirit.[101] To put it bluntly, the church's evangelistic "missions should never be conceptualized apart from the *missio dei*."[102] As our Lord himself teaches, "As the Father has sent me, I also send you." John continues, "After saying this, he breathed on them and said, 'Receive the Holy Spirit'" (John 20:21–22). The proclamation of the gospel involves attesting to the mission of the Son while speaking as empowered by the mission of the Holy Spirit. The theology of the divine missions is thus central not only to our understanding of the triune God but also to our understanding of the nature of the church and its ministry.

FOR FURTHER READING

On the Preexistence of Christ

Gathercole, Simon J. *The Preexistent Son: Recovering the Christologies of Matthew, Mark, and Luke*. Grand Rapids: Eerdmans, 2006.

> Gathercole argues that preexistence is present in the Synoptic Gospels, against the common assumption that the Synoptics ignore or deny such preexistence. Though his work has met some criticism, I find his basic insights compelling.

98. Hick, "Trinity and Incarnation," 207–10.
99. Hick, "Trinity and Incarnation," 204.
100. Joseph, *Indian Trinitarian Theology*, 182.
101. Costas, *Liberating News*, 83.
102. Tennent, *Invitation to World Missions*, 59.

Hamerton-Kelly, R. G. *Pre-existence, Wisdom, and the Son of Man: A Study of the Idea of Pre-existence in the New Testament*. Cambridge: Cambridge University Press, 1973.

> Hamerton-Kelly's maximalist treatment of preexistence sees the concept throughout the New Testament. Though a helpful guide, Hamerton-Kelly is nevertheless prone to overstate his case.

Kuschel, Karl-Josef. *Born before All Time? The Dispute over Christ's Origin*. New York: Crossroad, 1992.

> One of many noteworthy critics of the idea of the preexistence of the Son, Kuschel puts forward a well-rounded but ultimately unsuccessful critique of preexistence theology.

Relevant for Exploring Rahner's Rule

LaCugna, Catherine Mowry. *God for Us: The Trinity and Christian Life*. New York: HarperSanFrancisco, 1991.

> LaCugna influentially argues that we cannot divide *oikonomia* and *theologia* and that much trinitarian theology from the late patristic period to the modern era has abstracted the Trinity from redemption history, rendering it impractical and risking an unknowable God.

Rahner, Karl. *The Trinity*. Translated by Joseph Donceel. New York: Seabury, 1974.

> Rahner's work deserves a central place in scholarship about the divine missions due to the extensive impact of his rule. In addition, the work is widely discussed among theologians because it explores problems with modern concepts of personhood in trinitarian theology.

Sanders, Fred. *The Triune God*. Grand Rapids: Zondervan, 2016.

> *The Triune God* is a work largely focused on exploring trinitarian hermeneutics. Sanders conducts an impressive exploration of how the deep structure of the Bible, with its emphasis on two missions, rightly prompts the judgment that God is eternally three. Concurrently, Sanders gives extended attention to Rahner's Rule and to the eternal processions.

CHAPTER 7

Inseparable Operations

We come now to the final chapter that will treat the divine unity. In many respects this chapter is the most important. I have already explained that Father, Son, and Spirit are unified in that they share the same essence, that this essence is simple and thus is not divided by the divine processions, and, therefore, that the three mutually coinhere within one another. This chapter will seek to explain the doctrine of inseparable operations, which, in classical form, means that the *opera Dei ad extra indivisa sunt*—the *ad extra* works of God, the works that affect the created world, are indivisible. Much of what I have said so far could be interpreted along quasi-materialist lines. Affirming that Father, Son, and Spirit share a substance, for example, could lead us to think of divine unity in terms of the Father, Son, and Spirit being made of the same stuff, some sort of spiritual equivalent to created matter. There is some benefit to this conceptual scheme, and I find it intuitive to many students in my classroom, though we must be careful to avoid the impression that God is composite or material in any literal sense. Yet, some cultures are prone to think of being in different terms not rooted in material concepts. For example, African *ubuntu* philosophy identifies the essence of a thing with a particular force. "Every force is specific, thus different beings are characterized by different intensities and types of forces."[1] Such a conceptuality certainly fits within many classical accounts of the doctrine of God. As *actus purus*, God is, so to speak, the most intense force conceivable. Because he is the only simple, uncreated being, his force is also uniquely unlike all created forces.

1. Kombo, *Theological Models*, 102.

Pro-Nicene theology tended to think of divine unity by considering the power and acts of the divine persons, concepts loosely similar to the *ubuntu* notion of force.[2] By the 380s, this understanding of divine unity had become "the most fundamental conception and articulation in 'Nicene' trinitarian theology," to use the phrasing of Michel Barnes.[3] Putting the matter another way, G. L. Prestige argues that since the idea of inseparable operations was used to argue for consubstantiality (as we shall see), inseparable operations must have "occasioned less difficulty" and been "even more widely held" than consubstantiality.[4] Soon, inseparable operations became a litmus test for orthodoxy. A Roman council led by Pope Damasus I in 380 anathematized those who denied the doctrine, and it remained a standard of orthodoxy in such councils as the Lateran Synod of 649, Lateran IV (1215), and the Council of Florence (1438–45).[5] In numerous Protestant confessions and catechisms we see consistent affirmation of the one power of God, a major component of the classical doctrine of inseparable operations.[6]

Though the notion of inseparable operations was central to the classical understanding of the doctrine of the Trinity, some recent trinitarian theology has been critical of the notion. For example, Catherine Mowry LaCugna argues that Augustine's understanding of inseparable operations "tends to blur any real distinction among the divine persons," a common objection.[7] If this criticism has any weight, it is very serious. The unity of the persons in operation must be normed by their distinction through the eternal processions. Therefore, any effort to preserve the doctrine must show that it does not, in fact, obliterate the distinctions between the persons. There is also an exegetical objection to the doctrine. Writing from a more biblicist perspective, Wayne Grudem argues that the claim that all actions of the Trinity are actions "of every person in the Trinity" is an idea that comes "perilously close to denying what is taught by literally hundreds of passages of Scripture that speak of *different* actions carried out by different members of the Trinity."[8] My theology

---

2. I will provide more technical analysis of these concepts as the chapter unfolds.

3. Barnes, "Rereading Augustine's Theology of the Trinity," 156.

4. Prestige, *God in Patristic Thought*, 260.

5. Hugon, *Le mystère de la Très Ste Trinité*, 253–54.

6. The one power of God is affirmed in the Augsburg Confession §1; the Church of England's Thirty-Nine Articles of Religion §1; the Westminster Confession of Faith §2. The Second Helvetic Confession condemns those who think the Trinity is "in will diverse" (§3). Admittedly, the specific language of inseparable operations is absent from many of these confessions, though it is present in most of the theologians who would adhere to these confessions.

7. E.g., see LaCugna, *God for Us*, 97. Adonis Vidu provides an extensive survey of critics in *Same God*, 82–89. In his work Vidu offers an extensive treatment of objections to inseparable operations.

8. Grudem, "Biblical Evidence," 256. Adonis Vidu more accurately understands history when he notes that "the primary reason [for the doctrine] has been fidelity to scriptural revelation!" (Vidu, *Same God*, xiv).

of inseparable operations must strive to demonstrate the exegetical warrant for this position. Much is at stake. The pro-Nicene account of the Trinity stands and falls with the doctrine of inseparable operations, and fall it must if this doctrine is not biblical in its root or its fruit. I hope to show that the doctrine of inseparable operations is deeply biblical, fully compatible with personal distinctions (though this task will only be completed in chap. 8), and fundamental to understanding the doctrine of the Trinity.

This chapter will proceed by exploring two basic arguments. The first argument will consider the claim that natures are identified by distinctive powers and that Father, Son, and Holy Spirit all act according to powers that are unique to the divine nature. The second argument will show that all divine operations, not just key divine distinctives, are shared by Father, Son, and Holy Spirit. Each section will carefully explore biblical warrant for the arguments. I will conclude the chapter by exploring how the doctrine of inseparable operations does not obliterate the distinctions between the persons, with special attention to the doctrine of **appropriations**.

The One Power of the Father, Son, and Holy Spirit

Over time, the Nicene debates about the Trinity became increasingly preoccupied with the question of the power of God. Many anti-Nicene theologians made the divine power a prominent feature of their theology. Eusebius of Nicomedia, for example, thought the Son had only a likeness of power to the Father, as if the Son were a creature using divine power derived from God.[9] Eunomius of Cyzicus argued that God's acts were not proper to the divine essence, because if they were, then they would be eternal and necessary. Therefore, the Father and Son could do the same acts without sharing the same essence.[10] Eunomius also debated Gregory of Nyssa on whether there was a natural divine power of production—if there was, then eternal generation was possible.[11] Eunomius tended to eliminate the notion of a divine power internal to God, considering divine operations (*energeia*) as external to the divine essence, with the result that the Son and his generation must also be external to this essence.[12] Those who opposed Nicaea argued that the Father and Son could do similar acts because the Son was a creature empowered to share in the acts of the Father.

9. "Eusebius might be understood to be speaking of the Son's likeness to the Father as the Creator's instrument—that is, as one who works the ordering and power which stem from God" (Gregg and Groh, *Early Arianism*, 100).
10. Behr, *Formation of Christian Theology* II/2, 279–80.
11. Barnes, *Power of God*, 14.
12. Anatolios, *Retrieving Nicaea*, 74–75.

The pro-Nicene response was rooted in the argument that characteristic powers identify the nature of a thing. By the AD 300s, the time of the Nicene debates, this was a venerable philosophical tradition traceable to the 400s BC, when medical authors in the Hippocratic school linked power and nature. Michel Barnes explains that, for the Hippocratics, "power means the affective capacity (or capacities) of any given existent distinctive to the identity of that existent."[13] In other words, distinctive powers determine the identity of unique natures. Medical authors increasingly denied humans' ability to know the essence of a thing directly; power was crucially important for knowing what a thing is.[14] This sense of power was present at an early stage of trinitarian theology, though it was not yet fully developed. Tertullian spoke of Father, Son, and Spirit as being three, but not in substance or power, which are one.[15] Unfortunately, Tertullian tended to understand the personal distinctions in economic terms.[16] Origen's *Dialogue with Heraclides* included the surprising language of two gods, one power.[17] These and other examples show how early the philosophical concept of power was used to explain the unity of the divine persons.

Though the procedure of deriving a thing's nature from its power has deep philosophical roots, this history should not lead to the impression that the concept is a philosophical imposition onto purer scriptural ideas. There is certainly a biblical sensibility to the idea of deriving a thing's nature from its acts. The Bible frequently emphasizes that the moral character of an individual is known by the fruits of that individual's actions (1 Sam. 24:13; Prov. 20:11; Matt. 7:15–20; Luke 6:43–45; James 3:12). Similarly, we can distinguish between the living God and idols because the latter are mute and impotent while God acts and speaks (Pss. 115:4–8; 135:16–17; Jer. 14:22; Hab. 2:18). In fact, there is considerable biblical emphasis on identifying God by his acts of deliverance. For example, Robert Jenson notes that when God gives the Decalogue to Moses, he begins with "name and narrative side by side": "I am the LORD your God, who brought you out of the land of Egypt, out of the place of slavery" (Exod. 20:2).[18] God is known by the acts he has done. There are even those who would translate the divine name given to Moses as "I will be what I will be" (3:14; see the CSB footnote), as if God's nature is revealed to Israel by God's acts.

---

13. Anatolois, *Retrieving Nicaea*, 7. Later, Galen argued in a medical context that a distinct organ had a distinctive power and that a unique power in the body entailed the presence of a distinct organ (Anatolios, *Retrieving Nicaea*, 98).

14. Anatolios, *Retrieving Nicaea*, 41.

15. Tertullian, *Against Praxeas* §2.

16. Tertullian, *Against Praxeas* §§2, 8, 9. See Kelly, *Early Christian Doctrines*, 110–15.

17. Origen, *Dialogue with Heraclides*, 438.

18. Jenson, *Systematic Theology*, 1:44.

Pro-Nicene theology argues for the consubstantiality of the divine persons on the basis of the shared divine power. This is particularly evident in the arguments of Gregory of Nyssa. The logic here is that there are certain powers that are indicative of a particular nature. Michel Barnes explains clearly: "A bicycle and a horse both perform the same 'operation' of transportation, but they have completely different natures: unity of activity does not prove unity of nature. Obviously, Gregory's reasoning must pivot on designating a certain class of 'activities.' Not just any one. The presumption is that there are some functions which are distinctive to the nature or identity. . . . The name of the function unique to a nature is, of course, *power*."[19] In other words, we know God exists as spirit (John 4:24), but we cannot say that the Holy Spirit existing as spirit demonstrates the divinity of the Spirit, because angels exist immaterially as spirit too. Taken superficially, "existing as spirit" is not a distinctive act of God.[20] What is needed for a strong argument for consubstantiality are acts that are peculiar to the divine nature, powers in the technical sense of the term. Pro-Nicene theologians tended to identify substances as subsisting by particular powers, meaning that attributing a divine power to the Spirit or Son would entail their subsistence as God.[21] In Scripture we see various distinctive divine powers that are attributed to the Son and Spirit.

Gregory's *Answer to Ablabius* is perhaps the most well known of his works to deploy this strategy. In this text, Gregory traces the etymology of the word "God" (*theos*) to the word "beholding" (*theas*) to argue that God is the one who beholds all things.[22] Gregory cites Matthew 9:4, where Jesus knows the thoughts of others, and Acts 5:3, where the Spirit discloses to Peter the hidden thoughts of Ananias and Saphira, to argue that Son and Spirit behold all things, even our thoughts. Gregory concludes that we cannot exclude any person of the Trinity from the name "God" because they all possess this distinctive power and thus are divine. Gregory's rather limited citations could be expanded further. The Holy Spirit "searches everything, even the depths of God" (1 Cor. 2:10). Presumably, if the Holy Spirit knows the thoughts

19. Barnes, *Power of God*, 16; italics original.

20. Of course, a fully developed doctrine of analogy would insist that angels exist as spirit in a manner quite distinct from God. The point is taken, and yet, for the logic of this argument to hold (as well as its exegetical foundations), we must identify those powers that are distinctive of the divine nature more fully.

21. This is true of famous pro-Nicenes like Gregory of Nyssa, discussed in this chapter, and lesser-known ones like Phoabadius of Agen. See Hanson, *Search for the Christian Doctrine of God*, 518. The reader should not be misled to think that Gregory is somehow unique in this argument.

22. Gregory of Nyssa, *Answer to Ablabius*, 260.

of God (2:11), he knows and beholds all things, as does the Father. Given that the Bible indicates there are three who behold all things, could this not mean that there are three gods? Lewis Ayres summarizes why Gregory finds this conclusion misguided: "There is, then, no basis on which to speak of a divided divine nature, because the divine operation which has given rise to our conception of Godhead itself is not divided."[23] In other words, what we are dealing with is not the collective action of three distinct agents but rather a single threefold action. This point is more clearly made with reference to another distinctive divine action: creation.

Creation, a paradigmatic divine act, is shared by Father, Son, and Holy Spirit. The book of Isaiah in particular frequently links claims to God's uniqueness with his act of creating (Isa. 37:16; 40:25–26), for God alone created (44:24). In noncanonical Second Temple literature, even the most reverential treatments of mediatorial figures of the exalted-patriarch or angel categories do not involve these figures in the act of creation.[24] Personified attributes such as Wisdom do participate in creation (Prov. 8:30), but the New Testament identifies the Wisdom or Word of God with Jesus Christ (John 1:1; 1 Cor. 1:24, 30). In the New Testament, creation becomes an act of God through the Word (John 1:3), an act by, through, and for the Son (Col. 1:16). Similarly, we see biblical claims that God creates by the Spirit (Job 26:13; Ps. 33:6; cf. Gen. 1:2).[25] The prepositional linkage is best taken to be a "distinction within the singular creative activity of God."[26] There are many reasons for this conclusion, a historically important one being that the Son is the very power of God (1 Cor. 1:24, 30).[27] This means, in Petrus van Mastricht's words, that the Father acts through the Son and the Spirit and therefore that "the operative force indeed is only one, common to three, but the order of

23. Ayres, "On Not Three People," 29.
24. Fletcher-Lewis gives the example of angels prostrating themselves before Adam in the section of 1 Enoch called the Similitudes of Enoch or the Book of Parables (Fletcher-Louis, *Jesus Monotheism*, 1:144).
25. Note, however, that some commentators disagree with translating Gen. 1:2 as a reference to the Spirit. See, e.g., von Rad, *Genesis*, 49–50. Von Rad's claim that "the Old Testament nowhere knows of such a cosmological significance for the concept of the spirit of God" (49–50) seems too strong, given such passages as Ps. 33:6 and Job 26:13, which point to *ruach* in creation, or passages like Ps. 104:30 and Mal. 2:15, which associate God's *ruach* with the giving of life to humanity. Admittedly, the Hebrew phrase is ambiguous and can be translated as "breath" or "wind," among other possibilities. At the very least, then, the evidence suggests an ambiguous connection with the Spirit of God and creation. From a dogmatic standpoint, I am convinced of the Spirit's role in creation.
26. Köstenberger and Swain, *Father, Son and Spirit*, 114–15.
27. These were initially crucial texts in establishing the united power of the Son, but they were gradually made peripheral due to the Arian strategy of linking them with texts about wisdom being created. See the discussion in Barnes, *Power of God*, 112, 164.

operation, and also its terminus, is diverse."[28] On the other hand, we face tremendous problems if we treat the Son and Spirit as distinct agents and intermediaries in creation. Adonis Vidu names the problem succinctly: "Attempts to ascribe creation to an intermediary being inevitably imply that the Father is not Creator."[29]

I am claiming that there is a single power and act with a threefold distinction within it, not a collaboration between three persons with their own similar yet numerically distinct powers. I must belabor this tremendously important point a little longer by providing three further arguments for this interpretation. First, in the Bible we often see a depiction of the Father and the Son sharing a single authority. In Revelation, for example, the Lord Almighty and the Lamb are a single temple (21:22) on a single throne (22:1) before which people serve a singular "him" (22:3).[30] Second, there is the interesting example of Hebrews 1:10, which cites Psalm 102:25, originally about God creating the earth, and applies it to Jesus Christ, as if there is a single agency.[31] Creation is not depicted as collaborative, but as a single act fully attributable to each person. Third, as Theophylact of Ochrid notes, if the Father simply used the Son and Spirit as instruments or tools, then they would be regarded as lower than the created world. "The things made by a saw are more highly regarded than the saw itself, which is only a tool. The saw was made for the sake of the things it will produce; the crafted objects were not made for the sake of the saw."[32] If Son and Spirit were merely instruments, they would be less valuable than creation, but the clear implication of many of the passages incorporating these persons into the divine act of creation is that they are superior to the created world. This suggests that they are not mere instruments of the Father. Taken together, these points compel me to see a single divine power of creation, a power that definitively identifies the Son and Spirit as divine by virtue of sharing this power and that is inseparably shared by the three persons.

Let us consider one more paradigmatic divine power: the power to save to eternal life. By God's progressive revelation, the witness to eternal salvation

28. Van Mastricht, *Theoretical-Practical Theology* 1.2.24.10.
29. Vidu, *Same God*, 91.
30. Paul, "Trinitarian Dynamic of the Book of Revelation," 100.
31. See the discussions in Pierce, *Divine Discourse*, 56–59. Lewis Sperry Chafer remarks, "The fact that each One is announced as wholly achieving a given undertaking, quite apart from the Others, indicates the truth that the Persons maintain a distinction the One from the Others. On the other hand, the fact that each does completely and perfectly the given task and in a way that would imply that no other need undertake it, indicates a mysterious unity far more vitally concentrated than is known in any aspect of human experience" (*Systematic Theology*, 1:305).
32. Theophylact of Ochrid, *Explanation of the Holy Gospel according to John*, 12–13.

developed late in the Old Testament canon, but where eternal salvation is present in the canon—in Psalm 49, for example, or in Daniel 12—it is attributed to God alone.[33] In Isaiah, in one of the most monotheistic sections of the Old Testament, God identifies himself as the unique Savior (Isa. 43:11; cf. 45:21), contrasting himself with idols that cannot save (Isa. 44:17; 45:20).[34] Christian exegetes have long recognized that the Son's and Spirit's involvement in the act of salvation suggests their divinity, for this is a power of God alone. So, Thomas Aquinas notes that the Son is given the ability to raise the dead and give life (John 5:21), and the Spirit raises Jesus from the dead (Rom. 8:11) and gives life (John 6:63).[35] Paul's frequent use of the language of "in Christ" and "in the Spirit" demands that we see a single power of God by which the Father works through the Son and Spirit, who are agents of the same power. Neil Richardson explains that "in Christ" often

> occurs in contexts which suggest that it denotes the place ("field of force"), focus, or means of God's action. . . . Thus, God's grace is given to the Corinthians "in Christ Jesus" (1 Cor. 1:4); God's call is actualized "in Christ Jesus" (Phil. 3:14; cf. Gal. 5:1, 8); God's consolation is to be found "in Christ" (Phil. 2:1), for it was in him that God's act of liberation took place (Rom. 3:24); God's love is experienced "in Christ Jesus our Lord" (Rom. 8:39); "Christ Jesus" is the focus of the operation of God's Spirit of life (Rom. 8:2; cf. 6:23); the old dispensation is being abolished "in Christ" (2 Cor. 3:14; cf. Gal. 3:14).[36]

33. Wainwright, *The Trinity in the New Testament*, 157–58. Admittedly, this is not the case outside of the canon (see 1 Enoch 48:7; 51:2; Testament of Levi 18:11), but if we affirm the canon alone as inspired, then we see no competitor with God in the authoritative literature.
34. I agree with John Oswalt when he says that the conclusion that God alone is Savior is logical.
> God has insisted that Israel has witnessed the evidence that he alone is God. What had that evidence been? The promise to make Abraham a great nation; the promise to deliver his descendants from Egypt; the promise to give them the land of Canaan; the promise to make the dynasty of David secure over the throne of Jerusalem, and so on. What had the fulfillment of those promises required again and again? Deliverance, often over impossible odds. In the process of demonstrating his character as Yahweh to his people, he had demonstrated to them over and over his inclination and capacity to save. What Israel had witnessed and could not escape was the realization that "Yahweh" meant "Savior," and that as Yahweh was the only God, he was the only Savior. (Oswalt, *Book of Isaiah*, 148)
35. Aquinas, *Summa contra Gentiles* 4.16.4.
36. N. Richardson, *Paul's Language about God*, 245. Richardson is not unique in this conclusion. Constantine Campbell sees "instrumentality" (I find the word choice unfortunate insofar as it may imply that the Father is the agent and the Son merely a passive means by which the agent works) an important aspect of Paul's definition of union. "Apart from Christ, we are without God and without his acts toward us" (Campbell, *Paul and Union with Christ*, 409).

Though less frequently, Paul speaks in similar patterns about the Spirit. In Ephesians 1:3–14, Paul lays out salvation's grand scope. Every blessing is explicitly named as being "in Christ," and the series finds its completion in the Holy Spirit.[37] Put together, these suggest that Father, Son, and Spirit share the single power of saving, a power distinctive to the Godhead.

The Inseparable Operations of the Father, Son, and Holy Spirit

If the Father, Son, and Spirit all have the same powers that are distinctive of divinity—namely, creating, beholding all things, and bestowing eternal life—then what would prevent us from concluding that there are three gods? After all, three things that possess the same power of producing heat and light through gravity-induced fusion would be identified as three distinct stars.[38] Yet, early Christians tended to think of the distinction between the persons who shared the one power as that between a single star and its light, not as a distinction between three stars.[39] Why? Here we must move beyond the doctrine of the single power of God to a full-fledged doctrine of inseparable operations. The unity of the Father, Son, and Holy Spirit is not merely a unity of common powers, with other attributes and activities being distinctive to each person. Orthodox trinitarianism has long affirmed that Father, Son, and Spirit share all attributes of the single, simple divine essence, as discussed in chapter 3, and work all operations in unity with one another.

The doctrine of inseparable operations was given its famous wording from Augustine, who preferred to speak of the inseparable works (*opera insepara-bilia*), in contrast to later theology, which tended to speak of undivided works (*opera indivisa*). Arguably, "undivided works" emphasizes the unity of the divine nature more, while language of "inseparability" implies greater personal distinction within the works. For this reason, I find language of "inseparability" to be slightly superior because it focuses more clearly on the agents who work inseparably rather than on the work that is indivisible, thus more clearly communicating personal distinction amid unity.[40] The doctrine of inseparable operations is evident among all pro-Nicene theologians.[41] As Gregory

---

37. Letham, *The Holy Trinity*, 76.

38. Michel Barnes notes that, in ancient medical thought, common power might indicate belonging to a common genus (*Power of God*, 8).

39. Gregory of Nazianzus uses such an analogy, though he names more clearly than others how it falls short (*Theological Orations* 5.32).

40. Beckwith, *The Holy Trinity*, 326.

41. Indeed, Lewis Ayres identifies this as one of three distinguishing elements of pro-Nicene theology (*Nicaea and Its Legacy*, 236).

of Nyssa notes, "If . . . we understand that the operation of the Father, the Son, and the Holy Spirit is one, *differing or varying in nothing*, the oneness of their nature must needs be inferred from the identity of their operation."[42] Later theologians came to recognize the need to speak of four categories of divine actions: (1) the *ad intra* personal works of the divine processions, distinctive to certain persons; (2) the *ad intra* essential works, described by Reformed scholastics as the counsel or decree, which reference the Trinity's shared will or plan for the indivisible act of creation and redemption; (3) the essential *opera Dei ad extra*, which are indivisible; and (4) outward works that are considered personal "in a certain manner" because they terminate on a single person, though they are performed inseparably by all three persons.[43] This fourth category refers to such things as the incarnation. Our focus in this section will be on the third category of divine work.

The inseparability of all divine works *ad extra* can be rooted in three scriptural arguments. Crucially important to the pro-Nicenes was John 5:19.[44] In context, Jesus is criticized by Pharisees for healing on the Sabbath (5:16), and he responds by an appeal to a common rabbinic argument that God works on the Sabbath. "My Father is still working, and I am working also" (5:17). His critics believe he is making himself equal to God and plan to stone him (5:18), and Jesus, having the opportunity to clear up any misunderstanding, instead doubles down: "Truly I tell you, the Son is not able to do anything on his own, but only what he sees the Father doing. For whatever the Father does, the Son likewise does" (5:19). Hilary of Poitiers interprets the text in a significant way. The word "whatever" means that all acts of the Father and the Son are shared. The word "likewise" ensures that there are two persons doing these acts (and here Hilary would infer a third, the Holy Spirit, for good reason).[45] Jesus claims for himself the paradigmatic divine powers of giving life and judging (5:21–22)[46] before moving on, in subsequent chapters, to identify himself with major historic works of the Father. For example, on Passover, Jesus re-creates the distinctive acts of a miraculous crossing of the sea (6:19) and a miraculous provision of food (6:1–15), miracles mirroring those of the Father in Exodus 14:1–31 and 16:4–26. Therefore, John 5:19, considered in its context, gives us strong warrant for seeing the *ad extra* works of the Father and Son as inseparable.

42. Gregory of Nyssa, *On the Holy Trinity*, 328.
43. Muller, *Post-Reformation Reformed Dogmatics*, 4:258. Muller is here summarizing Amandus Polanus.
44. I offer a more extensive interpretation of this passage in Butner, *Son Who Learned Obedience*, 13–16, 32–35.
45. Hilary of Poitiers, *On the Trinity* 7.18.
46. Giving life is the most significant of the two, as at times other figures appear to share, by grace, in the divine prerogative of judgment, as, e.g., believers are said to do in 1 Cor. 6:3.

The second and third arguments provide exegetical evidence for the doctrine of inseparable operations while prompting the Spirit's inclusion in the doctrine. The second, focusing on triadic patterns of parallelism used to describe divine action, is the weaker of the two. For example, in 1 Corinthians 12:4–7, "the same Spirit," "the same Lord," and "the same God" are placed in parallel, working to achieve the same end.[47] Theologians have long pointed to Old Testament language of God acting by his Word and Spirit. For example, Wolfgang Musculus points to David's last words as evidence of inseparable operations: "The Spirit of the LORD spoke through me, his word was on my tongue. The God of Israel spoke . . ." (2 Sam. 23:2–3).[48] Similar juxtaposition of the Spirit and Word in divine action is occasionally evident in the Old Testament (e.g., Ps. 33:6).[49] Such parallelism suggests the possibility of inseparable operations, though given their poetic form, the passages may not intend to assert that all divine actions toward creation are shared.

The third argument identifies divine actions that are attributed to each of the three persons across a range of biblical texts. For example, we typically associate the Holy Spirit with sanctification (1 Cor. 6:11; 2 Thess. 2:13; 1 Pet. 1:2), but the New Testament also speaks of the Father sanctifying (John 17:17) and of the Son sanctifying (Heb. 10:10). Pro-Nicene theologians, and many since, have compiled large lists of actions attributed in different passages to different members of the Trinity. For example, Didymus the Blind compiles such a list to argue for the full divinity of the Holy Spirit against fourth-century theologians who deny the same. Didymus argues that Father, Son, and Spirit all give grace (Rom. 1:7; Heb. 10:29), all have communion with the believer (1 Cor. 1:9; 2 Cor. 13:13; 1 John 1:7), all call to ministry (Acts 6:4; 13:2; Gal. 2:9), and all indwell the believer (1 Cor. 3:16; 2 Cor. 6:16; Eph. 3:16–17), among other examples.[50] He concludes, "On the basis of all these passages it is proved that the activity of the Father and the Son and the Holy Spirit is the same. But those who have a single activity also have a single substance."[51]

Given the patterns of shared operations between Father, Son, and Holy Spirit, why infer that each and every action *ad extra* is inseparable? There are a number of reasons. John 5:19 demonstrates that this is the case for the Father and Son, so we might make the same argument for the Holy Spirit in

47. Thiselton, *Shorter Guide to the Holy Spirit*, 29. Thiselton notes that the divine unity of operation is set in contrast to human "varieties of gifts, . . . varieties of services, . . . and varieties of activities," highlighting the unity of the persons.

48. Musculus, *Commonplaces of the Christian Religion*, folio 6.

49. See also Isa. 59:21, where the plural "words" and Spirit are parallel.

50. Didymus the Blind, *On the Holy Spirit* §§75–76, 78, 96–98, 106–8.

51. Didymus the Blind, *On the Holy Spirit* §81.

order to avoid subordinating one of the divine persons, who is equally worshiped. If some actions were fully distinct to singular divine persons, then the nature of the relation between the divine persons might seem to depend on the economy, jeopardizing divine aseity.[52] Moreover, if divine persons operated unilaterally, we might find ourselves with divided allegiances, jeopardizing monotheism. A crude form of this conception of the Godhead might resemble pagan polytheism, with Father, Son, and Spirit being given their own respective domain of authority and responsibility, much as Poseidon was thought to rule the sea and Dionysius to govern agriculture. In polytheistic mythology, it was common for the gods of different domains to pick sides in human affairs, with humans reciprocating by claiming a special allegiance to a particular god. Most theological accounts could avoid such a crude division of labor, but even then, problems could arise. For example, if all divine acts contributing to salvation were not inseparable, we might find the need to have special allegiance to the person who contributed the most.[53] Alternately, if one person created us but another saved us, we could wonder whether we owed more to one than the other. Shared operations and powers entail a shared nature between Father, Son, and Holy Spirit, but following these patterns in Scripture to conclude that the doctrine of inseparable operations extends to all divine actions ensures the coequality of the persons, making sense of the worship directed to all three.

The logic of this argument may not convince a skeptical reader. After all, John 10:29 teaches that the Father is "greater than all," so one might be inclined to argue for the subordination of the Son and Spirit, perhaps by relegating some works *ad extra* entirely to him. Let me supplement my argument by further connecting the doctrine of inseparable operations to other trinitarian loci, as does John 10.[54] The doctrine of perichoresis insists on the mutual interpenetration and coinherence of the three divine persons. "The Father is in [the Son] and [he is] in the Father" (10:38). Perichoresis is the ground of inseparable operations.[55] In the words of Gregory of Sinai, "Wherever [God] expresses himself, none of the three persons is manifest or to be perceived apart

52. Vidu, *Same God*, 94.

53. Anselm uses a similar argument to assert that Jesus must be God, for we are indebted to whomever saves us. Unless God saves, we would still be indebted to someone other than God rather than freed from bondage so as to be completely devoted to God (Anselm, *Why God Became Man* 1.5). It seems that similar logic would apply even within the Godhead. If salvation were obtained or applied disproportionately by one divine person, we would be more indebted to that person than the others.

54. I am indebted to Adonis Vidu for the broad contours of this interpretation. See Vidu, *Same God*, 42–46.

55. Jüngel, *Doctrine of the Trinity*, 35; Meyendorff, *Byzantine Theology*, 186.

from or without the other two."[56] Perichoresis suggests, then, that no act of a divine person can be an act without the others. For external acts, this means that Father, Son, and Spirit act together. For internal actions like the processions, the Father generates the Son and spirates the Spirit within himself such that the procession of the Son is somehow in the Holy Spirit and the procession of the Holy Spirit is somehow in the Son. The doctrine of inseparable operations is also qualified by the consubstantiality of the persons. Jesus and his Father are one (10:29–30). Father, Son, and Spirit share the same simple essence, so we cannot distinguish the powers and acts of God from the essence of God. Therefore, Father, Son, and Spirit also perfectly share the power and acts of God and cannot divide these into parts. Within this context, claims about the Father's greatness cannot suggest that he has powers the Son and Spirit lack or that he is greater in essence. Rather, the greatness must refer to the trinitarian *taxis*.

At this point I must offer one careful clarification regarding the extent of the doctrine of inseparable operations. The doctrine of the incarnation complicates matters somewhat. Though a full explanation of the classical position exceeds the scope of this work, I can offer a brief treatment here.[57] Because the Son assumed a human nature, he is able to complete acts that are distinctive to himself by virtue of this human nature.[58] Traditionally, the incarnate actions of the Son are interpreted in line with the Third Council of Constantinople (681), which says that "each nature wills and works what is proper to it, in communion with the other."[59] Following the line of thought explored in this chapter, the theology of the council identifies powers with natures and thus posits that each nature produces specific operations by virtue of its distinctive powers. This allows certain human actions, such as eating, drinking, and sleeping, to be unique to the Son. Yet, the two natures are continually working in conjunction with one another through the single subject of the Son. This is why Jesus can attest that "the Father who lives in [him] does

56. Gregory of Sinai, *On Commandments and Doctrines* §30.

57. I have offered a more extensive treatment in Butner, *Son Who Learned Obedience*, 54–57, 62–94.

58. When I suggest that the Son is newly "able" to perform distinctive human acts because of the incarnation, I am not meaning to imply a lack or deficiency in the Father or Spirit who are unable to personally act through the humanity of the Son. Rather, if we were to suppose that a single person could complete an action *ad extra* without the others, only then would there be genuine lack because the full Godhead would not be involved in the action. The Son's distinctive human actions, such as dying on the cross, are lacking in the sense that they are acts of a nature that is not consubstantial with the divine persons of the Father and Spirit. This is simply another way of saying that they are created and contingent acts of a divine person, and thus inferior to the inseparable divine acts of Father, Son, and Spirit.

59. "The Statement of Faith of the Third Council of Constantinople," 384.

his works" (John 14:10). When Jesus heals, for example, he does so through human actions, such as spitting (Mark 7:31–37; John 9:6), touching (Matt. 8:3), or breaking and blessing bread (Mark 6:41). But simultaneous to these human acts, and convergent with them, are the divine acts by which the healings occur, and these divine acts are the work of all three persons inseparably, terminating on the Son as the agent who especially performs them. Thus, the Son alone spits to facilitate healing, but the healing itself is also the work of the Father and Spirit.[60]

We will now consider the nature of the shared actions of the three persons. Do they act like three coordinate yet distinct agents, or is there a single operation and act? To explore this question, consider the example of revelation. It is notable that when Jesus speaks, he does so authoritatively (Matt. 7:29). Maria Bingemer explains, "Unlike the prophets who dot their discourses with explicit references to the God of Israel in order to be very clear in whose name they speak—'Thus says the Lord' or 'Word of Yahweh'—Jesus does not distinguish his word from the word of God."[61] In fact, in Matthew 11:27 Jesus claims the exclusive right to reveal (*apokaluptein*) the Father, using the same verb attributed to the Father in 11:25.[62] Yet, the New Testament is also clear that all revelation given to the prophets was through the Holy Spirit (2 Pet. 1:21). It seems that the act of revelation is proper to each of the persons, and Jesus speaks as if he possesses divine authority. Here we might conclude that different aspects of revelation are accomplished by different persons. Perhaps the Father revealed the law to Moses, the Son offered much teaching for the Gospels, and the Spirit led the prophets, three distinct yet coordinated actions. Further examination, however, shows that this is not the best interpretation.

There are various Old Testament passages that are attributed to the Father but are attributed by the New Testament to the Son or Holy Spirit, as if the acts referenced by these passages are attributable to all three persons. This is particularly true of the Holy Spirit with respect to revelation. For example, Acts 28:25–27 attributes the words of the Lord in Isaiah 6:9–10 to the Holy Spirit. Similarly, Hebrews 10:15–17 attributes the words of the Lord in Jeremiah 31:33–34 to the Holy Spirit. Both instances suggest that the single word of God came from both the Holy Spirit and the Father. One thinks here of the three angels speaking as the single Lord in Genesis 16–18, a passage I discussed in chapter 1. The various close links found between the

---

60. The Spirit's involvement in this joint operation of healing is perhaps suggested in Jesus's casting out demons by the power of the Holy Spirit (Matt. 12:28).

61. Bingemer, *Face for God*, 46.

62. "This in principle places Jesus on the side of the Father in contrast to all humanity" (Hagner, *Matthew 1–13*, 320).

divine persons in divine actions explains the consensus in the tradition that the doctrine of inseparable operations does not refer to collaborative action. We find this in the East, with Gregory Palamas: "The energy of the three divine hypostases is one not in the sense that each has an energy similar to that of the others, as is the case with us, but in the sense of true numerical unity."[63] We see this in the West with Augustine, who in the course of several letters to Nebridius argues that humans cannot do the same identical act due to their finite, embodied state[64] but that the divine persons act perfectly in common.[65] Traditionally, it has been agreed that there is a single operation in threefold form, not three actors and agents.

If we are tempted to think of inseparable operations as collaborative works, this thinking is likely associated with changes to other trinitarian loci, changes that move beyond traditional interpretations. The doctrine of inseparable operations is connected to perichoresis, consubstantiality, simplicity, and the eternal processions. If we deny the processions, the biblical emphasis on personal distinction likely requires weakening the doctrine of inseparable operations. The persons are then distinguished by role, act, or function. If we overemphasize perichoresis, a single inseparable operation of the Trinity becomes an act jointly caused by three coordinated actors. If we reject the simplicity of the divine nature, or if we understand consubstantiality in terms of secondary substance, as if Father, Son, and Spirit are members of a genus, then we again wind up with a weak notion of inseparable operations where three distinct agents work jointly to produce an act. The historical and, more importantly, the biblically warranted notion of inseparable operations states that Father, Son, and Spirit share one power and through this power perform all acts inseparably, performing the acts as single, indivisible actions.

Inseparable Actions and Personal Distinctions

I return now to the modern fear that the doctrine of inseparable operations obliterates the personal distinctions between the persons. The rest of this chapter will address the metaphysics of inseparable operations to argue that this is not the case, while the final chapter of this book will explore, through an extended exploration of the doctrine of communion, the distinct human experience of the triune God who works inseparably. In terms of metaphysics, we can consider three issues, each corresponding to one category of divine

63. Palamas, *Topics of Natural and Theological Science* §138.
64. Augustine, *Letter 14 to Nebridius*.
65. Augustine, *Letter 11 to Nebridius*.

essential acts. I will begin by considering the *opera Dei ad extra*, which have been the focus of the above discussion. If we consider the works of God toward creation to be inseparable, does this obliterate personal distinctions? This question will lead me to clarify the doctrine of inseparable operations itself. Next, I will address the *ad intra* essential works, such as willing or knowing, by returning to that point made in chapter 4 that mind and will are proper to the divine being, not to the persons themselves. Having explored the doctrine of inseparable operations, I can offer some clarification about the divine mind and will. Finally, I will introduce the doctrine of appropriations in order to speak of God's works *ad extra* that are most closely associated with one person but are performed by all three.

Preserving Personal Distinction in the Inseparable Operations

I must begin by admitting that it is possible for a firm conviction about the indivisibility of the works of God to lead to an obliteration of personal distinctions. For example, some Oneness Pentecostals, such as the Iglesia Apostólica de la Fe en Cristo Jesús, reject the language of three eternal persons because (taking "person" in its popular and not its technical sense) it would imply three separate agents and thus three gods.[66] Such an approach sacrifices one dimension of biblical truth, the personal distinctions, for the sake of another dimension of biblical truth, the inseparability of divine operations. The best systematic theology has been able to preserve both truths. In the words of Tyler Wittman, "God enacts himself externally as God is internally: absolutely indivisible and relatively distinct."[67]

We must begin by recognizing that the persons simply are the essence; there is no real distinction between person and essence in God, or else we would have a **quaternity**. Therefore, there is no essence that can act without the divine persons. Rather, any act of God is an act of the three persons. Therefore, as Gilles Emery summarizes, "just as each divine person is characterized by a *distinct mode of existence*, each person possesses likewise a *distinct mode of action*."[68] Classically, this fact was manifest in the pro-Nicene claim that, in Gregory of Nyssa's words, "there is one motion and disposition of the good will which proceeds from the Father, through the Son, to the Spirit."[69] The linear ordering of actions from the Father, through the Son, to the Holy Spirit is a conceptual framework that reflects the order of the divine processions. The Son performs

66. Gill, *Toward a Contextualized Theology*, 187, 230.
67. Wittman, "On the Unity of the Trinity's External Works," 373.
68. Emery, *The Trinity*, 163.
69. Gregory of Nyssa, *Answer to Ablabius*, 262.

the same indivisible act as the Father and the Holy Spirit, except that he per-forms it uniquely as one uniquely begotten of the Father. The trinitarian *taxis* is preserved in the inseparable operations of the Trinity, though it must be clear that this order reflects only origin and relation, not nature, time, dignity, or rank.[70] Thus, there is an inherent relationality to all of God's acts, even though these acts remain indivisible, since the nature and power are shared.

While the linear explanation of all divine acts moving from the Father, through the Son, to the Holy Spirit is the most historically prevalent way of describing the distinction between the persons in the inseparable operations of God, it is not the only way of doing so. Sometimes theologians appeal to distinctions in the kind of causation. Basil of Caesarea speaks of the Father as the original cause, the Son as the creating cause, and the Holy Spirit as the perfecting cause.[71] Later theologians clarify this terminology. Bonaventure explains that the Father is the efficient cause, the Son is the formal cause, and the Spirit is the final cause.[72] This approach is helpful in that it suggests that a single act may be caused in a threefold way, with this threefold causation corresponding to the *taxis* of the processions. However, this approach is lim-ited in that it may still suggest three distinct agents working collaboratively. Another strategy has been to clarify the Augustinian formula: "The external works of the Trinity are undivided, *preserving, of course, the properties of each person*." Carl Beckwith traces the idea expressed in the italicized text to Reformation-era Lutheran theologians like Philip Melanchthon, Martin Chemnitz, and others.[73] This, too, can be a viable way of preserving the per-sonal distinctions, though in itself it lacks any explanation for how these are preserved. Combined, these strategies significantly deflate modern concerns.

Speculations on the Divine Consciousness

Recall from chapter 4 that I argued for a christological-compatibility criterion, which, on the basis of creedal understandings of the incarnation, requires that faculties like the mind and the will are proper to nature or essence, not to specific persons. This entails—counterintuitively, given our understanding of the concept of personhood—that there are not three minds or wills in a tri-personal God. I qualified this statement with an apophatic move in chapter 4,

70. Beckwith, *The Holy Trinity*, 332.
71. Basil, *On the Holy Spirit* 16.38.
72. Bonaventure, *Disputed Questions on the Mystery of the Trinity* Q. 4, A. 2, arg. 8. Bonaven-ture correlates these three causes with the appropriated qualities of power, wisdom, and goodness, which he says correspond to the persons and the causes. I am not certain whether Bonaventure would also consider the three forms of causation to be appropriations (which are explained below).
73. Beckwith, *The Holy Trinity*, 332; italics original.

suggesting that the unique otherness of God requires us to treat any language of divine dialogue *ad intra* as anthropomorphic. Any consideration of what it is like for God to be conscious remains equally subject to apophatic qualification. To put the matter bluntly, finite, created human beings cannot understand what the consciousness of God is like, if a word like "consciousness" is even appropriate to use of an infinite, eternal being whose perfect act of knowing does not require a physical brain. Nevertheless, having explored the doctrine of inseparable operations, I can now offer a cautious clarification of the one divine mind with the help of theologian Bernard Lonergan.

Lonergan has speculated more openly, and more precisely, about the divine consciousness than most theologians, who either avoid the subject or speak boldly without much dogmatic grounding. For this reason, his proposal strikes me as the strongest way of considering the essential acts *ad intra*. Writing in line with the Western tradition, Lonergan argues that anything in God that is not shaped by relations of opposition is one, so the divine consciousness must be one. Father, Son, and Spirit must therefore possess no unique or divided consciousness. However, Lonergan clarifies that each of the persons possess a unique mode of subsistence rooted in the processions, meaning that there are three conscious subjects. Recall that divine simplicity requires us to treat the divine essence and divine acts as the same. Simplicity also requires that the persons simply are the essence. Therefore, Lonergan rightly concludes that "the intellectually conscious Father generates the Son by intellectual consciousness," in other words, by his self, which is the divine being, which is also the divine consciousness. "The intellectually conscious Son," then, "is generated into intellectual consciousness by the Father." A similar claim can be made of the Spirit, who is spirated into intellectual consciousness by the Father. Therefore, the persons have the one consciousness in three distinct ways, the Son as a subject who has received the one consciousness as one generated, the Spirit as a subject who has the one consciousness by spiration, and the Father as a subject who has generated and spirated by the consciousness.[74]

Lonergan's proposal is helpful in showing how the essential acts *ad intra* do not obliterate personal distinctions. Rather, personal distinctions must norm divine unity once again, as I have argued is the case across all means of speaking of God's unity within the field of trinitarian dogmatics. At the same time, personal distinctions must be normed by divine unity so that the unique persons do not divide the one divine consciousness, mind, or will. Here, too, we see a pattern I have advocated throughout this work. Yet, having said this,

74. Lonergan, *Triune God*, 387.

I must again reassert the basic apophatic impulse. As finite humans, we cannot understand what it is like to possess an infinite, perfect consciousness by spiration as opposed to by generation any more than we can understand what it is to spirate or generate a divine consciousness. Our theological language presses against the ineffable here. These reflections ought not to be taken as helping us understand what it is to know or think as God. Rather, they should be understood as providing a meager, human manner of speaking about God's knowledge or consciousness in such a way that it does not obliterate divine plurality. God knows by inseparable act, but God also knows irreducibly as Father, Son, and Holy Spirit.

The Doctrine of Appropriations and Distinctive Personal Acts

Though I have made a biblical case that the doctrine of inseparable operations extends to all divine acts, some readers may still be uncomfortable, given the fact that there remain specific acts in the Bible that are explicitly attributed only to one of the divine persons. Yes, I have offered an explanation for how this is possible in the context of the incarnation, but what about other divine acts, like empowering the judges of the Old Testament, which is attributed only to the Holy Spirit (e.g., Judg. 3:10; 11:29; 13:25)? Does the doctrine of inseparable operations read against the grain of Scripture by attributing such acts to all three persons? The doctrine of appropriations helps us to understand these patterns. Before I explain appropriations, I should note that even in Judges, the events and authorship of which belong to a historical period or periods that came well before God fully revealed his tripersonality, we see language that implies a multipersonal divine agency. Language of the Holy Spirit filling the judges finds a parallel in the statements that "the LORD raised up" the judges (2:16, 18; 3:9, 15). Similarly, we see the angel of the Lord playing a role in calling various judges. Notably, the angel of the Lord appears to Manoah and his wife to announce the birth of Samson. When the angel departs, Manoah announces that he has seen God (13:22). Such statements lead many patristic writers to consider the angel of the Lord to be the Son. If this interpretation stands, then we do have evidence of threefold agency in the calling of judges, even if no specific action is attributed to all three persons. Nevertheless, to fully understand examples of seemingly isolated actions, we must turn to the doctrine of appropriations.

Put concisely, the doctrine of appropriations (from the Latin *ad* + *proprium*, "to draw toward the proper")[75] attributes a divine attribute or an action to

75. Emery, *The Trinity*, 165.

the divine person with whom one most closely associates it. The term "appropriation" was developed by Richard of St. Victor, though the practice was widespread in the West thanks to its frequent use by Augustine, who tended to use appropriations for titles alone, not for divine actions.[76] The doctrine of appropriations is rooted in the idea that any essential attributes or acts belong to the persons in a manner fitting their unique mode of subsistence and their personal properties.[77] If a particular act or attribute more closely resembles the unique hypostatic mode of a divine person, then we can appropriate that act or attribute to that person. For example, the Father is the source of the Son and Spirit, so the shared divine act of creating most clearly reveals the hypostatic mode of the Father, as does the shared attribute of power. Both the act of creating and the attribute of power can be appropriated to the Father for this reason. As Joseph Pohle remarks, "The *appropriata* are apt to lead to a knowledge of the *propria* [the personal properties of each person]."[78] Perhaps the doctrine of appropriations will become clearer with several examples of its use.

The most famous appropriation of attributes treats the Father as power, the Son as wisdom, and the Holy Spirit as goodness.[79] Because the Father is the source of the Son and Spirit, he is best associated with power, though technically all three share the same power. The Son is best associated with wisdom because he reveals truth. And the Spirit is associated with goodness because it is clearly revealed in his mode of existence, which in the West is often thought to be the bond of love between Father and Son. This triad is used by Hugh of St. Victor—not to be confused with Richard of St. Victor—to develop a psychological analogy of the Trinity and to appropriate different aspects of the economy to unique persons, where the Father is revealed under an economy of power and the law, the Son is revealed in wisdom that manifests truth, and the Spirit is revealed in love where the good is restored within Christians.[80] Likely drawing on Hugh, Peter Abelard develops a theology that attempts to distinguish between the three persons on

76. Ayres, *Augustine and the Trinity*, 228. For Augustine's appropriations, see esp. Augustine, *On the Holy Trinity* 7.1–3; 15.19.

77. Poirel, *Livre de la nature*, 282.

78. Pohle, *Divine Trinity*, 244.

79. Regarding the origin of this triad, Michel Barnes notes that this trio seems to harmonize "power and wisdom" (1 Cor. 1:24) with "power and goodness" in Plato's *Republic* 509B (Barnes, *Power of God*, 257). Recently, similar appropriations have emerged in non-Western contexts, contextualized to philosophies that are different than the Platonic and Stoic ones that shape this triad yet remaining quite similar in broad contours. For example, the Vedic triad of being (*Sat*), consciousness (*Chit*), and bliss (*Ananda*) can be appropriated to Father, Son, and Spirit. See Yung, *Mangoes or Bananas?*, 111–14.

80. Hugh of St. Victor, *On the Three Days* 2.21–22; 3.27.

the basis of these three attributes, believing that the divine persons signify aspects of the divine nature, each of which is a different way of defining the supreme good. The Father is power, the Son wisdom, and the Holy Spirit goodness, each person being one aspect of divine perfection. Abelard was condemned twice because his theology resembled Sabellianism and seemed to imply that not all of the divine persons were powerful, wise, or good. His initial work was burned at a council of Soissons in 1121, and his attempted revisions were condemned at Sens in 1140.[81] Abelard's theology reveals the limits of appropriations. They cannot fully distinguish the persons, as they do not meet all the criteria for personhood, discussed in chapter 4. If the Spirit is distinguished only by goodness, for example, the relationality criterion is not clearly satisfied, for how is goodness necessarily distinguished from power and wisdom by a relation rooted in the divine processions?[82] Given that these attributes are appropriated, Abelard also fails the uniqueness criterion; if the Spirit, as goodness, shares this goodness with Father and Son, the Spirit would lack a truly unique personal property and mode of subsistence. The triad of power, wisdom, and goodness may help us understand the persons somewhat more clearly, but appropriations alone cannot be the basis for personal distinctions.

An appropriation more common among modern theologians is to speak of Father, Son, and Holy Spirit as Creator, Redeemer, and Sanctifier. Often, this appropriation is made in an effort to avoid masculine names that may imply that God is male. The concern is understandable, since the notion that God is male is contrary to the fact of divine immateriality, which negates any biological sex in God, and contrary to the doctrine of analogy, which insists that there is a greater difference between human gender and God's "masculine" or "feminine" attributes than there is similarity. Though the proponents of this triad are well meaning, it does not follow the biblical norm for speaking of God, and its intentions are not fulfilled in the church catholic found across the world. Zaida Maldonado Pérez explains, "Because the Spanish language (and all Romance languages) has no neuter forms for persons and things, hearing God referred to as Creator, Redeemer, and Sanctifier did not, at least for me, achieve its intentions: God was still male."[83] Though, undoubtedly, not every Spanish speaker would understand

81. On Peter Abelard's life and trinitarianism, see Mews, *Abelard and Heloise*, 101–22, 226–49; Thom, *Logic of the Trinity*, 62–77.
82. Even Hugh's attempt to develop these attributes into a psychological analogy rooted in procession falls short.
83. Maldonado Pérez, "The Trinity *Es*," 54–55. The proposed terms are typically masculine in Spanish.

the language of Creator, Redeemer, Sanctifier in the same way, it seems probable that many others would share her conclusions. There is a second problem that moves beyond gender in different languages: such titles can seem to depersonalize God, undermining much Christian spirituality.[84] Besides, the formula reduces the divine names to a feature of the economy, eliminating any reference to the immanent Trinity.[85] Though these appropriations should not be used to distinguish the persons, we can nevertheless maintain them to help us gain some understanding of the divine persons in their inseparable operations. All three persons create, but the Father, as source of the Son and Spirit, is most clearly evident in creation, so we can appropriate "Creator" to him. All three persons redeem, but the Son alone was incarnate, as was fitting, given his eternal generation, so we can appropriate "Redeemer" to him. All three persons sanctify, but the Spirit is the perfecting cause of all divine actions, so God's perfecting work in us most clearly reveals the Holy Spirit, and we can rightly appropriate "Sanctifier" to him.

More must be said about appropriated actions, which are somewhat distinct from appropriated attributes.[86] In scholastic theology, it became common to speak of inseparable operations that terminated in the Son and the Spirit. Divine acts *ad extra* were said to have a *fundamentum*, or source, and a *terminus*, or conclusion. These terms are relational; the *terminus* is the person whose relation or hypostatic mode is most clearly revealed in the execution of the act, while the *fundamentum* is the person whose relation or hypostatic mode is most clearly revealed in the initiation of the act.[87] Certain acts might terminate on the Son, like the incarnation, while others, like the inspiration of the prophets, might terminate on the Holy Spirit. Though all three persons were technically involved in inspiring the prophets, the act terminated on the Holy Spirit, and though all three persons were technically involved in the Son's taking on flesh, the act terminated on the Son. The Father, as *fundamentum*, is alone said to send (e.g., John 3:16), though he does so through the Spirit (Matt. 1:18; Luke 1:25). The Son, as *terminus* of the act, is the one sent. This appropriation stands, even though in another sense we can say that the Son has come of his own accord.

84. Maldonado Pérez argues that this triad fails to connect with personal spirituality of *evangélicas* (Latina evangelicals, without the political connotations of "evangelical" in recent US culture), who do not "relate to the Trinity, nor address, praise, or pray to the Godhead specifically through these distinctions" ("The Trinity *Es*," 55, 64).

85. F. Sanders, *Image of the Immanent Trinity*, 10–11.

86. A helpful treatment is found in Barcellos, *Trinity & Creation*, 87–96.

87. See Muller, *Post-Reformation Reformed Dogmatics*, 268.

The appropriations take strides toward helping us understand how the doctrine of inseparable operations does not eliminate personal distinction but rather ensures that in all divine actions each person can be known, though one can perhaps be known most clearly according to that person's unique mode of subsistence. At times, appropriations have been used in too speculative a manner,[88] but when we derive them from Scripture, avoid arbitrary attributions, and refuse to distinguish the persons on the basis of appropriations,[89] they are a helpful tool in preserving personal distinction amid the unity of inseparable operations. However, they alone cannot do so sufficiently, so I turn now to the final dogmatic locus in my treatment of the doctrine of the Trinity: our communion with the triune God.

FOR FURTHER READING

Theological Treatments of Inseparable Operations

Lonergan, Bernard. *The Triune God: Systematics*. Translated by Michael G. Shields. Edited by Robert M. Doran and H. Daniel Monsour. Toronto: University of Toronto Press, 2007.

> Lonergan's text could be listed at the end of several chapters, but I place his work here due to his careful exploration of questions about God's trinitarian consciousness and his treatment of divine action in relation to contingent predication. Few texts are more careful in their analysis.

Vidu, Adonis. *The Same God Who Works All Things: Inseparable Operations in Trinitarian Theology*. Grand Rapids: Eerdmans, 2021.

> This work is a much-needed monograph exploring the doctrine of inseparable operations in theological perspective, the first English-language work of this sort of which I am aware. This is an invaluable treatment of an underexplored locus in theology.

The History of Inseparable Operations

Barnes, Michel René. *The Power of God: Δύναμις in Gregory of Nyssa's Trinitarian Theology*. Washington, DC: Catholic University of America Press, 2001.

> Michel Barnes offers the most expansive study of *dynamis* ("power") in print, exploring the ancient medical and philosophical histories of the word as well

88. As Catherine Mowry LaCugna summarizes, "The attributions are often arbitrary and sometimes contradict biblical ways of speaking about God's activity" (*God for Us*, 98).

89. I draw these three criteria for the appropriate use of appropriations from Barth, *Church Dogmatics* I/1, 429.

as the word's deployment among early trinitarians, with special emphasis on Gregory of Nyssa.

Beckwith, Carl L. *The Holy Trinity*. Fort Wayne: Luther Academy, 2016.

Beckwith's survey of the doctrine of the Trinity has an especially helpful treatment of the doctrine of inseparable operations, with particular attention given to its formulation in the history of Lutheran thought.

CHAPTER 8

Communion

Our exploration of the doctrine of the Trinity has thus far considered the need to adopt a trinitarian structure for worship as well as the trinitarian shape of the application of salvation that is evident in the overlap between perichoresis and union. Yet, I have not attended in adequate detail to the question of how Christians are intended to experience the triune God to whom we are united in salvation and whom we address in worship. Speaking anecdotally, I have often found that college students in my classes and adult learners I have taught in Sunday school lack a conceptual framework for making sense of the experience of God in a trinitarian way. We must worship God as one without ever allowing God's oneness to eliminate the distinctions between Father, Son, and Holy Spirit. The absence of any trinitarian framework for thinking through our spiritual life results in a trinitarianism that is largely intellectual and theoretical and is barely relevant at experiential and practical levels. Certainly this will not do, so it is necessary to develop a clear dogmatic account of our communion with God.

Several important disclaimers must be made before I move on with the task of describing the triune structure of Christian spirituality. The first disclaimer is that I do not believe it possible to derive a theology of the Trinity from generalized human experience, though I do believe that human experience has some relevance. I cannot quite accept the wording of Fred Sanders when he writes, "Though everyone who receives the gospel has an experience whose deep structure is Trinitarian, nobody constructs the doctrine of the Trinity from the deliverances of that experience." After all, the scriptural accounts of early Christians' experience of the Father, Son, and Holy Spirit, the same accounts that lead to the doctrine of the Trinity, are, in large part, based on the historical experiences of the disciples, who came to recognize Jesus as worthy of worship. While the direct teachings of Christ as recorded in the Bible certainly play a role in the disciples' thinking, these teachings were often experienced firsthand too. Nevertheless, the direct role of experience in grounding the doctrine of the Trinity ended with the completion of the inspired biblical canon, so today we are left in a different situation. Therefore, I fully support Sanders's broader point (and recognize my critique to be somewhat peripheral to that point): "What would result from that maneuver [of deriving the Trinity from experience], if it were possible, would be a codified account of the distinctions in our spiritual experience with no guarantee that it corresponds to distinctions in God."[1] We should expect that a triune God could produce a threefold spirituality, but there is no guarantee that plurality in religious experience corresponds to plurality in the Godhead. The foundations of the doctrine of the Trinity lie in exegesis.

Second, though Christian worship and spiritual experience should be the worship and experience of God as Father, Son, and Holy Spirit, the limits of human experience and language ultimately prevent our fully understanding the experience of God. As Maria Bingemer explains, "At the level of communication, therefore, silence is more suitable than a word for the experience of God. Silence is the companion of this experience, of the intimate understanding of it, of its enjoyment, and ultimately of the perception that concepts are insufficient to express it."[2] Here I am reminded of Thomas Aquinas, the great theologian whose trinitarian insights were so central to early chapters in this work and who, late in life, experienced God in a mystical way and stopped writing, concluding that his theological reflections were as chaff in comparison with the beatific vision. We await the coming of the Lord, when we shall see God face-to-face. At that eschatological end, we will truly know and experience God as Father, Son, and Holy Spirit. How extensively we will be able to explain that experience using human language in the new creation is something I do not know. In this life, however, our understanding of our spiritual experience must be normed by Scripture and those doctrines that arise as a good and necessary consequence of Scripture, though perhaps one may hope for an experience of God that exceeds what we can currently know and say. For now, I turn to what can be said and known about communion with God, beginning with the word "communion" itself and proceeding to analyze three possible models for understanding the trinitarian structure of Christian experience and worship.

1. F. Sanders, *Triune God*, 77.
2. Bingemer, *Face for God*, 26.

Koinōnia and Communion

Koinōnia is the ideal Greek word for the dogmatic exploration of our experience of the Trinity, though it is only used nineteen times in the New Testament. Thirteen of these instances are found in Paul's writings, with another four in 1 John 1:3, 6–7. The term may emphasize either giving or receiving, so it can be translated as "participation," "impartation," or "fellowship."[3] This ambiguity is further complicated in some verses. For example, 2 Corinthians 13:13 speaks of the "fellowship of the Holy Spirit." The genitive ("of the Holy Spirit") could be subjective, meaning that the Spirit is the "author and font" of fellowship, or it could have an objective sense, such that we are called to participate in the Spirit.[4] In broader Greco-Roman usage, *koinōnia* might refer to community, companionship, or even a unity of thought.[5] In figures like Plutarch, Philo, Josephus, and the Stoics, such unity typically assumes the need for human moral transformation rooted in knowledge and directed toward some concept of the divine.[6] In a similar fashion, *koinōnia* with God in the New Testament requires that we walk in the light (1 John 1:6–7); is frequently used to refer "strictly to the relation of faith to Christ" (1 Cor. 1:9; 2 Cor. 13:13; Phil. 1:5; Philem. 6),[7] which includes knowledge along with trust; and is aimed toward Christians being "partakers of the divine nature" (*theias koinōnoi phuseōs*; 2 Pet. 1:4 ESV). This specific phrase—"partakers of the divine nature"—is not found in other sources and thus is possibly unique to Peter.[8] In the context of 2 Peter, this phrase points to our participation in the present moral excellence of Christ and our future eternity and glory.[9] The term *koinōnia* is often found in or near duplex or triplex formulas in the New Testament, as in Paul's triadic benediction: "The grace of the Lord Jesus Christ, and the love of God, and the fellowship of the Holy Spirit be with you all" (2 Cor. 13:13). Elsewhere, "fellowship with the Spirit" is parallel to "encouragement in Christ" (Phil. 2:1), and John speaks of "fellowship . . . with the Father and with his Son, Jesus Christ" (1 John 1:3; cf. 1 Cor. 1:9). When 2 Peter speaks of Christians being partakers (*koinōnoi*) of the divine nature, the formula is introduced after a duplex formula pointing to the Father and the Son (1:1–2; cf. 2 Cor. 9:13). In summary, *koinōnia* occurs

3. Hauck, "κοινωνός [*koinōnos*]," 3:798.
4. Maleparampil, *"Trinitarian" Formulae in St. Paul*, 95. The fact that the other two clauses in this verse are subjective genitives suggests the same may be the case here.
5. *New International Dictionary*, s.v. "Koinos."
6. Starr, *Sharers in the Divine Nature*, 235.
7. *New International Dictionary*, s.v. "Koinos."
8. Starr, *Sharers in the Divine Nature*, 236–37.
9. Starr, *Sharers in the Divine Nature*, 227.

in trinitarian contexts and speaks of the Christian's knowledge of and faith in Father, Son, and Holy Spirit in a way that carries moral implications and produces transformation.

When the Greek New Testament was translated into the Latin Vulgate, *koinōnia* was rendered by a variety of words, including *societas* ("society"), *participatio* ("participation"), and *communio* ("communion"), though the latter was less common.[10] As *communio* filtered into the Indo-Germanic languages, it could be taken to derive from the Latin *mun*, meaning "entrenchment, dike or embankment," in which case it would refer to being behind a common embankment. It could also be taken to derive from the Latin *munus*, meaning "task/service," or "gift/present."[11] At times the term *communio* has been used to speak of the unity of the Trinity. For example, Novatian speaks of a *communio substantiae*, clarified to be a "reciprocal transfer" of glory and divinity by degrees.[12] Novatian's understanding of this unity is considerably weaker than the later concept of consubstantiality, and it contains many elements that are similar to later Arianism.[13] In modern theology, the notion of communion has made a resurgence in trinitarian thought. Gisbert Greshake summarizes his particularly noteworthy use of the term thus: "Whoever lives in communion puts himself at the service of another, hands on to this other a gift that shapes and forms him such that out of the giver and the receiver of communication, a third is constituted: the communio that is shared together."[14] Communion has also been central to the theology of John Zizioulas, who tends to take the term in both trinitarian and eucharistic directions.[15] This eucharistic emphasis on communion has a long history in Christian thought and is rooted in the use of *koinōnia* in 1 Corinthians 10:16.[16] The terms "Eucharist" and "communion," in fact, are often used synonymously with reference to the Lord's Supper. One more example is found in the Reformed tradition, which understands communion as being rooted in our union with Christ. Thus, John Owen defines communion as God's "communication of himself unto

10. Dewailly, "Communio-communicatio," 49. *Societas* was used for 1 Cor. 1:9; 2 Cor. 6:14; Gal. 2:9; Phil. 2:1, 3:10; 1 John 1:3, 6–7. *Participatio* was used for 1 Cor. 10:16b. *Communio* was used in Heb. 13:16.

11. Greshake, "Trinity as 'Communio,'" 333–34.

12. Novatian, *De Trinitate* 27.6.

13. Novatian considers the Father before the Son and appeals to John 10:36 to claim that the Son is inferior since the Son received sanctification from the Father (Novatian, *De Trinitate* §§27, 31). Novatian is concerned to preserve divine monarchy, and he tends to assert a volitional or moral unity, with this term an ambiguous exception. See Kelly, *Early Christian Doctrines*, 115, 125–26.

14. Greshake, "Trinity as 'Communio,'" 333–34.

15. Zizioulas, *Being as Communion*.

16. Dewailly, "Communio-communicatio."

us, with our return unto him of that which he requires and accepts, flowing from that union which in Jesus Christ we have with him."[17]

Three Models of Communion

Various models of communion provide a conceptual framework that helps explain the experience of God as Trinity through liturgical worship, prayer, and spiritual disciplines. For my present purposes, I will explore three broad models of communion, with several variants and practical applications being considered under each larger variant. In exploring these models, I will use two conceptual distinctions. The first is rooted in doxology. As Gilles Emery explains, we can distinguish between "**co-ordinate** address" doxologies (e.g., "glory to the Father and to the Son and to the Holy Spirit") and "mediatorial pattern" doxologies (e.g., "glory to the Father, through the Son, in the Holy Spirit"). Co-ordinate address "ranks the three persons together as equal," while mediatorial address "makes clear the order of the divine persons in the economy of salvation."[18] This distinction is a long-standing one that has played a major role in past trinitarian debates. For example, when Basil of Caesarea used both co-ordinate doxologies and the more linear mediatorial pattern, he was accused of inconsistency by **Pneumatomachians**, who rejected the co-ordinate versions and argued that the linear mediatorial pattern demonstrated a difference in nature and the Son's and Spirit's subordination, in rank, to the Father.[19] Rejecting this position, Basil rightly insisted that there was biblical warrant for both doxologies. The coordinate model of communion therefore serves as an important reminder that all three trinitarian persons can be addressed in the grammatical second person—for example, "you" rather than "him"—as God.

Sarah Coakley provides a second distinction when she explores a **linear model**, which Emery designated as mediatorial, in contrast with an **incorporative model**. In the incorporative model, Coakley says, "the Holy Spirit is perceived as the primary means of incorporation into the trinitarian life of God, and as constantly and 'reflexively' at work in believers in the circle of response to the Father's call." In contrast, the linear model gives "primary focus . . . to the Father-Son relationship, and the Holy Spirit becomes the secondary purveyor of that relationship to the church."[20] The difference here

17. Owen, *Communion with the Triune God*, 94.
18. Emery, *The Trinity*, 7.
19. Basil, *On the Holy Spirit* §§3–5.
20. Coakley, *God, Sexuality, and the Self*, 111.

is partially a degree of emphasis, with the incorporative model focusing on the Spirit as the divine person drawing us into the life of God and the linear model emphasizing the Father-Son relationship into which we are drawn. However, Coakley argues that this difference in emphasis has consequences in terms of the freedom each model appears to give to noninstitutional and individual expressions of communion. The incorporative model is thus particularly common among Pentecostals, mystics, and historical theological movements that did not conform to the more hierarchical institutional church, with its linear emphasis. All three models have biblical warrant, and all three can benefit the church today, so I will explore each in due course.

The Co-ordinate Model

The co-ordinate model is rooted in the various passages of Scripture that link the three persons together in liturgical contexts and in biblical passages that speak of fellowship with, or communication from, each person distinctly. Paul's benediction in 2 Corinthians 13:13[21] is a noteworthy example: "The grace of the Lord Jesus Christ, and the love of God, and the fellowship of the Holy Spirit be with you all." Similarly, the Bible speaks distinctly of communion with the Father (1 John 1:3), with the Son (1 Cor. 1:9), and with the Spirit (2 Cor. 13:13).[22] If communion is a reciprocal communication, then biblical texts that speak of unique communications from the Father, Son, and Spirit to the church provide further evidence of co-ordinate communion.[23] Kevin Vanhoozer notes passages where the Father (e.g., Mark 1:11), Son (e.g., John 11:41), and Spirit (e.g., John 16:13–14) are identified as uniquely communicative. Affirming the doctrine of inseparable operations, he concludes, "The three persons are distinct communicative agents that share a common communicative agency."[24] The co-ordinate model of communion is rooted in this basic theological claim: each divine person may be addressed directly in prayer and speech.

When the co-ordinate model seeks to foster direct address to each divine person, it prompts the obvious question of how the speaker might discern the three persons addressed from one another. A number of spiritual and mystical theologies throughout the centuries have sought to identify the basic features of the human spiritual perception of each divine person. For example, medieval mystical theology in various forms sought vocabulary that

---

21. This verse is 13:14 in some versions (e.g., ESV, NIV).
22. Owen, *Communion with the Triune God*, 97.
23. Owen, *Communion with the Triune God*, 102–4.
24. Vanhoozer, *Remythologizing Theology*, 246–47.

could capture the unique human experience of each divine person. Thus, Hildegard von Bingen describes the Holy Spirit in terms of *viriditas*. As Anne Hunt explains, "Virtually untranslatable into English, *viriditas* literally means greenness, verdure (*viridis*, green, fresh). . . . It connotes life, vitality, freshness, life force, fecundity. By it, she means all life, physical as well as spiritual, is quickened, nurtured, sustained by the Holy Spirit, giver of life."[25] Using a similar concept, Julian of Norwich frequently speaks of the Holy Spirit as the enkindling one, a description that Hunt summarizes as "effectively [signifying] the soul's entry into the trinitarian communion."[26] The language Julian uses to describe the Spirit automatically tends toward the incorporative model; the three models of communion are not always sharply distinguished. Such words seeking to articulate the unique hypostatic mode of each person may leave one equally unclear—What, precisely, is the human experience of the *viriditas* or enkindling of the Spirit?

Modern theologians have sometimes sought an explanation of trinitarian communion in distinctions in human religious experience. For example, Raimundo Panikkar argues that there are three basic types of spirituality, those rooted in ritual action (*karma*), those rooted in love (*bhakti*), and those rooted in knowledge (*jñāna*), which correspond to apophatic iconolatry, personalism, and *advaita*.[27] Panikkar believes that these three approaches to spirituality can be reconciled only in the Trinity, though he believes that this reconciliation involves strands of authentic spirituality from many religions.[28] Panikkar argues that the Father is the absolute, ineffable God, who is known only through his icon, the Son. We must ultimately remain in apophatic silence about the Father.[29] By virtue of the incarnation, Panikkar argues, only the Son can be known personally.[30] The Spirit is radically immanent to us, experienced as a consciousness of our place in reality or as authentic existence, which Panikkar links with the Hindu notion of *advaita*, the unity of self with God.[31] In the Spirit, then, is true knowledge of the self as constituted by God, our end. Panikkar's theology is clearly in service of interreligious dialogue, and he makes interesting connections between three traditional forms of Hindu spirituality—*karma*, *bhakti*, and *jñāna*—and the Christian doctrine of the Trinity. Yet, if what we have said about consubstantiality,

25. Hunt, *The Trinity: Insights from the Mystics*, 37.
26. Hunt, *The Trinity: Insights from the Mystics*, 137.
27. Panikkar, *The Trinity and the Religious Experience of Man*, 16.
28. Panikkar, *The Trinity and the Religious Experience of Man*, 41.
29. Panikkar, *The Trinity and the Religious Experience of Man*, 44, 47.
30. Panikkar, *The Trinity and the Religious Experience of Man*, 52.
31. Panikkar, *The Trinity and the Religious Experience of Man*, 64–65.

inseparable operations, and the appropriations is true, then Panikkar's attribution of immanence to the Spirit and transcendence to the Father can be nothing more than appropriation and is thus not finally a distinction in how we know the divine persons. Moreover, Panikkar's vision has been accused of being more like a Christian inculturation of Hinduism than an orthodox account of the Trinity expressed in interfaith terms.[32]

It seems likely that attempts to express the distinct experience of Father, Son, and Holy Spirit would be better rooted in the history of the Father's self-revelation through the Son and the Spirit. This brings us to an interesting yet underdeveloped aspect of Vladimir Lossky's trinitarian thought. Lossky argues, "In his *kenōsis*, the Son revealed himself as a person, but he concealed his divine nature under 'the form of a slave.'" Here one thinks of John's teaching that "the world did not recognize him" (John 1:10), the so-called messianic secret in the Gospel of Mark whereby Jesus keeps his true identity hidden (e.g., Mark 1:34; 7:36; 8:27–30), or the transfiguration, where the true nature of Christ is briefly revealed (Matt. 17:1–8 and pars.). Turning to pneumatology, Lossky writes, "The Spirit, through a complementary economy, manifests the divine nature, but conceals his person."[33] Such a hiddenness of person explains the debate surrounding the personality of the Holy Spirit, discussed in chapter 4. The mission of the Son thus reveals the unique person of the Son in filial relation with the Father and empowered by the Holy Spirit, who rests on him. Conversely, the mission of the Spirit reveals what is common to God: the power of the charismatic gifts and miracles and the goodness and love of God manifest in the fruits of the Spirit (Gal. 5:22–26). The Father remains hidden in both nature and person. Interestingly, Lossky reverses this distinction between person and nature in the work of salvation: "The Holy Spirit communicates himself *to persons*, marking each member of the Church with a seal of personal and unique relationship to the Trinity, becoming present in each person."[34] Conversely, the Son overcomes the "triple barrier which separates us from God—death, sin, and nature" by uniting the human and divine natures in his person and then defeating sin and death.[35] Through the cross, the entirety of the human nature in its corruption and death has been transformed into the means of salvation.[36]

---

32. See the critique found in Tanchanpongs, "Asian Reformulations of the Trinity," 120–39.
33. Lossky, *Dogmatic Theology*, 143. See also Lossky, *Mystical Theology of the Eastern Church*, 166–67.
34. Lossky, *Mystical Theology of the Eastern Church*, 168.
35. Lossky, *Mystical Theology of the Eastern Church*, 136. Here Lossky draws on a concept from Nicholas Cabasilas.
36. Lossky, *Mystical Theology of the Eastern Church*, 154.

Lossky's approach has several benefits but ultimately requires modification. Rooting the unique human relation to Son and Spirit in the person-nature distinction moves beyond those approaches, like Panikkar's, that treat the distinction primarily in terms of different forms of human religion and experience. Though Panikkar does draw on the divine missions, particularly the incarnation of the Son, to explain the personalist relation to the Son, Lossky goes even further in rooting communion in the missions by noting features of the Spirit's mission that are different from the Son's. Though a distinction between experiencing the nature of a hypostasis and experiencing the person of hypostasis remains abstract, this abstraction must partly be situated within Lossky's larger apophatic project; ultimately, God exceeds conceptual explanation. Perhaps the claim that the Son is known in person, the Spirit is known in nature, and the Father is hidden rightly collapses into that ineffable experience of what we may call "super-sensible sensation," which cannot be described in theological terminology.[37] Nevertheless, several objections must push us further in our search for a theological understanding of co-ordinate communion with Father, Son, and Spirit.

Perhaps Lossky's largest weakness here is the disconnect between the economic and immanent Trinity. This is a feature of Lossky's larger trinitarian project, which remains so apophatic that one can question the extent to which the missions reveal something eternal about God.[38] In the case of the theology of God revealed in the missions, one wonders how the Spirit can reveal the divine nature if that nature is invisible and ineffable. Some early Christians, including Novatian and Tertullian, took a structurally similar approach to the mission of the Son, who was thought to reveal the divine nature, which was invisible in the Father. Such an approach may distinguish between the Father and the Son, but it is open to a homoian interpretation in which the Son's visible nature is somehow only similar (Greek *homoios*) to the Father's invisible one rather than being the same (Greek *homos*) simple consubstantial nature.[39] Simplicity is also difficult to fit with Lossky's proposal. If, as simplicity entails, the persons are the nature, then how is the nature of the Spirit manifest, but not the person?[40] Lossky prompts us to

---

37. Symeon the New Theologian, *Practical and Theological Chapters* 2.1.

38. So, Aristotle Papanikolaou can critique Lossky because "the link between God's *oikonomia* and the *theologia* of God's immanent life is slim, and God's immanent life as Trinity remains shrouded in an apophatic cloud" (*Being with God*, 51, 91–98).

39. See the discussion in Boersma, *Seeing God*, 104.

40. Papanikolaou argues that Lossky has difficulty maintaining a strong doctrine of simplicity throughout his work (see *Being with God*, 63). Admittedly, the problem of distinguishing person and nature in the Spirit's manifestation is but one particular permutation of the larger theological questions that arise with divine simplicity, so we ought not to make the point too forcefully.

ground unique union with Father, Son, and Spirit in the missions, but more work remains to be done.

Given the ambiguities of the metaphysical explanations offered by Lossky and the religious ones offered by Panikkar, theologians are often rightly driven to the biblical text to seek patterns by which the divine persons may be distinguished in devotional experience. Consider the historical example of John Owen. He explains that "communion consists in *giving* and *receiving*."[41] With this in mind, Owen can argue that communion with the Father consists in love, which the elect receive by faith and return to God in love.[42] He also offers a detailed and complex analysis of the various dimensions of purchased grace and communion with the Son, which can be briefly summarized thus: in communion with the Son, Christians receive the grace of Christ's personal presence and the purchased grace attained through the cross.[43] Owen says that the saints receive communion with the Son when they "cordially approve of this righteousness," by which he means that they recognize themselves as lacking the righteousness necessary to stand before God and therefore rely on and trust in the Son.[44] We have communion with the Holy Spirit as he performs such acts as bringing to mind things spoken by Christ (John 14:26), bearing witness to our adoption (Rom. 8:16), and anointing us.[45] Owen names the condition of Christians who receive these gifts "consolation."

Owen's theology relies on the divine missions and a robust doctrine of appropriations. Communion with the Trinity is through the love of God, the grace of the Son, and the consolation of the indwelling of the Spirit, a distinction that helps us identify the personal distinctiveness of each person in the process, but one that is ultimately an appropriation to each person. When we have communion with one person, we have communion with the others "secondarily."[46] This conclusion follows from the perichoresis of the divine persons and from the inseparability of their operations *ad extra*.[47] Yet, these appropriations are not arbitrary. They are rooted both in Scripture and in the divine missions. Here is where Owen's use of appropriations seems clearer than Pannikar's, though perhaps the latter's thought could be connected more

---

41. Owen, *Communion with the Triune God*, 111. This distinguishes communion from union, which is a unilateral act of God in Owen's mind. See the discussion in Kapic, "Worshipping the Triune God," 21.

42. Owen, *Communion with the Triune God*, 107, 111–14.

43. Owen, *Communion with the Triune God*, 143, 271.

44. Owen, *Communion with the Triune God*, 310–14; see also 157–58.

45. Owen, *Communion with the Triune God*, 373–87.

46. Owen, *Communion with the Triune God*, 95, 105.

47. See the discussion in McGraw, "Trinitarian Doxology," 304–5.

clearly with Scripture. Owen's larger pattern of communion with the Father in love, the Son in grace, and the Spirit through indwelling and consolation mirrors the pattern of 2 Corinthians 13:13, which attributes grace, love, and communion to Son, Father, and Spirit, respectively. Owen's explanation of the purchasing grace of the Son and the consolation of the Holy Spirit depends on the missions of each person, which are rooted in the divine processions and are thus uniquely the missions of that trinitarian person, not in such a way that the persons are divided, but in a way that the persons are uniquely knowable by virtue of these missions.[48]

To summarize, the co-ordinate model shows that Christians have communion with each of the divine persons in a distinct way, receiving from each through the inseparable works that terminate on one or another person. Such appropriations are not arbitrary but are rooted in the divine processions, which characterize the unique hypostatic mode of each person, and in the missions through which these processions are manifest in historical works of the Son and Spirit. When we receive purchased grace from the Son or consolation from the Spirit through works appropriated to them or founded in their missions, we still have communion secondarily with the other two persons. Any experience primarily of one divine person, or any term intended to describe this experience, derives from these missions and appropriations. To set aside the technical language for a moment, the above point can be summarized as follows: God is given in acts that most clearly reveal the Father, Son, or Spirit, the most notable of these being the missions of the Son and Spirit. While we can never have communion with the Father, Son, or Spirit in isolation from the other persons, we can more clearly receive from and speak to one of the divine persons in any particular divine act. This means that the co-ordinate model can provide a dogmatic foundation for our unique fellowship with Father, Son, and Spirit. However, this model does not exhaust the ways in which our fellowship with one person relates to fellowship with the others. To explore this question further, I must now turn to two further models of communion: the linear and the incorporative.

The Linear Model

The linear model of communion describes our fellowship with the Father through the Son in the Spirit. It finds New Testament textual support in the

---

48. Owen treats the missions as the "foundation" of our communion with the Spirit and Son (Owen, *Communion with the Triune God*, 91, 355). According to Owen, this is true in the sense that without the missions, sin would prohibit any such communion, but also in the sense that the contours of fellowship with the Son and Spirit are rooted in their missional work.

common triadic pattern found in various texts. For example, Paul explains the great scope of salvation in Romans by moving from the judgment of God (1:18–3:20) to justification through Christ (3:21–8:1) and then to sanctification in the Spirit (8:2–30).[49] This linear pattern fits the patristic rule that says the inseparable *ad extra* work of God moves from the Father, through the Son, to the Spirit. The book of Hebrews lines up even more clearly with the linear model, a model, Coakley explains, in which the Spirit is the "secondary purveyor of [the Father-Son] relationship to the church."[50] Madison Pierce explores the prosopological exegesis in the book of Hebrews, finding evidence of a clear pattern in the first two sections of the book. In these sections, the Father speaks to confirm the superiority and identity of the Son (1:5–13; 5:5–6; 7:17, 21; 8:7–12), the Son speaks to accept his role in saving humanity (2:12–13; 10:5–7), and the Spirit exhorts the community not to neglect the salvation available through the Son (3:7–4:11; 10:15–17).[51] The Spirit's role in Hebrews is to address the reader in order to testify to the Father and Son, while the other two divine persons address one another. The linear pattern in Romans and Hebrews mirrors the larger pattern of the biblical canon, where covenants with Israel appropriated to the Father result in the later incarnation of the Son and, following his ascent, the outpouring of the Holy Spirit at Pentecost.

Though we have clear exegetical reasons for thinking of communion with God according to the linear model, it is worth noting that this is not the only way to conceive of communion with God in the Bible. Romans follows this linear triadic pattern, but other key epistles such as 1 Corinthians and Galatians remain triadic but discuss the divine persons in different orders. Even the clear linear pattern in Hebrews breaks down in the third section, perhaps due to a shift from intratrinitarian discourse toward God's speech to us in the Son.[52] Speaking of the triplex formulas more broadly, we must note Paul's many variations in ordering the names, suggesting that Paul does not intend to give a fixed order.[53] The linear model is important, though not exclusive, in our understanding of *koinōnia*.

To a large extent, the linear model has been dominant in the history of theology, largely due to its inclusion as a key dimension of the doctrine of inseparable operations, discussed in the previous chapter. During the Nicene

49. Erickson, *God in Three Persons*, 190–91.
50. Coakley, *God, Sexuality, and the Self*, 111.
51. Pierce, *Divine Discourse*, 2, 178–82.
52. Pierce, *Divine Discourse*, 194–97.
53. Maleparampil, *"Trinitarian" Formulae in St. Paul*, 238. Maleparampil cites Rom. 8:11; 15:15–16, 30; 1 Cor. 12:4–6; 2 Cor. 1:21–22; 13:13; Gal. 4:6.

debates, Athanasius could write, "[The] grace and gift given in the Trinity
is given by the Father through the Son in the Holy Spirit. Just as the grace
given through the Son is from the Father, so too we cannot have fellowship
[*koinōnia*] with the gift except in the Holy Spirit."[54] Many centuries later,
Petrus van Mastricht argued that the linear pattern of economic operations
should lead to an "economic worship," wherein we seek the various benefits
of salvation from the specific person to whom the benefit is appropriated and
wherein we are to thank each person specifically for the gifts appropriated
to him.[55] Such economic worship renders the *taxis* of inseparable operations into a conceptual framework whereby we have distinct requests of, and
thanksgiving toward, each divine person.

The linear model of communion is perhaps most apparent in prayer. Perhaps it is clearer to say that that the linear model gives conceptual formulation
to the prior practice of prayer.[56] In the words of Francesca Murphy, "At its
fullest, prayer is brought about not by an innate religious sense but by the
Mediator in whose name it is made, and in whose Spirit it is inspired. This is
why prayer is Trinitarian."[57] Here we can apply the patristic formula for the
proper tripersonal shape of inseparable operations.

Prayer is in the Spirit, through the Son, to the Father. This statement
deserves explication. Prayer is in the Spirit (Eph. 6:18; Jude 20). It is the
Spirit who convicts us of sin (John 16:8), prompting prayer, and who guides
our words when we do not know what to pray (Rom. 8:26–27). Augustine adds that the Spirit asks on our behalf because "God's love has been
poured out in our hearts through the Holy Spirit" (Rom. 5:5). He adds that
when we ask in love of God and of neighbor, praying in the love from the
Spirit, we are keeping the commandments and so shall receive from God
(cf. 1 John 3:22).[58]

Prayer is through the Son by virtue of the mediatorial office of high priest
that he assumed through the incarnation. The Son took on human nature,
praying intercessory prayers for those around him (Luke 22:31; John 17:9–19;
presumably Luke 6:12) in the fashion of a faithful first-century Jew. Jesus
now fulfills this intercessory role as our great high priest (Heb. 7:23–28) who
has ascended to the right hand of the Father. As James Torrance notes, Jesus

54. Athanasius, *Letters to Serapion on the Holy Spirit* 1.30.6. Athanasius is commenting
here on 2 Cor. 13:14.
55. Van Mastricht, *Theoretical-Practical Theology* 1.2.24.15.
56. This is true in a historical sense as well. As Robert Louis Wilken remarks succinctly,
"Before there was a 'doctrine' of the Trinity, Christian prayers invoked the Holy Trinity" (*Spirit
of Early Christian Thought*, 31).
57. Murphy, "The Trinity and Prayer," 507.
58. Augustine, *Homilies on the First Epistle of John* 6.8.

212 Trinitarian Dogmatics

taking on our prayers, cleansing them, and making them his own is part of the "wonderful exchange" (*mirifica commutatio, commercium admirabile*) of the incarnation.[59] The Son's mediatorial role is also a role of the human and divine natures in harmony, which is significant for our prayer. Jesus is not only a human representative to the Father in prayer but also a divine representative to us. Contrary to popular conceptions that may treat the Son as our ally against a wrathful Father, the consubstantiality of the Father, Son, and Spirit requires that they are one in will and inseparable in operation, meaning that, as Carl Trueman explains, "God the Father, God the Son, and God the Holy Spirit are one God and all desire the same things. Thus, Christ as God-man asks the Father only for that which the Father desires to give him."[60] The Son's mediatorial prayer perfectly reflects the will of the Father, with whom he is consubstantial. Moreover, the Spirit can work to conform our humanity to Christ's, and our human will to his, because the Spirit shares the divine *ousia* of the Son and Father. The Spirit, too, is our intercessor (Rom. 8:27; John 14:16).

Prayer is to the Father, as is seen in the Lord's Prayer (Matt. 6:9–15; Luke 11:1–4). This is the normal pattern in Scripture, a fact that leads some to argue that prayer to the Son or Spirit, though permissible, should be de-emphasized in favor of prayer to the Father.[61] However, too much de-emphasis based on such scriptural patterns would minimize the experiences of many Christians and various aspects of the Christian tradition. More significantly, it could give the impression of a subordination of the Son and especially the Spirit, which is one risk of the linear model of communion when it is not supplemented with other models. Nevertheless, given the distinctive missions of the Son and Spirit and the typical pattern of inseparable divine operations, it is fitting to make prayer to the Father the common expression of Christian faith, provided that adequate theological safeguards are in place to ensure the full equality of the Son and Spirit. The Father as *fons divinatis*, the font of divinity, is in this sense the source of our salvation.

The risks of subordination associated with the linear approach are evident in Western iconography. Sarah Coakley demonstrates this by examining the growing centrality of the cross in Western religious art. Frequently, the

---

59. J. B. Torrance, *Worship, Community, and the Triune God of Grace*, 46. Attributing this prayer to the incarnation ensures that this mediation and prayer is an act proper to the assumed human nature.

60. Trueman, "The Trinity and Prayer," 226.

61. See Cole, *He Who Gives Life*, 84–87; Grudem, *Systematic Theology*, 380–81. Grudem admits that this dominant pattern is slightly skewed by the facts that many New Testament prayers are by Jesus to the Father and that in the Old Testament the Trinity was not yet clearly revealed.

Father is prominently displayed behind the cross, while the Spirit is increasingly marginalized, sometimes even being replaced with Mary the mother of God.[62] In fairness, the Spirit is not named at the crucifixion, unless perhaps in Jesus's cry—"Father, into your hands I commit my spirit" (Luke 23:46 ESV), though such an interpretation is unusual because it can imply adoptionism. Even granting this qualification, it remains noteworthy that where the cross had once been the Western means of presenting the Trinity visually, it gradually depicted more of a dyad. One can also see in much Western spirituality a growing emphasis on the Father and Son with a corresponding neglect of the Spirit. Though it is beyond the scope of my present analysis to explore reasons for this downplaying of the Spirit, such a de-emphasis does suggest the need for alternative models of communion that highlight the Spirit's role more clearly. Depictions of the Father and Son without the Spirit are certainly distinct from the Rublev icon discussed in chapter 1, where Father, Son, and Spirit are depicted so similarly that any notion of subordination is excluded. Rublev's depiction is more theologically defensible, though like all such depictions, it has its problems. What are needed are further conceptual models that might prevent the subordination of the Spirit. One such model is what Coakley calls the incorporative model. Before exploring this model, however, it would be helpful to note the potential spiritual risks of having a theology of communion that is imbalanced in its treatment on the divine persons.

Simon Chan provides a helpful and accurate summary of the risks that can come from emphasizing one divine person to the neglect of others. Appropriation of the role of Creator to the Father means that a spirituality focused on the Father tends to be more sacramental, seeking the presence of God in creation and tending to partner with an ecological ethic and the recognition of the equal value of all humans. Yet, there are risks with too exclusive an emphasis on the Father, notably a trend toward universalism that neglects the cross and the possible sense of a distant God who is "cold, formalistic, and aloof"[63] rather than a God made present through the Son and Spirit. A spirituality that emphasizes the mission of the Son can take various forms, from the spirituality of liberation that focuses on Christ's ministry to the poor to a more ascetic approach that focuses on following him through suffering and trials. In pietistic and evangelical circles, the notion of Jesus as personal Savior often leads to a lively faith filled with an emphasis on personal devotional practices and evangelism. This pietistic strand risks being too individualistic, missing the Spirit's role in knitting together a global body for Christ. Christians can

---

62. Coakley, God, Sexuality, and the Self, 197, 212–20.
63. Chan, Spiritual Theology, 46.

have a difficult time balancing the emphasis on Christ the liberator with the emphasis on Christ the sufferer; one risks reducing theology to a political program, and the other risks quietism, though the best forms of a spirituality of Christ as liberator or sufferer can avoid these risks. A spirituality focused on the Holy Spirit, Chan argues, results in a "heightened sense of the divine presence"[64] through an emphasis on the charismatic gifts or the fruits of the Spirit, or both. However, such a sense can be difficult to maintain in the mundane routines of normal life, and the pursuit of such experience can lead to a church turned inward toward worship experiences and neglecting ethical and evangelistic responsibilities.[65] Trinitarian spirituality, then, must balance the missions and appropriations and thus also balance personal conversion, spiritual experience, ethical service, and an appreciation of God as manifest through nature in natural revelation. Since the linear model risks subordinating the Spirit and causing an imbalance, it would be helpful for Christians to have a framework that would help with the maintenance of proper balance. The incorporative model is a biblical approach that can fulfill such a purpose.

The Incorporative Model

Against the backdrop of the risk of subordinationist interpretations and applications of the linear model, but with that model's intention of rooting Christian communion with God in the divine economy, Sarah Coakley develops an incorporative model of divine-human communion. While the linear model can often take the form of a binary Father-Son relationship to which the Spirit bears witness in a secondary manner, Coakley sees the incorporative approach centering the Holy Spirit. "In it the Holy Spirit is perceived as the primary means of incorporation into the trinitarian life of God, and as constantly and 'reflexively' at work in believers in the circle of response to the Father's call."[66] Coakley finds this model to be rooted in Romans 8, in tradition in Origen's allegorical readings of the Song of Songs, and in the experience of charismatic and Pentecostal Christians. The incorporative approach takes two forms: an ecstatic form centered on charismatic gifts and an ascetic form where the Spirit facilitates a spirituality of ascent, yet not one that leaves the Spirit behind. The Spirit is not the first rung on the ladder but the harness that ensures safe progression to the heights of our presence before the Father.[67]

64. Chan, *Spiritual Theology*, 47.
65. Chan, *Spiritual Theology*, 48–49.
66. Coakley, *God, Sexuality, and the Self*, 111.
67. Coakley, *God, Sexuality, and the Self*, 133, 140, 142.

To an extent, the incorporative model of communion could be understood as a reversal of the order of inseparable operations. Alternatively, one might follow Orlando Costas in appropriating to the Father and Son the "movement from God to the world" and appropriating to the Holy Spirit the movement drawing creation back to God.[68] These approaches are akin to the incorporative approach, but Coakley has something more in mind, something involving the Father as the "source and ultimate object" of desire and the Spirit as that which makes creation share in this ultimate desire. On this account, the Son "is that divine and perfected creation."[69] The Spirit is the one bringing life to creation by joining creation to Christ (Rom. 8:9–11). To put the matter another way, "No one can say 'Jesus is Lord,' except by the Holy Spirit" (1 Cor. 12:3). Here, the profession of Jesus as Lord represents the faithful affirmation necessary for salvation and union with Christ.[70] The Holy Spirit's incorporative work is necessary for any faith in Jesus and therefore for any adoption as beloved sons and daughters of the Father. For this reason, it is no surprise that pro-Nicene theologians such as Gregory of Nyssa appeal to the necessary role of the Spirit in sanctification as a reason to accept the Spirit's inclusion in inseparable operations, this inclusion being a reason to affirm the Spirit's consubstantiality with Father and Son.[71] Salvation is rooted in the Spirit's incorporative work, through which communion with Father and Son is made possible.

The incorporative model is frequently seen in eucharistic theology. For example, John Zizioulas emphasizes that the Eucharist is fundamentally a communion between persons.[72] The Spirit plays an important role in this process, for the work of Christ is "always conditioned by the coming of the Spirit."[73] If Christ is present in the Eucharist, this is also by the Holy Spirit.[74]

68. "The gospel presupposes a twofold movement: from God to the world and from the world back to God. The first of these movements discloses God as the holy and loving Father of Jesus, and as the loving and obedient Son of the Father. The second reveals God as uniting Spirit" (Costas, *Liberating News*, 73).

69. Coakley, *God, Sexuality, and the Self*, 114.

70. Werner Kramer argues that the formula of Jesus as Lord often occurs in a liturgical setting such as the Philippians Christ hymn or, as in the case of 1 Cor. 12:3, in affirmations of faith accompanying charismatic gifts in congregational settings (*Christ, Lord, Son of God*, 65). Larry Hurtado notes that 1 Cor. 11:2–14:40 is considering questions of worship and that Paul identifies believers as those who "call on" Jesus Christ as Lord. Together, these points suggest that a public affirmation of faith is in mind (see Hurtado, *Lord Jesus Christ*, 142, 198).

71. See the discussion in Anatolios, *Retrieving Nicaea*, 207.

72. A helpful summary is in Papanikolaou, *Being with God*, 138–39.

73. Zizioulas, *Eucharistic Communion and the World*, 9.

74. Zizioulas, *Eucharistic Communion and the World*, 138–39; see also 45.

In Zizioulas's words, "The Spirit as 'power' or 'giver of life' opens up our existence to become relational, so that he may at the same time be 'communion.'"[75]
Zizioulas is following the broad contours of an ancient pattern when he links
the Holy Spirit to the Eucharist. One of the earliest liturgical manuals, *On
the Apostolic Tradition*, describes the liturgy for the Eucharist as part of a
service welcoming a new bishop to ecclesiastical office. After recounting the
biblical narrative of Jesus's act of instituting the Supper, and after giving
thanks to the Father, the new bishop says, "And we ask that you should send
your Holy Spirit on the presbytery of the holy church. Gathering us into one,
may you grant to all the saints who receive for the fullness of the Holy Spirit,
for the confirmation of their faith in truth that we may praise and glorify you
through your child Jesus Christ."[76] Here we see a close conceptual association
between the communion of the community, the work of the Holy Spirit, and
eucharistic communion with the Son.

The association between the Spirit, *koinōnia*, and the Eucharist in tradition is rooted in New Testament patterns of thought that are clear enough to
provide some degree of unity among the wide range of eucharistic theologies.
The Spirit is associated, at times, with *koinōnia* (2 Cor. 13:13; Phil. 2:1), and
the Lord's Supper is called *koinōnia* in the body and blood of Christ (1 Cor.
10:16). Similarly, Acts 2:42 places *koinōnia* and the breaking of bread in
juxtaposition, associating that communion of the church with the act by
which we personally commune with the Son. If the Lord's Supper is done in
remembrance of Christ (Luke 22:19), then we cannot forget that the Holy
Spirit is identified with the role of reminding us of all things about Christ
(John 14:26). It is noteworthy that among the few things concerning the Lord's
Supper that Martin Luther, Huldrich Zwingli, and the other signers of the
Marburg Articles could agree on during the early stages of the Reformation
was the claim that "the use of the sacrament . . . is given and ordained by God
almighty so that weak consciences might be moved to faith through the Holy
Spirit."[77] However deeply Protestants may have been divided over what hap-

75. Zizioulas, *Being as Communion*, 112.

76. Hippolytus, *On the Apostolic Tradition* 4.12. I should note that the Greek is somewhat
unclear in this passage, leading some to reject the epiclesis here, though there are good reasons
for its acceptance. See the discussion by Alistair Stewart in *On the Apostolic Tradition*, 79–81,
86–88. Coakley herself points to Hippolytus and Cyril of Jerusalem as early representatives of
the incorporative approach (*God, Sexuality, and the Self*, 133). The authorship of *On the Apostolic Tradition* is debated, though the theological point stands regardless of whether or how this
debate is resolved. On the debate, see Bradshaw, Johnson, and Phillips, *Apostolic Tradition*, 1–6.

77. *Marburg Articles* §15. The articles were signed by Martin Luther, Justus Jonas, Philip
Melanchthon, Andreas Osiander, Stephan Agricola, Johannes Brenz, Johannes Oecolampadius,
Huldrich Zwingli, Martin Bucer, and Caspar Hedio.

pened to the bread and wine or over the spiritual outcome of the sacrament, the magisterial Reformers were in basic agreement that the Lord's Supper was used by the Holy Spirit to draw new believers into the fellowship of Christians and to reinforce the faith of those who were already members of the body. The same can be said of the various medieval Catholic views of the Eucharist. As Henri de Lubac explains, no matter one's view, "all are agreed on this: the result of the sacrament is unity."[78] Though the polity, identity, and theology of the church are still debated by Protestants, Roman Catholics, and Orthodox, many theological perspectives seem to agree with a basic ecclesiological point de Lubac draws out through a citation of Pope Pelagius: "Those who do not wish to be in unity cannot have the sacrifice [Eucharist], since they do not have the Spirit that dwells in the body of Christ."[79]

   I have presented the Eucharist here as one particularly significant example of the incorporative model, but I do not want this particular instance to distract from the larger argument I am making. The co-ordinate model of communion encourages Christians to direct prayer, worship, and other spiritual disciplines to Father, Son, and Spirit as distinct persons who may be addressed specifically, with the implication that Christian worship is fundamentally a pursuit of a threefold communion with God. The co-ordinate model raises questions about how Christians may think dogmatically about this threefold spiritual address. Appeals to three distinct dimensions of Christian religious experience alone are insufficient to ground the doctrine of the Trinity, so my exploration of the eight key dogmatic loci of the Trinity began in chapter 1 by moving from the threefold worship of the church toward a dogmatic account of the Trinity that flows from the doctrine of consubstantiality. Here, in chapter 8, having developed an extensive account of the Trinity, I added two further models of communion. The linear model of communion with the Trinity draws on the processions, missions, and inseparable operations to provide a conceptual framework that allows us to see how all three divine persons are united in their actions in a manner that reflects the particular hypostatic mode of each person. This linear pattern is particularly clear in Christian prayer, which is in the Spirit and addressed to the Father through the mediatorial role of the Son, our great high priest. Despite the many benefits of this model, when used exclusively, it could lead to a sense of subordination of the Holy Spirit, a danger that prompts us toward the final incorporative model. Drawing on the theme of indwelling, which parallels, in certain respects, the doctrine of perichoresis from which it

---

78. De Lubac, *Catholicism*, 93.
   79. Pelagius I, *Epist. Viatori et Pancratio*, cited in de Lubac, *Splendor of the Church*, 159.

must be carefully distinguished, the incorporative model focuses on how the Holy Spirit's indwelling presence draws the church and individual Christians into participation, by grace, in that communion that is constitutive of the divine life. The disciples are required to wait in Jerusalem until the coming of the Holy Spirit (Luke 24:49; Acts 1:4), but after Pentecost and the Spirit's indwelling, they can truly proclaim the good news: the Edenic fellowship with God that had been lost after the fall was now restored through the atoning work of the Son and the indwelling power of the Holy Spirit. This incorporative model of communion is particularly evident in our eucharistic anticipation of that day when the Lord himself will drink of the cup again in the coming kingdom (Matt. 26:29), a kingdom where God will be "all in all" (1 Cor. 15:28).

The doctrine of the Trinity is fundamental to Christian faith in numerous ways. The Christian God is a God who is eternally Father, Son, and Holy Spirit, so any personal advance in theological knowledge of this God will always be coupled with and rooted in trinitarian doctrine. The very structure of salvation is trinitarian, both in the missions, because the Father sends his Son and Spirit as his two hands of salvation, and in terms of perichoresis, because believers' union with Christ is a created analogue for the perichoretic mutual indwelling of the divine persons. The Christian conception of revelation is that of the self-revelation of the Father through the Son in the Spirit. I have attempted to explain aspects of these areas of dogmatic significance throughout this work, yet above all I have attempted to highlight the connections between the doctrine of the Trinity and worship. If all worship of God must be in Spirit and in truth (John 4:24), and if there is but one Spirit who is worshiped and one Son who is himself truth (John 14:6), then all worship is fundamentally trinitarian—in its object, as three divine persons are addressed; in its structure, as worship proceeds in the Spirit through the Son to the Father; and in its mode, as Christians enabled by the indwelling Holy Spirit are incorporated into spiritual communion with Father, Son, and Spirit. So, the ancient dictum holds true: *Lex orandi, lex credendi*; "The law of worship is the law of belief." May the church's worship of the triune God always drive it to a faithful dogmatic account of the Trinity, and may this dogmatic account itself inspire worship.[80]

---

80. I was first prompted to contemplate, at least in a deep manner, the cycle in which worship inspires a thirst for doctrine and doctrine inspires a thirst for worship by Catherine of Siena, who argues that the soul begins to advance in the spiritual life through the teaching of Christ crucified and through self-knowledge. Self-knowledge in light of Christ, however, sees that there is no way to attain salvation, driving us to wait for the coming of God and to pray fervently for his gracious aid. The soul who thirsts in this way is drawn to the Eucharist for nourishment

FOR FURTHER READING

Relevant Historical Material

Hunt, Anne. *The Trinity: Insights from the Mystics*. Collegeville, MN: Liturgical Press, 2010.

> Hunt offers the most extensive survey of the trinitarian theology of the mystics, to the great benefit of the reader. Typically, these figures are neglected in introductions to the Trinity (as I fear they are in mine).

Theological Treatments of Communion

Coakley, Sarah. *God, Sexuality, and the Self: An Essay "On the Trinity."* Cambridge: Cambridge University Press, 2013.

> Coakley's volume introduces what she calls a *théologie totale*, a method that draws on a wider range of sources than is typically used in considerations of the Trinity. Using this method, she analyses trinitarian theology in light of its connection with human desire, gender, and sex. Her analysis spans patristic documents on the Trinity and prayer, the history of iconography, and field work among charismatic Anglicans.

Panikkar, Raimundo. *The Trinity and the Religious Experience of Man: Icon— Person—Mystery*. Maryknoll, NY: Orbis Books, 1973.

> Panikkar's exploration of the unique spiritualities associated with each divine person is a fine example of the intersection of constructive and spiritual theologies.

Papanikolaou, Aristotle. *Being with God: Trinity, Apophaticism, and Divine-Human Communion*. Notre Dame, IN: University of Notre Dame Press, 2006.

> Papanikolaou's treatment of Vladimir Lossky and John Zizioulas explores the relationship between theological epistemology and trinitarian ontology, the extent to which apophaticism should limit our willingness to conceptualize the God to whom we relate, and whether communion takes place primarily through the divine energies or from (human) person to (divine) person.

---

as it waits. In due course, the soul that has waited in the worship of prayer and the Eucharist is granted the "wisdom of [the] Son," God's truth, and deeper self-knowledge. Presumably, this can bring the cycle to its beginning again (Catherine of Siena, *Dialogue* §§65–66, 74).

Glossary

The following terms are particularly pertinent to the doctrine of the Trinity, and the definitions provided are given with trinitarian implications and usage especially in mind.[1]

accidents In Aristotelian thought, accidents are the properties of a being that are contingent and caused in some sense by substance. The doctrine of divine simplicity prohibits speaking of accidents in the divine substance or being.

actus purus A Latin phrase referring to pure act or actualization. In Thomist and later scholastic metaphysics, God is thought to have no potency that he can actualize, meaning he has no attribute or faculty that he can begin to possess or possess to a greater degree. Therefore, he is immutable, impassible, and absolutely perfect.

ad extra A Latin phrase that literally means "toward the outside." In this context it typically refers to God's acts that terminate on creation. See also *ad intra*.

ad intra A Latin phrase that literally means "toward the inside." In this context it typically refers to God's acts that terminate within the Godhead, such as the divine processions. See also *ad extra*.

adoptionism An ancient heresy that states that Jesus was a human person adopted by God to become his Son at some point in history after that person's birth, usually identified as his baptism.

---

1. When crafting the glossary, I defined each term in my own words, then cross-referenced several theological dictionaries, making adjustments to my wording where necessary. Sources consulted: Muller, *Dictionary of Latin and Greek Theological Terms*; McKim, *Westminster Dictionary of Theological Terms*; Grenz, Guretzki, and Nordling, *Pocket Dictionary of Theological Terms*; the glossary in Emery, *The Trinity*, 199–203.

analogy, doctrine of   The treatment of God as like or proportionate to creation yet fundamentally dissimilar. As a result of the doctrine of analogy, all human language of God must be qualified to identify properly the ways that the meaning of words differs when applied to God rather than to creation. *See also* univocity.

anarthrous noun   Noun lacking an article.

apophatic theology   Theology that relies on the way of negation, understanding God by denying that which cannot be said of him. *See also* cataphatic theology; way of negation.

appropriation   Attributing a divine attribute or action to the divine person with whom one most closely associates it. The term comes from the Latin *ad* + *proprium*, "to draw toward the proper."

archetypal theology   The knowledge that God has of himself, in which human theology attempts to participate.

aseity   God's attribute of needing and receiving nothing from creation, having his existence entirely determined by himself. The term is synonymous with "self-existence."

being   See *ousia*.

***bhakti*, spirituality of**   A spirituality rooted in love and personalism, attributed by Raimundo Panikkar to our communion with the Son. The word *bhakti* is Sanskrit. See also *jñāna*, spirituality of; *karma*, spirituality of.

Blachernae, Council of (1285)   A Byzantine Orthodox council that rejected a politicized movement to reconcile East and West over the *filioque*. Blachernae proposed that the Holy Spirit is eternally manifest through the Son.

cataphatic theology   Theology that makes positive claims or statements about the nature of God. *See also* apophatic theology.

Colwell's Rule   A (now-contested) rule of Greek grammar stating that definite predicate nouns that come before the verb typically lack the article for the purpose of indicating that they are the predicate.

communicable divine attributes   The attributes of God in which creatures are graciously allowed to participate analogically.

communion   Fellowship or mutual receiving and giving. The term can apply to the relationship between Christians or to the relationship between Christians and the persons of the Trinity.

Constantinople, First Council of (381)   This council clarified the original Nicene Creed by expanding the article on the Holy Spirit to include him in worship, by updating the creed to fit with the new conceptual distinction between *hypostasis* and *ousia*, and by adding content to resist Marcellus of Ancyra's belief that the reign of the Son would one day end. The creed it produced is properly named the Niceano-Constantinopolitan Creed, though it is commonly called the Nicene Creed. *See also* Niceano-Constantinopolitan Creed.

Constantinople, Second Council of (553)   The fifth ecumenical council, which condemned Origenism.

consubstantiality   Derived from the Latin translation of *homoousios*, the term refers to sharing substance, which entails sharing all attributes that are essential to a particular type of thing. When deployed in the doctrine of the Trinity, "consubstantiality" refers to the Father, Son, and Holy Spirit sharing the same single primary substance without division.

co-ordinate model of communion   A model of communion with God that focuses on the unique human address to each divine person, particularly in worship.

correlatives   The paired terms of a relation; two reciprocally related things.

cultic worship   Reverence or devotion offered in a formal liturgical setting. Larry Hurtado claims that cultic worship is offered only to persons viewed as divine.

economic Trinity   A somewhat imprecise term signifying the Trinity in terms of its acts toward and revelation within created history. *See also* immanent Trinity.

economy   Derived from the Greek *oikonomia*, which refers to oversight of a household or management according to a plan, the divine economy refers to the work of the Father, Son, and Spirit in history. It includes creation, redemption, and the future eschatological renewal of all things.

ectypal theology   Knowledge of God in a human mode that attempts to mirror the knowledge that God has of himself.

energies   The operations produced by the power of a nature. In much Eastern Orthodox theology, the divine energies are a third ontological aspect of the Trinity, in addition to hypostases and *ousia*.

essence   The "whatness" of a thing, typically considered in the abstract. It is that which explains a thing's properties.

Eternal Functional Subordination (EFS)   A common evangelical theology of the Trinity that argues that the Son eternally submits to the Father, being subordinate in role or function but not in ontology or being. This position is also called Eternal Relations of Authority and Submission (ERAS) and the Eternal Submission of the Son (ESS).

eternal generation   The Father's eternal, intimate, and personal causing of the Son without change, division, or imperfection.

eternal manifestation   Rooted in the theology of Gregory of Cyprus, eternal manifestation explains the relation between Son and Spirit in a form that is an alternative to the *filioque*.

filiation   The unique, eternal relation of the Son to the Father.

filioque   A Latin word that literally means "and the Son." Western Christians added the word (likely unknowingly) to the Latin Niceano-Constantinopolitan Creed to claim that the Holy Spirit proceeds from the Father *and the Son*.

formal distinction   In theology, a distinction between two divine attributes where the attributes are not different things but, rather, are different formal aspects of the same thing. *See also* virtual distinction.

Florence, Council of (1438–45)   A council, viewed as ecumenical by the Roman Catholic Church, that unsuccessfully sought unity between the Orthodox and Catholic Churches. This council incorporated relational opposition into its definition of the Trinity.

fundamentum   A Latin word referring to the foundation of a thing. In the doctrine of inseparable operations, the *fundamentum* is the person who initiates a particular divine act.

genus   A class of similar things.

homoousios   A Greek term meaning "of the same being." This term was used at the Council of Nicaea (325) to refer to what was common between Father and Son, and it was later extended to the Holy Spirit. It is somewhat ambiguous and was likely a compromise position for various parties at Nicaea. *See also* consubstantiality.

hypostasis   A Greek term that refers to that which makes a thing real. It is used in a nonmaterial sense in pro-Nicene thought to refer to a particular, individuated divine person.

identicals   Things that have no discernibly different properties. *See also* indiscernibility of identicals.

immanent Trinity   A somewhat imprecise term signifying the Trinity in terms of its eternal existence apart from considerations of creation, often particularly emphasizing the processions. *See also* economic Trinity.

immutability   The doctrine that states that God does not and cannot change.

incommunicable attributes   Those divine attributes in which creatures do not participate.

incorporative model of communion   A model of communion, named by Sarah Coakley, that focuses on the Spirit's role of drawing us to God.

indiscernibility of identicals   A principle, made famous by G. W. Leibniz, that argues that two identicals can have no discernibly different properties.

Much analytic philosophy and theology sets up the philosophical problem of the doctrine of the Trinity by appeal to this principle, treating the three persons as identicals. *See also* identicals.

in se   A Latin phrase meaning "in itself." Often, "Trinity *in se*" is used as a less confusing alternative to the language of "immanent Trinity." *See also* immanent Trinity.

inseparable operations   A doctrine explaining that the Father, Son, and Holy Spirit work all divine acts *ad extra* inseparably. See also *ad extra*.

jñāna, **spirituality of**   A spirituality rooted in knowledge and personal self-transcendence (*advaita*), attributed by Raimundo Panikkar to our communion with the Holy Spirit. The terms *jñāna* and *advaita* are Sanskrit. See also *bhakti*, spirituality of; *karma*, spirituality of.

karma, **spirituality of**   A spirituality rooted in action and apophaticism, attributed by Raimundo Panikkar to our communion with the Father. The word *karma* is Sanskrit. See also *bhakti*, spirituality of; *jñāna*, spirituality of.

kind   *See* genus.

koinōnia   *See* communion.

Lateran Council, Fourth (1215)   A council, accepted by the Roman Catholic Church, that affirmed the doctrine of analogy with the caveat that the dissimilarity between God and creation was greater than the similarity. The council also condemned Joachim of Fiore's version of trinitarianism.

linear model of communion   A model of communion emphasizing our ability to discern each divine person in God's inseparable operations and in God-enabled human actions by recognizing a linear order in the actions. God's own operations come from the Father, through the Son, to the Spirit, and God-enabled human actions are conducted in the Spirit, through the Son, to the Father.

Lyons, Second Council of (1274)   A joint council between the Eastern and Western churches that resulted in a brief and contested affirmation of the *filioque*. Roman Catholics and some Protestants view this as the fourteenth ecumenical council.

mediatorial figures   Intermediary figures prevalent in Second Temple Judaism that were thought to make God present in some fashion even though they were distinct from God. Mediatorial figures could take the form of a personified divine attribute, an ideal figure such as a biblical king, or an exalted angel or human figure such as a charismatic prophet.

Metatron The name given to Enoch in noncanonical literature after he is transformed into an angel. Metatron is closely linked with the divine identity in some Second Temple literature.

mission The voluntary extension of a procession into space and time through a created term.

modalism An ancient heresy that treats the three divine persons as temporary, economic modes of the one single God. This heresy is also known as Sabellianism and modalistic monarchianism.

modes of subsistence A distinct way of possessing the divine nature according to each person's unique relations to one another. The term is roughly equivalent to *hypostasis*.

monarchy A term, literally meaning "single rule," that in the context of trinitarian theology refers to the fact that the Father is the source of all things, including the divine persons.

monogenēs A disputed Greek term used of the Son in the New Testament that may mean "only begotten" or "unique." It is central to some modern debates about the validity of the doctrine of eternal generation.

nature The character of a thing considered particularly in terms of its distinctive powers and resulting operations.

Nicaea, Council of (325) The council that established the original Nicene Creed, which was later modified at the First Council of Constantinople (381). The council condemned Arius, affirmed the eternal generation of the Son, used the word *homoousios* to speak of Father and Son, and left the Spirit's status and nature undefined. Nicaea prompted decades of subsequent trinitarian debate, but its modified creed became the norm for orthodoxy in Orthodox, Roman Catholic, and Protestant churches.

Niceano-Constantinopolitan Creed The revision of the Nicene Creed that was the product of the First Council of Constantinople (381) and is used as a standard of orthodoxy by confessional Orthodox, Roman Catholic, and Protestant Christians. Most nonspecialists know it simply as the Nicene Creed, even though that title is more properly restricted to the original Nicene Creed, produced by the Council of Nicaea in 325. *See also* Constantinople, First Council of (381); Nicaea, Council of (325).

oikonomia *See* economy.

oneness of God In the thought of Abū Rā'iṭa, the oneness of God is not a oneness of number, since the unique God cannot be part of a series, nor oneness of genus, since God is one of a kind. Therefore, the divine oneness is the oneness of species, meaning that there is one being that is God.

operation   Any act of God through use of a power.

ousia   A Greek term referring to that which makes a thing what it is. In pro-Nicene thought, the term refers to what is undifferentiated or what is common to the divine persons.

passive spiration   The unique relation of the Spirit to the Father and, in most Western theology, to the Son.

paternity   The unique, eternal relation of the Father to the Son.

perichoresis   A term referring to the mutual interpenetration and coinherence of the divine persons and of the two natures in Christ. This concept is often explained with reference to metaphors of motion and space and to unity of love, consciousness, and will.

personality of the Holy Spirit   The doctrine that treats the Holy Spirit as a rational, volitional agent in contrast to those that see the Spirit as an impersonal force.

personal properties   That which is proper to the persons due to the processions. The Father is unbegotten, the Son is begotten, and the Spirit is spirated.

personified divine attributes   *See* mediatorial figures.

persons, divine   A unique subsistence of the singular and rational divine nature that is distinguished from, yet inseparably united with, the other divine persons by the divine relations.

Pneumatomachians   Literally "Spirit-fighters," the proponents of this fourth-century Christian heresy denied the full divinity of the Holy Spirit. The heresy is also called Macedonianism.

power   A causal capacity distinctive of a given kind of nature.

preexistence, actual   The real, not potential, existence of a being prior to a specific time, typically its manifestation in history. This may be protological, where a being exists prior to creation, or eschatological, where a being exists prior to its eschatological manifestation.

preexistence, ideal   The existence of a being in the mind of God in potency prior to its creation.

primary substance   That which exists. In contrast to secondary substance, which conceives of the whatness of a thing in an abstract manner, primary substance refers to a specific thing.

processions   A term used among Protestants and Catholics to refer to the eternal generation of the Son and spiration of the Holy Spirit. Among the Orthodox, "procession" is typically used exclusively of the Holy Spirit, who proceeds from the Father.

pro-Nicene   A term popularized by Lewis Ayres, "pro-Nicene" describes those theologians who defended the theology of the Council of Nicaea while emphasizing the inseparability of divine operations, the eternal generation of the Son, and a terminological distinction between the one divine essence and the three divine persons. *See also* Nicaea, Council of (325).

prosopological exegesis   An ancient method of interpreting texts that reads a passage as if it is a dialogue between multiple unnamed characters, identifying shifts in speaker based on small textual clues. The New Testament often reads Old Testament passages through prosopological exegesis, identifying speakers as one or more of the divine persons.

prosopon   Used in Greek to signify the persons, the word *prosopon* originally meant "face," "gaze," or "that which is seen."

psychological analogy   A common means of clarifying how there may be two divine processions within the Godhead by comparing generation and spiration to two distinct processions within a mind. Generation is like the procession of a word, thought, or self-image within the mind, and spiration is like the procession of an emotion, especially love. Both processions are distinct yet internal to the mind.

quaternity   A conception of God as having four things, not three. This term contrasts with "Trinity." Theologians who make too great a distinction between the divine persons and the divine essence are often accused of affirming four things in God, the three persons and the essence.

Rahner's Rule   The widely debated claim of Karl Rahner that the economic Trinity is the immanent Trinity and the immanent Trinity is the economic Trinity. *See also* economic Trinity; immanent Trinity.

relational opposition   The idea that the divine persons are identical in all things except the personal properties, which, as relatives, require an opposite correlative (e.g., "begotten" requires a begetter). In much Western trinitarianism, this concept is used to argue for the necessity of the *filioque*.

relations, divine   The divine relations describe the manner in which each divine person is oriented toward the others.

Sabellianism   *See* modalism.

secondary substance   That which a thing is, but considered abstractly. *See also* primary substance.

Shema   The liturgical affirmation of God's oneness in Judaism, based on Deuteronomy 6:4.

simplicity, doctrine of   The doctrine that God is not composed of parts. In its strongest form, simplicity denies material parts, a real distinction between the divine attributes, and a distinction between God's essence and God's existence.

social trinitarianism An approach to the Trinity that emphasizes the distinctions between the persons and tends to identify divine persons as distinct minds or centers of consciousness.

spiration The act by which the Father (and the Son, if the *filioque* is affirmed) is the eternal source of the Holy Spirit, who proceeds without division, change, or imperfection. The term may also refer to the relation of the Father (and the Son, if the *filioque* is affirmed) to the Holy Spirit.

subordinationism A trinitarian heresy that either treats the Son as lesser in being, authority, and/or dignity than the Father or treats the Spirit as lesser in being, authority, and/or dignity than the Father and Son.

subsist To exist in particular, individual form.

substance The fundamental reality that is the bearer of properties. *See also* primary substance; secondary substance.

tawhid The Muslim understanding of the absolute oneness and uniqueness of God. The term is Arabic.

theophany A manifestation or self-revelation of God in creation.

Toledo, Third Council of (589) The first council that included the *filioque* in the Niceano-Constantinopolitan Creed, likely believing this was original to the creed.

triplex formula A series of the names for all three divine persons that is found in the New Testament.

tritheism A heresy that so distinguishes the three divine persons that they are practically different gods.

tropikoi Proponents of a fourth-century heresy that denied the divinity of the Holy Spirit based largely on several prooftexts, such as Amos 4:13, where God claims to create wind/spirit.

ubuntu philosophy An African philosophy that emphasizes relationality, social unity, and the idea that each life is a distinct force.

univocity An alternative to the doctrine of analogy that treats words used of God as if they mean the same thing in the same way as when they are used of creation. *See also* analogy, doctrine of.

viriditas A Latin word that can be translated as "life-giving fecundity," "verdure," or "greenness." The term was popularized in the Middle Ages by Hildegaard von Bingen, who used it to refer to the unique experience of the Holy Spirit.

virtual distinction   In theology, a mental distinction between two divine attributes where the distinction is rooted in something that is real in the divine essence but is distinct only in a created human mind. *See also* formal distinction.

way of negation   The means of describing God through the denial of various concepts that do not apply to him. *See also* apophatic theology.

Bibliography

à Brakel, Wilhelmus. *The Christian's Reasonable Service*. Vol. 1, *God, Man, and Christ*. Edited by Joel R. Beeke. Translated by Bartel Elshout. Grand Rapids: Reformation Heritage, 1992.

Abū Rā'iṭa al-Takrītī, 'Ḥabīb ibn Khidma. *The First* Risālah *on the Holy Trinity*. In *Defending the "People of Truth" in the Early Islamic Period: The Christian Apologies of Abu Ra'itah*, edited and translated by Sandra Toenies Keating, 164–216. Leiden: Brill, 2006.

Alcuin. *Commentary on the Gospel of John*. In *Photius and the Carolingians: The Trinitarian Controversy*. Translated by Richard Haugh. Belmont, MA: Nordland, 1975.

Alexopoulos, Theodoros. "The Eternal Manifestation of the Spirit 'through the Son' (*dia tou 'Hoiou*) according to Nikephoros Blemmydes and Gregory of Cyprus." In *Ecumenical Perspectives on the* Filioque *for the Twenty-First Century*, edited by Myk Habets, 65–86. London: Bloomsbury, 2014.

Ambrose. *Of the Christian Faith*. Translated by H. de Romestin, E. de Romestin, and H. T. F. Duckworth. In *The Nicene and Post-Nicene Fathers*, series 2, edited by Philip Schaff and Henry Wace, 10:199–314. Reprint, Grand Rapids: Eerdmans, 1955.

———. *On the Holy Spirit*. Translated by H. de Romestin, E. de Romestin, and H. T. F. Duckworth. In *The Nicene and Post-Nicene Fathers*, series 2, edited by Philip Schaff and Henry Wace, 10:91–158. Reprint, Grand Rapids: Eerdmans, 1955.

Ames, William. *The Marrow of Theology*. Translated by John D. Eusden. Boston: Pilgrim, 1968.

Anatolios, Khaled. *Retrieving Nicaea: The Development and Meaning of Trinitarian Doctrine*. Grand Rapids: Baker Academic, 2011.

Anselm. *On the Incarnation of the Word*. Translated by Richard Regan. In *Anselm of Canterbury: The Major Works*, edited by Brian Davies and G. R. Evans, 233–59. Oxford: Oxford University Press, 1998.

———. *On the Procession of the Holy Spirit.* Translated by Richard Regan. In *Anselm of Canterbury: The Major Works,* edited by Brian Davies and G. R. Evans, 390–434. Oxford: Oxford University Press, 1998.

———. *Proslogion.* Translated by M. J. Charlesworth. In *Anselm of Canterbury: The Major Works,* edited by Brian Davies and G. R. Evans, 82–104. Oxford: Oxford University Press, 1998.

———. *Why God Became Man.* Translated by Janet Fairweather. In *Anselm of Canterbury: The Major Works,* edited by Brian Davies and G. R. Evans, 260–356. Oxford: Oxford University Press, 1998.

Aquinas, Thomas. *Commentary on the Gospel of John: Chapters 13–21.* Translated by Fabian Larcher and James A. Weisheipl. Washington, DC: Catholic University of America Press, 2010.

———. *On Being and Essence.* Translated by Joseph Bobik. In *Aquinas on Being and Essence: A Translation and Interpretation,* by Joseph Bobik. Notre Dame, IN: University of Notre Dame Press, 1965.

———. *Summa contra Gentiles.* Translated by Charles J. O'Niel. 4 vols. 1957. Reprint, Notre Dame, IN: University of Notre Dame Press, 1975.

———. *Summa Theologica.* Translated by fathers of the English Dominican Province. 5 vols. 1911. Reprint, Allen, TX: Christian Classics, 1981.

Aristotle. *Categoriae.* Translated by E. M. Edghill. In *The Basic Works of Aristotle,* edited by Richard McKeon, 7–39. New York: Random House, 1941.

Arius. *The Letter of Arius to Eusebius of Nicomedia.* Translated by Edward Rochie Hardy. In *Christology of the Later Fathers,* edited by Edward Rochie Hardy, 329–31. Louisville: Westminster John Knox, 1954.

Athanasius. *Defense of the Nicene Definition (De Decretis).* Translated by John Henry Newman. In *The Nicene and Post-Nicene Fathers,* series 2, edited by Philip Schaff and Henry Wace, 4:149–72. Reprint, Grand Rapids: Eerdmans, 1975.

———. *Letters to Serapion on the Holy Spirit.* In *Works on the Spirit,* translated by Mark DelCogliano, Andrew Radde-Gallwitz, and Lewis Ayres, 51–138. Yonkers, NY: St. Vladimir's Seminary Press, 2011.

———. *On the Councils of Ariminum and Seleuca (De Synodis).* Translated by John Henry Newman. In *The Nicene and Post-Nicene Fathers,* series 2, edited by Philip Schaff and Henry Wace, 4:448–80. Reprint, Grand Rapids: Eerdmans, 1975.

———. *Orations against the Arians.* In *Athanasius,* translated and edited by Khaled Anatolios, 70–141. New York: Routledge, 2004.

———. *To the Bishops of Africa.* Translated by A. Robertson. In *The Nicene and Post-Nicene Fathers,* series 2, edited by Philip Schaff and Henry Wace, 4:489–94. Reprint, Grand Rapids: Eerdmans, 1975.

———. *To the Bishops of Egypt.* Translated by M. Atkinson. In *The Nicene and Post-Nicene Fathers,* series 2, edited by Philip Schaff and Henry Wace, 4:223–35. Reprint, Grand Rapids: Eerdmans, 1975.

Athenagoras. *A Plea regarding Christians*. Translated by Eugene Fairweather. In *Early Christian Fathers*, edited by Cyril C. Richardson, 300–42. Philadelphia: Westminster, 1953.

Augustine. *Homilies on the First Epistle of John*. Translated by Boniface Ramsey. Edited by Daniel E. Doyle and Thomas Martin. Hyde Park, NY: New City, 2008.

———. "Letter 11 to Nebridius." Translated by J. G. Cunningham. In *Nicene and Post-Nicene Fathers*, series 1, edited by Philip Schaff, 1:228–30. Reprint, Grand Rapids: Eerdmans, 1956.

———. "Letter 14 to Nebridius." Translated by J. G. Cunningham. In *Nicene and Post-Nicene Fathers*, series 1, edited by Philip Schaff, 1:231–32. Reprint, Grand Rapids: Eerdmans, 1956.

———. *On Christian Teaching*. Translated by R. P. H. Green. Oxford: Oxford University Press, 1997.

———. *On the Holy Trinity*. Translated by Arthur West Haddan. In *Nicene and Post-Nicene Fathers*, series 1, edited by Philip Schaff, 3:1–228. Reprint, Grand Rapids: Eerdmans, 1956.

Awad, Najib George. *Orthodoxy in Arabic Terms: A Study of Theodore Abū Qurrah's Theology in Its Islamic Context*. Berlin: De Gruyter, 2016.

Ayres, Lewis. "At the Origins of Eternal Generation." In *Retrieving Eternal Generation*, edited by Fred Sanders and Scott R. Swain, 149–62. Grand Rapids: Zondervan, 2017.

———. *Augustine and the Trinity*. Cambridge: Cambridge University Press, 2014.

———. *Nicaea and Its Legacy: An Approach to Fourth-Century Trinitarian Theology*. Oxford: Oxford University Press, 2004.

———. "On Not Three People: The Fundamental Themes of Gregory of Nyssa's Trinitarian Theology as Seen in *To Ablabius: On Not Three Gods*." In *Re-thinking Gregory of Nyssa*, edited by Sarah Coakley, 15–44. Malden, MA: Blackwell, 2003.

Baber, H. E. *The Trinity: A Philosophical Investigation*. London: SCM, 2019.

Baker-Fletcher, Karen. *Dancing with God: The Trinity from a Womanist Perspective*. St. Louis: Chalice, 2006.

Barcellos, Richard C. *Trinity & Creation: A Scriptural and Confessional Account*. Eugene, OR: Resource, 2020.

Barnes, Michel René. "Irenaeus's Trinitarian Theology." *Nova et Vetera* 7, no. 1 (2009): 67–106.

———. *The Power of God: Δύναμις in Gregory of Nyssa's Trinitarain Theology*. Washington, DC: Catholic University of America Press, 2001.

———. "Rereading Augustine's Theology of the Trinity." In *The Trinity: An Interdisciplinary Symposium on the Trinity*, edited by Stephen T. Davis, Daniel Kendall, and Gerald O'Collins, 143–76. Oxford: Oxford University Press, 1999.

Barrett, C. K. *The Gospel according to St. John*. 2nd ed. Philadelphia: Westminster, 1978.

Barth, Karl. *Church Dogmatics*. Edited by G. W. Bromiley and T. F. Torrance. Translated by G. W. Bromiley, G. T. Thomson, et al. Four volumes in 13 parts. Edinburgh: T&T Clark, 1936–77.

———. *The Epistle to the Romans*. Translated by Edwyn C. Hoskyns. 6th ed. London: Oxford University Press, 1933.

Basil. *Against Eunomius*. Translated by Mark Delcogliano and Andrew Radde-Gallwitz. Washington, DC: Catholic University of America Press, 2011.

———. *Letters*. Translated by Blomfield Jackson. In *Nicene and Post-Nicene Fathers*, series 2, edited by Philip Schaff and Henry Wace, 8:109–327. Reprint, Grand Rapids: Eerdmans, 1955.

———. *On the Holy Spirit*. Translated by David Anderson. Crestwood, NY: St. Vladimir's Seminary Press, 1980.

Bates, Matthew W. *The Birth of the Trinity: Jesus, God, and Spirit in New Testament and Early Christian Interpretations of the Old Testament*. Oxford: Oxford University Press, 2015.

Bauckham, Richard. "The Trinity and the Gospel of John." In *The Essential Trinity: New Testament Foundations and Practical Relevance*, edited by Brandon D. Crowe and Carl R. Trueman, 91–117. Phillipsburg, NJ: P&R, 2016.

Beckwith, Carl L. *The Holy Trinity*. Fort Wayne: Luther Academy, 2016.

Behr, John. *The Formation of Christian Theology*. Vol. 2, *The Nicene Faith*. Part 2, *One of the Holy Trinity*. Crestwood, NY: St. Vladimir's Seminary Press, 2004.

Beyer, Hermann Wolfgang. "βλασφημία [blasphēmia]." In *Theological Dictionary of the New Testament*, vol. 1, edited by Gerhard Kittel, translated by Geoffrey W. Bromiley, 621–25. Grand Rapids: Eerdmans, 1964.

Billings, J. Todd. *Calvin, Participation, and the Gift*. New York: Oxford University Press, 2007.

Bingemer, Maria Clara Lucchetti. *A Face for God*. Translated by Jovelino Ramos and Joan Ramos. Miami: Convivium, 2014.

Bobik, Joseph. *Aquinas on Being and Essence: A Translation and Interpretation*. Notre Dame, IN: University of Notre Dame Press, 1965.

Bobrinskoy, Boris. *The Mystery of the Trinity: Trinitarian Experience and Vision in the Biblical and Patristic Tradition*. Translated by Anthony P. Gythiel. Crestwood, NY: St. Vladimir's Seminary Press, 1999.

Boersma, Hans. *Seeing God: The Beatific Vision in Christian Tradition*. Grand Rapids: Eerdmans, 2018.

Boethius. *Contra Eutychen*. In *Boethius: The Theological Tractates and the Consolation of Philosophy*, translated by H. F. Stewart and E. K. Rand, 72–127. Cambridge, MA: Harvard University Press, 1918.

————. *De Trinitate*. In *Boethius: The Theological Tractates and the Consolation of Philosophy*, translated by H. F. Stewart and E. K. Rand, 2–31. Cambridge, MA: Harvard University Press, 1918.

Boff, Leonardo. *Trinity and Society*. Translated by Paul Burns. Maryknoll, NY: Orbis Books, 1988.

Bonaventure. *Commentary on the Sentences: Philosophy of God*. Translated by R. E. Houser and Timothy B. Noone. St. Bonaventure, NY: Franciscan Institute Publications, 2013.

————. *Disputed Questions on the Mystery of the Trinity*. Translated by Zachary Hayes. New York: Franciscan Institute of St. Bonaventure University, 1979.

Boston, Thomas. *An Illustration of the Doctrines of the Christian Religion with Respect to Faith and Practice upon the Plan of the Assembly's Shorter Catechism: Comprehending a Complete Body of Divinity*. 2 vols. Aberdeen: George and Robert King, 1848.

Bourassa, François. *Questions de théologie trinitaire*. Rome: Gregorian University Press, 1970.

Boyd, Gregory A. *God of the Possible: A Biblical Introduction to the Open View of God*. Grand Rapids: Baker, 2006.

Bradshaw, David. *Aristotle East and West: Metaphysics and the Division of Christendom*. Cambridge: Cambridge University Press, 2004.

Bradshaw, Paul F., Maxwell E. Johnson, and L. Edward Phillips. *The Apostolic Tradition: A Commentary*. Edited by Harold W. Attridge. Minneapolis: Fortress, 2002.

Brown, Raymond E. *An Introduction to New Testament Christology*. New York: Paulist, 1994.

————. *An Introduction to the Gospel of John*. Edited by Francis J. Moloney. New Haven: Yale, 2003.

Bruce, F. F. *The Epistle to the Hebrews*. Rev. ed. Grand Rapids: Eerdmans, 1990.

Brunner, Emil. *Dogmatics*. Vol. 1, *The Christian Doctrine of God*. Translated by Olive Wyon. Philadelphia: Westminster, 1950.

Buchanan, George Wesley. *To the Hebrews*. Garden City, NY: Doubleday, 1981.

Büchsel, F. "μονογενής [*monogenēs*]." In *Theological Dictionary of the New Testament*, vol. 4, edited by Gerhard Kittel, translated by Geoffrey W. Bromiley, 737–41. Grand Rapids: Eerdmans, 1967.

Bulgakov, Sergius. *The Comforter*. Translated by Boris Jakim. Grand Rapids: Eerdmans, 2004.

Bultmann, Rudolf. *Theology of the New Testament: Complete in One Volume*. Translated by Kendrick Grobel. New York: Scribners, 1951.

Burton, Ernest DeWitt. *A Critical and Exegetical Commentary on the Epistle to the Galatians*. Edinburgh: T&T Clark, 1921.

Buswell, James Oliver, Jr. *A Systematic Theology of the Christian Religion*. 2 vols. Grand Rapids: Zondervan, 1962.

Butner, D. Glenn, Jr. "Communion with God: An Energetic Defense of Gregory Palamas." *Modern Theology* 32, no. 1 (January 2016): 20–44.

———. "For and against de Régnon: Trinitarianism East and West." *International Journal of Systematic Theology* 17, no. 4 (October 2015): 399–412.

———. "Probing the Exegetical Foundations of Consubstantiality: Worship, Mediatorial Figures, and the *Homoousion*." *Modern Theology* 37, no. 3 (July 2020): 679–702.

———. *The Son Who Learned Obedience: A Theological Case against the Eternal Submission of the Son*. Eugene, OR: Pickwick, 2018.

Calvin, John. *Institutes of the Christian Religion*. Translated by Henry Beveridge. Peabody, MA: Hendrickson, 2008.

Campbell, Constantine R. *Paul and Union with Christ: An Exegetical and Theological Study*. Grand Rapids: Zondervan, 2012.

Carraway, George. *Christ Is God over All: Romans 9:5 in the Context of Romans 9–11*. London: Bloomsbury, 2013.

Carson, D. A. *Exegetical Fallacies*. 2nd ed. Grand Rapids: Baker, 1996.

Catherine of Siena. *The Dialogue*. Translated by Suzanne Noffke. New York: Paulist, 1980.

Chafer, Lewis Sperry. *Systematic Theology*. Dallas: Dallas Seminary Press, 1947.

Chan, Simon. *Spiritual Theology: A Systematic Study of the Christian Life*. Downers Grove, IL: IVP Academic, 1998.

Chester, Andrew. "Jewish Messianic Expectations and Mediatorial Figures and Pauline Christology." In *Paulus und das antike Judentum*, edited by Martin Hengel and Ulrich Heckel, 17–90. Tübingen: Mohr, 1991.

Childs, Brevard S. *Biblical Theology of the Old and New Testaments: Theological Reflection on the Christian Bible*. Minneapolis: Fortress, 1992.

Clarke, W. Norris. *The One and the Many: A Contemporary Thomistic Metaphysics*. Notre Dame, IL: University of Notre Dame Press, 2001.

Coakley, Sarah. *God, Sexuality, and the Self: An Essay "On the Trinity."* Cambridge: Cambridge University Press, 2013.

———. "'Persons' in the 'Social' Doctrine of the Trinity: A Critique of Current Analytic Discussion." In *The Trinity: An Interdisciplinary Symposium on the Trinity*, edited by Stephen T. Davis, Daniel Kendall, and Gerald O'Collins, 123–44. Oxford: Oxford University Press, 1999.

Cole, Graham A. *He Who Gives Life: The Doctrine of the Holy Spirit*. Wheaton: Crossway, 2007.

Colwell, E. C. "A Definite Rule for the Use of the Article in the Greek New Testament." *Journal of Biblical Literature* 52 (1933): 12–21.

Congar, Yves. *I Believe in the Holy Spirit.* Vol. 3, *The River of Life Flows in the East and in the West.* Translated by David Smith. New York: Seabury, 1983.

Copleston, F. C. *Aquinas.* Baltimore: Penguin, 1955.

Cordovilla Pérez, Ángel. "The Trinitarian Concept of Person." In *Rethinking Trinitarian Theology: Disputed Questions and Contemporary Issues in Trinitarian Theology,* edited by Giulio Maspero and Robert J. Wozniak, 105–45. London: T&T Clark, 2012.

Costas, Orlando E. *Liberating News: A Theology of Contextual Evangelization.* Eugene, OR: Wipf & Stock, 2002.

Cross, Richard. *Duns Scotus.* Great Medieval Thinkers. Oxford: Oxford University Press, 1999.

Crouzel, Henri. *Théologie de l'image de Dieu chez Origène.* Paris: Aubier, 1955.

Crowe, Brandon D. "The Trinity and the Gospel of Matthew." In *The Essential Trinity: New Testament Foundations and Practical Relevance,* edited by Brandon D. Crowe and Carl R. Trueman, 25–43. Philipsburg, NJ: P&R, 2016.

Cullman, Oscar. *The Christology of the New Testament.* Rev. ed. Translated by Shirley C. Guthrie and Charles A. M. Hall. Philadelphia: Westminster, 1963.

Dahms, John V. "Johannine Use of *Monogenēs.*" *New Testament Studies* 29, no. 2 (April 1983): 222–32.

Daly-Denton, Margaret. "Singing Hymns to Christ as to a God." In *The Jewish Roots of Christological Monotheism: Papers from the St. Andrews Conference on the Historical Origins of the Worship of Jesus,* edited by Carey C. Newman, James R. Davila, and Gladys S. Lewis, 272–92. Leiden: Brill, 1999.

Davies, Brian. *The Thought of Thomas Aquinas.* Oxford: Clarendon, 1992.

Davies, Richard N. *The Doctrine of the Trinity: The Biblical Evidence.* Cincinnati: Granston & Stowe, 1891.

Davila, James R. "Of Methodology, Monotheism and Metatron: Introductory Reflections on Divine Mediators and the Origins of the Worship of Jesus." In *The Jewish Roots of Christological Monotheism: Papers from the St. Andrews Conference on the Historical Origins of the Worship of Jesus,* edited by Carey C. Newman, James R. Davila, and Gladys S. Lewis, 3–18. Leiden: Brill, 1999.

Davis, Leo Donald. *The First Seven Ecumenical Councils (325–787): Their History and Theology.* Collegeville, MN: Liturgical, 1983.

de Lubac, Henri. *Catholicism: Christ and the Common Destiny of Man.* Translated by Lancelot C. Sheppard and Elizabeth Englund. San Francisco: Ignatius, 1988.

Del Colle, Ralph. *The Splendor of the Church.* Translated by Michael Mason. San Francisco: Ignatius, 1986.

———. "The Triune God." In *The Cambridge Companion to Christian Doctrine,* edited by Colin E. Gunton, 121–40. London: Cambridge University Press, 1997.

de Régnon, Théodore. *Études de théologie positive sur la Sainte Trinité.* Vol. 1, *Exposé du Dogme.* Paris: Victor Retaux, 1892.

DeSilva, David A. *The Letter to the Galatians*. Grand Rapids: Eerdmans, 2018.

Dewailly, L. M. "Communio-communicatio." *Revue des sciences philosophiques et théologiques* 54, no. 1 (January 1970): 46–63.

Dewan, Lawrence. *Form and Being: Studies in Thomistic Metaphysics*. Washington, DC: Catholic University of America Press, 2006.

Didymus the Blind. *On the Holy Spirit*. In *Works on the Spirit: Athanasius the Great and Didymus the Blind*, translated by Mark DelCogliano, Andrew Radde-Gallwitz, and Lewis Ayres, 143–227. Yonkers, NY: St. Vladimir's Seminary Press, 2011.

Dolezal, James E. *All That Is in God: Evangelical Theology and the Challenge of Classical Theism*. Grand Rapids: Reformation Heritage, 2016.

———. *God without Parts: Divine Simplicity and the Metaphysics of God's Absoluteness*. Eugene, OR: Pickwick, 2011.

———. "Trinity, Simplicity and the Status of God's Personal Relations." *International Journal of Systematic Theology* 16, no. 1 (January 2014): 79–98.

Doran, Robert M. *The Trinity in History: A Theology of the Divine Missions*. Vol. 1, *Missions and Processions*. Toronto: University of Toronto Press, 2012.

Dorner, I. A. *System of Christian Religion*. Translated by Alfred Cave. Rev. ed. Edinburgh: T&T Clark, 1888.

Duby, Steven J. *Divine Simplicity: A Dogmatic Account*. London: T&T Clark, 2016.

Dunn, James D. G. "Christ, Adam, and Preexistence." In *Where Christology Began*, edited by Ralph P. Martin and Brian J. Dodd, 74–83. Louisville: Westminster John Knox, 1998.

———. *Christology in the Making: A New Testament Inquiry into the Origins of the Doctrine of the Incarnation*. Philadelphia: Westminster, 1980.

———. *Jesus and the Spirit: A Study of the Religious and Charismatic Experience of Jesus and the First Christians as Reflected in the New Testament*. Philadelphia: Westminster, 1975.

———. *Romans 1–8*. Nashville: Thomas Nelson, 1988.

———. *Romans 9–16*. Nashville: Thomas Nelson, 1988.

———. *The Theology of Paul the Apostle*. Grand Rapids: Eerdmans, 1998.

Durand, Emmanuel. *La périchorèse des personnes divines: Immanence mutuelle; Réciprocité et communion*. Paris: Les Éditions du Cerf, 2005.

Ellis, Brannon. *Calvin, Classical Trinitarianism, and the Aseity of the Son*. Oxford: Oxford University Press, 2012.

Emery, Gilles. "Central Aristotelian Themes in Aquinas's Trinitarian Theology." In *Aristotle in Aquinas's Theology*, edited by Gilles Emery and Matthew Levering, 1–28. Oxford: Oxford University Press, 2015.

———. *The Trinitarian Theology of St. Thomas Aquinas*. Translated by Francesca Aran Murphy. Oxford: Oxford University Press, 2010.

———. *The Trinity: An Introduction to Catholic Doctrine on the Triune God*. Translated by Matthew Levering. Washington, DC: Catholic University of America Press, 2011.

———. *Trinity in Aquinas*. Ypsilanti, MI: Sapientia Press of Ave Maria College, 2003.

Erickson, Millard J. *God in Three Persons: A Contemporary Interpretation of the Trinity*. Grand Rapids: Baker, 1995.

Erismann, Christophe. "The Trinity, Universals, and Particular Substances: Philoponus and Roscelin." *Traditio* 63 (2008): 277–305.

Feser, Edward. *Scholastic Metaphysics: A Contemporary Introduction*. Heusenstamm, Germany: Editiones Scholasticae, 2014.

Fletcher-Louis, Crispin. *Jesus Monotheism*. Vol. 1, *Christological Origins: The Emerging Consensus and Beyond*. Eugene, OR: Cascade, 2015.

Fossum, Jarl E. *The Image of the Invisible God: Essays on the Influence of Jewish Mysticism on Early Christology*. Göttingen: Vandenhoeck & Ruprecht, 1995.

Frame, John. *Systematic Theology*. Philadelphia: P&R, 2013.

Galot, Jean. "La generation éternelle du Fils." *Gregorianum* 71, no. 4 (1990): 657–78.

Garrigou-Lagrange, Réginald. *The Trinity and God the Creator: A Commentary on St. Thomas' Theological Summa, Ia, q. 27–119*. Translated by Frederic C. Eckhoff. St. Louis: B. Herder, 1952.

Gathercole, Simon J. *The Preexistent Son: Recovering the Christologies of Matthew, Mark, and Luke*. Grand Rapids: Eerdmans, 2006.

Gemeinhardt, Peter. "Logic, Tradition and Ecumenics: Latin Developments of Trinitarian Theology between c. 1075 and c. 1160." In *Trinitarian Theology in the Medieval West*, edited by Pekka Kärkkäinen, 10–68. Helsinki: Luther-Agricola-Society, 2007.

Gerhard, Johann. *Commonplace III (1625 Exegesis): On the Most Holy Mystery of the All-Hallowed and Ineffable Trinity*. In *On the Nature of God and On the Most Holy Mystery of the Trinity*, edited by Benjamin T. G. Mayes, translated by Richard J. Dinda, 267–418. St. Louis: Concordia, 2007.

Gieschen, Charles A. *Angelomorphic Christology: Antecedents and Early Evidence*. Leiden: Brill, 1998.

———. "The Divine Name in Ante-Nicene Christology." *Vigiliae Christianae* 57, no. 2 (2003): 115–58.

Giles, Kevin. *The Eternal Generation of the Son: Maintaining Orthodoxy in Trinitarian Theology*. Downers Grove, IL: IVP Academic, 2012.

Gill, Kenneth D. *Toward a Contextualized Theology for the Third World: The Emergence and Development of Jesus' Name Pentecostalism in Mexico*. Frankfurt: Peter Lang, 1994.

Gilson, Étienne. *John Duns Scotus: Introduction to His Fundamental Positions*. Translated by James G. Colbert. London: T&T Clark, 2019.

Gorman, Michael J. *Inhabiting the Cruciform God: Kenosis, Justification, and Theosis in Paul's Narrative Soteriology*. Grand Rapids: Eerdmans, 2009.

Gregg, Robert C., and Dennis E. Groh. *Early Arianism: A View of Salvation*. 1981. Reprint, Eugene, OR: Wipf & Stock, 2002.

Grégoire, José. "La relation éternelle de l'Esprit au Fils d'aprés les écrits de Jean de Damas." *Revue d'histoire ecclesiastique* 64, no. 3 (January 1969): 713–55.

Gregory of Cyprus. *Exposition of the Tomus of Faith against Beccus*. Translated by Aristeides Papadakis. In *Crisis in Byzantium: The Filioque Controversy in the Patriarchate of Gregory II of Cyprus (1283–1289)*, by Aristeides Papadakis, 212–26. Rev. ed. Crestwood, NY: St. Vladimir's Seminary Press, 1997.

Gregory of Nazianzus. *Oration on Holy Baptism*. Translated by Charles Gordon Browne and James Edward Swallow. In *Nicene and Post-Nicene Fathers*, series 2, edited by Philip Schaff and Henry Wace, 7:360–77. Reprint, Grand Rapids: Eerdmans, 1955.

———. *The Second Letter to Cledonius against Apollinaris (Epistle 102)*. Translated by Charles Gordon Browne and James Edward Swallow. In *Christology of the Later Fathers*, edited by Edward Rochie Hardy, 225–29. Louisville: Westminster John Knox, 1954.

———. *The Theological Orations*. Translated by Charles Gordon Browne and James Edward Swallow. In *Christology of the Later Fathers*, edited by Edward Rochie Hardy, 128–214. Louisville: Westminster John Knox, 1954.

———. *To Cledonius against Apollinaris (Epistle 101)*. Translated by Charles Gordon Browne and James Edward Swallow. In *Christology of the Later Fathers*, edited by Edward Rochie Hardy, 215–24. Louisville: Westminster John Knox, 1954.

Gregory of Nyssa. *Against Eunomius* and *Answer to Eunomius' Second Book*. Translated by William Moore and Henry Austin Wilson. In *Nicene and Post-Nicene Fathers*, series 2, edited by Philip Schaff and Henry Wace, 5:33–248. Reprint, Grand Rapids: Eerdmans, 1954. [Note: the works are now treated as a single work called *Contra Eunomius*.]

———. *An Answer to Ablabius: That We Should Not Think of Saying There Are Three Gods*. Edited and translated by Cyril C. Richardson. In *Christology of the Later Fathers*, edited by Edward Rochie Hardy, 256–67. Louisville: Westminster John Knox, 1954, 256–67.

———. *On the Holy Spirit against the Followers of Macedonius*. Translated by William Moore and Henry Austin Wilson. In *Nicene and Post-Nicene Fathers*, series 2, edited by Philip Schaff and Henry Wace, 5:315–25. Reprint, Grand Rapids: Eerdmans, 1954.

———. *On the Holy Trinity, and of the Godhead of the Holy Spirit: To Eustathius*. Translated by William Moore and Henry Austin Wilson. In *Nicene and Post-Nicene Fathers*, series 2, edited by Philip Schaff and Henry Wace, 5:326–30. Reprint, Grand Rapids: Eerdmans, 1954.

Gregory of Sinai. *On Commandments and Doctrines, Warnings and Promises; on Thoughts, Passions and Virtues, and also on Stillness and Prayer: One Hundred and Thirty-Seven Texts.* In *The Philokalia*, compiled by St. Nikodimos of the Holy Mountain and St. Makarios of Corinth, translated and edited by G. E. H. Palmer, Philip Sherrard, and Kallistos Ware, 4:212–52. London: Faber & Faber, 1995.

Grenz, Stanley J. *Rediscovering the Triune God: The Trinity in Contemporary Theology.* Minneapolis: Fortress, 2004.

Grenz, Stanley J., David Guretzki, and Cherith Fee Nordling. *Pocket Dictionary of Theological Terms.* Downers Grove, IL: InterVarsity, 1999.

Greshake, Gisbert. "Trinity as 'Communio.'" In *Rethinking Trinitarian Theology: Disputed Questions and Contemporary Issues in Trinitarian Theology*, edited by Giulio Maspero and Robert J. Wozniak, 331–45. London: T&T Clark, 2012.

Grudem, Wayne. "Biblical Evidence for the Eternal Submission of the Son to the Father." In *The New Evangelical Subordinationism? Perspectives on the Equality of God the Father and God the Son*, edited by Dennis W. Jowers and H. Wayne House, 223–61. Eugene, OR: Pickwick, 2012.

———. *Systematic Theology: An Introduction to Biblical Doctrine.* Grand Rapids: Zondervan, 1994.

Gunton, Colin E. *The Promise of Trinitarian Theology.* Edinburgh: T&T Clark, 1991.

Hagner, Donald A. *Matthew 1–13.* Dallas: Word, 1993.

Hamerton-Kelly, R. G. *Pre-existence, Wisdom, and the Son of Man: A Study of the Idea of Pre-existence in the New Testament.* Cambridge: Cambridge University Press, 1973.

Hamilton, Victor P. *The Book of Genesis: Chapters 1–17.* Grand Rapids: Eerdmans, 1990.

Hanson, R. P. C. *The Search for the Christian Doctrine of God: The Arian Controversy 318–381.* Grand Rapids: Baker Academic, 1988.

Harnack, Adolf von. *History of Dogma.* Translated by Neil Bucanan. 7 vols. New York: Dover, 1961.

———. *What Is Christianity?* Translated by Thomas Bailey Saunders. Philadelphia: Fortress, 1986.

Harner, Philip D. "Qualitative Anarthrous Predicate Nouns: Mark 15:39 and John 1:1." *Journal of Biblical Literature* 92, no. 1 (March 1973): 75–87.

Harris, Murray J. *Jesus as God: The New Testament Use of Theos in Reference to Jesus.* Grand Rapids: Baker, 1992.

Harrison, Verna. "Perichoresis in the Greek Fathers." *St. Vladimir's Theological Quarterly* 35, no. 1 (1991): 53–66.

Harrower, Scott. *Trinitarian Self and Salvation: An Evangelical Engagement with Rahner's Rule.* Eugene, OR: Pickwick, 2012.

Hartman, Lars. *"Into the Name of the Lord Jesus": Baptism in the Early Church.* Edinburgh: T&T Clark, 1997.

Hasker, William. *Metaphysics and the Tri-personal God.* Oxford: Oxford University Press, 2013.

Hauck, Friedrich. "κοινωνός [*koinōnos*]." In *Theological Dictionary of the New Testament*, vol. 3, edited by Gerhard Kittel, translated by Geoffrey W. Bromiley, 797–809. Grand Rapids: Eerdmans, 1965.

Haugh, Richard. *Photius and the Carolingians: The Trinitarian Controversy.* Belmont, MA: Nordland, 1975.

Helmer, Christine. *The Trinity and Martin Luther.* Rev. ed. Bellingham, WA: Lexham, 2017.

Hengel, Martin. *Between Jesus and Paul: Studies in the Earliest History of Christianity.* Waco: Baylor University Press, 2013.

Henninger, Mark G. *Relations: Medieval Theories 1250–1325.* Oxford: Clarendon Press, 1989.

Henry of Ghent. *Summa of Ordinary Questions.* In *On the Divine Persons: Henry of Ghent's Summa, Articles 53–55*, translated by Roland J. Teske. Mediaeval Philosophical Texts in Translation. Milwaukee: Marquette University Press, 2015.

Heppe, Heinrich. *Reformed Dogmatics: Set Out and Illustrated from the Sources.* Edited by Ernst Bizer. Translated by G. T. Thomson. Grand Rapids: Baker, 1950.

Hick, John. "Trinity and Incarnation in Light of Religious Pluralism." In *Three Faiths—One God: A Jewish, Christian, Muslim Encounter*, edited by John Hick and Edmund S. Meltzer, 197–210. Albany, NY: State University of New York Press, 1989.

Hilary of Poitiers. *On the Trinity.* Translated by E. W. Watson and L. Pullan. In *Nicene and Post-Nicene Fathers*, series 2, edited by Philip Schaff and Henry Wace, 9:40–233. Reprint, Grand Rapids: Eerdmans, 1955.

Hildebrand, Stephen. *The Trinitarian Theology of Basil of Caesarea: A Synthesis of Greek Thought and Biblical Truth.* Washington, DC: Catholic University of America Press, 2007.

Hill, Wesley. *Paul and the Trinity: Persons, Relations, and the Pauline Letters.* Grand Rapids: Eerdmans, 2015.

Hinlicky, Paul R. *Divine Complexity: The Rise of Creedal Christianity.* Minneapolis: Fortress, 2011.

Hippolytus. *On the Apostolic Tradition.* Translated and edited by Alistair C. Stewart. 2nd ed. Yonkers, NY: St. Vladimir's Seminary Press, 2015.

Hodge, Archibald Alexander. *Popular Lectures on Theological Themes.* Philadelphia: Presbyterian Board of Publication, 1887.

Hodge, Charles. *Commentary on the Epistle to the Romans.* Rev. ed. 1886. Reprint, Grand Rapids: Eerdmans, 1950.

———. *Systematic Theology.* 3 vols. Grand Rapids: Eerdmans, 1940.

Hodgson, Leonard. *The Doctrine of the Trinity: Croall Lectures, 1942–1943*. London: Nisbet, 1946.

Holmes, Stephen R. "The Attributes of God." In *The Oxford Handbook of Systematic Theology*, edited by John Webster, Kathryn Tanner, and Iain Torrance, 54–71. Oxford: Oxford University Press, 2007.

———. *The Quest for the Trinity: The Doctrine of God in Scripture, History, and Modernity*. Downers Grove, IL: IVP Academic, 2012.

Holzer, Vincent. "Rahner, Balthasar, and Catholic Currents." In *The Oxford Handbook of the Trinity*, edited by Gilles Emery and Matthew Levering, 314–27. Oxford: Oxford University Press, 2011.

Hughes, Christopher. *On a Complex Theory of a Simple God: An Investigation in Aquinas' Philosophical Theology*. Ithaca, NY: Cornell University Press, 1989.

Hugh of St. Victor. *On the Three Days*. In *Trinity and Creation: A Selection of Works from Hugh, Richard and Adam of St. Victor*, edited by Boyd Taylor Coolman and Dale M. Coulter, 49–102. Hyde Park, NY: New City, 2011.

Hugon, R. P. Édouard. *Le mystère de la Très Ste Trinité*. Paris: Pierre Téqui, 1912.

Hunsinger, George. "Robert Jenson's *Systematic Theology*: A Review Essay." *Scottish Journal of Theology* 55, no. 2 (2002): 161–200.

Hunt, Anne. *The Trinity: Insights from the Mystics*. Collegeville, MN: Liturgical Press, 2010.

———. *Trinity: Nexus of the Mysteries of the Christian Faith*. Maryknoll, NY: Orbis Books, 2005.

Hur, Ju. *A Dynamic Reading of the Holy Spirit in Luke-Acts*. New York: T&T Clark, 2004.

Hurtado, Larry W. "The Binitarian Shape of Early Christian Worship." In *The Jewish Roots of Christological Monotheism: Papers from the St. Andrews Conference on the Historical Origins of the Worship of Jesus*, edited by Carey C. Newman, James R. Davila, and Gladys S. Lewis, 187–213. Leiden: Brill, 1999.

———. *Lord Jesus Christ: Devotion to Jesus in Earliest Christianity*. Grand Rapids: Eerdmans, 2003.

———. *One God, One Lord: Early Christian Devotion and Ancient Jewish Monotheism*. Philadelphia: Fortress, 1988.

Husseini, Sara Leila. *Early Christian-Muslim Debate on the Unity of God: Three Christian Scholars and Their Engagement with Islamic Thought (9th Century C.E.)*. Leiden: Brill, 2014.

Irenaeus of Lyons. *Against Heresies*. Translated by W. H. Rambaut. In *The Ante-Nicene Fathers*, edited by Alexander Roberts and James Donaldson, 1:309–565. Reprint, Grand Rapids: Eerdmans, 1956.

Irons, Charles Lee. "A Lexical Defense of the Johannine 'Only Begotten.'" In *Retrieving Eternal Generation*, edited by Fred Sanders and Scott R. Swain, 98–116. Grand Rapids: Zondervan, 2017.

Isasi-Díaz, Ada María. *En la Lucha: Elaborating a Mujerista Theology.* Minneapolis: Fortress, 1993.

————. *Mujerista Theology: A Theology for the Twenty-First Century.* Maryknoll, NY: Orbis Books, 1997.

Jenson, Robert W. *Systematic Theology.* Vol. 1, *The Triune God.* Oxford: Oxford University Press, 1997.

————. *The Triune Identity: God according to the Gospel.* Philadelphia: Fortress, 1982.

John of Damascus. *Exposition of the Orthodox Faith.* In *Saint John of Damascus: Writings,* translated by Frederic H. Chase Jr., 165–406. Washington, DC: Catholic University of America Press, 1958.

Johnson, Elizabeth A. *She Who Is: The Mystery of God in Feminist Discourse.* New York: Crossroad, 1992.

Johnson, Luke Timothy. *Hebrews: A Commentary.* Louisville: Westminster John Knox, 2006.

Johnson, Marcus Peter. *One with Christ: An Evangelical Theology of Salvation.* Wheaton: Crossway, 2013.

Joseph, P. V. *An Indian Trinitarian Theology of Missio Dei: Insights from St. Augustine and Brahmabandhab Upadhyay.* Eugene, OR: Pickwick, 2019.

Jüngel, Eberhard. *The Doctrine of the Trinity: God's Being Is in Becoming.* Grand Rapids: Eerdmans, 1976.

Justin Martyr. *Dialogue with Trypho, a Jew.* Translated by Marcus Dods and George Reith. In *The Ante-Nicene Fathers,* edited by Alexander Roberts and James Donaldson, 1:194–270. Reprint, Grand Rapids: Eerdmans, 1956.

Kapic, Kelly M. "Worshipping the Triune God: The Shape of John Owen's Trinitarian Spirituality." In *Communion with the Triune God,* by John Owen, edited by Kelly M. Kapic and Justin Taylor, 17–49. Wheaton: Crossway, 2007.

Kärkkäinen, Veli-Matti. *The Trinity: Global Perspectives.* Louisville: Westminster John Knox, 2007.

Kasper, Walter. *The God of Jesus Christ.* Rev. ed. London: T&T Clark, 2012.

Kaye, Bruce N. "The New Testament." In *One God in Trinity: An Analysis of the Primary Dogma of Christianity,* edited by Peter Toon and James D. Spiceland, 11–26. Westchester, IL: Cornerstone, 1980.

Keck, Leander E. *Why Christ Matters: Toward a New Testament Christology.* Waco: Baylor University Press, 2015.

Keener, Craig S. *The Gospel of John: A Commentary.* 2 vols. Grand Rapids: Baker, 2003.

Keller, Catherine. *Face of the Deep.* Abingdon, UK: Routledge, 2003.

Kelly, J. N. D. *Early Christian Creeds.* 3rd ed. New York: Longman, 1972.

————. *Early Christian Doctrines.* Rev. ed. San Francisco: HarperSanFrancisco, 1978.

Kilby, Karen. "Perichoresis and Projection: Problems with Social Doctrines of the Trinity." *New Blackfriars* 81, no. 956 (October 2000): 432–45.

Kombo, James Henry Owino. *The Doctrine of God in African Christian Thought: The Holy Trinity, Theological Hermeneutics and the African Intellectual Culture.* Leiden: Brill, 2007.

———. *Theological Models of the Doctrine of the Trinity: The Trinity, Diversity and Theological Hermeneutics.* Carlisle, UK: Langham, 2016.

Köstenberger, Andreas J., and Scott R. Swain. *Father, Son and Spirit: The Trinity and John's Gospel.* Downers Grove, IL: InterVarsity, 2008.

Kramer, Werner. *Christ, Lord, Son of God.* Translated by Brian Hardy. London: SCM, 1966.

Kuschel, Karl-Josef. *Born before All Time? The Dispute over Christ's Origin.* New York: Crossroad, 1992.

LaCugna, Catherine Mowry. *God for Us: The Trinity and Christian Life.* New York: HarperSanFrancisco, 1991.

———. "The Trinitarian Mystery of God." In *Systematic Theology: Roman Catholic Perspectives,* edited by Francis Schüssler Fiorenza and John P. Galvin, 1:151–92. 2 vols. Minneapolis: Fortress, 1991.

Lane, William L. *Hebrews 1–8.* Dallas: Word, 1991.

Lashier, Jackson. *Irenaeus on the Trinity.* Leiden: Brill, 2014.

Leibniz, G. W. "Leibniz's Comments on Note L to Bayle's *Dictionary* Article 'Rorarius' (1705?)." In *G. W. Leibniz: Philosophical Texts,* translated and edited by R. S. Woolhouse and Richard Francks, 198–200. Oxford: Oxford University Press, 1998.

Letham, Robert. *The Holy Trinity: In Scripture, History, Theology, and Worship.* Phillipsburg, NJ: P&R, 2004.

Levering, Matthew. *Engaging the Doctrine of the Holy Spirit: Love and Gift in the Trinity and the Church.* Grand Rapids: Baker, 2016.

Lombard, Peter. *The Sentences.* Book 1, *The Mystery of the Trinity.* Translated by Giulio Silano. Toronto: Pontifical Institute of Mediaeval Studies, 2007.

Lonergan, Bernard. *The Triune God: Systematics.* Edited by Robert M. Doran and H. Daniel Monsour. Translated by Michael G. Shields. Toronto: University of Toronto Press, 2007.

Long, D. Stephen. *The Perfectly Simple Triune God: Aquinas and His Legacy.* Minneapolis: Fortress, 2013.

Longenecker, Richard N. *The Epistle to the Romans: A Commentary on the Greek Text.* Grand Rapids: Eerdmans, 2016.

Lossky, Vladimir. *Dogmatic Theology: Creation, God's Image in Man, and the Redeeming Work of the Trinity.* Edited by Olivier Clément and Michel Stavrou. Translated by Anthony P. Gythiel. Yonkers, NY: St. Vladimir's Seminary Press, 2017.

―――. *The Mystical Theology of the Eastern Church.* Translated by members of the Fellowship of St. Alban and St. Sergius. London: James Clarke, 1957.

Maldonado Pérez, Zaida. "The Trinity *Es* and *Son Familia.*" In *Latina Evangélicas: A Theological Survey from the Margins,* edited by Loida I. Martell-Otero, Zaida Maldonado Pérez, and Elizabeth Conde-Frazier, 52–72. Eugene, OR: Cascade, 2013.

Maleparampil, Joseph. *The "Trinitarian" Formulae in St. Paul: An Exegetical Investigation into the Meaning and Function of Those Pauline Sayings Which Compositely Make Mention of God, Christ and the Holy Spirit.* Frankfurt: Peter Lang, 1995.

Mantzaridis, Georgios I. *The Deification of Man: St. Gregory Palamas and the Orthodox Tradition.* Translated by Liadain Sherrard. Crestwood, NY: St. Vladmir's Seminary Press, 1984.

The Marburg Articles (1529). In *Martin Luther's Basic Theological Writings,* edited by Timothy F. Lull and William R. Russell, 280–82. 3rd ed. Minneapolis: Fortress, 2012.

Maximus the Confessor. *Disputation with Pyrrhus.* Translated by Joseph P. Farrell. Waymart, PA: St. Tikhon's Monastery Press, 2014.

McCall, Thomas. *Whose Monotheism? Which Trinity? Philosophical and Systematic Theologians on the Metaphysics of Trinitarian Theology.* Grand Rapids: Eerdmans, 2010.

McCready, Douglas. *He Came Down from Heaven: The Preexistence of Christ and the Christian Faith.* Downers Grove, IL: Intervarsity, 2005.

McGrath, James F. *The Only True God: Early Christian Monotheism in Its Jewish Context.* Urbana: University of Illinois Press, 2009.

McGraw, Ryan M. "Trinitarian Doxology: Reassessing John Owen's Contributions to Reformed Orthodox Trinitarian Theology." *Westminster Theological Journal* 77, no. 2 (Fall 2015): 293–316.

McKim, Donald K. *Westminster Dictionary of Theological Terms.* Louisville: Westminster John Knox, 1996.

Mews, Constant J. *Abelard and Heloise.* New York: Oxford University Press, 2005.

Meyendorff, John. *Byzantine Theology: Historical Trends and Doctrinal Themes.* New York: Fordham University Press, 1979.

Meyer, Hans. *The Philosophy of St. Thomas Aquinas.* Translated by Frederic Eckhoff. St. Louis: B. Herder, 1944.

Miyahira, Nozomu. *Towards a Theology of the Concord of God: A Japanese Perspective on the Trinity.* Carlisle, UK: Paternoster, 2000.

Molnar, Paul D. "Classical Trinity: Catholic Perspective." In *Two Views on the Doctrine of the Trinity,* edited by Jason Sexton and Stanley N. Gundry, 69–95. Grand Rapids: Zondervan, 2014.

―――. *Divine Freedom and the Doctrine of the Immanent Trinity: In Dialogue with Karl Barth and Contemporary Theology.* London: T&T Clark, 2002.

Moltmann, Jürgen. *Experiences in Theology: Ways and Forms of Christian Theology*. Translated by Margaret Kohl. London: SCM, 2000.

———. *The Future of Creation*. Translated by Margaret Kohl. Philadelphia: Fortress, 1979.

———. *God in Creation*. Translated by Margaret Kohl. Minneapolis: Fortress, 1993.

———. *The Trinity and the Kingdom*. Translated by Margaret Kohl. San Francisco: Harper & Row, 1981.

Montague, George T. *The Holy Spirit: Growth of a Biblical Tradition*. New York: Paulist, 1976.

Moody, Dale. "God's Only Son: The Translation of John 3:16 in the Revised Standard Version." *Journal of Biblical Literature* 72, no. 4 (December 1953): 213–19.

Moreland, J. P., and William Lane Craig. *Philosophical Foundations for a Christian Worldview*. Downers Grove, IL: IVP Academic, 2003.

Muller, Richard A. *Dictionary of Latin and Greek Theological Terms Drawn Principally from Protestant Scholastic Theology*. Grand Rapids: Baker, 1985.

———. *Post-Reformation Reformed Dogmatics: The Rise and Development of Reformed Orthodoxy, ca. 1520 to ca. 1725*. Vol. 4, *The Triunity of God*. Grand Rapids: Baker Academic, 2003.

Murphy, Francesca Aran. *God Is Not a Story: Realism Revisited*. Oxford: Oxford University Press, 2007.

———. "The Trinity and Prayer." In *The Oxford Handbook of the Trinity*, edited by Gilles Emery and Matthew Levering, 505–18. Oxford: Oxford University Press, 2011.

Musculus, Wolfgang. *Commonplaces of the Christian Religion: For the Use of Such as Desire the Knowledge of Godly Truth*. Translated by John Man. London: R. Woulfe, 1563.

New International Dictionary of New Testament Theology and Exegesis. Edited by Moisés Silva. 5 vols. Grand Rapids: Zondervan, 2014.

Nielson, Lauge O. "Trinitarian Theology from Alcuin to Anselm." In *The Oxford Handbook of the Trinity*, edited by Gilles Emery and Matthew Levering, 162–67. New York: Oxford University Press, 2011.

Novatian. *De Trinitate*. Translated by Robert Ernest Wallis. In *The Ante-Nicene Fathers*, edited by Alexander Roberts and James Donaldson, 5:611–44. Reprint, Grand Rapids: Eerdmans, 1957.

O'Collins, Gerald. *The Tripersonal God: Understanding and Interpreting the Trinity*. Rev. ed. New York: Paulist, 2014.

Origen. *Commentary on the Gospel according to John: Books 1–10*. Translated by Ronald E. Heine. Washington, DC: Catholic University of America Press, 1989.

———. *Dialogue with Heraclides*. In *Alexandrian Christianity*, edited and translated by Henry Chadwick and J. E. L. Oulton, 437–55. Philadelphia: Westminster, 1954.

———. *On First Principles*. Translated by G. W. Butterworth. New York: Harper & Row, 1966.

Orlov, Andrei A. *The Enoch-Metatron Tradition*. Tübingen: Mohr Siebeck, 2005.

Oswalt, John N. *The Book of Isaiah: Chapters 40–66*. Grand Rapids: Eerdmans, 1998.

Otto, Randall E. "The Use and Abuse of Perichoresis in Recent Theology." *Scottish Journal of Theology* 54, no. 3 (2001): 366–84.

Owen, John. *A Brief Declaration and Vindication of the Doctrine of the Trinity*. In *The Works of John Owen*, edited by William H. Goold, 2:366–440. 16 vols. Philadelphia: Leighton, 1862.

———. *Communion with the Triune God*. Edited by Kelly M. Kapic and Justin Taylor. Wheaton, IL: Crossway, 2007.

———. *The Holy Spirit: His Gifts and Power*. Grand Rapids: Kregel, 1954.

Palamas, Gregory. *Dialogue Between an Orthodox and a Barlaamite*. Translated by Rein Ferwerda. Binghamton, NY: Global, 1999.

———. *Topics of Natural and Theological Science and on the Moral and Ascetic Life: One Hundred and Fifty Texts*. In *The Philokalia*, compiled by St. Nikodimos of the Holy Mountain and St. Makarios of Corinth, translated and edited by G. E. H. Palmer, Philip Sherrard, and Kallistos Ware, 4:346–417. London: Faber & Faber, 1995.

Panikkar, Raimundo. *The Trinity and the Religious Experience of Man: Icon—Person—Mystery*. Maryknoll, NY: Orbis Books, 1973.

Papadakis, Aristeides. *Crisis in Byzantium: The Filioque Controversy in the Patriarchate of Gregory II of Cyprus (1283–1289)*. Rev. ed. Crestwood, NY: St. Vladimir's Seminary Press, 1997.

Papanikolaou, Aristotle. *Being with God: Trinity, Apophaticism, and Divine-Human Communion*. Notre Dame, IN: University of Notre Dame Press, 2006.

———. "From Sophia to Personhood: The Development of 20th Century Orthodox Trinitarian Theology." *Phronema* 33, no. 2 (2018): 1–20.

———. "Is John Zizioulas an Existentialist in Disguise? A Response to Lucian Turcescu." *Modern Theology* 20, no. 4 (October 2004): 601–7.

Paul, Ian. "The Trinitarian Dynamic of the Book of Revelation." In *Trinity without Hierarchy: Reclaiming Nicene Orthodoxy in Evangelical Theology*, edited by Michael F. Bird and Scott Harrower, 85–108. Grand Rapids: Kregel, 2019.

Pelikan, Jaroslav. *The Christian Tradition: A History of the Development of Doctrine*. Vol. 1, *The Emergence of the Catholic Tradition (100–600)*. Chicago: University of Chicago Press, 1971.

Pendrick, Gerard. "*Monogenēs*." *New Testament Studies* 41, no. 4 (October 1995): 587–600.

Photius of Constantinople. *The Mystagogy of the Holy Spirit*. Translated by Joseph P. Farrell. Brookline, MA: Holy Cross Orthodox, 1987.

Pierce, Madison. *Divine Discourse in the Epistle to the Hebrews: The Recontextualization of Spoken Quotations of Scripture.* Cambridge: Cambridge University Press, 2020.

Plantinga, Cornelius. "The Threeness/Oneness Problem of the Trinity." *Calvin Theological Journal* 23, no. 1 (April 1988): 37–53.

Plantinga, Richard J., Thomas R. Thompson, and Matthew D. Lundberg. *An Introduction to Christian Theology.* Cambridge: Cambridge University Press, 2010.

Plested, Marcus. "St. Gregory Palamas on the Divine Simplicity." *Modern Theology* 35, no. 3 (July 2019): 508–21.

Podles, Mary Elizabeth. "*The Trinity* by Andrei Rublev." *Touchstone* 26, no. 1 (January/February 2013): 54–55.

Pohle, Joseph. *The Divine Trinity: A Dogmatic Treatise.* Translated by Arthur Preuss. St. Louis: Herder, 1912.

Poirel, Dominique. *Livre de la nature et débat trinitaire au XIIᵉ siècle: Le De tribus diebus de Hugues de Saint-Victor.* Turnhout, Belgium: Brepols, 2002.

Pope, William Burt. *A Compendium of Christian Theology.* 3 vols. 2nd ed. New York: Phillips & Hunt, 1881.

Prestige, G. L. *God in Patristic Thought.* 2nd ed. London: SPCK, 1952.

———. "ΠΕΡΙΧΩΡΕΩ and ΠΕΡΙΧΩΡΗΣΙΣ in the Fathers." *Journal of Theological Studies* 29, no. 115 (April 1928): 242–52.

Radde-Gallwitz, Andrew. *Basil of Caesarea, Gregory of Nyssa, and the Transformation of Divine Simplicity.* Oxford: Oxford University Press, 2009.

Rahner, Karl. *Foundations of Christian Faith: An Introduction to the Idea of Christianity.* Translated by William V. Dych. New York: Seabury, 1978.

———. "Oneness and Threefoldness of God in Discussion with Islam." In *Theological Investigations*, vol. 28, *God and Revelation*, translated by Edward Quinn, 105–21. New York: Crossroad, 1983.

———. *The Trinity.* Translated by Joseph Donceel. New York: Seabury, 1974.

Ramelli, Ilara. "Origen's Anti-subordinationism and Its Heritage in the Nicene and Cappadocian Line." *Vigiliae Christianae* 65, no. 1 (2011): 21–49.

Ray, Ron C. "Was Paul a Trinitarian? A Look at Romans 8." In *Paul and His Theology*, edited by Stanley E. Porter, 327–46. Leiden: Brill, 2006.

Renczes, Philipp Gabriel. "The Scope of Rahner's Fundamental Axiom in the Patristic Perspective: A Dialogue of Systematic and Historical Theology." In *Rethinking Trinitarian Theology: Disputed Questions and Contemporary Issues in Trinitarian Theology*, edited by Giulio Maspero and Robert J. Wozniak, 255–88. London: T&T Clark, 2012.

Richard of St. Victor. *On the Trinity.* In *Trinity and Creation*, edited by Boyd Taylor Coolman and Dale M. Coulter, 195–382. Hyde Park, NY: New City, 2011.

Richardson, Kurt Andres. "Uncreated and Created Perichoretic Relations." In *Revisioning, Renewing, Rediscovering the Triune Center: Essays in Honor of Stanley J.*

Grenz, edited by Derek J. Tidball, Brian S. Harris, and Jason S. Sexton, 79–94. Eugene, OR: Cascade, 2014.

Richardson, Neil. *Paul's Language about God*. Sheffield, UK: Sheffield Academic, 1994.

Ridderbos, Herman. *Paul: An Outline of His Theology*. Translated by John Richard de Witt. Grand Rapids: Eerdmans, 1975.

Routley, Jonathan J. *Eternal Submission: A Biblical and Theological Examination*. Eugene, OR: Wipf & Stock, 2019.

Rowland, Christopher. *The Open Heaven: A Study of Apocalyptic in Judaism and Early Christianity*. New York: Crossroad, 1982.

Russell, Norman. *The Doctrine of Deification in the Greek Patristic Tradition*. Oxford: Oxford University Press, 2005.

Sanders, Fred. *The Image of the Immanent Trinity: Rahner's Rule and the Theological Interpretation of Scripture*. New York: Peter Lang, 2005.

———. *The Triune God*. Grand Rapids: Zondervan, 2016.

Sanders, Fred, and Scott R. Swain, eds. *Retrieving Eternal Generation*. Grand Rapids: Zondervan, 2017.

Sanders, John. *The God Who Risks: A Theology of Divine Providence*. 2nd ed. Downers Grove, IL: IVP Academic, 2007.

Schelkle, Karl Hermann. *Theology of the New Testament*. Vol. 2, *Salvation History— Revelation*. Translated by William A. Jurgens. Collegeville, MN: Liturgical Press, 1976.

Schnackenburg, Rudolf. *The Gospel according to St. John*. Translated by Kevin Smith. 3 vols. New York: Seabury, 1980.

Scouteris, Constantine B. *Ecclesial Being: Contributions to Theological Dialogue*. Edited by Christopher Veniamin. South Canaan, PA: Mount Thabor Publishing, 2006.

Segal, Alan F. *Two Powers in Heaven: Early Rabbinic Reports about Christianity and Gnosticism*. 1977. Reprint, Waco: Baylor University Press, 2012.

Shehadeh, Imad N. *God with Us and God without Us*. Vol. 1, *Oneness in Trinity versus Absolute Oneness*. Carlisle, UK: Langham, 2018.

Shenuda III. *Trinity & Unity: A Lecture by Pope Shenuda III Delivered at the Cathedral of Mark in Cairo*. Ironton, OH: Al-Nour, 1970.

Siddiqui, Mona. *Christians, Muslims, & Jesus*. New Haven: Yale University Press, 2013.

Sieben, Hermann Josef. "Herméneutique de l'exégèse dogmatique d'Athanase." In *Politique et théologie chez Athanase d'Alexandrie*, edited by Charles Kannengiesser, 195–214. Paris: Beauchesne, 1974.

Siecienski, A. Edward. *The Filioque: History of a Doctrinal Controversy*. Oxford: Oxford University Press, 2010.

Slotemaker, John T. *Anselm of Canterbury and the Search for God*. Lanham, MD: Lexington, 2018.

Sonderegger, Katherine. *Systematic Theology*. 2 vols. Minneapolis: Fortress, 2015–20.

Soskice, Janet Martin. *The Kindness of God: Metaphor, Gender, and Religious Language*. Oxford: Oxford University Press, 2007.

Speiser, E. A. *Genesis*. Garden City, NY: Doubleday, 1981.

Stamatović, Slobodan. "The Meaning of Perichoresis." *Open Theology* 2 (2016): 303–23.

Starr, James M. *Sharers in the Divine Nature: 2 Peter 1:4 in Its Hellenistic Context*. Stockholm: Almqvist & Wicksell, 2000.

"The Statement of Faith of the Third Council of Constantinople (Sixth Ecumenical)." Translated by Edward Rochie Hardy. In *Christology of the Later Fathers*, edited by Edward Rochie Hardy, 382–85. Louisville: Westminster John Knox, 1954.

Stead, Christopher. *Divine Substance*. Oxford: Oxford University Press, 1977.

Steenburg, David. "The Case against the Synonymity of MORPHĒ and EIKŌN." *Journal for the Study of the New Testament* 34 (1988): 77–86.

Steward, James S. *A Man in Christ: The Vital Elements of St. Paul's Religion*. New York: Harper & Row, 1964.

Stramara, Daniel F. "Gregory of Nyssa's Terminology for Trinitarian Perichoresis." *Vigilae Christianae* 53, no. 3 (August 1998): 257–63.

Strezova, Anita. *Hesychasm and Art: The Appearance of New Iconographic Trends in Byzantine and Slavic Lands in the 14th and 15th Centuries*. Canberra, Australia: Australian National University Press, 2014.

Stuckenbruck, Loren T. *Angel Veneration and Christology: A Study in Early Judaism and in the Christology of the Apocalypse of John*. 1995. Reprint, Waco: Baylor University Press, 2017.

Symeon the New Theologian. *Practical and Theological Chapters*. In *Symeon the New Theologian: The Practical and Theological Chapters and The Three Theological Discourses*, translated by Paul McGuckin, 33–103. Kalamazoo, MI: Cistercian, 1982.

Tanchanpongs, Natee. "Asian Reformulations of the Trinity: An Evaluation." In *The Trinity among the Nations: The Doctrine of God in the Majority World*, edited by Gene L. Green, Stephen T. Pardue, and K. K. Yeo, 120–39. Carlisle, UK: Langham, 2015.

Tanner, Kathryn. "Beyond the East/West Divide." In *Ecumenical Perspectives on the Filioque for the Twenty-First Century*, edited by Myk Habets, 198–210. London: Bloomsbury, 2014.

———. *God and Creation in Christian Theology: Tyranny or Empowerment?* Minneapolis: Fortress, 1988.

———. "Is God in Charge?" In *Essentials of Christian Theology*, edited by William C. Placher, 116–31. Louisville: Westminster John Knox, 2002.

———. *Jesus, Humanity and the Trinity: A Brief Systematic Theology.* Minneapolis: Fortress, 2001.

Tennent, Timothy C. *Invitation to World Missions: A Trinitarian Missiology for the Twenty-First Century.* Grand Rapids: Kregel, 2010.

Tertullian. *Against Praxeas.* Translated by Dr. Holmes. In *The Ante-Nicene Fathers,* edited by Alexander Roberts and James Donaldson, 3:597–632. Reprint, Grand Rapids, Eerdmans: 1957.

Theophylact of Ochrid. *The Explanation of the Holy Gospel according to John.* Translated by Christopher Stade. House Springs, MO: Chrysostom, 2007.

Thiselton, Anthony C. *A Shorter Guide to the Holy Spirit: Bible, Doctrine, Experience.* Grand Rapids: Eerdmans, 2016.

Thom, Paul. *The Logic of the Trinity: Augustine to Ockham.* New York: Fordham University Press, 2012.

Toon, Peter. *Our Triune God: A Biblical Portrayal of the Trinity.* Wheaton: Bridgepoint, 1996.

Torrance, Alan J. *Persons in Communion: Trinitarian Description and Human Participation.* Edinburgh: T&T Clark, 1996.

Torrance, James B. *Worship, Community, and the Triune God of Grace.* Downers Grove, IL: InterVarsity, 1996.

Torrance, Thomas F. *The Christian Doctrine of God: One Being, Three Persons.* London: T&T Clark, 1996.

———. *Divine Meaning: Studies in Patristic Hermeneutics.* Edinburgh: T&T Clark, 1995.

———. *Karl Barth: An Introduction to His Early Theology, 1910–1931.* London: SCM, 1962.

Treier, Daniel J. *Introducing Evangelical Theology.* Grand Rapids: Baker, 2019.

Trueman, Carl. "The Trinity and Prayer." In *The Essential Trinity: New Testament Foundations and Practical Relevance,* edited by Brandon D. Crowe and Carl R. Trueman, 222–40. Phillipsburg, NJ: P&R, 2017.

Turcescu, Lucian. *Gregory of Nyssa and the Concept of Divine Persons.* Oxford: Oxford University Press, 2005.

Turner, C. J. G. "George-Gannadius Scholarius and the Union of Florence." *Journal of Theological Studies* 18, no. 1 (April 1967): 83–103.

Turretin, Francis. *Institutes of Elenctic Theology.* Edited by James T. Dennison Jr. Translated by George Musgrave Giger. Philipsburg, NJ: P&R, 1992.

Twombly, Charles C. *Perichoresis and Personhood: God, Christ, and Salvation in John of Damascus.* Eugene, OR: Pickwick, 2015.

Ursinus, Zacharias. *Commentary on the Heidelberg Catechism.* Translated by G. W. Williard. Philipsburg, NJ: P&R, 1985.

Vanhoozer, Kevin J. *Remythologizing Theology: Divine Action, Passion, and Authorship*. Cambridge: Cambridge University Press, 2010.

van Mastricht, Petrus. *Theoretical-Practical Theology*. Vol. 2, *Faith in the Triune God*. Translated by Todd M. Rester and Michael T. Spangler. Edited by Joel R. Beeke and Michael T. Spangler. Grand Rapids: Reformation Heritage, 2019.

Vidu, Adonis. *The Same God Who Works in All Things: Inseparable Operations in Trinitarian Theology*. Grand Rapids: Eerdmans, 2021.

Vogt, Berard. "Note on the 'Formal Distinction' in Scotus." *Franciscan Studies* 3 (August 1925): 38–42.

von Rad, Gerhard. *Genesis: A Commentary*. Rev. ed. Translated by John H. Marks. Philadelphia: Westminster, 1972.

Wainwright, Arthur W. *The Trinity in the New Testament*. London: SPCK, 1969.

Warden, Francis M. "God's Only Son." *Review and Expositor* 50, no. 2 (April 1953): 216–23.

Ware, Bruce A. "Does Affirming an Eternal Authority-Submission Relationship in the Trinity Entail a Denial of *Homoousios*?" In *One God in Three Persons: Unity of Essence, Distinction of Persons, Implications for Life*, edited by Bruce A. Ware and John Starke, 237–48. Wheaton: Crossway, 2015.

———. *Father, Son, and Holy Spirit: Relationships, Roles, and Relevance*. Wheaton: Crossway, 2005.

Watson, Francis. "The Bible." In *The Cambridge Companion to Karl Barth*, edited by John Webster, 57–71. Cambridge: Cambridge University Press, 2000.

Webster, John. *Holy Scripture: A Dogmatic Sketch*. Cambridge: Cambridge University Press, 2003.

Wegner, Paul D. "Isaiah 48:16: A Trinitarian Enigma?" In *Presence, Power, and Promise: The Role of the Spirit of God in the Old Testament*, edited by David G. Firth and Paul D. Wegner, 233–44. Downers Grove, IL: IVP Academic, 2011.

Weinandy, Thomas G. *Athanasius: A Theological Introduction*. Burlington, VT: Ashgate, 2007.

Wenham, Gordon. *Genesis 16–50*. Dallas: Word, 1994.

Westcott, Brooke Foss. *The Epistles of St. John*. Grand Rapids: Eerdmans, 1966.

Westermann, Claus. *Genesis: A Practical Commentary*. Translated by David E. Green. Grand Rapids: Eerdmans, 1987.

Wiles, Maurice. "Some Reflections on the Origins of the Doctrine of the Trinity." *Journal of Theological Studies* 8, no. 1 (April 1957): 92–106.

Wilken, Robert Louis. *The Spirit of Early Christian Thought: Seeing the Face of God*. New Haven: Yale University Press, 2003.

William of Auvergne. *The Trinity, or the First Principles*. Translated by Roland J. Teske and Francis C. Wade. Milwaukee: Marquette University Press, 1989.

Williams, A. N. *The Ground of Union: Deification in Aquinas and Palamas.* New York: Oxford University Press, 1999.

Williams, Rowan. *Arius.* Rev. ed. Grand Rapids: Eerdmans, 2001.

Winston, David. *The Wisdom of Solomon.* Garden City, NY: Doubleday, 1979.

Wippel, John F. "Metaphysics." In *The Cambridge Companion to Aquinas*, edited by Norman Kretzmann and Eleonore Stump, 85–127. Cambridge: Cambridge University Press, 1993.

Wittman, Tyler R. "On the Unity of the Trinity's External Works: Archaeology and Grammar." *International Journal of Systematic Theology* 20, no. 3 (July 2018): 359–80.

Woznicki, Christopher. "Dancing around the Black Box: The Problem of Metaphysics and Perichoresis." *Philosophia Christi* 22, no. 1 (2020): 103–21.

Wright, N. T. *The New Testament and the People of God.* Christian Origins and the Question of God 1. Minneapolis: Fortress, 1992.

Yandell, Keith. "How Many Times Does Three Go into One?" In *Philosophical and Theological Essays on the Trinity*, edited by Thomas McCall and Michael C. Rea. Oxford: Oxford University Press, 2009.

Yong, Amos. *Renewing Christian Theology: Systematics for a Global Christianity.* Waco: Baylor University Press, 2014.

Yung, Hwa. *Mangoes or Bananas? The Quest for an Authentic Asian Christian Theology.* 2nd ed. Maryknoll, NY: Orbis Books, 2015.

Zizioulas, John D. *Being as Communion.* Crestwood, NY: St. Vladimir's Seminary Press, 1985.

———. *Communion and Otherness: Further Studies in Personhood and the Church.* New York: T&T Clark, 2006.

———. *The Eucharistic Communion and the World.* Edited by Luke Ben Tallon. London: Bloomsbury, 2011.

Index of Names

Abelard, Peter, 194–95
à Brakel, Wilhelmus, 59, 67n93
Abū Qurrah, Theodore, 42
Abū Rā'iṭa al-Takrītī, 'Ḥabīb ibn Khidma, 40–42
Agricola, Stephan, 216n77
Akindynos, Gregory, 81, 82n33
al-Baṣrī, 'Ammār, 41
Alcuin of York, 102
Alexander of Alexandria, 25
Alexopoulos, Theodoros, 121n92
al-Kindī, 40n120
al-Warrāq, 40n120
Ambrose of Milan, 27, 155
Ames, William, 114n53, 149n81
Anatolios, Khaled, 55, 56n40, 77, 143n55, 177n12, 178nn13–14, 215n71
Anselm of Canterbury, 7, 97, 98n100, 103–5, 114n53, 123, 186n53
Aquinas, Thomas, 18, 29, 33–39, 49, 53, 56–58, 78, 79, 80, 81n27, 82, 85n48, 94, 95n87, 98, 121n88, 122nn95–96, 138, 149n83, 171, 171n96, 182, 200
Aristotle, 34, 38, 39, 61, 81, 122n96, 123
Arius of Alexandria, 1n3, 25, 26n47, 52, 83, 84, 159
Asterius, 143n55, 159
Athanasius of Alexandria, 26, 47, 61n66, 83, 84, 85n47, 115, 124–25, 155, 159n32, 171n95, 211
Athenagoras, 75, 137n29
Augustine of Hippo, 3n6, 26n51, 60, 101, 114n53, 176, 183, 189, 194, 211
Awad, Najib George, 40, 42n129

Ayres, Lewis, 13, 30, 55, 56n40, 71n107, 159n31, 180, 183n41

Baber, H. E., 37n107, 45
Baker-Fletcher, Karen, 134–35, 152
Barcellos, Richard C., 196n86
Barnes, Michel René, 48, 154n5, 161nn42–44, 176, 177n11, 178–79, 183n38, 194n79, 197
Barrett, C. K., 91
Barth, Karl, 1, 3–5, 7–9, 13, 84, 85, 94, 109, 110, 111, 140, 171n95, 197n89
Basil of Caesarea, 18, 27, 29, 30–33, 35, 36, 71, 77–78, 82, 126, 160n36, 191, 203
Bates, Matthew W., 12, 18n13, 117n73
Bauckham, Richard, 24, 91n69, 92n79, 143
Bavinck, Herman, 94
Beckwith, Carl L., 183n40, 191, 198
Behr, John, 29n66, 30, 77n6, 177n10
Billings, J. Todd, 113n47
Bingemer, Maria Clara Lucchetti, 14, 111n40, 188, 200
Bobik, Joseph, 35n92
Bobrinskoy, Boris, 129n122
Boersma, Hans, 207n39
Boethius, 106–7, 110
Boff, Leonardo, 14, 128, 142
Bolotov, V. V., 130n126
Bonaventure, 61n60, 96, 97, 137n24, 170n90, 191
Boston, Thomas, 94n85
Bourassa, François, 139n36
Boyd, Gregory A., 95n90
Bradshaw, David, 35n94
Bradshaw, Paul F., 216n76

255

Gregory of Sinai, 186, 187n56
Grenz, Stanley J., 142n51, 167n80
Greshake, Gisbert, 202
Groh, Dennis E., 26n48, 83n36
Grudem, Wayne, 114n54, 176, 212n61
Gunton, Colin E., 11, 118–19, 138n30

Hagner, Donald A., 188n62
Hamerton-Kelly, R. G., 156n12, 158n27, 173
Hamilton, Victor P., 16
Hanson, R. P. C., 44, 77n3, 84n39, 85, 179n21
Harnack, Adolf von, 2n5, 49n7, 156n10, 158n28
Harner, Philip D., 90n67
Harris, Murray J., 87n51, 90n65, 90n68, 91n71, 92, 99, 117n70
Harrison, Verna, 135n13, 137n29, 150n85, 151n87
Harrower, Scott, 167n75, 167n79
Hartman, Lars, 23n36
Hasker, William, 28n63, 32n80, 45, 114, 115
Hauck, Friedrich, 201n3
Haugh, Richard, 102n2
Hedio, Caspar, 216n77
Helmer, Christine, 7n23, 61n67
Hengel, Martin, 23
Henninger, Mark, 35n96
Henry of Ghent, 126n115
Heppe, Heinrich, 62n69
Hick, John, 171–72
Hilary of Poitiers, 26, 60n64, 159n32, 184
Hildebrand, Stephen, 31n78, 45, 160n36
Hildegard von Bingen, 205
Hill, Wesley, 12, 22n31, 69n103, 120
Hinlicky, Paul R., 84n39
Hippolytus, 216n76
Hodge, A. A., 7
Hodge, Charles, 7n21, 87n55, 138, 139n37
Hodgson, Leonard, 108
Holmes, Stephen R., 10n31, 57n47, 82, 83n34, 105n19, 126n110
Holzer, Vincent, 167n78
Hughes, Christopher, 78n8, 83n34
Hugh of St. Victor, 195
Hugon, R. P. Édouard, 35n98, 176n5
Hunsinger, George, 164n61
Hunt, Anne, 135n14, 205, 219
Hur, Ju, 160n38
Hurtado, Larry W., 19n20, 20n20, 22, 23n38, 44, 215n70
Husseini, Sara Leila, 40n120, 41n123, 45

Irenaeus of Lyons, 153–54, 161nn42–44
Irons, Charles Lee, 50n13, 51n17, 51n21
Isasi-Díaz, Ada María, 9

Jenson, Robert W., 70n104, 162n45, 163–64, 178
John Beccus, 129
John of Damascus, 61n66, 114n53, 129, 136, 137, 138, 139n35, 151
Johnson, Elizabeth A., 110, 111
Johnson, Luke Timothy, 68
Johnson, Marcus Peter, 147n76
Johnson, Maxwell, 216n76
Jonas, Justus, 216n77
Joseph, P. V., 116n68, 172
Josephus, 201
Julian of Norwich, 205
Jüngle, Eberhard, 137n24, 186n55
Justin Martyr, 117

Kapic, Kelly M., 208n41
Kärkkäinen, Veli-Matti, 128n119
Kasper, Walter, 162nn45–46, 165n64
Kaye, Bruce N., 70n116
Keck, Leander E., 1n3
Keener, Craig S., 21n25, 68n100, 90n65, 92, 108n32
Keller, Catherine, 66n91
Kelly, J. N. D., 28n58, 28n60, 121n87, 154n3, 178n16
Kilby, Karen, 143, 144nn61–62
Kombo, James Henry Owino, 8n27, 14, 168, 169nn84–85, 175n1
Köstenberger, Andreas J., 147, 151, 180n26
Kramer, Werner, 22n32, 120n83, 215n70
Kuschel, Karl-Josef, 156, 159n34, 173

LaCugna, Catherine Mowry, 110n39, 111n42, 162n45, 165, 173, 176, 197n88
Lane, William L., 68n97, 117n70
Lashier, Jackson, 154n1, 161nn40–41
Leibniz, G. W., 28, 32, 33n86
Letham, Robert, 183n37
Levering, Matthew, 58, 105n19
Lombard, Peter, 61n68
Lonergan, Bernard, 10n32, 169–70, 192–93, 197
Long, D. Stephen, 34n88, 78, 94n83, 99
Longenecker, Bruce, 87n54
Lossky, Vladimir, 32, 206–8, 209
Lundberg, Matthew, 76
Luther, Martin, 7n23, 216

Maldonado Pérez, Zaida, 195–96
Maleparampil, Joseph, 201n4, 210n53
Mantzaridis, Georgios I., 82n33
Maximus the Confessor, 102n3, 135, 136, 151
McCall, Thomas, 29, 36n103, 45, 143n60
McCready, Douglas, 156n17, 158n24, 170n92
McGrath, James F., 18n12, 19n18, 22n31,
   23n39, 24n41, 24n43, 44, 91n74
McGraw, Ryan M., 208
Melanchthon, Philip, 191, 216n77
Mews, Constant J., 195n81
Meyendorff, John, 56n41, 82n31, 137, 186n55
Meyer, Hans, 35n97
Miyahira, Nozomu, 8n27, 119, 130
Molnar, Paul D., 4, 5
Moltmann, Jürgen, 134, 140–44, 145, 152, 167
Montague, George T., 108n30
Moody, Dale, 50n11
Moreland, J. P., 33, 78n8, 115n61
Muller, Richard A., 13, 184n43, 196n87
Murphy, Francesca Aran, 164, 211
Musculus, Wolfgang, 185

Nebridius, 189
Nielson, Lauge O., 123n99
Novatian, 202, 207

O'Collins, Gerald, 18n15, 19n16
Oecolampadius, Johannes, 216n77
Olson, Roger, 165n64
Origin of Alexandria, 49, 52, 53, 54, 55, 56, 59,
   84, 116n65, 155, 178, 214
Orlov, Andrei A., 88n59
Osiander, Andreas, 216n77
Oswalt, John N., 155n8, 182n34
Otto, Randall E., 1n58
Owen, John, 109, 161n39, 202, 208–9

Palamas, Gregory, 61n66, 81, 82, 113n47,
   114n53, 149n80, 149n84, 189
Panikkar, Raimundo, 205–6, 207, 208, 219
Papadakis, Aristeides, 104n13, 121n89, 121n91,
   129n122, 131
Papanikolaou, Aristotle, 62n70, 106n24,
   126n110, 207n38, 207n40, 215n72, 219
Paul, Ian, 88n61, 181n30
Paul of Samosata, 28
Pelagius I, 217
Pelikan, Jaroslav, 31
Pendrick, Gerard, 50n13, 50n15
Peters, Ted, 165n64
Phillips, Edward, 216n76

Philo, 16n6, 21, 201
Philoponus, John, 123
Phoabadius of Agen, 179n21
Photius of Constantinople, 102–5, 121, 123,
   126–27
Pierce, Madison, 13, 67n95, 116n64, 116n69,
   156n14, 181n31, 210
Plantinga, Cornelius, 114n57
Plantinga, Richard J., 76
Plato, 194n79
Plested, Marcus, 81n25, 82
Plutarch, 201
Podles, Mary Elizabeth, 15
Pohle, Joseph, 126n113, 194
Polanus, Amandus, 184n43
Pope, William Burt, 62n71
Prestige, G. L., 30n70, 106n22, 136n18, 137n28,
   176

Radde-Gallwitz, Andrew, 77n4, 78n9, 99
Rahner, Karl, 38, 39n114, 60n63, 109–11, 140,
   164–67, 173
Ramelli, Ilara, 56n40
Ray, Ron C., 147n73
Reccard of the Visigoths, 101
Renczes, Philipp Gabriel, 167n79, 168n82
Richardson, K. A., 134n5, 150n85
Richardson, Neil, 119n81, 182
Richard of St. Victor, 71, 72, 104n14, 122, 125,
   194
Ridderbos, Herman, 146n66
Roscelin of Compiègne, 123, 140
Routley, Jonathan J., 114n54
Rowland, Christopher, 93n82
Rublev, Andrei, 15, 17, 18
Ruusbroec, Jan van, 135
Russell, Norman, 112n46

Sabellius, 121
Sanders, Fred, 64, 66, 73, 162, 163n48, 164n63,
   165n64, 166n73, 173, 196n85, 199–200
Sanders, John, 66n91
Schelkle, Karl Hermann, 69n102
Schnackenburg, Rudolf, 91n72, 92
Scotus, John Duns, 79, 80, 81, 82, 85, 122
Scouteris, Constantine B., 151
Segal, Alan F., 20n22, 24n41
Shehadeh, Imad N., 42, 43
Shenuda III, 41
Siddiqui, Mona, 40n116, 41n120
Sieben, Hermann Josef, 116n67
Siecienski, A. Edward, 102n7, 103, 131

Index of Scripture

Index of Subjects

Abū Rā'iṭa al-Takrītī, 40–42
accidents, 35, 38
accommodation, 118
actus purus, 61, 78, 175
ad extra operations, 137, 184, 186
adoptionism, 162, 213
analogy, 8, 52, 56–57, 59, 66, 94, 142, 179n20
angels. *See* mediatorial figures
anomianism, 77
anthropopathism, 95
apophatic theology, 76–77, 115, 126, 168, 193, 205, 207
Appolinarianism, 113
appropriations, 177, 193–97, 205–6, 208, 211
  of Creator, Redeemer, Sanctifier, 195
  of movement to and from creation, 215
  of power, wisdom, and goodness, 194–95
  of *sat*, *chit*, and *ananda* (being, consciousness, and bliss), 194n79
Arianism, 51, 83, 102, 116, 143, 149, 180n27, 202
aseity, 61, 62–63, 95, 142, 148, 167, 170, 186

baptism, 23, 147–48
beatific vision, 166, 200
being, 29, 30, 35
  real vs. propositional, 35
bhakti, 205
Blachernae, Council of (1285), 121

canonical principle of hermeneutics, 6, 24–25, 93, 108
cataphatic theology, 168
categories, 34, 81
Chalcedon, Council of (451), 112–15, 118, 136

circumincessio, 137. *See also* perichoresis
circuminsessio, 137. *See also* perichoresis
Colwell's Rule, 90
communicable attributes, 148
communion, 115
  communio, 202
  co-ordinate model, 203, 204–9, 217
  definition, 201–3, 208
  incorporative model, 203, 214–17
  linear model, 190, 203, 209–14
  risks of de-emphasizing one person in, 213–14
consciousness and the Trinity, 114–15, 138, 191–93
consolation, 208
Constantinople, First Council of (381), 17, 28
Constantinople, Second Council of (553), 56
Constantinople, Third Council of (681), 187
consubstantiality, 75, 123, 125, 129, 136, 144, 149, 153, 176
  biblical basis, 18–25, 26, 86
  derived from singular divine power, 179
  logical problem of, 33, 36–37
  meaning, 28, 43
  modern criticism of, 140
  oneness of number, genus, and species, 40–41
correlatives, 39
creation *ex nihilo*, 84
cultural bias, 9

de Régnon hypothesis, 11, 60, 103
docetism, 157
dogmatics, definition of, 2–3
doxology. *See* worship
duplex formulas, 69, 201